PENGUIN BOOKS

THE ONES WE'VE BEEN WAITING FOR

Charlotte Alter is a national correspondent for *Time*, covering the 2016, 2018, and 2020 campaigns, youth social movements, and women in politics. Her work has also appeared in *The New York Times* and *The Wall Street Journal*.

* * *

Praise for *The Ones We've Been Waiting For*

"[Alter] does an excellent job detailing—with persuasive data—what has shaped and motivated this young generation so far.... Thanks to [her] timely book we can have a better understanding of why an entire generation was set back and what's driving it now." —*The New York Times Book Review*

"When it comes to political prescience today, *Time* magazine writer Charlotte Alter is arguably peerless.... Each of Alter's chosen ones emerges as an individual with his or her own history and path. The result is a more nuanced picture of a generation than previously reported." —*Los Angeles Times*

"These stories are all buoyed by Alter's sharp writing and engaging voice. She is by turns sarcastic, funny, and sincere, but always conversational.... Alter's book will come as a tonic to millennials who have grown weary of boomers' well-worn complaints about them. That's because *The Ones We've Been Waiting For* takes millennials seriously—and likewise takes seriously older generations' responsibility for millennial woes, such as economic insecurity. To Alter, social media and complaints about student debt aren't symptoms of an infantilized generation. They are simply facts of millennial life and are entering political office along with all the new millennials who ascend to power—boomers' complaints be damned." —*The Washington Post*

"Alter is an exceptional storyteller. . . . This nuanced and comprehensive guide does an admirable job illuminating the next generation of political leaders and the issues that drive them." —*Publishers Weekly*

"*The Ones We've Been Waiting For* is an excellent and timely look at the young leaders who are at the gates, and a lesson in what we have to learn from them. If you're curious about what the future looks like, this book is a thorough, thoughtful place to start."

—Rebecca Traister, *New York Times* bestselling author of *Good and Mad* and *All the Single Ladies*

"For anyone who has dismissed millennials or who cares about our country's future, Charlotte Alter has written a riveting, essential book. In bringing to vivid life the young upstarts who will ultimately inherit our democracy, Alter has inadvertently given us another vital young voice that will shape our political future: hers."

—Amy Chozick, *New York Times* bestselling author of *Chasing Hillary*

"Just when we need it, a new generational wave is poised to sweep away the aging politicians who are part of a divisive and dysfunctional system. In this valuable and richly reported book, Charlotte Alter weaves together the tale of ten millennials who are disrupting our stale politics. By the end you'll smile and say to yourself, 'There's hope.'"

—Walter Isaacson, *New York Times* bestselling author of *Leonardo da Vinci* and *Steve Jobs*

"Millennials are pissed off and burnt out and ready for change—and *The Ones We've Been Waiting For* brilliantly profiles the leaders of our own generation who will make it happen. These leaders have been influenced (and radicalized) by pivotal millennial experiences, whether witnessing 9/11 as a young adult or taking out staggering amounts of student debt—which is part of what makes the book feel so relatable, infuriating, and hopeful, all at once."

—Anne Helen Petersen, author of *Too Fat, Too Slutty, Too Loud*

THE ONES
WE'VE BEEN
WAITING FOR

HOW A NEW GENERATION
OF LEADERS WILL
TRANSFORM AMERICA

CHARLOTTE ALTER

PENGUIN BOOKS

PENGUIN BOOKS
An imprint of Penguin Random House LLC
penguinrandomhouse.com

First published in the United States of America by Viking,
an imprint of Penguin Random House LLC, 2020
Published with a new epilogue in Penguin Books 2021

ISBN 9780525561521 (paperback)

THE LIBRARY OF CONGRESS HAS CATALOGED THE HARDCOVER EDITION AS FOLLOWS:
Names: Alter, Charlotte, author.
Title: The ones we've been waiting for : how a new generation of leaders
will transform America / Charlotte Alter.
Other titles: Ones we have been waiting for
Description: New York : Viking, 2020. | Includes bibliographical references and index.
Identifiers: LCCN 2019053404 (print) | LCCN 2019053405 (ebook) |
ISBN 9780525561507 (hardcover) | ISBN 9780525561514 (ebook)
Subjects: LCSH: Political participation—United States. | Generation
Y—Political activity—United States. | Political leadership—United
States. | United States—Politics and government—21st century.
Classification: LCC JK1764 .A46 2020 (print) | LCC JK1764 (ebook) |
DDC 320.973—dc23
LC record available at https://lccn.loc.gov/2019053404
LC ebook record available at https://lccn.loc.gov/2019053405

Printed in the United States of America
1st Printing

Book design by Daniel Lagin

For my mom and dad, who taught me everything

The cruelties and obstacles of this swiftly changing planet will not yield to obsolete dogmas and outworn slogans. It cannot be moved by those who cling to a present which is already dying, who prefer the illusion of security to the excitement and danger which comes with even the most peaceful progress. This world demands the qualities of youth; not a time of life but a state of mind, a temper of the will, a quality of the imagination . . .

—ROBERT F. KENNEDY, CAPETOWN, SOUTH AFRICA, JUNE 6, 1966

CONTENTS

PART THREE

INTRODUCTION

L ove 'em or hate 'em, this much is true: one day soon, millennials will rule America.

This is neither wish nor warning but a fact, rooted in the physics of time and the biology of human cells. Millennials—born between 1981 and 1996—are already the largest living generation, the majority of the workforce, and will soon eclipse their parents as the biggest bloc of eligible voters. But even as America gets younger and more diverse, our national leadership is overwhelmingly dominated by white men in their seventies carrying baggage from the previous century. I offer this book as a reminder of the only real truth, in politics and in life: this, too, shall pass.

Millennial attitudes already define most other aspects of American society: their startups have revolutionized the economy, their tastes have shifted the culture, and their enormous appetite for social media has transformed human interaction. Politics is just the latest arena ripe for disruption.

This book is about those disrupters, the stepper-uppers, the young leaders attempting to drag our government into the twenty-first century. Others have written well about the millennial social identity in general, their unique economic peril, and the young activists and organizers who spurred the enormous social movements of the last twenty years. This is not that book.

Instead, this is about the "electeds"—the young mayors and city council

members and state legislators and members of Congress who ran for office
and won, the first in their generation to gain political power. While a septua-
genarian president strutted and fretted in the Oval Office, I spent the last
three years crisscrossing the country meeting the young politicians trying
to build a new America from the ground up. The thirty-two-year-old mayor
who renovated downtown Ithaca, the twenty-nine-year-old bartender who
proposed a Green New Deal days after she arrived in Congress, the thirty-
five-year-old congresswoman trying to attract more women to the GOP, the
thirty-eight-year-old gay veteran who ran for president of the United States:
these young leaders are the vanguard of millennial political power, and they're
only the first of their cohort to step up to the plate.

I don't pretend to know what will happen to any of their individual political careers. I'm not trying to predict who will be in the Senate in 2022, or
in congressional leadership in 2024, or president in 2028. But no matter what
happens to them individually, studying their lives—the experiences that define their attitudes, the attitudes that define their politics—can give us a pre-
view of what America might look like when their generation is in charge. I
am not arguing that millennials will save America: they will surely bring
their own flawed assumptions and misguided ideas into the political realm,
just as their parents did. But a country run by millennials will look different
than the boomer-built America, and this book attempts to figure out what
those differences might look like.

Like all younger generations, millennials get a bad rap: boomers and Gen
Xers think they're entitled, overly sensitive, obsessed with social media, and
naive about the ways of the world. Each of those stereotypes has a grain of
truth—just ask anyone who's ever hired an annoying millennial. But when
taken collectively, the qualities that seem grating on an individual level actually hint at a broader political disposition. Individually, millennials are
stereotyped as entitled; collectively, they demand broad government investment in a twenty-first-century social safety net. Individually, they're cari-
catured as oversensitive to "microaggressions"; collectively, they're pushing
toward a more comprehensive vision of social justice. Individually, they seem
glued to their phones; collectively, their intuitive use of social networks has
given them a fresh understanding of how individuals work within systems.

Individually, they come off as naive or demanding; collectively, that looks a lot like idealism.

Politics is supposed to be about the future, even if the last four years have apparently been aimed at making America "great again." This may be an era defined by smartphones, but the Speaker of the House, the Senate Majority Leader, and three of the top Democratic presidential candidates were all born in the 1940s, well before the invention of the color television, the polio vaccine, and the bikini. In 2017, President Donald Trump took the oath of office as the oldest first-term president ever, elected mostly by white voters over sixty-five and enabled by one of the oldest Congresses in history; in 2021, seventy-eight-year-old president Joe Biden beat his record by nearly eight years. There are only three other American presidents (William Henry Harrison, James Buchanan, and Ronald Reagan) who were older than sixty-five on Inauguration day.

The graying of US politics feels especially claustrophobic given that America's most visionary leaders have typically been young. Alexander Hamilton was just thirty-two when he became the first secretary of the Treasury, Thomas Jefferson was thirty-three when he wrote the Declaration of Independence, Martin Luther King Jr. was thirty-four when he led the March on Washington, and John F. Kennedy was forty-four when he promised to send a man to the moon. Even the middle-aged presidents have historically been much younger than our current leadership: Abraham Lincoln was in his early fifties when he preserved the Union in the Civil War, roughly the same age Franklin Delano Roosevelt was at the time of the New Deal. The powdered wigs and black-and-white photographs make American history look like a succession of old men, but actually, some of the most momentous shifts have resulted from younger generations replacing older ones.

Of course, age itself does not determine political relevance—just look at Supreme Court Justice Ruth Bader Ginsburg (b. 1933), an improbable cult figure among young women, or Bernie Sanders (b. 1941), a seventy-eight-year-old socialist whose popularity with young voters has buoyed two presidential campaigns or Joe Biden (b. 1942) who was counted out as a too-old has-been before he defeated Donald Trump with more votes than any presidential candidate in history.

But as Alexis de Tocqueville observed in the early decades of the American experiment, "Among democratic nations, each generation is a new people." And those generations are defined not by age or by family relationships, but by the major historical and social events of their lifetimes, or what generational theorists William Strauss and Neil Howe called the study of "people moving through time." Building off the work of German sociologist Karl Mannheim, Strauss and Howe concluded that each generation develops some shared general attitudes based on their formative experiences: the generation that fought World War II, they suggest, gravitated toward civic engagement (the so-called Greatest Generation), while their children—the baby boomers—tended to be more individualistic. Although their theory is surely overgeneralized, there are glimmers of truth within the stereotypes. In what now reads like an eerie premonition, Strauss and Howe picked a young New York businessman as the archetypal boomer in their 1991 opus *Generations*: "Like Donald Trump," they wrote, "a prototype Boomer sees himself capable of becoming a titan of whatever world he chooses fully to inhabit—providing cover for personal disappointments or (as a Boomer might put it) 'deferred ambitions.'"

Since each of us is a product of historical experiences as well as personal ones, age is a useful proxy for understanding the forces that shape political attitudes. Social scientists have found that, along with typical indicators such as race, religion, and family, the historical events experienced in early adulthood significantly shape lifelong political leanings. In the same way that the first few years of education determine the way children learn, the first few years of political awareness determine the way adults vote and lead. Therefore, what leaders experienced—or didn't experience—when they were young can affect their priorities when they're older. Trump, for example, learned to read before *Brown v. Board of Education*, graduated from college during the protests against the Vietnam War, and was well into middle age by the time scientists started to realize the seriousness of human impact on climate change. Joe Biden (b. 1942) was a young adult when JFK was elected, a grown man during the civil rights movement, and already a grieving dad in the US Senate during the 1970s push for women's liberation. Age can also determine how quickly leaders adapt to new technology and ideas: when

Facebook was created in 2004, Mitch McConnell (b. 1942) was eligible for Social Security.

Age, then, is not just a number; it can help measure whether our leaders are closer to the past than they are to the future. Many of the assumptions of the twentieth century seem hopelessly outdated in the twenty-first, and where boomers see icons, many millennials see relics. Longtime Democratic Senator Diane Feinstein—who in 2018 won a reelection that would keep her in the Senate until her nineties—highlighted this generational tension when she dismissed a sixteen-year-old climate activist because "you didn't vote for me."

When I started writing this book in 2017, there were shockingly few millennials in elected office: just five in Congress, even though if representation were proportional to population there should have been about ninety-seven.

But millennials were already making changes on the state and local level. When I first met Mayor Pete Buttigieg for coffee in 2017, he mentioned a Jon Stewart graduation speech that he had recently found on YouTube. "He said, 'Here's the thing about the real world: we broke it, sorry'—I think he meant grown-ups," Pete told me, shouting over the noise in a coffee shop in Midtown Manhattan. "He said, 'We broke it, but the thing is, if you figure out how to fix it, you get to be the next Greatest Generation.'" Back then, Pete was just the ambitious mayor of a small American city, but clearly angling for something bigger: he was already working with top Democratic strategists and hobnobbing with national reporters in preparation for his next move.

New York congresswoman Alexandria Ocasio-Cortez doesn't have much in common with Pete Buttigieg politically, but on this they agree: "The America we grew up in is nothing like the America our parents or our grandparents grew up in," she told me in her office on Capitol Hill. "A lot of what we have to deal with are issues and decisions that were made by people in generations before us."

Over the last three years, the quiet rumblings of generational change have become a deafening roar. You can hear it in the din of the crowds at campaign rallies, in the youthful voices singing at global climate marches, in the staticky silence after Mark Zuckerberg has to explain to retirement-age senators how Facebook makes money. You can sense it in the urgency around tackling police violence, the demands to address the student debt crisis, and the drumbeat of youth-led activism around reforming America's gun laws. You can see it in the young mayors implementing progressive policies on the local level, in the first-time women candidates who seized congressional seats in the 2018 midterms, and in the massive youth voter turnout that helped oust Donald Trump from office.

Still, millennials will have to continue to significantly increase their voter turnout in order to turn their social power into real political gains. They're already stirring: while young voters still vote less reliably than their grandparents, millennial turnout doubled in the 2018 midterms, and surged again in the 2020 presidential election, suggesting that their phase of political apathy may be coming to an end. It's also worth noting that young voters don't necessarily favor young candidates: just look at the youth movement sustaining seventy-eight-year-old Bernie Sanders's political ambitions.

The first wave of the millennial vanguard came after the 2008 election, when a handful of young people—many of them young black men—heeded Obama's call to be "the change that we seek" and stepped up to run for state and local offices around the country. From Stockton, California, to Ithaca, New York, millennials took their first steps toward civic leadership by revitalizing American cities for the twenty-first century.

Then, in 2016, Hillary Clinton tried to become the first woman president, and Donald Trump was elected instead. That election shifted the calculus for many young people, as Obama's rosy vision of American progress was suddenly cast in shadow. One of the most racially diverse generations in history saw a president defend white nationalists while denigrating immigrants and nonwhite Americans. The generation that would inherit a dying planet saw a seventy-one-year-old withdraw from the Paris Climate Agreement. The most openly LGBTQ generation in history saw him ban transgender people from the military. The generation raised on third-wave feminism saw a man who bragged about grabbing women "by the pussy" beat the first woman to have a serious chance at the presidency.

Some despaired, but others mobilized. And as young black men had stepped up to emulate Obama after 2008, young women stepped up to confront Trump after 2016. In the wake of his election, a historic wave of young first-time women candidates ran for offices as big as Congress and as small as town council. Because of women like Alexandria Ocasio-Cortez of New York, Haley Stevens of Michigan, and Lauren Underwood of Illinois, there were more women in Congress in 2019 than ever before, and millennial representation had jumped fivefold in one cycle.

This book is not a forty-under-forty list of Washington, DC, power players, nor is it a comprehensive account of the most powerful millennials in the country (which would include generational outliers such as Trump advisors Stephen Miller and Jared Kushner, who are not elected, and not exactly representative of their generation). It's also not an up-to-the-minute news account of the inner workings of Washington, DC: I finished reporting this book in the fall of 2019, but the unprecedented events of 2020 have only sharpened the point. And while I include Republicans such as Dan Crenshaw and Elise Stefanik, the majority of young leaders in this book are Democrats. That's a reflection of the political identity of this generation, which leans to the left by almost every available metric. A 2018 Pew Research Center survey found that nearly 60 percent of millennials say they're "consistently" or "mostly" liberal, while only 12 percent say they're "consistently" or "mostly" conservative.

I selected characters whose lives were marked by the major events of the first decades of the twenty-first century: 9/11, the wars in Iraq and Afghanistan, the Great Recession, the election of Barack Obama and then Donald Trump. These events shaped their personal experiences—they fought overseas, or experienced the economic collapse firsthand, or worked in the Obama White House—but also informed the broader attitudes of their peers. Millennials are more financially precarious, less likely to support war overseas, and significantly more progressive than their parents on most issues. They've largely abandoned the sexual politics of the Christian right and feel significantly more urgency around addressing climate change. They grew up in an America that is more diverse and more socially progressive than any time in history, and their lives reflect both the increased opportunities for women and people of color, and the work still left to do. Their lifetimes have been punctuated by school shootings and extreme weather events, and their reality has been defined by the failure of old structures and the rise of new systems. By learning where they've been, we can get a sense of where we're going.

Every couple of decades, American politics experiences a generational turnover. The Greatest Generation, the ones who fought WWII, led the civic revival of the 1950s and '60s, building everything from the national highway system to world class research universities to the rockets that took men to the moon. The Silent Generation came into office in the 1970s as "Watergate babies" determined to reform Washington after Nixon's scandal. The boomers began their takeover in the 1980s and '90s with an emphasis on individualism that led them toward privatization, tax cuts, and an emphasis on "personal responsibility." Generation X (born in the late 1960s and '70s) is on the ascent, with leaders like Kamala Harris and Stacey Abrams entering center stage.

Millennials are next to seize the torch. This book is about what they believe and why they believe it, and what America might look like when they're in charge.

AUTHOR'S NOTE

I am writing about politicians who were a particular age at a particular time, not just any young "hotshots." So I had to be ruthless about the age cutoff: nobody born before 1980 or after 1996 is included here at significant length. (Pew says the first millennials were born in 1981, but politics moves a little slower than everything else, so I extended the window to 1980 in order to include Carlos Curbelo.) Unfortunately, that meant leaving out exciting Gen X-ers such as Rep. Katie Porter (b. 1974), Rep. Ayanna Pressley (b. 1974), and GOP senator Josh Hawley (b. 1979), and powerful Gen-Z activists like Emma Gonzalez (b. 1999), David Hogg (b. 2000), and Greta Thunberg (b. 2003). They are all poised to make their mark on American politics, and they would be great characters in another book.

If I had been writing in the mid-twentieth century, I would have followed the convention of calling public officials by their last names, mostly because so many of the white men in power at that time had the same first names: John, Michael, Robert, or James. The fact that none of the main characters in this book have the same first name reflects the astonishing shift toward racial and gender diversity of the early twenty-first century. Besides, this is also a book about that uniquely American alchemy through which an ordinary person becomes a public official. Because this is about human transformations as well as political ones, I am using first names throughout.

Just as the last twenty years have been punctuated by mass shootings and increasingly severe hurricanes, this narrative is periodically interrupted by short episodes about these events. The shooting episodes are constructed almost entirely from contemporaneous news and social media, while the hurricane episodes are short summaries of the human cost of these major storms.

Finally, you may be wondering what I mean by "the ones we've been waiting for." Who are "we" supposed to be, anyway, and who am I to suggest what we're "waiting for"? The title of this book is taken from a pivotal Barack Obama speech during the 2008 primary. He may have adapted the line from author Alice Walker, who may have borrowed it from the poet June Jordan, but on Super Tuesday, 2008, he transformed the words into a rallying cry:

> You see, the challenges we face will not be solved with one meeting in one night. It will not be resolved on even a Super Duper Tuesday. Change will not come if we wait for some other person or if we wait for some other time. We are the ones we've been waiting for. We are the change that we seek.

It may seem overly triumphant to use this line to describe an entire generation, even one that was so heavily influenced by Obama's example. The optimism of the Obama era was exciting but incomplete: his hope came with blind spots, and his work was unfinished. Besides, the millennial-led future won't be a rosy utopia: the next generation of leaders will no doubt create as many problems as they solve, and many of those new problems aren't yet apparent. America in 2050 won't necessarily be better than America in 2020 just because millennials will be in charge.

But the phrase is prophetic in its plurality: the sense that America's future will not be built in one night, but in an era; not by one, but by ones.

THE ONES
(IN BIRTH ORDER)

Pete Buttigieg, born 1982, the one who ran for president (Indiana).

Haley Stevens, born 1983, the one who worked on the auto rescue (Michigan).

Braxton Winston, born 1983, the one who protested to defend black lives (North Carolina).

Elise Stefanik, born 1984, the one who tried to recruit more women to the GOP (New York).

Dan Crenshaw, born 1984, the one who lost his eye in Afghanistan (Texas).

Eric Lesser, born 1985, the one who handled bags for Barack Obama (Massachusetts).

Max Rose, born 1986, the one who's not a fucking socialist (New York).

Lauren Underwood, born 1986, the one with a preexisting condition (Illinois).

Svante Myrick, born 1987, the one who rebuilt downtown Ithaca (New York).

Alexandria Ocasio-Cortez, born 1989, the one who proposed a Green New Deal (New York).

PART ONE

This is the millennium of Aftermath.

—DR. DRE

CHAPTER I

One Sunny Tuesday

I t was a Tuesday morning and a heartless sun was shining. It burned through the windows of fresh September classrooms, reminding students that they still had ten months of school before summer vacation. It slashed the blinds of darkened college dorm rooms and beamed at early risers shuffling to class. It flashed against big glass buildings and made short shadows in Lower Manhattan, where it glinted off the fuselage of low-flying airplanes.

The leaves in Cambridge, Massachusetts, had not yet started to turn. It was still summer, and still hot, and classes hadn't begun at Harvard, which meant that sophomore Pete Buttigieg was lying on his bottom bunk in Leverett House on that Tuesday morning when his roommate Uzo knocked on the door. Uzo was out of breath because he had just run back from the bank in Harvard Square. He had gone there early to sort out a problem with his debit card, and the bank teller had said, "You know, a plane just flew into the World Trade Center." Uzo said, "That's weird," but he figured it was probably an accident. By the time he was done fixing the debit card issue, the teller had seen a news alert that there was a second plane.

When Pete and Uzo turned on the TV, every channel had the same video on loop: the planes flying into the towers, the cloud of gray smoke against a blue sky. On the *Today* show, Katie Couric and Matt Lauer were taking calls from people on the ground in Lower Manhattan. By then the other guys had woken up, and they were all sitting on the floor of their half-unpacked common room, watching the footage replay over and over.

It was class registration day, and Pete didn't know what else to do, so after a few hours of watching the news he went out. He walked away from the river, up past the Harvard Lampoon Building, which looked like a castle designed by a circus clown, past the newspaper and the bookstore and all the old buildings that had been standing since before the Civil War. He walked around the back of Widener Library, and into Harvard Yard.

Someone had organized an interfaith prayer service on the steps of Memorial Church, and when Pete—or Peter, as he was called back then—paused to join it, he looked up and saw a lone fighter jet in the cloudless sky. Pete, who was already a tad more grandiose than your average nineteen-year-old boy, began to rethink his cohort's "generational purpose." He realized that he was living through what historians might call a "fulcrum of history." These were the kinds of things Pete thought about often, but on this day, his usual sense of momentousness seemed to match the moment.

Pete was a dorky kid, with a chubby face and a smile that actually turned up at the edges, like something drawn by Dr. Seuss. He was one of the only freshman kids at Harvard from South Bend, Indiana, and when he first arrived he felt as if he were entering an X-Men universe where everyone else had superpowers. Some kids at Harvard were tech wizards (like Mark Zuckerberg, who lived a few dorms over in Kirkland House), others were artistic prodigies (like his roommate Uzo, better known as Uzodinma Iweala, who wrote the bestselling novel *Beasts of No Nation* while still in college), and others were so rich and connected they might as well have been born wearing tuxedos.

Pete wasn't any of those things. Back then he was a fashion disaster: he mostly wore too-big polo shirts with baggy khakis and Clarks. His eyebrows looked like two caterpillars huddled in intense conversation about James Joyce. His friends recall him having an "old man calm," a sort of hokey sophistication that was at once impressive and a little weird, but still genuine. Like how when everyone else was drinking Miller Lite out of Solo Cups, Pete would drink nice whiskey from a glass. Or like how he would rather smoke a pipe or a cigar than a cigarette or a joint. (On one of the few times he did take a hit of a joint, he almost got busted for it in a police encounter that he knew would surely have gone differently if he wasn't white.) While other college sophomores were figuring out where they could get a game of beer pong going, Pete was installing a real wood bar in their dorm room. His room-mates remembered that he would bring smoked fish into the room some-times, or get gift hampers full of jams and fancy snacks, all in beautiful little tins that didn't seem as if they belonged next to all the potato chips in a college dorm room. He had a girlfriend briefly—a smart, nice girl by all recollection—but when his roommates gathered on Sunday mornings to compare hookup stories from the night before, he never joined in. Instead, he was the one who would insist that five college bros put up an actual, live Christmas tree with real decorations. He reminded his roommates of Jed Bartlet, the president in *The West Wing*: kind, intellectual, listening for a higher calling.

When he wasn't studying Puritan texts or running meetings as the stu-dent president of the Institute of Politics, Pete spent his time writing col-umns for *The Harvard Crimson*. His favorite subject was the battle over political language, which he knew Republicans were winning. "The real chal-lenge for the Democratic Party, and its presidential candidates in particular, is to figure out how to reverse the Right's stranglehold on our political vo-cabulary," he wrote. "If the Dems don't act fast to reclaim our language, they risk losing the word battle before they realize they're fighting it." A year later, he returned to the subject. "Establishing a new vocabulary is not the point," he wrote. "We need to take the old vocabulary and make it make sense again."

Pete was raised amid long conversations about the meanings of words: how they work, what they mean, and how they could become imbued with power. He was born in 1982, the only child of two Notre Dame professors: his mother taught linguistics; his father, who had emigrated from the tiny Med-iterranean island of Malta, taught English. By the time he was born, South Bend was already deep in nostalgia for another era. It had been two de-cades since the Studebaker plant—once the largest automotive factory in the world—shut its doors forever. Pete didn't even ask about the massive old crumbling building he saw from the back seat of his dad's car on the way to the grocery store. Studebaker was to his South Bend childhood what the Colosseum is to modern Rome: a landmark, a relic, something to drive by.

Pete had always been a Very Good Boy. So good that nobody who knew him—not his mother, his mother's friends, his high school friends, his teachers, his college classmates—can remember a cross word or an outburst or a screw-up of any kind. No rough patches, no flameouts, no big fights with his parents or embarrassing moments or awkward phases. Sure, Pete's whole adolescence could look like one big awkward phase, mainly because he had a truly awful bowl cut. He seemed like the kind of kid other kids should hate—a multilingual only child who was trained in classical piano and wasn't an athlete—except they just . . . didn't. He was friendly and eager to help with homework, and he didn't talk about himself very often. He had enough humility to offset his accomplishments, enough curiosity to endear him to strangers, and enough of a sense of humor to laugh at himself when he needed to. He was a perfect concoction of immense talent and impressiveness with just the right amount of likability to keep him from being insufferable. "At times it was a little frustrating," one of his high school friends remembered. "Like: What is this, who are you?"

He moved schools a lot, and he had a weird last name—he was constantly having to explain that it was Maltese, that it was pronounced "Boot-edge-edge"—but none of that ever seemed to really bother him. He had an old-fashioned kind of way about him, a solidity that might once have been called "good sense." He was the type of boy who would arrange for all the kids on the block to pool their Halloween candy for the one kid whose candy got stolen. Pete's mother, Dr. Anne Montgomery, calls these kids his "pals" and "neighborhood fellows," a phrase that conjures images of stickball and knee socks even though Pete and his friends spent their time playing *Mario Kart* on Super Nintendo in the basement. His friends sensed something sad about him, that he was a little apart, but they mostly figured it was just that he didn't have any siblings.

As an only child, he never developed the instinct for conflict. Once, when he was about three or four, Pete was playing in the backyard with a family friend when the girl's mother looked out the window and noticed they were hitting each other over the head with big plastic gardening tools, calmly and deliberately. The girl's mother called out to ask what they were doing. "We're not fighting," young Pete explained. "We're playing monster."

"Then why are you hitting each other?" the mother asked.

"Because that's what monsters do."

Years later, the little girl's father would ask her why she didn't date that nice young man, Peter Buttigieg. "Dad," the girl would say. "He's obviously gay."

In retrospect, of course, it all made sense. In 1973, writer Andrew Tobias first popularized the "best little boy in the world" hypothesis, which suggests that closeted young men often become overachievers in order to deflect attention from their sexuality. In 2013, this theory was substantiated in a study that found that young men who were hiding their sexual orientation were more likely to derive their self-worth from academics, appearance, and competitive performance—and that the longer they stayed in the closet, the more they achieved. Pete knew in high school that he was, as he told me later, "really strongly attracted to other young men." But he tried to believe that his sexuality was on a sliding scale, and he focused on the part of himself he insisted must be straight.

In the meantime, he was keeping himself extraordinarily busy with nearly every academic accomplishment he could find. In high school, he entered an essay competition sponsored by the John F. Kennedy Presidential Library's Profile in Courage Award. Almost two decades before millions of other young people would become enamored with his subject, Pete chose to write about a lawmaker who was at that point fairly obscure: Senator Bernie Sanders of Vermont.

The essay started off as predictable high school drivel ("There are a daunting number of important issues which are to be confronted if we are to progress as a nation") and ended up a premonition. He lamented the moral timidity of politics ("Candidates have discovered that it is easier to be elected by not offending anyone rather than by impressing voters") and politicians who "outgrow their convictions in order to win power." Sanders, he thought, represented an important distinction in American politics: compromise was not the same as centrism, and collaboration was not the same as capitulation.

He ended with a hint at his own ambitions: "I commend Bernie Sanders for giving me an answer to those who say American young people see politics as a cesspool of corruption, beyond redemption," he wrote. "I have heard that no sensible young person today would want to give his or her life to public service. I can personally assure you this is untrue."

A year later, he arrived at Harvard. As a freshman, he ate his meals in Memorial Hall, built in honor of the Harvard men who fought and died for the Union in the Civil War. Their names were inscribed on the neo-Gothic walls in neat letters on slabs of marble. Sometimes, he liked to stand in the cool silence and read the lists of dead boys, very good boys just like him, who had slept where he slept and studied where he studied, who seemed different from him only because of the times in which they lived.

He thought of those names that day, as he looked up and saw the fighter jet pierce the sky. He hadn't even realized how peaceful his childhood had been until it was over.

✳ ✳ ✳

Haley Stevens slept through the sunlight. She was having a dream where she was in grave danger, surrounded by smoke and noise. She could hear sirens and somebody screaming at her, "Get out! Get out! Get out!" When she opened her eyes, her dorm phone was ringing, and when she picked up she heard Kari's mom's voice on the other end of the line. Kari, who slept in the standard twin bed a few feet away from Haley's in Letts Hall 307, was already on the way to her early-morning class, but her mom was screaming into the phone. Haley turned on the tiny TV in her dorm room just in time to see the second tower fall.

She was a freshman at American University in Washington, DC, the first in her family to go to an elite school. Haley was short, with thick dark hair and a low forehead and a sharp chin. She had a heavy Michigan accent and a loud voice and an ability to both grin widely and say "Nice to meetcha!" at the same time. Haley was a worker, a doer, a show-up-early-and-stay-up-late kind of person. She buzzed through her days in a frenzy of activity, and by 2:00 a.m., unable to sleep, she would stay up late writing mediocre poetry in her journal.

Here, in Letts 307, she was on her own for the first time; she could do what she wanted and be who she wanted to be. She and her roommate, Kari, were opposites—Kari was more of an Urban Outfitters type, with low-cut jeans and T-shirts that said things like "Gettin' Lucky in Kentucky." Haley wore sweatshirts, red running shorts, and a side ponytail, sort of a *Wet Hot American Summer* camp counselor look. Kari was vaguely Republican; Haley was a die-hard Democrat. Haley surprised Kari for her nineteenth birthday by taking her out to dinner wearing fake fur coats and tiaras and smoking cigars.

On that sunny Tuesday, when Kari finally made it home from class, she found Haley sitting in bed, wrapped in a blanket, looking at the television. Nobody seemed to know what was going on, but Haley was instantly sure. "It's an attack," she said, and then looked back at the TV.

By that point, the cell phones were down, and almost nobody in DC could talk to anybody that they couldn't see face-to-face. Groups of freshmen slowly gathered in the halls of Letts, swapping different versions of the same information, every hour another rumor of a plane hitting the place their parents lived. The professors and RAs—the adults who were supposed to know things—had no answers. People started talking about whether they should call their parents to say goodbye.

A few days after she arrived at college, Haley had called her mother, Maria, to tell her about her courses. Maria was Haley's best friend: they had the same big smile and loud laugh. Haley told Maria she was taking writing and literature, and that her political science class would take field trips to government buildings around DC. She told her they were going to the Pentagon next.

So on that Tuesday, when someone turned on the TV at Maria's office and said, "A plane just hit the Pentagon." Maria's body went numb. She tried to call Haley's dorm phone, but the call wouldn't connect because all the phone lines in DC were jammed up. Her child was in a city where planes were falling out of the sky, possibly in a building that was a target of a terrorist attack. Everyone in her office began calling Haley's dorm phone, trying to reach her. She spent the day frantic until she finally thought to log on to AOL Instant Messenger, and there was a message from Haley: she was all right.

Haley had Michigan in her veins. Her parents ran a landscaping company in the suburbs of Detroit. Bad weather meant good snowplow business, and the company did OK for a while. Maria and her husband, Jim, were Reagan Republicans, like lots of people in Michigan: commonsense conservatives, not particularly religious, just trying to do what was best for small business. But more importantly, they were a Ford family: Jim's dad had been a Ford union worker, Jim drove a Ford pickup truck for landscaping, Haley learned to drive in a Ford Expedition (the giant SUV), and after her parents' divorce, her father drove around in a Ford Bronco—white, just like OJ's. Haley didn't know it yet, but the auto industry would help determine her future.

After Maria and Jim's divorce, Maria got a job at her sister's advertising agency and moved with the kids to Birmingham, Michigan, a neat suburb about forty minutes from Detroit. Most people there worked for Chrysler or GM, or for a supplier that sold parts to Chrysler or GM, or for a company that sold things to people who worked for Chrysler or GM.

Around the time of the divorce, Haley started journaling more. Mostly it was just dispatches from camp, or middle school social cartography, or bad poetry. Once, she wrote an in-depth account of her road trip to the Lip Smackers factory. But her parents read the newspaper and watched the evening news, and she wasn't ignorant to the things that were happening in the world. And so on Christmas Eve 1999, sixteen-year-old Haley opened her journal, gripped a purple marker, and wrote in large round letters, "Haley's Millennium Ideas."

"The polar ice caps are going to melt and flood California and Seattle and some other West Coast states," she wrote. "We have two years to stop the floods and wars and the human destruction. But what are we going to do about it in the meantime? Sit on our naive asses and laugh?" Filled with indignation and a heavy dose of drama, she spent her Christmas Eve listing her geopolitical concerns. "Natural disasters and mad leaders at war (Saddam Hussein) . . . What we read and what we do became so unbalanced and money driven. . . . Pick up a magazine and I bet all it talks about is who's doing and wearing what."

"We won't hear what the prophets say," she wrote. "We won't stop our mistakes. So what the prophets predict will come true."

Haley may have been writing in magic marker, in a fit of teenage ennui, but she wasn't wrong: she was entering a screwed-up world, and even in 1999, she knew it. Two years later, sitting in her dorm room bed wrapped in a blanket, it seemed as if she had been right.

* * *

More than 150 miles away from Ground Zero, Elise Stefanik was sitting in her senior AP English class at the Albany Academy for Girls. They were in the middle of a critical writing exercise that morning when the dean of the high school came into class and pulled the English teacher outside. A few minutes later the teacher came back and her face had changed. Elise could tell that something had happened, but the teacher just sat in silence while the girls finished their exercise. Elise looked around, trying to sense if anybody knew what was going on, but everybody had their head down over their papers.

When they finally left class and saw the news, Elise's friend Kate collapsed to the floor: Her sister worked in the World Trade Center. They all tried to comfort her, but there was nothing they could say: nobody could reach Kate's sister, which meant nobody could be sure of anything. Elise says she will never forget that sick feeling of watching her friend on the floor, surrounded by helpless teenage girls.

Everything in Albany shut down that day. Everyone who had a flag flew it out their window. The Old Navy where Elise worked after school was closed. Elise and the senior council president planned a fundraiser for the Red Cross. Kate's sister, it turned out, had been late to work that day and hadn't been in the towers when they fell.

The school year chugged forward. Eventually, the flags came down and the Old Navy reopened. But it was caught in her memory: the look on her teacher's face, Kate on the floor, the flags. "It's one of the reasons why I wanted to go into public policy," she told me later. "On that day, we became a globally aware generation."

Elise had bright eyes and long dark hair and round cheeks, like a living version of Samantha the American Girl doll. She liked listening to Broadway musical soundtracks—especially *The Sound of Music* and *My Fair Lady*—but she also liked *NSYNC, loved Billy Joel, and was a Gloria Estefan superfan. She played varsity lacrosse and was president of the student council and captain of the mock trial team. People who knew her in high school say she was "driven" and "competitive," but also recall her being true to her word. She was widely respected. "As much as I wanted to hate her for certain things, I never really could," recalled one classmate who described herself as "frenemies" with Elise. "Because along with the drive and the boldness, I also sensed a lot of integrity."

Albany Academy was one of the oldest continuous all-girls schools in the country, but it was small—less than fifty girls in the whole class. They had a uniform: a navy plaid skirt, with a yellow or navy sweater or blazer and brown shoes. Being surrounded by girls gave Elise a certain confidence: all the best students were girls, and everyone who raised their hand in math was a girl, and the best athletes were girls. Her ethos was simple: do the work, step up to the plate, look grown-ups in the eye, don't rock the boat. In sixth grade, she ran for student council on a platform of getting a new snack machine. She and her friend Melissa DeRosa negotiated a deal with the janitors to ensure that kids would help clean up the candy wrappers, Melissa said, then negotiated a deal with the vending machine company so that a certain portion of the profits would go to the school. In the end, they got it done, and Elise and Melissa would stay lifelong friends, even as Melissa went on to be a top aide to Democratic governor Andrew Cuomo.

"Even in high school she was a young Republican," one friend recalls. "I think that her father being this business owner probably had a lot to do with it." Elise's father had gotten his first job cutting door frames and worked his way up in the wood industry until he started Premium Plywood Products, which distributed plywood to companies around the Northeast. The business did very well: high school friends remember visiting her at home and immediately thinking her family was rich. "When I went to her house, I was embarrassed for when she would come to mine," said one friend. "Her house was so big and expensive and fancy looking." But her parents hadn't graduated from college, which meant that academics was very important for them; college, for Elise, would be the next step toward the Stefanik family's American dream.

Elise took that very seriously. By the time she was a senior, the Stefanik family had been talking about college for years—Georgetown and the

University of Chicago were on her list—but classmates remembered that Elise was obsessed with Harvard. "From the moment I set foot in Albany Academy," a classmate said, "someone pointed out Elise and said 'That's Elise, she's the smartest person in the class, she's going to Harvard.'" On the day she was finally accepted, friends remember her sobbing in the halls.

When she got to Harvard, she joined the Institute of Politics, where Pete was already pretty much in charge.

✳ ✳ ✳

That morning doesn't stick out in Dan Crenshaw's mind very much at all. He was a junior in high school, living in Colombia, where his father was working as a petroleum engineer. Nobody turned on the TV at school; no announcement came over the loudspeaker. To his Colombian friends, this was something that was happening to other people in another country, but Dan felt like he was watching from afar as his nation was attacked. Besides, Dan was already 100 percent sure of the only thing in his life that really mattered, which was that he would be a Navy SEAL. What happened in New York just gave him something to fight for when he joined.

Dan was born to American parents in Scotland, but he spent the first years of his life in Katy, Texas, a Houston exurb that was mostly soccer fields and football fields and neatly planned communities of people who socialized on soccer fields and football fields. When he was five, all apple cheeks and sandy hair, his mother was diagnosed with breast cancer. He spent most of elementary school shuffling through chemo wards with her and his brother, carrying his books and his spy toys and learning how to not complain.

Dan's mom hated feeling sorry for herself, and she couldn't stand it when other people felt sorry for her either. There was a stench of pity that surrounded cancer treatment, and Dan's mom wanted no part of it. People tell themselves different stories in this life, he learned, and you could tell yourself a victimhood story or you could tell yourself a story of overcoming adversity. If you told yourself a victimhood story, then you would always be trapped in that story: your life would be defined by things that happen to you, and everything would always be somebody else's fault. Dan's mother told herself the other story, the one where she was the protagonist who overcame adversity. Mental toughness, it was called. A sense of responsibility for yourself, regardless of your circumstances. She died when he was ten.

Around that time, Dan picked up *Rogue Warrior* by former Navy SEAL Richard Marcinko. It was "the Explosive, #1 *New York Times* Bestselling Autobiography of the Controversial, Death-Defying Founder of the U.S. Navy's Top Secret Counterterrorist Unit, SEAL Team Six," according to the cover. The book had Marcinko on the cover looking like a badass, all bulging muscles and manly beard, staring out from the book as though he was deciding whether you were worth a bullet or if he should kill you with his bare hands.

Marcinko was usually posing holding a huge gun, or with his face superimposed over an explosion. Dan read every book Marcinko ever wrote: *Red Cell*, *Echo Platoon*, *SEAL Force Alpha*. By the time he was in middle school, Dan knew he wanted to be a Navy SEAL, to defy death.

By then, his dad had moved them from Katy to Ecuador, and then Ecuador to Colombia. Dan grew up going to international schools and speaking fluent Spanish and missing a lot of what was happening in the United States. It didn't make him less patriotic—if anything, it made being American more fundamental; it was his identifying characteristic. He didn't move back to the United States until he went to college two years after that Tuesday, on an ROTC scholarship to Tufts University.

He had always planned on doing ROTC or the Naval Academy, so figuring out how to pay for college wasn't a problem for him. Still, "it's not totally fair to say that I had no student loan debt," he said later. "I paid in blood."

✳ ✳ ✳

A few hours after the sun rose that Tuesday on the too-green lawns of Naperville, Illinois, Lauren Underwood was walking to first-period Honors Algebra II and saw a screen full of smoke on a school TV. She wondered why they were playing a movie so early in the morning. She was a sophomore, one of only a few black students at Neuqua Valley High School in Naperville. She had never had a black teacher.

With nearly 150,000 residents, Naperville—thirty minutes west of

Chicago—was what white people call "comfortable." It was affluent, but not like Winnetka or Lake Forest, and the Underwoods were friends with the handful of other black families in their neighborhood.

Lauren was a Girl Scout. She loved Whitney Houston and *Little House on the Prairie* and soapy novels about teens with cancer who fall in love. She smiled a lot, almost too much, and would greet any good news (a lost shoe found, a school team victory) with an exuberant grin. She smiled so much that sometimes people wondered, "What is she smiling about? What's such good news?" and then wondered if she was faking. But that's just what she was like. She emoted with people. She was full of plans and solutions and schedules, and she didn't have funks; she wasn't the type to go hang out in her friends' bedrooms and complain. It made it hard to connect with people, being so "on" all the time. She didn't have as many friends in high school as her younger sister, Lindsey, who didn't really smile as often, who liked to gossip and whine about teachers. Lindsey was cool. Lauren was warm and hardworking and smart and diligent, but she was never cool.

Second period that morning was social studies. Nobody knew what was going on in New York, so Lauren just sat there, listening to her teacher without understanding or writing much down. When she and Lindsey got home from school, their father was watching TV. On the news they said that people were jumping out of the towers.

A few days later she and her friends went out to buy patriotic T-shirts to show solidarity with the victims—hers was Ralph Lauren, red, white, and blue. Some people got those T-shirts with "I Heart New York" on them. If you were a fourteen-year-old girl in central Illinois, what else could you do?

That weekend the Underwood family went to church. Because there were so few black people in Naperville, Lauren's parents wanted them to go to a black church in Chicago. So Sundays, Lauren and Lindsey would have to get up at eight thirty to make it to Trinity United Church of Christ services that started at eleven on the South Side. *And* they had to wear pantyhose, which sucked. Church was supposed to end at one thirty, but if somebody caught the spirit (and somebody always caught the spirit), they'd be there until two, and they wouldn't get home until three o'clock. Every. Single. Week.

On that particular week, the Underwoods filed past the well-dressed older ladies into their usual seats, on the balcony right in the middle. And after some singing and prayers and some more singing and more prayers, Rev. Jeremiah Wright walked across the ruby-red carpet in the center of the church and reached the pulpit and began to speak.

"There's a move in Psalm 137 from thoughts of paying tithes"—he paused—"to thoughts of paying back." He waved his hand from right to left, as if he were turning a page in a massive book. "A move, if you will, from worship to war." He continued, building his voice. "It is a move that spotlights the insanity of the cycle of violence and the cycle of hatred."

Lauren and Lindsey sat there. Maybe they listened, maybe they didn't. They were basically kids, so they weren't necessarily paying attention. Church was something their religious parents made them do. This was one of the most prominent black churches in the city: Obama, who was then teaching at the University of Chicago, also belonged there, but the Underwoods didn't know him. Their dad was in the choir but the church was an hour away from their house in Naperville, too far for them to have any real friends there, so they mostly just sat through the services until it was time to go home. Besides, their parents wanted less politics and more religion from Rev. Wright. They all agreed that he was a little much.

"We have moved from the hatred of armed enemies to the hatred of unarmed innocents." He pointed his finger. "We want revenge, we want paybacks, and we don't care who gets hurt in the process."

Then Reverend Wright went into what he calls a "faith footnote." Everyone in the congregation turned to their neighbor and said, "Faith footnote." Lauren might have turned to Lindsey and said, "Faith footnote." Lindsey might have rolled her eyes.

He listed all the atrocities America had committed against innocents, and then finished in a grand and controversial crescendo. "America's chickens," he said, twirling around and waving his hand in the air, "are coming home"—he paused again, for dramatic effect—"to roost!"

Lindsey and Lauren don't remember much about that day. Lauren wouldn't even think about the speech until years later, when it was used as a political attack against Barack Obama when he was running for president. To them, it was just another day of getting up, finding a skirt, going to church, and sitting through a sermon.

❋ ❋ ❋*

On Monday, Max Rose's biggest concern was that he was about six inches shorter than every other tenth grader in Brooklyn, or at least that's what it seemed like. Also: a ginger. Also: freckles.

On Tuesday, he was a fourteen-year-old sophomore listening to an announcement over the loudspeaker in a moment of cold fear. His mother usually worked in Lower Manhattan, near the towers, at the Borough of Manhattan Community College. If there was a terrorist attack on downtown Manhattan, he thought, then his mother might be dead.

As it happened, she had been teaching uptown that morning, and she wasn't near the towers when they fell. Lisa Rose called her husband, Hal, who ran a medical lab in Brooklyn, and they agreed he should go pick up Max and his sister from school. Then she walked downtown to take an F train home, underneath nervous helicopters, with a smell of burning in the air.

Some of the kids Max knew had dads who were firefighters. These were kids he grew up with, kids that played *Madden* on Nintendo 64 and Sega Genesis at his house, the ones who would sit on stoops in Park Slope and drink beer they'd gotten from the one bodega that would sell to underage kids. He asked his parents, "How many people can't get back to Manhattan? How many people can come sleep over?"

At the time, Lisa says, she didn't fully realize how much it had impacted him. It seemed as if nothing could rattle him, but the attacks did. For weeks afterward, people would stop each other on the street and say, "Your family OK?" Max noticed a sense of people looking out for one another, a new cohesion. He suddenly found himself more patriotic than his parents. A few weeks later, Lisa noticed that Max had put an American flag up in his room.

He grew up in Park Slope—after it got gentrified but before it was full of vegan mommies. He was into all the things that '90s kids were into: Teenage Mutant Ninja Turtles (he liked Leonardo) and NBA video games and playing *Oregon Trail* on his desktop computer.

He was very short, always, and kids could be mean about it. Sometimes kids would say, "You're nine? You look like you're six!" and Max would get upset. Later he would tell his mom that "people have no filter when it comes to height." As a kid in Brooklyn, being very short and a ginger meant only one thing: you had to be, as Max put it, an "intense fucking asshole"—otherwise you were toast.

Puberty seemed as though it would never come, and when it finally did, it didn't make him much taller. But he kept working out, so he got beefy instead. He was like a diamond, a condensed block of male energy made hard and brilliant by sustained pressure, small but sharp and unbreakable. He developed a habit of looking at people straight in the eyes, almost without blinking, daring them to laugh at him.

He was a huge Knicks fan but he didn't even try to play basketball—he wrestled instead, which was the perfect outlet for his intensity and aggression. By the time he was in middle school he loved movies about big guys who exploded things: *Die Hard* was his favorite, but he liked basically anything with Steven Seagal or Jean-Claude Van Damme or Bruce Willis or Arnold Schwarzenegger. He would go to the Pavilion movie theater when it opened in Brooklyn and watch guys in black leather jackets blow things up and then walk away slowly. His personal World Series was when the Rock wrestled "Stone Cold" Steve Austin in 1999. But he was also a guy who watched Hugh Grant romantic comedies with his sister and still had his tap shoes somewhere in his messy room. (The tap lessons had been Lisa's idea; Max insists he "took one fucking class.")

Max had a short fuse. He broke the rules and didn't care. He didn't do drugs, but he drank a lot, and he would have house parties when his parents were out of town and not really bother to clean up, just accept whatever punishment was coming to him, like a man.

Later, people would ask him if he decided to join the military on 9/11, and he would get annoyed, because why was everybody so interested in his reasons for joining the military anyway? Was there something so strange about it? And even if he had decided on that day—which, by the way, he didn't—it wouldn't have been the right way to decide. It's not a lightning bolt. Asking how he became a patriot, he said later, is like asking someone how they decided to fall in love.

Still, his mom thinks what happened that Tuesday did have something to do with his decision to serve. "We were attacked," he told her. "It's different for me, Ma, than it was for you."

✳ ✳ ✳

In Earlville, New York (population ~800), Svante Myrick rolled out of bed around seven fifteen, fought his brothers and sister for hot water and a sliver of soap, and ran out to catch the school bus. He was a ninth grader, just starting high school, trying to be a cool kid the way his brothers had been. His mom left the house at 6:00 a.m. for her job as a cook at a nursing home (or, as Svante called it, "The Home for Healthyish Old Ladies"), but she'd usually leave a big pan of eggs or a hunk of cornbread for breakfast, and they'd pour milk over the cornbread as if it was cereal and mush it up and eat it.

Svante was a small, half-black, tubby kid with a long nose and a wide smile, a middle kid in a troubled family, a peacemaker. He had a minor speech impediment that garbled his Ls and Rs and Ws, so he always thought three sentences ahead to avoid saying words he couldn't pronounce. But with his natural friendliness and sense of humor, that formality became charisma, and the kid who couldn't say his Ls became known as a kid who had a way with words.

He had been born blue, in March 1987 in Florida, strangled by his own umbilical cord. When his mother, Leslie Myrick, finally got home from the hospital, her husband had disappeared (again) and she had been evicted from their apartment. Their church put her and her two toddlers and a newborn up in a hotel for a little while, but they eventually landed in a homeless shelter, where she finally updated Svante's baby book. "Cord around neck 2x," she wrote in neat cursive. "Funny gray color but we loved our third boy!" She named him Svante because she thought it meant "young swan" in Teutonic German. It seemed masculine, she thought, and swans are strong. Later, she would learn that the actual meaning was closer to "anointed."

Leslie had a Janis Joplin look, with curly red hair and small, sharp eyes and a long nose. She met Jesse Myrick at a dance club in '81. He was tall and handsome, with long legs and thick eyelashes and nicely shaped brows. They got married in a civil ceremony and settled in Tampa, Florida. First Mykel was born, then Neith. Leslie's parents, Red and Phyllis, embraced their black son-in-law and their biracial grandsons, and for a while, things were OK. But one day Jesse's sister and brother-in-law came to visit them in their apartment in Tampa, and when somebody brought out a joint, the brother-in-law said, "Let's put this stuff in it." Leslie immediately realized this wasn't the normal weed they smoked. She remembers feeling very happy, ecstatic almost, but she knew something was wrong, and she tried to compartmentalize the feeling. She said it was as if she had a little can in the back of her mind, and she had to put the feeling in the little can so that she wouldn't go toward it again. Jesse didn't have a little can. It turned out the stuff was crack cocaine.

Jesse started getting fired from jobs, disappearing for weeks, stealing money. At the time, Leslie thought there was another woman. Addiction wasn't something people talked about much, and she didn't have the vocabulary to recognize it for what it was. Plus, she was pregnant again, for the third time.

They lived in a homeless shelter in Florida for the first six months of Svante's life. Leslie and Jesse split and reconciled over and over during those first ten years, and the family bounced around to different apartments, sometimes with Jesse, sometimes with a new boyfriend. Wherever they lived, they didn't live there long. Eventually, Leslie took the kids back to Earlville, New York, to live with her parents.

For some kids, all that upheaval would breed resentment, but not for Svante. Somehow, he grew into a relentless optimist. Yes, he was born into a homeless family—but the people who ran the homeless shelter gave his mother a job there. Yes, his family was too poor to afford meals and clothes—but people donated to the food pantry and gave out clothes from the church basement. Yes, there were white kids who would ask him, "Where are you from?" and when he'd say, "New York," they'd say, "No, really, where are you *from*?"—but there were also white kids who befriended him, white teachers who mentored him, white grandparents who raised him. Where others saw

America as a constellation of fatal flaws, Svante saw a country in constant battle with its darker impulses. America was imperfect, but Svante was already used to loving things that weren't perfect.

Finally, when Svante was about eleven, his grandparents bought a house down the street from theirs in Earlville, and Svante and his mother and siblings moved in. It was a small Victorian house, yellow with red trim, just a block down from the only real intersection in Earlville, where North Main Street becomes South Main Street and East Main Street becomes West Main Street. There were five bedrooms, one for each of them, and the bedrooms on the second floor had doors in the walls so that the kids could get in and out of one another's rooms without going into the hallway. Svante decorated his bedroom with pictures of basketball players he cut out from *Sports Illustrated* and *Slam* magazine: Allen Iverson, Tracy McGrady, Vince Carter.

Before the house, they were living so close to the edge that Svante had a constant sense of existential dread. Being poor meant being afraid all the time. There was always a possibility that that they would be kicked out of wherever they were living and have to find someplace else, and then Svante would have to put his books and clothes into garbage bags again. Svante couldn't think about the future because he was just thinking about that day— he couldn't focus on his homework if he didn't know whether they'd be moving the next week.

The house changed everything because it changed almost nothing. Leslie could afford the rent, and even if she couldn't, the kids knew that their grandparents were the landlords so they would never really be evicted. But the stability was the biggest change. For the first time, Svante's life entered a period where his only uncertainties were small and adolescent—his body morphing, his friendships reshuffling, his classwork accelerating. But his bus number didn't change. His bedroom didn't change. The time he got home from school didn't change.

Safe in the house, he blossomed like a normal kid. He'd had a growth spurt in eighth grade, and he started hanging out with kids who had names like Brock and Tyler and wore Nike headbands and watched *The Fast and the Furious*. Being one of the only black kids in his mostly white high school meant that the boys thought he was cool and the girls wanted to date him, and by tenth or eleventh grade he would be one of the popular kids.

His favorite teacher was Mr. Jonathan Sherry, who got Svante into the Gifted and Talented program, and who mentored him so well that he later got accepted to Cornell. Mr. Sherry's classroom was decorated with iconic photographs with big questions underneath, like "What do YOU think?" Mr. Sherry said Svante was a once-in-a-lifetime student, because there was something inspired about him. He was compelling. You wanted to listen to him, because you got the sense he had something important to say.

In ninth grade, Svante was still basically a kid. He still loved *Magic: The Gathering* and was still holding onto Pokémon cards. He had an after-school job at a grocery store, and he spent his earnings on Vanilla Coke and Twizzlers and Oatmeal Creme Pies, which he ate while watching *Scarface* for the millionth time. He held strong opinions about Red Vines (which were garbage) and about *Dragon Ball Z* (which was the best show on television).

It was Tuesday, so he had band first period, which woke everybody up, and then second period was biology. Mr. Hoff was talking about mitochondria, which are the energy factory of the cell. He had a bumper sticker in his classroom that said "Biologists Are Mitochondriacs," and he would stand in front of the bumper sticker and jump up and down so that his students would associate mitochondria with energy. Svante was sitting next to Matt, who was older, cooler, and more popular. Matt wore Nike headbands, and Svante knew better than to ask him about which comic books he was reading (he wasn't).

There was a knock on the door, and someone came into the room and whispered something in Mr. Hoff's ear. Mr. Hoff continued to recite facts about mitochondria for a few seconds, and then paused.

"There's something happening and I think you deserve to know about it," he said. Then he pulled out the classroom TV and turned it on. The first plane had already hit, but the class watched the second plane hit the second tower and then saw the news coverage of the plane that crashed in Pennsylvania and the plane that hit the Pentagon. Mr. Hoff explained Lower Manhattan, how dense it was, how high the buildings were. There were kids in

Earlville who had never been in an elevator or seen a building more than a few stories tall. The idea of a building that high, of people jumping and splattering on the pavement, was baffling to them.

Next to Svante, Matt started hysterically laughing. "We're fucked," he said between chortles. "We're at war." For the first time, it occurred to Svante that America was not alone in the world.

※ ※ ※

On that Tuesday, Alexandria Ocasio-Cortez was sitting in her seventh-grade math class when an announcement came on over the PA. She went to Mildred E. Strang Middle School, in Yorktown Heights, where nearly everyone had a parent working in Manhattan: her dad was an architect, and he worked most days in the city, often getting permits at the Department of Buildings downtown. All the rich stay-at-home moms came to pick their kids up from school. Within an hour, half the class was gone.

Her father was miles away, trying to get out of the city himself, her mother was at work cleaning houses. Nobody could get through to anybody on their cell phones, and even if they could, her parents couldn't come pick her up. School was dismissed early and when Alexandria went outside to get on the school bus, the air was tinged grayish blue. She could see the smoke hanging in the air from the towers fifty miles away. She got home before the rest of her family, walked alone into their ranch house, and turned on the TV. Every channel showed a picture of the towers standing with smoke billowing out of the top. "This is like the apocalypse," she thought. "Is my mom going to get home before the world ends?"

She was born in the Bronx in 1989. Her family and close friends called her Sandy; other kids at school called her Alex. She was very tiny, with bones so small that if you shook her hand too hard it could feel as though you might break them, and big dark eyes that peered out of her perfectly symmetrical face. She usually wore her shiny dark hair pulled back from a straight, off-center part. Her early childhood was spent in the Bronx—her mom was born in Puerto Rico, her dad a native of the South Bronx—but they moved to Yorktown Heights when she was about five so she and her younger brother, Gabriel, could go to better schools. Yorktown Heights was a culture shock: in the Bronx, she had been surrounded by kids wearing nameplates and hoop earrings and styling their baby hair, but she quickly learned that things were different in the suburbs. She knew that if she wore certain things and said certain words, she would be trapped in a stereotype that had been created for people like her.

There were only a handful of other kids in their school who weren't white. Their parents were strict, and their grandmother lived with them for a while, which meant they were raised to be extremely respectful of their elders. Alexandria and Gabriel weren't allowed to roll their eyes at their parents or curse in their house—*ever*—but they heard white kids from school saying things like "Fuck you, Mom!" Sometimes they missed field trips because their parents couldn't afford the fees, and when other kids came to the Scholastic Book Fair with blank checks signed by their parents, Alexandria and Gabriel would go window shopping.

Their father, Sergio, was a big man with a bushy mustache and heavy eyebrows that he wiggled when he was joking, and big eyes that he would widen when he was making a point. He had a "keep it real" philosophy. He wanted people to be having fun, but he also wanted people to say what they thought, to be honest with themselves and with him. He was always knocking on their old neighbors' doors in the Bronx to check up on them, or buying coffee for his coworkers on random Monday mornings. Their mother, Blanca, was small like Alexandria, with the same wide smile and a sort of gentleness about her. She had been raised in poverty in Puerto Rico, moved to New York and taught herself English, and cleaned houses to make money. Alexandria says her mom was a "soft foil" to her intense and gregarious dad, the one who instilled compassion along with conviction. "Listen, if someone's picking on you, that's their problem," she would say. "What they're doing is they're vocalizing their insecurities."

Alexandria was the kind of kid who asked for a microscope for her birthday. She loved math and science, and she had a grown-up poise that impressed people and helped her out-argue anyone. Her teacher once said that when she was presenting her science project at seventeen, a school administrator mistook her for a professional businesswoman instead of a high school senior.

She had friends, but she wasn't popular. The popular kids had flat-ironed hair and wore polo shirts from Abercrombie & Fitch, sometimes two at the same time, pink over green or green over pink. Sometimes Alexandria would go with her mother to clean rich people's houses that were bigger and nicer, with more expensive furniture and fancier decorations. Once, her mom cleaned a woman's home in exchange for SAT lessons for Alexandria. "I saw and interpreted a lot subconsciously about income inequality," she said later. "We were an economic underclass. We were part of the service class." Gabriel had once gone on a job with their mom and realized halfway through that he was cleaning the home of one of his classmates. "That was one of the first moments that I felt shame," he remembered.

Another time, Blanca was cleaning the house of an older man whose wife was in the hospital. His wife wasn't doing well, and the old man didn't know how to take care of the house without her. So Blanca and Alexandria went in and cleaned out his refrigerator, which was crammed full of rotting food. They threw out bottles of Mylanta that were ten years old, leftovers from months ago, old vegetables that never got eaten, milk that had gone sour. They weren't on the clock: they did it as a favor to him, because his wife was dying. Sometimes, she learned, the most helpful thing you can do is just clean out someone's refrigerator when they're grieving. She remembered that rotting refrigerator for years, the way her mother scrubbed the shelves not because it was her job, but because it was the right thing to do. She ended up writing her college essay about it.

But that Tuesday morning in 2001, years before Alexandria competed in a science fair or applied to college, the Ocasio-Cortez family didn't know how to react, so they didn't. Gabriel came home on the school bus a little while after Alexandria. When Blanca came home, she turned on the TV and then turned it off right away and didn't say anything. When Sergio returned safe—he hadn't been in danger after all—the family sat around their glass table eating in total silence. This was unusual, because Sergio loved to talk, and Alexandria loved to talk, and everyone loved to be up in everyone else's business. But that night, nobody spoke. Finally, Gabriel recalls, Sergio broke the silence: "Our economy will never be the same."

He didn't really mean it. It was just something to say.

✳ ✳ ✳

What happened that morning would change everything for an entire generation, even if they didn't know it yet. Nine in ten millennials would name
9/11 as one of the most important events of their lifetime. This day would
become a dividing line between Before and After. Before: the peace and prosperity of the 1980s and 1990s, the sense of safety, the widespread illusion that
America was on top of the world. Millennials would be the first to grow up
in the After.

THOUGHTS & PRAYERS

APRIL 20, 1999
LITTLETON, COLORADO

"Good evening, everyone. The reaction of so many people today was, oh, no, not again—another high school: Columbine." . . . **COLUMBINE HIGH SCHOOL SHOOTING LEAVES 15 DEAD, 28 HURT: The shootings were the latest in a series of school shootings since 1997 that have shocked the nation and led to calls for tighter security and closer monitoring of troubled students. . . .** We currently have four, Peter. We have two girls and two boys, they're all in serious condition. We have one young woman who has at least nine gunshots to the chest. . . . Well, Roz, they wore black trench coats, combat boots, and some wore Nazi crosses. They hated jocks, loved the internet, and were fascinated by WWII. They were known as the Trenchcoat Mafia. . . . *"There was a girl crouched beneath a desk in the library, and the guy came over and said, 'Peekaboo,' and shot her in the neck."* . . . We now know that one of them, Eric Harris, also posted violent lyrics and recipes for pipe bombs on the internet, and his final entry in an AOL chat room posted yesterday morning at 8:41 read, "Today is my last day on earth." . . . **TEENS EASY PURCHASE SHOWS FLAWS IN LAW, GUN FOES CLAIM: . . .** *"I have only five words for you," actor Charlton Heston said as he hoisted his rifle into the air at an NRA convention: "From my cold dead hands!"* . . . *"For the past three months, the gun lobby has been calling the shots on Capitol Hill," said President Bill Clinton. "Now it's time for Congress to listen to the lobbyists who truly matter: our children."* . . . *"'We are the students of today, the voters of next year, and the leaders of tomorrow,' said Denver student David Winkler. 'We will be heard.'"* . . . *The students' overtures to several congressmen opposed to gun-control legislation were sternly rebuffed. . . .* ("I would like you to write me a letter," "I'm busy, write me a letter") . . . **SENATE VOTES GUN CURBS, HOURS AFTER SCHOOL SHOOTING:** *"This is a turning point for our country," Mr. Gore, a radiant smile on his face, said at a news conference after he left the Senate floor. . . .* **HOUSE DEFEATS GUN CONTROL BILL: The drive for expanded gun controls abruptly collapsed in the House yesterday, raising doubts that Congress will pass any gun measures this year. . . .**

CHAPTER 2

Harry Potter and the Spawn of the Boomers

The baby boomers are the most spoiled, most self-centered, most narcissistic generation the country's ever produced.

—STEVE BANNON

O nce upon a time in America, a generation of middle-class young people graduated from publicly funded high schools and went to highly subsidized, rapidly diversifying, and increasingly competitive colleges. They outworked their aristocratic classmates and entered a new "knowledge economy" of lawyers, bankers, and lobbyists, where they made hundreds of thousands of dollars a year helping other rich people stay rich. They *deserved* to keep that money, they told each other. They had made it themselves, after all, through *meritocracy*—ever heard of it? They had *worked hard* for their wealth, and if keeping it meant changing a few rules and cutting a few taxes and kneecapping a few regulations, then so be it. Wasn't that the meaning of American freedom, after all? Weren't they the embodiment of the American dream?

Their dream transformed the American economy and political system. They developed obscure new financial tools—leveraged buyouts, derivatives, credit default swaps—that made the financial system more about short-term trading than long-term productivity. They flooded Washington, DC, with litigators and lobbyists who made money helping big business make more money. Armed with the conviction of their own "meritocracy," they perpetuated the myth of deserved destiny: that the rich were rich because they worked hard, and that the poor were poor because they didn't. They were, as Steven Brill put it in *Tailspin: The People and Forces Behind America's Fifty-Year Fall—and Those Fighting to Reverse It*, "really, really good at taking advantage of what the American system gave them." Their generation was named *TIME*'s Man of the Year in 1967, nicknamed "the Inheritor" because "cushioned by unprecedented affluence and the welfare state, he has a sense of economic security unmatched in history." When they were young, they were called the "Me Generation." You probably know them as the baby boomers.

The boomers' parents were nicknamed the "Greatest Generation," the ones who lived through the Great Depression and fought World War II, endured unfathomable hardship, and wanted their kids to have a better life. They did that by building structures and systems that would benefit an entire cohort of American kids, including a strong social safety net, robust national infrastructure, and an American higher education system that became the envy of the world. There were serious faults—most of their institutions, particularly the education system, were racially segregated, and they generally integrated their schools and companies only under pressure—but their impulse was toward civic engagement and institutional health. Their motto was best articulated by John F. Kennedy: "Ask not what your country can do for you—ask what you can do for your country."

To their credit, the boomers (born between 1946 and 1966) had much more progressive social politics than their parents: the Greatest Generation largely excluded women and nonwhites from almost all the prosperity they created, and boomers radically expanded rights and opportunities for people who weren't white men. The boomer activists who protested the Vietnam War, agitated for women's equality, and marched in the civil rights movement certainly deserve real credit for the immense social progress made in the 1960s and 1970s. Boomers didn't lead those movements—they were mostly organized by nonboomers such as Gloria Steinem (b. 1934), Malcolm X (b. 1925), and Martin Luther King Jr. (b. 1929). Still, they were the generation that made once-fringe ideas like racial justice and feminism central to the American social compact.

But by the 1980s, many boomers had stopped asking what they could do for their country and started asking what their country could do for them. They liked the idea of being "socially liberal but fiscally conservative." After a decade of economic malaise in the 1970s, boomers largely embraced the exuberant materialism and cynical individualism that characterized much of the late twentieth century. They voted for Ronald Reagan (especially in 1984) and supported the tax cuts and financial deregulation that laid the groundwork for soaring income inequality.

The two decades spanning the Reagan and Clinton presidencies amounted to a lurch to the right in American politics. Reagan oversaw a radical reduction in government investment, and Clinton's "Third Way" attempted to triangulate a path forward for Democrats that prioritized market solutions over government programs and ended up boosting corporate profit more than middle-class wealth. For the boomers and Gen X, Reagan's antigovernment conservatism and Clinton's Third Way centrism defined the parameters of political debate for the next twenty years. "These Republican children of Reagan and Democratic children of Clinton comprise America's reigning political generation," wrote journalist Peter Beinart.

By the 1990s, when Bill Clinton became the first boomer president, baby boomers had been building power for long enough that they held important positions in the White House, Congress, and the courts: America was tilting their way. Clinton greatly expanded the earned income tax credit—the most successful antipoverty program in a generation—which, along with a rising economy, sharply raised the incomes of the working poor. But despite some rational justifications at the time, many of the policies implemented by Clinton and his fellow boomers in the 1990s would prove to be disastrously shortsighted. The bill he signed to "end welfare as we know it" helped some welfare recipients find jobs, but cut off desperately needed cash for families stuck in deep poverty. His 1994 crime bill had a few redeeming qualities (including the assault weapons ban and the Violence Against Women Act) but ultimately accelerated the mass incarceration of a generation of young black men. Boomers shored up Social Security for just long enough so that they'll have it when they retire—the Social Security Trust Fund is expected to be exhausted by 2035, when the youngest boomers will be in their seventies and the average millennial is still hard at work. Meanwhile, by repealing the Glass-Steagall Act and a few other forms of financial regulation, Clinton and later George W. Bush (also a boomer) built on Reagan-era policies that favored finance capital over labor. At least Clinton balanced the budget; with massive tax cuts and trillions for his "War on Terror," President George W. Bush exploded both the annual budget deficit and the cumulative national debt, which more than doubled since the 1970s.

Even if you put aside the age-old squabbles over taxation and government spending, Reagan, Clinton, and their political heirs utterly failed at perhaps the most urgent demand of their time: addressing climate change. Despite decades of scientific warnings about the effects of burning fossil fuels, the reigning political generation failed to take any meaningful action to mitigate global warming in the decades when it could have been seriously fixed or slowed. They had their reasons—not wanting to disrupt the economy, not wanting to jeopardize competition with China—but in retrospect, their children would believe that none of those reasons were good enough. Al Gore and several other Clinton-era environmentalists tried hard to push the issue, but they couldn't build any real political momentum around it.

"Individually, boomers might be as selfless and as interested in the future as anybody else," says Svante Myrick. "As a body politic, they've made a series of choices that increase their short-term prosperity and shortchanged us. At every opportunity, they decided instead that they wanted a short-term tax cut."

Even many boomers themselves don't think they did so great. *New York Times* columnist David Brooks gives his generation a C minus for its political contributions. "During the years of boomer dominance—from Bill Clinton through Donald Trump—America's political institutions have become dysfunctional, civic debate has crumbled, debt has soared and few major pieces of legislation have passed," he wrote.

"In the world that boomers will pass along to their children," wrote boomer Michael Kinsley in *The Atlantic*, "America is widely held in contempt, prosperity looks to more and more people like a mirage, and things are generally going to hell."

But boomers were really good at one thing: raising kids.

✳ ✳ ✳

The boomers—the ultimate individualists—didn't think much about the next generation in a broad political sense, but they thought *a lot* about the next generation in a specific, individual sense. Boomer political calculations were often rooted in where their sons would go to college, whether their daughters would be able to play soccer, all the triumphs and failures of their own individual progeny.

Something had changed for parents in the 1980s and 1990s. The average first-time mother was older and better-educated than at any time in history. The average married father spent more time with his kids than his dad had. Contraceptives were widely available, abortion was legal, and for most women, unintended pregnancies declined. Boomer women were more free than ever to start families when and how they chose—which meant that when most boomers had kids, it was because they really wanted them.

By 1984, a majority of women with small children were working. For the first time ever, large numbers of highly educated mothers were navigating how to raise kids while working full-time in professional, male-dominated industries—a departure from their own mothers, who had mostly stayed home. In 1975, fewer than half of American mothers worked outside the home—by 1999, that number had jumped to more than 60 percent. As women got more education and better jobs, they married later and had fewer kids; by the 1990s, the average mother had around two kids, while in their parents' generation most mothers had at least three.

That meant that there were more, higher-income mothers (and fathers) heaping their parental attention on fewer, more precious children. "Parenting," a word that barely existed in 1950, more than tripled in usage between 1980 and 2000, partly to validate moms and dads who chose to stay home.

Raising kids—something that had been done in countless ways since the beginning of human society—was suddenly dissected as something that could be done "right" or done "wrong."

All that created a sense of widespread anxiety around parenting that produced several contradictory trends: the "latchkey kids" of working moms, who entertained themselves after school every day; the "helicopter moms," who decided to forgo professional work and doubled down on raising their kids; and the "mommy wars" between those who chose to balance work and family and those who did not. Much of the culture of the late 1980s and early 1990s reflected boomers' generational preoccupation with parenthood: think *Full House, Look Who's Talking, Three Men and a Baby, Parenthood*—and, later, *Mrs. Doubtfire*. It was the decade of minivans, snack packs, and soccer practice; even the quintessential high-waisted pants of the decade were ultimately called "mom jeans."

Parents who could afford it—largely white, suburban ones—became obsessed with "enrichment" activities for their kids. Many began to feel intimidated by the pressures of global competition and haunted by rumors that kids in India and China were years ahead in math. College-educated parents who had climbed the ladder of social mobility looked down and realized that the lower rungs had disappeared, and that people without college degrees were falling further and further behind. The message was clear: if your kid failed at school, your kid would fail at life. So parents gobbled up special picture books and Mozart CDs and encyclopedia video games and Hooked on Phonics reading primers for toddlers to help them move from ordinary to extraordinary, with a stop in between for "excellent." After three decades of largely hands-off parenting, college-educated parents began to spend much more time with their kids starting in the mid-1990s. The spike didn't come from increased time with babies: this was time with older kids, often shuttling them back and forth from various activities to help them get an edge in the competitive college process. By 2001, one in five parents said they spent more than seven hours a week driving their kids to and from organized activities. By 2008, adults spent about 20 percent of their workweek on childcare, which amounted to spending about $300 billion worth of time on their kids per year.

The boomers were defined by a sense of individualism, so when they had kids, they weren't just *any* kids: the boomers' kids must be super-duper special. So special that the boomers gave them names that they thought would "stand out"—such as Tiffany, Stephanie, and Madison—unlike their own parents, who picked names they thought would "fit in"—such as Mary, Susan, and Barbara. Parents loved anything that reminded their kids how special they were, so teachers began giving out gold stars for class participation, and coaches began giving out trophies to every kid who showed up to soccer practice. Childhood became at once more competitive and more coddled: because losing was so treacherous, everyone had to become a winner.

At the same time, boomer parents began to believe that any problem—from grades to friendships to misbehavior—could be tied to kids' self-confidence. And so millennials became the first generation to be coached in the dubious science of self-esteem. Kids' movies, books, and songs all drove home a central message: believe in yourself, and you will succeed. The phrase "Just be yourself" became eight times more popular between 1960 and 2008; "Believe in yourself" increased sixfold in usage.

These kids, writes Jean Twenge in her excellent book *Generation Me*, "simply take it for granted that we should all feel good about ourselves, we are all special, and we all deserve to follow our dreams." She described it as "a way of moving through the world beholden to few social rules and with the unshakable belief that you're important."

This, of course, has led to the widespread perception that millennials are entitled, selfie-obsessed narcissists more concerned with their personal brand than the state of the world, a stereotype that is firmly rooted in obnoxious truth: Twenge outlines in her book all the ways in which millennials do have higher self-esteem than previous generations, whether it's warranted or not. By 2007, 80 percent of millennials scored higher in self-esteem than Gen Xers had in 1988. No wonder so many of their elders found them so irritating.

Raised by parents obsessed with overachievement, millennial kids also began to work harder in school. A lot harder. Thanks to increased understanding of the importance of early childhood education, they began their educations earlier than their parents had, and tended to do more homework at a younger age. Toddlers were being taught second languages; preschoolers were parked in front of educational CD-ROMs. Between 1981 and 2003, kids between nine and twelve spent 30 percent more time on homework; for kids between six and eight, their studying time tripled.

Underneath all the "parenting" and the shuttling and the enrichment was the frantic realization that these children would be entering an adulthood in which twentieth-century style professional security would be increasingly precarious. Childhood in the 1980s and '90s, writes millennial thinker Malcolm Harris, was an elaborate obstacle course to train kids for a world where they would have to work more for less pay. "Efficiency is our existential purpose," he wrote in his engrossing book *Kids These Days*. "We are a generation of finely honed tools, crafted from embryos to be lean, mean production machines."

For middle-class and upper-income kids, every hour of their day became an opportunity for optimization. Even when they did play, it was monitored and organized by adults. Sports were transformed from games played with neighbors in the backyard to hypercompetitive extracurricular activities with the demands of a part-time job and the (rare) promise of a college scholarship. If it wasn't soccer it was tennis, if it wasn't tennis it was basketball, if it wasn't basketball it was ballet. Every kid had to compete, every kid had to play, everyone had to have something at which they were the best.

This experiment in super-parenting also exacerbated the already vast disparity between well-off kids with hyperinvolved parents and low-income kids without them. As kids with resources were getting further and further ahead—with early reading lessons, private art classes, and exclusive test prep—less lucky kids were being left behind. While earlier generations of parents may have been satisfied providing their children with inherited property or social status alone, rich boomer parents had been raised in the illusory twentieth-century meritocracy, so they wanted more than that. Their kids wouldn't just inherit wealth: they also had to inherit potential. It wasn't enough that their kids would be richer than the others: they also had to be smarter, tougher, faster, *better*.

Boomer parents were right that kids internalize the things they're exposed to at an early age, whether it's music classes or languages. Ironically, all that societal pressure to maximize their parenting and optimize their children meant that millennials also internalized that stress: a generalized sense that only the best is good enough. So it's not a coincidence that the babies whose parents fretted over how to play Mozart CDs during bath time grew up into a generation of adults with record levels of anxiety.

Of course, boomers weren't trying to make their kids into basket cases. They just wanted them to be the best they could be.

✳ ✳ ✳

But the other side of "Be the best you can be" is "Avoid the worst that can happen." Boomer parents were determined to protect their kids from anything that could possibly throw them off track, from pedophiles to bullies.

The 1980s and 1990s were a time of nearly unprecedented paranoia about the safety of children. In the late 1970s, parents began to sue city park districts after their children got hurt on public playgrounds—by the 1980s, cities were replacing old playgrounds with new, more boring playgrounds that radically reduced the possibility that kids could be injured. In 1979, six-year-old Etan Patz begged his mother to let him walk by himself to a Manhattan school bus stop. When his mother finally agreed, he was kidnapped and went missing for years, his face plastered on milk cartons across the country. (His killer was finally convicted in 2017.) That kicked off an era of morbid preoccupation with missing and abused children, which made parents even more paranoid about watching their kids' every move.

All this meant that millennials weren't raised with the personal autonomy and childhood freedom that their parents and grandparents had enjoyed. Thanks to a few high-profile kidnappings in the 1980s and widespread fear about child molesters, most kids were no longer allowed to roam their neighborhoods the way they once did. Parents began shuttling their kids around in cars rather than letting them get themselves from place to place. In 1969, 41 percent of kids biked to school—by 2001, only 13 percent did. "Playdate" (a word that barely existed before 1970) became the dominant structure of children's social lives by the 1980s and 1990s, as more and more aspects of

kids' lives—down to the games they played and the kids they played with—
were decided by their parents.

Even school behavior changed. In the 1990s, bullying in school began
to be seen as a public crisis instead of just an unpleasant reality of childhood. Schools began teaching antibullying workshops and cracking down
on kids tormenting other kids. In 1999, Georgia became the first state to
pass antibullying legislation, and the 2001 No Child Left Behind Act included provisions to increase school safety. Violent altercations in school declined 74 percent between 1992 and 2010, and school-related thefts dropped
82 percent.

Meanwhile, "zero tolerance" policies were sweeping America's schools,
imposing predetermined draconian punishments on even minor childhood
misbehavior, such as pushing other kids on the playground or calling names.
Black and brown kids bore the brunt of these punishments and were more
likely to be suspended, kicked out of school, or arrested for even minor infractions. This was the beginning of the "school-to-prison pipeline," in
which over-policing of school misconduct leads kids into a pattern where
they face real-life jail time. These zero tolerance policies echoed the criminal
justice system, where flawed mandatory minimum sentencing guidelines
forced judges to impose tough sentences for drug possession and other minor
infractions, a brutal overreach that unfairly targeted young people of color.
Decades later, in 2008, the American Psychological Association found that
zero tolerance policies were often "severe and punitive in nature" and not
particularly effective at keeping schools safe.

By then, the lessons had been learned. Millennials were raised in a system where even a little misbehavior could get you suspended, expelled, or
even imprisoned. Is it any surprise that these kids grew up to impose strict
social codes on each other and themselves? The kids who grew up under zero
tolerance policies for playground name-calling are the same ones who now
"cancel" each other for bad jokes and insist on campus "trigger warnings" to
protect themselves from harmful language. The kids who faced expulsion
for pushing each other on the playground have now significantly expanded
the definition of assault to mean anything from groping to rape. There's a

direct line between zero tolerance school behavior policies and the some-times merciless nature of millennial morality, in which anyone who violates the social code risks total ostracization for even a minor misstep.

✳ ✳ ✳

Of course, millennials had no idea that any of this was happening. They were busy playing Nintendo and buying low-cut jeans and listening to the Back-street Boys and watching *Friends*; they didn't know that they were being raised by the most actively involved parents in history. So maybe it's not a coincidence that a generation of super-parented, overly safe kids became ob-sessed with an orphan who defies death: Harry Potter.

Alexandria Ocasio-Cortez had the Potter bug. She got every book as soon as it came out, even though her parents wouldn't let her go to the mid-night releases at the local bookstore, and she carried it everywhere until she was finished. In retrospect, Gabriel thought his sister related to a book about a poor kid who got plucked from obscurity for a chance at something bigger. "It's definitely about a kid struggling, going under the radar and then getting an opportunity," he says. "It's about having somebody identify something special in you." In retrospect, Gabriel says, "maybe that's what she wanted."

Svante's grandmother got him the first three books, and he estimates he probably read each book five times. He and his sister would sit on the couch and read them together, side by side, each waiting until the other was fin-ished before they would turn the page. Something about the antiracist, anti-fascist allegory appealed to him, a sort of X-Men-style, kids-against-the-world thing. It tickled a particular part of his brain that wondered, "What if you weren't just different—what if you were *special*?"

When *Harry Potter and the Sorcerer's Stone*, the first in the series, was published in 1997, Harry was eleven—right around the age of an average mil-lennial. The books were written for young-adult readers, and as the series progressed and Harry grew older, they got more and more sophisticated. The series was long enough that the audience grew up with the characters—you might read about eleven-year-old Harry in elementary school and sixteen-year-old Harry in high school.

It wasn't just the most popular book series for this generation of kids;

Harry Potter was the most popular children's book series of all time. When the third book came out, Harry Potter took up the top three spots on the *New York Times* bestseller list—*The New York Times Book Review* eventually created a separate list for children's books because so many authors of adult fiction had been bumped off the list by the Potter juggernaut, or "Pottered." By the fifth book (*Harry Potter and the Order of the Phoenix*), the nine-hundred-page tome sold 8.5 million copies in the largest first printing ever, became a bestseller two hours after it became available for Amazon preorder, and proved so valuable that a forklift driver was forced to pay a fine after he stole pages from a printing plant and tried to sell them to the press. When the seventh and final book came out in 2007, it sold 8.3 million US copies in twenty-four hours, the fastest-selling book ever.

Kids waited outside bookstores in freezing temperatures at midnight for the next book. Despite the laws of gravity, more than three hundred high schools and colleges had actual Quidditch teams. In 2000, *TIME* compared Rowling to Charles Dickens in her ability to command a whole society—then quickly concluded that Rowling was actually more influential than Dickens, and that the Potter phenomenon was "literally unprecedented."

Kids heard about it through word of mouth, on sleepovers and at camp, stealing each other's copies and lining up to buy the next one. Parents reported kids' reading levels jumping four grades in two years, a development—if true—that seemed miraculous in the age of video games and VHS tapes. "For an entire generation of children," wrote *TIME* in 2003, "the most powerful entertainment experience of their lives comes not on a screen or a monitor or a disc but on a page."

That was partly because Harry Potter represented an escape from all the pressures of being a kid at this particularly pressurized moment near the turn of the century. He was an orphan with little adult supervision and few parental figures in his life, a fantasy of power and independence for a generation of overscheduled kids who weren't allowed to do anything on their own. Harry Potter's realm was free of technology and thus indifferent to anxieties of new gadgets and systems. Rowling's magical society had its own inequality—such as the treatment of house-elves and Muggle-borns—but real-world social distinctions were entirely erased. Women and people of different races were all treated equally in the Potter universe, and, most important, always had been: two of the four Hogwarts houses were founded by women, a fact that seems so obvious to the characters in the book that it's unremarkable. Years later, Rowling announced that Hogwarts headmaster Dumbledore was gay, and that Hermione—who was depicted by a white actress in the movies—could just as easily be black.

In 2009, University of Vermont professor Anthony Gierzynski tried to quantify exactly how Harry Potter impacted the millennial generation. He surveyed more than a thousand millennials in Vermont, Mississippi, upstate New York, California, Iowa, and Washington state about their experience of Harry Potter and how it shaped them. His survey included standard questions, personal interviews, and also Harry Potter trivia questions to determine the respondents' level of fandom. Two-thirds of the people he surveyed had read at least some of the Harry Potter books, nearly 90 percent had seen at least one of the movies, and almost a third considered themselves superfans of the series.

Even when controlling for other factors such as parental influences, Gierzynski found that Harry Potter fans were significantly more progressive than their peers who hadn't read the books or seen the movies. People who had read all the Harry Potter books tended to have a deeper appreciation of diversity and tended to be more tolerant toward outsiders than people who hadn't—Gierzynski found that fans displayed warmer feelings toward historically persecuted groups such as Muslims, African Americans, LGBTQ people, and undocumented immigrants. Harry Potter fans tended to have a highly developed sense of social injustice. (One fan pointed out that the lovable Weasleys are a quintessential working-class family, while the evil Malfoys represent an entrenched elite.) They tended to exhibit a lower predisposition for authoritarian tendencies (even when they were presented as "good manners" or "respect for elders") and disapproved of the death penalty and torture more than nonfans did. They disliked President Bush and liked Barack Obama: nearly two-thirds of Harry Potter fans voted for Obama, while fewer than half of nonfans did. Perhaps most important, Gierzynski found, Harry Potter fans seemed to believe not only in a progressive vision of right and wrong, but in their own personal responsibility to fight for good in the face of evil. They identified with Harry's agency as well as his values. These findings have been replicated elsewhere: a 2014 peer-reviewed study in the *Journal of Social Psychology* found that kids who read Harry Potter had more tolerance toward social outsiders than kids who didn't.

It's hard to establish whether millennials were influenced by Harry Potter or if the series took off because it touched on themes that were already brewing in young minds in the late 1990s and early 2000s. Most likely, the huge influence of Harry Potter and the rise of progressive attitudes among millennials are correlated, not causational. Harry's world—the heroes and villains, the assumptions and challenges—largely mirrors millennial attitudes about what's good (teamwork, diversity, tolerance) and what's bad (bigotry, racial purity, authoritarianism). Not everyone was happy about it: evangelical pastors condemned the book, Pope Benedict XVI warned that it might "distort Christianity," and it topped the American Library Association's list of most frequently challenged books, primarily in conservative communities.

But by the mid-2000s, Harry Potter fans had grown up enough that the series became part of the political conversation. In 2007, a group called the Harry Potter Alliance raised awareness about the genocide in Darfur, which led to a 52 percent increase in calls to an antigenocide hotline. President Obama was reported to be a fan after he read at least some of the books to his daughter Malia. When Trump appointed Mick Mulvaney to take over the Consumer Financial Protection Bureau in 2017, a small internal resistance group within the agency called "Dumbledore's Army" tried to block his agenda. More than a decade after the last novel was released, a small group of school shooting survivors in Parkland, Florida, compared their struggle against the seemingly all-powerful gun lobby to Potter's struggle against the Death Eaters. They, too, were a brave group of children using only the skills they learned in school (illumination, protection, disarmament) to battle corrupt, power-hungry adults. "This is kind of like Harry Potter," eighteen-year-old activist David Hogg told me in the aftermath of the Parkland shooting. "Like kids versus evil."

And as the kids of Pottermania reached political maturity, the novels became a generational touchstone, a shorthand reference to the moral clarity of the young. The archvillain in Potterworld is Lord Voldemort, but his reign was supported by adults—from the Minister of Magic to Hogwarts parents—who were too foolish or cynical to resist him. Decades after the books first came out, Rowling herself became a controversial figure after her criticism of trans-rights activism put her at odds with many of her more gender-inclusive fans. The Potter generation, Rowling would learn, had very little tolerance for intolerance, and very little deference to the presumed wisdom of adults. This was part of the enduring power of Potter: it was a story about youthful idealism over adult corruption, about kids forced to act when the adults won't.

THE BIG ONE

Everyone said this was the Big One.

The city's levees burst and water poured into the Ninth Ward of New Orleans—filled mostly with poor black people—and soon 80 percent of the city was flooded. People camped out on their roofs for days, screaming in vain at helicopters ignoring them overhead. Old people stood neck deep in snake-infested swamp water. People floated to safety on doors and air mattresses. Roofs were ripped off houses, brick buildings collapsed, hospitals flooded, coffins dislodged from graves.

People who could afford it moved into motels; people who couldn't went to the Superdome. About thirty thousand people camped out there, with the electricity flickering on and off; food rotted, the toilets were clogged. Women reported being raped, someone jumped off a fifty-foot-high walkway to their death. People were evacuated haphazardly, without knowing where they were going—some separated families took months to find each other. After everyone in the region was accounted for, nearly two thousand people were dead.

More than four hundred thousand people were displaced by the storm, many without the resources to start all over again in a new city. The government failed to provide adequate help to the destroyed black communities. More than seven hundred schools were forced to close. Houston took so many people fleeing the hurricane that they began to call them "refugees," while others bounced around the country looking for a place to live.

One in five displaced kids was not going to school regularly after the storm, and a third of the kids displaced by Katrina were a year behind in school. Ten years later, 20 percent of Louisiana young people were neither working nor in school. There was a surge in demand for GED programs and low-wage job training, to help Katrina dropouts complete their education.

Some scientists argued that climate change was making hurricanes more frequent and more intense, but there wasn't enough data to be certain. So the city eventually began to rebuild the places that were flooded. After all, they figured, storms like that probably only come around once every five hundred years or so.

CHAPTER 3

Getting Into College, Getting Out of Debt

Alexandria Ocasio-Cortez was a student who did everything right. She got good grades, did lots of extracurriculars, studied for the big tests, and scored high on the SAT. She even won second place in the microbiology category of Intel's International Science and Engineering Fair for a project on the effects of antioxidants on roundworms. There was no question of whether she would get into college: the question was how the Ocasio-Cortez family would pay for it.

In 2007, Alexandria was accepted to Boston University. If she had attended in 1980, tuition would have been $5,500, which would be roughly $13,000 when adjusted for inflation in 2007. Her actual tuition with room and board was more than triple that amount: just over $46,000 per year.

That number determined the next ten years of her life. After a series of scholarships and part-time jobs, she graduated with almost $30,000 in debt. Throughout her twenties, she paid roughly $300 a month, and when she worked as a waitress, she made so little she had to go into an income-based repayment plan. But she didn't even have it that bad: she knew people who were paying $800, $1,000 a month, even before they could think about paying rent.

"We have an entire generation that is delaying or forgoing purchasing houses; they're not buying second versions of everything because they have roommates," she told me later. "This is a crisis that is bubbling over into our entire economy."

Progressive organizer Jess Morales Rocketto (b. 1986) was loud and bubbly, with a big laugh and an Instagram presence that was half progressive organizing, half reviews of makeup products she liked at Sephora. She had been the digital organizing director for Hillary for America in 2016 (the texts from the Hillary campaign that started, "Hi, it's Jess," were hers), and after the election, she quickly emerged as a ubiquitous organizer of the anti-Trump resistance. Jess came from a Mexican-American family where the top priority was for her and her three siblings to go to college. She took out $35,000 in loans to pay tuition; her twin sister took out $45,000; her little sister took out $80,000; and their father took out $200,000 to cover the rest. The family agreed to sign for each others' loans so that the siblings would help each other through school and pay back their parents' debt. By the time she was in her thirties, Jess and her twin sister were together shouldering $280,000 of student debt taken on by their family. Her husband, Ross Morales Rocketto—who cofounded Run for Something, an organization that recruits and trains millennials to run for office—had another $80,000 on top of that. The debt was like a heavy purse she could never put down. "We will never pay off our debt," Jess told me once. "We will die with our debt."

Braxton Winston was raised in Crown Heights, Brooklyn, the son of a New York City fireman and a math teacher. He was tall and athletic, with a wide smile that showed the gap between his two front teeth. He got into an educational program called Prep for Prep in middle school, and was then admitted to Andover for high school, where he played football and thrived. But he was sick of the cold, and in college he wanted to play football someplace with good academics but without the frigid windchills. So he applied and was accepted to Davidson College in North Carolina, where he was one of only a handful of black students. But when it was time to do the paperwork, Braxton realized that his parents—both city employees—were technically making too much money for him to qualify for financial aid. With a stroke of a pen, he was eighteen years old and $80,000 in debt.

It made him angry. Braxton knew he deserved to go to Davidson: he had the grades, he had the extracurriculars, he had worked hard for twelve years to get into a good college. After all that work, he had his college degree but was living paycheck to paycheck. The government would take $100 a month from every paycheck for the next thirty years. By the time he was in his thirties, he was behind on paying back his private loans and figured he'd make a big payment one day if he got rich. "Why should I limit the opportunities I give myself just because the commas on some paperwork don't match up?" he says. "Do you stop life because you decided to go to fucking college?"

✳ ✳ ✳

Kids like Alexandria and Jess and Braxton were taught that a college education would open the doors to a prosperous and meaningful career—but nobody told them that the future would come with hidden fees. And while millennials are not the only generation carrying the $1.6 trillion student debt burden in the United States, they're the generation whose post-college futures have been the most fully defined by it. The average student debt for a Gen X college graduate was a little over $4,000—for millennials, it's nearly $15,000.

All this is because of the so-called education gospel, which boomers wholeheartedly swallowed and then passed on to their kids. As explained by historians W. Norton Grubb and Marvin Lazerson, the education gospel preaches that more people getting more education is the key to a democratic society, and that all young Americans—even those who couldn't afford it and never would be able to—should not just be going to college, but going to the most prestigious school they could find. For most parents in the 1980s and '90s, the single biggest goal of raising their children wasn't to get them married or get them into the family business: it was to get them into college.

That made sense in 1988, when the average annual tuition at a four-year college was just under $7,000 (roughly $15,000 in 2018 dollars). But thirty years later that cost had increased sevenfold—with room and board, books, and transportation, a year at a private four-year college cost more than $52,000. Even public schools had become much more expensive: the average public four-year college was three times as expensive in 2018 as it was in 1988.

For boomers, college was hoped for but not expected. Most boomers were raised by mothers who didn't have degrees, and since many elite colleges and universities only started accepting women in the 1970s, it wasn't necessarily assumed that all women would go to college. But thanks to the feminist movement, boomer women started going to college in record numbers. In 1982, for the first time in American history, more women than men earned undergraduate degrees. In 1960, only 18 percent of mothers of infants had any college education, but by the early 1990s a mother of a new infant was more likely to have some college education than none at all. Those moms—often married to college-educated men—wanted to ensure that all their kids had the same opportunities they did. College wasn't just for boys anymore.

And thanks to strong labor unions and a robust midcentury manufacturing economy, boomers didn't necessarily have to go to college to get a well-paying job. Many low-income families in the mid-twentieth century didn't think of college as an option, let alone a requirement: only about a quarter of baby boomers have a bachelor's degree or more, while 40 percent have only a high school degree. But by the turn of the twenty-first century, that educational divide had flipped: only a quarter of millennials had only a high school degree, while nearly 40 percent had finished college. And postsecondary education was increasingly becoming a prerequisite for a career. Even jobs that were once available to high school graduates, such as daycare teachers or hairdressers, now required some kind of certification.

Meanwhile, international student enrollment was skyrocketing, thanks in part to the United States' changing relationship with China. In 1980, fewer than three hundred thousand international students studied at US universities—by 2015, they numbered nearly a million. Chinese students went from only fifty in 1979 to more than 250,000 in 2001. This added valuable geographical diversity to elite schools, but it also made American students feel even more squeezed.

So over the last few decades of the twentieth century, the universe of people who expected to go to college radically expanded. Daughters as well as sons, preschool teachers as well as doctors, international students as well as American ones: according to the education gospel, college was for everyone. By 2006, there were 62 percent more students attending college than in the 1960s.

That presented a problem: the pool of people who wanted their kids to go to good colleges had exploded, but the number of spots at elite colleges had stayed roughly the same. In 1961, Harvard University accepted 27 percent of the students who sent applications; in 1976 it was 20 percent. By 2019, Harvard's admission rate hovered around 5 percent. And the "safety schools" of the past that once regularly admitted students with decent but unspectacular records were increasingly difficult to get into.

As their kids grew up, the baby boomers who graduated from college in the 1970s and 1980s began to realize that for their kids, getting into college was going to be at once more difficult and more necessary than it had been when they did it. College was a status symbol, a sorting system, a way to figure out where your child stood in the pecking order of "meritocracy." Meanwhile, as lucrative blue-collar jobs grew harder to find, parents knew that college admission was the single biggest indicator of their child's future professional success. And they weren't wrong: by 2018, a household led by a millennial with a bachelor's degree had twice the earnings of one led by someone with only a high school diploma.

All the features of a privileged millennial childhood—the encyclopedia CD-ROMs, the parental anxiety, the endless soccer practice—had been preparation for this moment. The "college process," as it was called, was seen by boomer parents as the ultimate way to prove their child's excellence, which was intrinsically tied to their own self-worth. Elite college students, wrote William Deresiewicz in *Excellent Sheep*, are the "academic equivalent of all-American athletes, coached and drilled and dieted from the earliest years of life" in a culture he calls "credentialism," in which "the purpose of life becomes the accumulation of gold stars."

Meanwhile, the No Child Left Behind Act led to a rise in standardized testing, which further raised the stakes for parents and kids as excruciating tests became an educational norm. The SAT and ACT, once seen as a three-hour chore on a Saturday morning, turned into a months-long ordeal as well-off parents tried to game the system by training their kids to ace the test and less affluent parents amassed new debts paying for test prep for their kids.

As colleges sought out more diverse students and began weighing a broader set of admissions criteria in the 1990s and early 2000s, some white parents accused schools of favoring students of color. White students sued schools for perceived discrimination, which led to tortured debates about how far colleges should go to ensure diversity on their campuses. In 2003, the year before Lauren Underwood would arrive at the University of Michigan for her freshman year, the Supreme Court ruled that the university could use race as a factor in admissions but couldn't assign "points" to particular racial groups. Lauren would become one of just a handful of out-of-state black students at the school, and many of the others decided to withdraw because of the scrutiny around the case. "They thought it would be a hostile environment where people thought they had only gotten in because of their race," she told me. "It was very isolating." Three years later, when she was a sophomore, Michigan passed a ballot initiative that prohibited public institutions from making any decisions based on race, a veiled attack on affirmative action programs. Lauren immediately felt a chill on campus. There were only a few black students in the School of Nursing, and once her classmates started handing out anti–affirmative action flyers, Lauren felt even more isolated. Even small interactions would remind her that some of her classmates were questioning her qualifications. "I was having to account for how I got in," she said. "Why I deserve to be there."

For many millennials, applying to college felt like a full-time job. After the Common Application went online in 1998, it became the norm for one student to apply to more than a dozen schools. In 2005, the SAT got longer and harder, with the addition of an essay section and more advanced math. Between 1996 and 2006, enrollment in degree-granting postsecondary schools increased 24 percent, and then jumped another 18 percent in the next five years.

The college frenzy became a self-fulfilling prophecy. It was true that college would determine millennials' futures, just not exactly the way their parents thought it would. Kids spent the first eighteen years of their lives training to get into college—and the rest of their lives trying to pay for it.

✳ ✳ ✳

Some millennials borrowed tens of thousands of dollars before they could legally buy a beer. Others graduated into the job market and struggled to find work—so they went back to get a graduate degree and took on even more debt to pay for it. Others took out loans to go to college and then dropped out halfway through, leaving them in the worst of both worlds: with crushing student debt but no degree to show for it.

But why was all this debt even necessary? Why was college suddenly so much more expensive?

One reason is that conservative boomer politicians radically slashed funding for public universities starting in the 1980s, which forced students to pick up the bill. Colorado state funding for education dropped 70 percent between 1980 and 2011, South Carolina cut more than 66 percent of higher education funding, and Arizona cut 62 percent, according to the American Council on Education. In 1987, more than half of Michigan State's revenue came from state funding—by 2012, it was just 18 percent. The University of California schools saw their funding cut in half over the same period. The Great Recession caused state governments to cut even more education funding, and because Republicans won control of state legislatures in the 2010 elections, much of that funding never came back. The only way to keep educating kids was to hike their tuitions, shifting the cost of education from the state to the student.

The college feeding frenzy also triggered a crisis for universities, which found themselves faced with skyrocketing costs even though their budgets were slashed. As more and more kids applied to more and more colleges, the yield rate (the number of accepted students who decide to enroll) plummeted drastically. In 2002, roughly half the students who were accepted ended up enrolling—by 2016, only a third of the kids who got acceptance letters said yes. This meant that colleges needed to compete harder to get the students they wanted—and their tuition dollars. They had to invest in fancy gyms, gourmet food, luxurious dorm rooms, anything to get the rich kids who could pay full tuition to choose their school over their other options.

And even as they were losing state funding, universities were adding administrators at a much faster rate than new professors. Colleges hired administrators to handle everything from student life and counseling (to meet student demands that campuses feel like safe spaces) to fundraising and fancier athletic programs (to help bring in more cash). Between 1987 and 2011, American colleges and universities collectively added more than 517,000 new administrators and nonacademic staff members—an average of eighty-seven every day.

Many top administrators were being paid salaries comparable to CEO pay, even as adjunct professors scraped by on poverty wages. Ken Starr, the former independent counsel who investigated Bill Clinton's affair with Monica Lewinsky, made almost $5 million in 2016 as president of Baylor University. The president of Columbia, Lee Bollinger, made nearly $4 million, and the president of the University of Pennsylvania, Amy Gutmann, made more than $3 million. Coaches made even more money: In Alabama, where state funding had decreased 30 percent since the recession, football coach Nick Saban made $8.3 million in 2018. Football coaches at Ohio State and the University of Michigan both raked in more than $7.5 million that year. Meanwhile, adjunct professors—who usually end up teaching the students who took out such crushing loans to get to college—were being paid less than pet-sitters or nannies, and were often eligible for food stamps.

All this meant that the state was spending less, universities were spending more, and students were left to pick up the difference.

Between 2006 and 2018, student debt doubled as a share of GDP. The average millennial in 2018 had about $36,000 in debt (not including mortgages) and spent about 34 percent of their monthly income paying it down—and most of that is student debt. Earlier generations went to college back when tuitions were within the realm of affordable: when Senate Majority Leader Mitch McConnell graduated from the University of Louisville in 1964, tuition cost $330 (about $2,800 in today's dollars)—today, it's up more than 300 percent, even when adjusted for inflation. The concept of "working your way through school" is now effectively impossible, because college costs too much and jobs pay too little. In 1987, for example, a student could pay her tuition at the University of Kansas working a part-time, minimum wage job and still have a little cash left over; in 2016, that same job would only cover a little over half of her tuition, leaving her more than $38,000 short.

That's why millennials have four times as much student debt as their parents ever did. But as with everything else in American life, that debt is not equally distributed. White millennials with college-educated parents tend to have less debt, because their parents were more likely to help them pay for their education. Their grandparents took advantage of twentieth-century college funding such as the GI Bill, which gave their families a two-generation head start at building wealth. When *BuzzFeed* journalist Anne Helen Petersen surveyed the "debt genealogies" of millennials, she found that the overwhelming majority of people whose parents and grandparents had been to college were white—and most of them had graduated with little or no debt.

But college funding like the GI Bill was less accessible to black veterans, because some segregationist lawmakers had structured the bill to make it more difficult for black veterans to access educational opportunities. Even if they could get the funding, many universities in the 1940s and '50s would not accept black students. As newly educated white veterans hurtled into the middle class in the 1950s and '60s, widespread discrimination in jobs and housing caused black families to fall further behind. Without two generations of wealth accumulation, fewer black families could afford to foot the bill for their kids to go to college. So black millennials—especially the ones who were the first in their families to go to college—often took on the biggest debt burdens. Four years after graduation, black millennials had twice as much student debt per capita as white millennials and were much more likely to be behind on their payments.

The rise of private, for-profit colleges made the education system even more predatory and unequal. Lured by the promise of the education gospel, first-generation college students—many of them black and Latino—forked over thousands of dollars to scam universities that offer little real education. Enrollment at these dubious "universities" doubled between 1998 and 2014, and the average "graduate" leaves with almost $40,000 of debt and a worthless degree.

The debt has kept millennials from getting married, buying homes, having kids. It has eaten into their salaries, their savings, and their buying power. Because of the debt, one in fifteen student borrowers has considered suicide.

It turned out the boomer parents had been right that college education would determine their kids' financial security. Just not in the way they thought.

THOUGHTS & PRAYERS

APRIL 16, 2007
BLACKSBURG, VIRGINIA

"We are live here on the campus of Virginia Tech, the location of the deadliest shooting in US history: 33 dead, 29 wounded, 15 still in the hospital tonight." . . . **VIRGINIA TECH SHOOTING LEAVES 33 DEAD:** She walked toward her class, preoccupied with an upcoming exam and listening to music on her iPod. On the way, she said, she heard some loud cracks, and only later concluded they had been gunshots from the second round of shootings. . . . "All this comes at a sobering moment, just five days before the anniversary of the Columbine high school massacre." . . . **THAT WAS THE DESK I CHOSE TO DIE UNDER:** The first thing he saw was a gun, then the gunman. *"I quickly dove under a desk." . . . After every shot, he thought, "OK, the next one is me." But shot after shot, and he felt nothing. He played dead. . . . "He came into our class, shot the person who was sitting next to me, shot our professor, and then I hid under the desk, and then he proceeded to shoot everyone else in our class." . . .* **HOLOCAUST SURVIVOR BLOCKED SHOOTER, LETTING STUDENTS FLEE:** *"I just remember looking back and seeing him at the door," the Virginia Tech senior recalled of her professor. "I don't think I would be here if it wasn't for him." . . .* **VIRGINIA CLOSES LOOPHOLE THAT ARMED GUNMAN:** The fact that he was able to purchase firearms despite his mental health history focused scrutiny on the adequacy of background checks on potential gun buyers. . . . "On the gun control debate," President George W. Bush told Katie Couric, "my hope is that the country puts people in prayer, not only those who have lost a loved one, but the kids here really need prayer." . . . "People who have never met you are praying for you," he said in a speech later. "There's a power in these prayers, real power." . . . **BUSH SIGNS BILL GEARED TO TOUGHEN SCREENING OF GUN BUYERS:** It seeks to expand the federal database to screen gun buyers. . . . *"It's certainly not this huge victory that the Brady Campaign is making it out to be." . . . The bill represents a shift from the last major gun measure, which shielded gun makers and sellers from lawsuits arising from misuse of their weapons. . . . The year before, Congress allowed the 10-year-old ban on assault weapons to expire.*

CHAPTER 4

The Last Dinosaurs

In July 1999, sixteen-year-old Haley Stevens sat in the mall and waited for her friend Rachel to show up. They didn't have cell phones, and Haley's mini-purse contained only a few tubes of Lip Smackers, so she waited and wrote in her journal in large scrawling letters, "Where the hell is Rachel!"

Since she had no idea where Rachel was or when she would arrive, she passed the time scribbling in her notebook. "I haven't smoked pot yet and I bet a lot of people are waiting for me to," she wrote. "Still no goddamn Rachel," she wrote, observing that a "devil-haired woman is prancing around the front of the shitty mall with a cell phone blubbering on like a prattering parrot." Haley had no way to check on Rachel to see whether she was close. They couldn't text each other, or drop a pin, or confirm the location on Google Maps, because Google Maps wouldn't be invented for another six years.

Haley looked at her watch. "Rachel still isn't here, I bet she's waiting for me on the other side of the damn mall," she wrote. "Here's my plan: I'm not going to move for another hour in case Rachel gets here and I leave."

Back then, Haley didn't have Facebook or Instagram, and she may have only just gotten an email address that she could check on her desktop computer. But over the next twenty years, almost every aspect of the way Haley communicated with everybody in her life would change. She didn't know it at the time, but those moments of boredom, of writing in her diary while waiting for a late friend, would soon be a thing of the past.

✳ ✳ ✳

Millennials like Haley are both the first digital natives and the last dinosaurs: young enough to have grown up online but old enough to remember what it was like before the ubiquity of the internet.

Their young lives spanned the biggest technological shift since the industrial revolution: most millennials were born before cell phones were widely used, yet now almost all carry one in their pocket. They grew up before the internet was available to ordinary people in most homes; now most of their professional and social lives take place online. Social media didn't exist in their early adolescence; now social media companies have the power to shape not only their personal lives, but their democracy. According to Walter Isaacson, one of the great chroniclers of the digital revolution, the transformation to a digital world included three big shifts: the rise of search engines (Google was founded in 1998), the rise of crowd-sourced collaboration (Wikipedia launched in 2001), and the transition to mobile (the iPhone was released in 2007). All three of these shifts happened right smack in the middle of the millennial adolescence.

Most technological revolutions this massive don't happen this fast. The telephone, for example, dates to the late nineteenth century and quickly became a popular luxury, but it was out of reach for millions until seventy-five years after it was invented. Radio and television took years to reach every living room in America. The rapid acceleration of technology in the first years of the twenty-first century is literally unprecedented. Never before has so much technology changed so fast, for so many people.

Unlike members of Generation Z, who were born into a digital universe and have never known anything different, millennials are acutely aware of how much has changed since they were children. They remember what it was like before the internet: calling up friends on home phone lines, calling Moviefone to find movie times, fighting over CDs in the car. Of course, Gen Xers and boomers also remember the analog age—probably much better than millennials do—and many of them are just as digitally nimble even if they spent more of their adult lives in a pre-internet world. But one day, far in the future, millennials will be the last people on earth who remember what it was like before the internet changed everything.

Being a kid in the 1980s meant getting a remote control for the first time, recording birthday parties on a camcorder, and trying to reach your parents on their pagers. In 1984, only about 8 percent of households had a computer, but households with kids were more likely to have one. These kids were the first to spend hours playing video games. They went to Blockbuster to rent VHS tapes of *E.T.* or *The Princess Bride* that had to be rewound after each viewing ("Be kind! Please rewind!"). They listened to tapes on Sony Walkmans (you'd have to flip the tape after forty-five minutes or so), and then, once the '90s rolled around, they could listen to Spice Girls CDs on a Sony Discman.

Things started to accelerate in the 1990s. In 1990, only 4 percent of Americans had a cell phone—ten years later, more than half would have one (mostly those block Nokia phones—flip phones would come later). By 1993, almost a quarter of US households had a computer, but they were mostly used for word processing, games, and calculations. When millennials were in elementary school and middle school in the mid-1990s, internet access was just beginning to spread.

Max Rose spent the 1990s with a beeper that his mom would use to reach him if it was an emergency. If he wanted to talk to his friends, he'd call their home landline and would have to say, "Hi, Mrs. So-and-So," and then ask for the kid. Finally, in 2001, he got a flip phone which could store only a hundred numbers.

The kids of the late 1990s were the first in history to have their social experiences mediated through screens. Kids like Max (screen name: SmallRedR) would race home from school, rush to the desktop computer, log in to AIM, and wait there until his friends logged in or his crush's screen name popped up. Haley (screen name: HaleyBooyah) spent high school printing out her AIM chats with boys from camp and putting them in a little folder to save for later analysis.

But between 2000 and 2007, America experienced a technological inflection point. By the year 2000, 65 percent of kids under seventeen had access to a home computer and 30 percent had internet access at home. It was also the first year that more people had internet than didn't (even if it wasn't quite home broadband yet) and the first year that Americans were more likely to have a cell phone than not (53 percent of Americans had cell phones by 2000). The iPod was invented in 2001. DVDs eclipsed VHS tapes in 2002. Facebook was launched in 2004, YouTube in 2005, Twitter in 2006, the iPhone in 2007. In the course of a few short years, technology had changed the way people found information, listened to music, and kept in touch with their friends. For millennials, it meant being born in an analog world and growing up in a digital one. In February 2005, only 5 percent of millennials used a social networking site—by early 2010, three-quarters did.

So someone like Haley would have started high school in 1997 listening to music on a Discman, calling her friends on their landlines, and pasting disposable-camera photos into her scrapbooks. By the time she graduated from college in 2005, she would be listening to music on her iPod, texting her friends on her cell phone, and posting her photos to Facebook. In less than ten years, everything had changed.

✳ ✳ ✳

It's impossible to quantify all the ways the digital revolution transformed how millennials thought. It might be easier to list the things that *weren't* affected by the digital revolution, such as the temperature at which an egg will boil, or that people still put their pants on one leg at a time. The full extent of how digital technology has fundamentally shaped millennial and post-millennial social behavior, psychology, and even brain chemistry won't be fully understood for years.

So it's not a surprise that nearly a quarter of millennials say their use of technology is the single most defining characteristic of their generation. And the contours of early internet culture—democratized information, an ethos of disruption, the power of networks, an emphasis on identity—would define millennial politics as well.

Search engines totally changed young people's relationship to information. Knowledge became something that could be accessed at the click of a button, not something accumulated over years of research. Facts became more easily available, arguments more forcefully made, and a universe of information was opened up to young people who were just beginning to interrogate their own beliefs and ideas. This democratization of information meant millennials had less use for gatekeepers who once shaped public discourse, or for experts who were once considered the arbiters of truth. That came with some benefits, such as more access to diverse perspectives that had been historically ignored by traditional news outlets. But it also came with dangers: with the rise of misleading blogs, easily edited Wikipedia pages, and pompous but ill-informed Facebook posts imploring followers to "do your research," misinformation spread so fast that it became difficult to tell what was true online and what was false. This glut of information bred widespread skepticism of institutions: by 2015 only about a quarter of millennials said they trusted the national news media (older generations were similarly skeptical). In the online information ecosystem, accuracy was sacrificed for scale.

The easy availability of information—and the new social networks that could quickly organize and disperse it—would transform the way political campaigns worked. Before, voters would rely on reporters to dig up candidates' old statements or past positions; now almost everything any candidate had ever done was easily searchable online. This could hurt candidates who had waffled in the past, but it could also help: some say Barack Obama's early rise could be partly attributed to the invention of YouTube in 2006, because it allowed young supporters to watch his electrifying 2004 Democratic Convention speech online. Once, candidates would have to rely on established political machines in order to reach voters; now they could easily spread their message on YouTube and Twitter, soliciting volunteers and donations along the way. Ad dollars once spent on interrupting local news programs would soon be spent targeting specific likely voters on Facebook. The campaigns of Barack Obama, Bernie Sanders, and Donald Trump would all thrive on this new model of viral fame and digital campaigning.

But because millennials grew up navigating this jungle of online information, they are often much better than older people at deciphering what's true and what's false. Millennials are more likely than boomers to get their news from Facebook—but because they're digital natives, they're also better at understanding how to interpret it. One study found that people over sixty-five were seven times more likely than younger people to share fake news during the 2016 election. People under fifty are significantly better than older people at distinguishing facts from opinions, according to a Pew study, and boomers are most likely to find themselves in Facebook "bubbles," surrounded by posts that reinforce their own views. Still, even if millennials are better at metabolizing online information than their parents, the spread and weaponization of misleading information will likely be a permanent feature of millennial political life.

The demise of the old gatekeepers led to the rise of a new kind of archetype: the disrupter. The infinite new opportunities in the digital space and the thrilling freedom of a vast, unregulated digital ecosystem gave young upstarts the courage to, as Mark Zuckerberg put it, "move fast and break things." Why should they respect the old ways when this was a whole new world? The future, they thought, belonged to the innovator, the coder, the breaker of rules, not the cog in some outdated machine. So it's probably not a coincidence that individualistic millennials raised in this bold new world had little reverence for the institutions of the old one: they became more skeptical than older Americans of organized religion, political parties, corporations, and labor unions.

The rise of the disrupter mind-set meant that millennials would always be looking for ways to use technology to make things work better—everything from managing their exercise routines to designing better bus routes. Technology brought an instant gratification that often translated into political impatience. If they could stream a sports game from a computer in their pocket at the push of a button, why couldn't they get a transit system that worked? Slow progress was for the analog world: with digital technology, things happened with a click or a swipe, a magical swiftness that obscured millions of smaller steps. This led to a general impatience, a sense that things *should just work*, and a frustration for all the ways they didn't. And it meant that millennials had little reverence for outdated systems, and wouldn't be afraid to challenge established leaders or torch flawed assumptions and begin to build new ones in their place. They were always looking for the latest upgrade.

And when millennials did build new systems, they tended to resemble networks more than hierarchies. Even though the companies were often run by near-dictators like Mark Zuckerberg, platforms such as Facebook and Twitter had created a new blueprint for digital social structures, in which everyone participates but nobody is in charge. In the early years of the internet, that mostly meant that cat photos could be easily shared among large groups of people. But as the networks grew more sophisticated, they became the perfect vehicles for nearly seamless collaboration between people who would never meet. They enabled the rise of leaderless political movements that allowed thousands of people to speak with a single voice, without the complications and vulnerabilities of a single leader: #Occupy, #BlackLives Matter, and #MeToo all took root on social networks before they existed in the physical world.

On a more practical level, the skills required to navigate social media were also skills that could help a political career. Millennials became used to having their words scrutinized, because they knew that old pictures could be dredged up at any time, and they didn't have the illusion of privacy that now seemed like the luxury of a previous generation. Early socializing on Facebook—inviting friends to events, circulating form letters and petitions, promoting new hashtags—used all the same skills that would become useful in twenty-first-century politics. Young people quickly learned how to groom themselves for public consumption, present themselves in the best light possible, and play to the camera. After years of selfies and cell phone videos, millennials (and their younger siblings in Gen Z) are the most camera-ready generation in history. When Alexandria Ocasio-Cortez skyrocketed into political fame in 2018, nobody had to teach her how to talk to a camera—she already knew.

"I think everyone is sort of a public figure in their own minds," says Jess Morales Rocketto. "There's a piece of life as a millennial that is public, regardless of whether or not you want it to be."

The networks were so elegant because they allowed people to maintain their individual identities as part of a larger whole, and to learn about themselves by communicating with people they'd probably never meet. Social media became a platform for finding solidarity with other people with shared interests, even if they lived thousands of miles away. It was the perfect mechanism for building both individual identities and collective ones. From race to sexuality to fandom of a particular video game, these new digital natives built online communities around self-definition, often embracing many overlapping identities at once. It was perfect for a generation of kids raised to "express yourself."

No wonder, then, that as they reached political maturity, millennials seemed more concerned with issues of identity than previous generations. Many of the most effective political movements of the first decades of the twenty-first century were rooted in questions of race, gender, and sexuality. "Identity politics" is often scorned for its emphasis on difference over commonality, but it made perfect sense for the most racially diverse and sexually empowered generation in history, raised in an online world built around a shared sense of self. It also comes as no surprise that millennials overwhelmingly believe that racial diversity is good for America, that women should be treated equally, that immigrants strengthen the country, and that gay people should be allowed to get married.

Of course, not all millennials subscribed to the gospel of social justice. The online alt-right—made up disproportionately of white millennial men— rose in backlash to the flourishing of identity politics and the successful social justice movements that began online. The young trolls in the antifeminist men's rights movement and the racist alt-right movement are also creatures of the digital ecosystem. They, too, owe their existence to social media platforms (including Reddit and 4chan as well as Facebook and Twitter), and their sexism and racism constitutes its own kind of online political identity rooted in white male grievance.

✳ ✳ ✳

None of this was abstract: the rapid expansion of information, development of social networks, and explosion of online identities were changing how ordinary millennials thought about themselves and their place in the world.

Pete Buttigieg saw the digital transformation firsthand. When he first got to Harvard in the fall of 2000, his internet usage was mostly just logging on to WNDU.com to look at a grainy picture of South Bend. That year, the homepage of Harvard's own website was just text with the Harvard logo and a tiny picture of campus. He called home by dialing a 1-800 number on his dorm room "cordless" phone. By sophomore year, he had a Sprint flip phone (with caller ID!), and a year later he had a dinky Ericsson T68i (with a color pixel display!) that could miraculously download his address book from his computer onto his phone. Soon he began to see people walking around campus tapping away on their BlackBerrys.

He had one of those big bubble iMac computers that came in bright colors—his was blue—and in the early aughts, AIM was the main way college kids communicated with one another. He and his roommates would even AIM each other when they were sitting five feet away in their redbrick dorm room in Harvard Yard.

By senior spring, Pete was one of the student leaders of the Institute of Politics, working on an impressive history and literature thesis about Puritan rhetoric and the Vietnam War, and applying for a Rhodes Scholarship. His friends figured he was just the type of person who was too busy to have a girlfriend. He was also too busy to pay much attention to the new website being invented by a handful of sophomores a few dorms down from his. In February 2004, when "The Facebook" began to circulate on campus, Pete thought of it as a campus website, as Harvard-specific as the *Crimson* or Widener Library. At first, people used it to compare women and decide who was more attractive, but soon it became the locus of all campus gossip, where people could see who was dating whom, who was in which clique, who was cool and who was not.

By the end of senior year, Pete would find himself up late, his round face lit in the blue computer screen glare, looking at Facebook profiles of men who said they were interested in men. He told himself it was just out of curiosity, that he found it intellectually interesting that these men were so public about their sexuality online, especially when he knew almost nobody who was openly gay. He knew that politics required stability, a family, someone to stand next to him onstage. Only a handful of states allowed same-sex couples to marry, and nobody with a successful political career was openly gay.

He never sent a message. He always ended up shutting down his iMac and going to sleep.

CHAPTER 5

This Is the War That Never Ends

D an Crenshaw graduated from Tufts in 2006 and was commissioned into the navy immediately afterward. But before he could be a Navy SEAL, he had to get through Hell Week: five and a half days designed to break your body and crush your spirit. Over nearly a week with only four hours of sleep, he and the other guys would be put through a seemingly endless cycle of grueling physical exertion spent running, swimming, and carrying logs and boats. Some guys got overwhelmed after the first few hours; others couldn't handle not knowing what the next physical labor might be; others dropped out when their friends gave up. Hell Week was designed to break you, because the instructors wanted to see what you looked like when you broke. It was more about mental discipline than physical strength, and the ones who had what it took were the ones who could silence the voice in their head telling them to quit. It was all about the story you told yourself: Were you the guy who was overcome by challenges, or were you the guy who conquered them? Ever since his mother's cancer treatments, Dan had been used to telling himself the second story. On his first Hell Week, Dan broke his tibia. On his next try, he made it through.

Dan served five tours in his ten years as a Navy SEAL, retiring with the rank of lieutenant commander. On his first deployment, in Fallujah, Iraq, he led convoys around the region and ended up in Basra sleeping on a cot in what had once been Saddam Hussein's palace. On his second deployment, he was unexpectedly moved into a platoon commander position, leading a SEAL platoon conducting missions to capture or kill al-Qaeda operatives in Iraq and training Iraqi soldiers on how to collect evidence and create warrants, all to advance American strategic interests and help the Iraqis build a criminal justice system.

His third tour was in Afghanistan, based in Kandahar. In June 2012 his unit was sent to support a Marine Special Operations unit that had been in a firefight in the nearby Helmand Province. The Marines had called in air strikes and kept the enemy at bay, but they'd taken wounded, were running low on ammunition and supplies, and were unable to maintain their position. The enemy compound was destroyed, but senior military leadership wanted to maintain a presence at the site of the engagement, and needed to ensure that the results of the airstrike were properly documented and that the air strikes had been justified. So Dan and his team went in to relieve the Marines and complete their mission, which included a battle damage assessment (BDA)—and taking pictures of the destroyed compound.

Later, Dan would think this mission was an example of flawed Obama-era priorities in Afghanistan. Dan thought Obama's Pentagon was so intent on avoiding bad PR that they'd sent American forces into harm's way. It wasn't as if Dan's team was actively storming the compound—they were taking pictures to justify an air strike that had already happened. And Helmand was so littered with IEDs that it was safer to crouch in place under sniper fire than run for cover over uncleared ground. "The idea that you would go all the way there on foot just to take pictures of it and prove that they weren't doing anything wrong is a crazy thing to do," Dan said later. "It's not like we were saving the Marines."

SEAL Team Three landed a couple of hours before daylight on June 15, 2012, and briefed the Marines on the plan: they would travel to a different, more abandoned compound, which would be the base for the battle damage assessment mission. But to get there, they had to cross a field and go through compounds that hadn't been cleared of IEDs, so the SEAL team was walking in single file, which was standard operation procedure but still tactically dangerous. Dan was walking behind the guy with the metal

detector. They were in the initial stages of clearing a compound when someone called out to one of the Afghan interpreters, Raqman, to come translate
something. Raqman cut in front of Dan to answer the call, and suddenly Dan
was on the ground.

He wasn't unconscious. He could feel his legs, he could hear, so he knew
he wasn't the one who had stepped on something. But it felt as if he'd been
hit by a truck. He couldn't see anything, but he figured he just had dirt in his
eyes. There was pain everywhere, but SEALs are trained to just think, "OK,
we've been through this before," and put mind over body. So he followed the
procedure, which is to sit there until the medic reached him. The worst thing
he could do would be to start running, because first of all, he could step on
another bomb, and second of all, he couldn't see anything. So he just sat there
and waited, and a few minutes later the medic showed up. "Dude," Dan said
to him, "don't get blown up, it sucks."

Raqman, the interpreter, lost all four limbs. His foot flew over to the next
compound and hit one of Dan's friends in the chest. Dan remembers hearing
him groaning, not a high shriek like something you'd hear in a movie, more
like a low moan from deep in his throat. He died a few hours later. The IED
he had stepped on was bigger than normal, and it was in hard ground, so
there was no way he could have survived a blast like that. Forty-five minutes
later Dan walked to the medevac holding on to somebody's shoulders. There
was still so much dirt in his eyes that he couldn't see anything, but he didn't
want to put more guys in harm's way by having multiple men carry him on a
stretcher. Once he got on the helicopter, they put him under.

Dan woke up in Germany five days later, barely able to move and still
blind. It hadn't been dirt in his eyes, after all: his right eye was completely
destroyed and had to be removed, and his left eye was so damaged that they
weren't sure if he would be able to see out of it at all. He had a tube in his
throat; his arms and legs were swollen as if they'd been hit with a bunch of
shotgun blasts.

But he was optimistic for no good reason. When the doctors told him
they had removed his right eye, he thought, "That's OK—I have another one."
When a copper wire was removed from his left eye and doctors explained
there was a very small chance he would be able to see again, Dan took it as

good news: he would see again! Later, he couldn't explain how he maintained that delusion, except that he thought God gave it to him to help him stay sane.

Otherwise, he knew he would have gone nuts. He had to lie facedown and sightless for weeks while his remaining eye healed. He could handle the loss of his eye, and the pain, and the tube in his throat—the thing he couldn't handle was the hallucinations. His optic nerve was still firing, showing him things as if he had a phantom eye. He looked around his hospital bed and saw Afghanistan, even when he knew he wasn't dreaming. He didn't see Raqman running, or the line of men, or the open field, or the compound. He never saw anything on a base. He saw a village: mud walls, mud rooms, piles of weapons. It wasn't necessarily a specific village he recognized, more just the combined images of all the villages he'd been to. And there was an old Afghan man sitting next to him. He had never seen this man before, he didn't recognize him, and the man never said or did anything, just sat there next to Dan in his hospital bed. Day after day he would wake up and look around and see the village and the man. His brain knew he was in Germany, but his eyes were showing him Afghanistan.

After a while, the doctors finally gave him some Ativan, and the village and the man faded away. His left eye had a broken iris and a scarred retina, but the doctors were able to save his sight. He would never be great at catching a baseball, and most of the times he poured water he would spill it, but he could see enough to read and live in the world. The next year, he married his longtime girlfriend, Tara. He deployed overseas twice more—to Bahrain and South Korea—before he was medically retired in 2016 with two Bronze Star Medals including one with valor, the Purple Heart, and the Navy and Marine Corps Commendation Medal with valor.

✳ ✳ ✳

Dan was a believer: he believed that American presence abroad could deter terrorists; he believed that military intervention in the Middle East was necessary and productive; he believed that US forces "go there so they don't come here." After all that time overseas, he was far better informed than most of his peers about the practicalities of the War on Terror.

But Dan was in the minority: after nearly two decades of combat, most millennials were deeply skeptical about the War on Terror. Most had initially supported sending troops to Afghanistan to capture the al-Qaeda terrorists who had plotted 9/11, but the presence went on much longer than anybody expected. Many believed that the invasion of Iraq was based on either staggering incompetence or an outright lie, depending on whom you asked. The endless war that followed set the stage for millennial disillusionment with US foreign policy in general, and with the Republican Party in particular.

Over the next decade, more than 4,500 Americans were killed and 32,000 were wounded in Iraq. By some counts, more than 250,000 Americans and Iraqis were killed in that war, including roughly 200,000 civilians. The war lasted so long that by 2017, there were young people enlisting in the military who didn't even remember 9/11. Fathers served in Iraq at the same time as their sons, mothers with their daughters. By late 2018, the military was recruiting teenagers to enlist in a war that had started before they were born, a war without beginning or end, a conflict *New York Times* correspondent Dexter Filkins called the "forever war."

Unlike World War II, a massive mobilization that enlisted almost an entire generation of young men, or Vietnam, which drafted enough baby boomers to cause widespread social unrest, the post-9/11 wars dragged on silently in the background of most people's lives. With no draft, the wars were fought almost entirely by young people like Dan, who had raised their hands and volunteered. But it also meant that public opposition to the wars was erratic and ineffective, and there was little sustained public pressure to force the conflict to end.

"The fact that we can project power and fight and win wars without having to resort to a draft is a blessing," says Rep. Mike Gallagher (b. 1984), who represents Green Bay, Wisconsin, in Congress and deployed twice to Iraq as a US Marine. "The risk is that it makes perpetual war more likely. If the society doesn't feel the cost of war, then we'd be more likely to find ourselves continually in wars."

The end of the draft meant that military service was concentrated in a small population, and people from military families were often the most likely to enlist. By one count, more than 80 percent of recruits in 2015 had a family member in the military, and more than a quarter had a military parent.

That meant that the war was being fought by a shrinking population of young people: at the end of World War II, nearly 10 percent of the US population was on active military duty—by 2015, less than 1 percent of Americans had served in Afghanistan or Iraq in the fourteen years since 9/11, many of them on multiple tours.

And as the war dragged on, military enlistment became increasingly segregated by income and geography. About 80 percent of active-duty military in the post-9/11 wars didn't have a college degree. One study found that 40 percent of newly enlisted military personnel came from the South, with another quarter coming from the West, while less than 15 percent of recruits came from the Northeast. By 2015, there were more young people studying abroad than joining the military.

A rift began to emerge between those millennials who served and those who didn't. For some, the war was the most significant event of their early adulthood—but for most, it was something they saw only on TV, if at all. Veterans like Dan Crenshaw or Mike Gallagher had a sophisticated understanding of what the United States was doing in Iraq, but ordinary young people began to see the whole thing as a huge, endless mistake.

. ✳ ✳ ✳

Nobody around Max Rose could understand why he felt such a sense of duty. It wasn't as if anybody was expecting him to enlist—his mom was a professor, his dad ran a medical lab, they were a Brooklyn family who didn't know many people in the military. But sometime in the years since the towers fell, Max had decided that he would fight in the war, not because he believed in it, but because it was there.

"I don't care what your position is on Iraq and Afghanistan," he said. "I was going to enlist because there was a war on." It spoke to something deeper for Max, some small voice that believed in the power of the American project. Even in the face of the epic fuckups on the federal level, Max still felt that the nation that put a man on the moon was capable of confronting any challenge. "We're going to take back this idea that being patriotic means that we think in a very bold way about how American society can conquer problems," he told me years later, at an Italian festival on Staten Island.

When his mother came to visit him at the London School of Economics, they took a long walk and he told her he was planning to enlist. Lisa Rose tried every argument she could think of to get him to reconsider. "You're not a rule follower, you lose things, you're an iconoclast," she said. She pointed out that she could have saved a lot of money on college if he had enrolled in ROTC. "You can't even make a bed that good," she said.

But Max hated it when people questioned his decision to join the military. It was like a tribunal: people asked him why he was joining, whether he believed in the invasion in Iraq, whether he could kill somebody with his bare hands. "Whoa, bro," he thought, "I'm just a twenty-two-year-old that made a life decision—back off." He had friends who were going to work at Goldman Sachs at the height of the financial crisis, and nobody asked them any big moral questions about why they decided to do what they did. But everywhere he went, there was this question of why. Why did he want to go fight a flawed war for a bad reason? Why did he want to stand around in the heat and the dust? Why did he want to be part of this institution?

That attitude bothered him. He got the sense that people assumed that the military was either for poor kids who had no other options or for war-hungry animals who wanted to become killing machines. He hated when people acted surprised, as if he were making some kind of crazy choice, when actually he was just doing his duty, unlike the millions of other Americans of fighting age who decided to sit it out. Besides, if he thought too hard about it ("Why am I doing this? What's my purpose? Why am I here?"), it would drive him crazy, so he just decided to not think too hard about it, which was easy since nobody else seemed to be thinking too hard about it either. Ultimately, it didn't matter whether he was there for a reason or not, or whether he wanted to or not, or whether he was fulfilling some deeper purpose or not. Those were special snowflake questions, and the military wasn't the place for special snowflakes.

Afghanistan didn't change him much. He figured he was an intense asshole before, on account of being short and ginger and all, and he was an intense asshole afterward. Military culture wasn't so different from law enforcement culture or fire department culture, and he had grown up around cops and firefighters, so it was familiar to him in a way. It was a bullshit-free zone, and that's why he liked it.

By the time Max got to Afghanistan in 2012, the United States had already been fighting there for more than ten years. Max was somebody who was usually good at most things he tried to do, but he sucked at being in the military. He hadn't had much experience with weapons until training, and he didn't know anything about operating military vehicles. Most of military training is being in the right place at the right time, wearing the right thing and understanding your mission. It turned out his mom had been right: he wasn't organized enough. He'd lose things, or he'd get confused or lost. All the intellectual ways he had been trained to think were useless here.

When he finally became a Ranger-qualified infantry platoon leader, he was in charge of thirty enlisted US personnel and about sixty Afghan National Army soldiers. The idea was for his platoon to gain the trust of the villagers, establish a secure zone, and train the Afghan National Army to maintain control. They'd go to a village, meet a village elder, "give him some Bobby Kennedy speech," as Max put it, try to figure out whether there were any IEDs in the area, then step back and let the Afghan National Army take it from there. It was just a stability operation, a signal to the Afghan army that the United States had its back. He thought of it like being a cop on community patrol. He was there to win hearts and minds, not kill people. This wasn't the bin Laden raid: he wasn't Rambo.

He and his unit usually got around on Strykers. The Stryker was an awkward beast: an eight-wheeled vehicle that was supposed to be bigger than a Humvee but lighter than a tank, and still transportable by air. It could be deployed relatively fast and used for a variety of operations; it offered more protection than a truck and gave soldiers the agility they needed to deal with an enemy that seemed to be everywhere at once. The military ordered almost 2,900 Strykers in a $13 billion program.

But when the Strykers debuted in Afghanistan in 2009 with the Fifth Stryker Brigade in Kandahar, it was a disaster. That brigade had two dozen troops killed and more than seventy wounded that year, in part because the Stryker wasn't built to withstand buried IEDs. Insurgents would surround the IEDs with cement, so they'd explode straight upward into the flat-bottomed vehicles. The Stryker made more sense in Iraq: a denser road network meant more plausible routes, so it was harder for insurgents to know exactly where to plant their bombs. But in Afghanistan, villages were often linked by a single road, so insurgents knew precisely where to bury the IEDs. The roads became booby traps. Soldiers started calling the Stryker "the Kevlar coffin."

In 2010, Congress ordered a study of how to make combat vehicles safer. In 2011, the army began sending "double V-hull" Strykers to Afghanistan, with a special V-shaped base that directed explosions outward, rather than up into the vehicle. In 2013, Max was riding in a double V-hull Stryker on his way back from a presence patrol in a village in northern Kandahar province.

There were poppy farms in the area—he remembers that. It was him and five other guys and his interpreter, Andish. Max doesn't like it when you ask him about what the explosion felt like, because it was an explosion—what do you think it felt like? But he also likes to compare it to something out of *Mission: Impossible*. Afterward, he woke up in Andish's lap. He had taken a bad cut to his head when the hatch of the vehicle came undone, and a bad cut to his knee. His guys called the medevac and they came and got him and brought him to Kandahar Air Force Base, where a two-star general came to his bed, looked at him for a second, and said, "Son, five years ago, you'd be dead." The V-hull on the Stryker had saved his life.

Max saw his time in the military as evidence of what this country could do if it really put its mind to it. He didn't come away disillusioned—he came away optimistic. Of course, there were lessons: don't invade Iraq; don't withdraw hastily after you invade Iraq; don't announce eighteen-month timetables in Afghanistan. But he had to admit that Bush's 2007 surge of troops into Iraq had been successful, mostly because it had been a surge of ideas: it was a military surge, sure, but it also involved training, investment, and diplomacy. It was a holistic, all-hands-on-deck approach, he thought. General Stanley McChrystal designed a military structure that was more decentralized, flatter, and empowered individual outposts with more authority to hand the war over to the Afghan army. They weren't getting top-down orders from the Pentagon. He figured this was how America should be solving all its problems—by attacking them from all sides at once, informed by locals on the ground.

Max thought America needed what he liked to call a "domestic surge": a massive investment in government resources to solve problems at home the way the military solved problems abroad. A surge could solve the opioid crisis. A surge could repair American infrastructure. He thought it was bullshit that George W. Bush kept talking about government being the problem at home, but when it came to another country's challenges, American government was the solution. "We are fucking Americans," Max liked to say. "And that means we fix stuff."

Like Dan, Max came away from the military with a greater belief in American capabilities abroad, but most young Americans remained skeptical. Even if they had begrudging respect for the military itself, most millennials were turning against the foreign policy attitudes that led us into Iraq in the first place. According to a 2011 Pew survey, about two-thirds of millennials believed that too much military intervention creates hatred that leads to more terrorism, while fewer than half of boomers agreed. Millennials overwhelmingly favored diplomacy and compromise over military presence abroad. They were also much less likely than their parents or grandparents to suspect that American Muslims held extremist views.

But mostly, Americans at home had almost no idea what Max and his platoon had experienced, because after years of skirmishes without victory or defeat, Iraq and Afghanistan had faded from the headlines. Unlike veterans returning from Vietnam, veterans of the 9/11 wars were rarely harassed— people tended to mumble "thank you for your service" and go about their day. Max began to get irritated whenever people thanked him for his service—it was a kind of empty, dutiful hero worship that just further distanced the 9/11 veterans from the American people. Veterans were returning to groups of friends who had spent the war swiping on their phones in a state of pleasant obliviousness, neither afraid of being drafted nor outraged at Americans dying overseas. Many thought of enlisting as a vaguely unpleasant endeavor that other people had chosen to sign up for, like running a triathlon. By 2011, more than eight in ten post-9/11 veterans said they felt misunderstood by the American public. Between 2001 and 2014, veteran suicides spiked 35 percent, according to the Department of Veteran Affairs, with a sharp increase among young veterans.

More important, the "forever war" dented a long-standing sense of exceptionalism and global mission for an entire generation of young Americans. In 2017, only about half of millennials said they thought the United States should take an active part in world affairs, compared to almost three-quarters of baby boomers. Only about a third of millennials said they thought the United States was the greatest country in the world. This lack of chauvinism has its value; unlike prior generations, millennial isolationism isn't entwined with nationalism, which could provide a check on the bristling nationalistic fervor and help keep the United States out of unnecessary wars abroad. But it could also become an abdication of America's role as a global leader, if the rising generation no longer believes that protecting and promoting democracy in the name of American ideals is worth the trouble.

Dan and Max's brand of patriotism had become the exception, not the rule.

✳ ✳ ✳

None of Pete Buttigieg's Harvard friends joined the military or even considered it. If you were a Harvard kid in the Zuckerberg era, you were trying to create another Facebook, or win a place at Goldman Sachs, or go into Teach for America or apply to law school or, as Pete himself did briefly, get a consulting job with McKinsey. For most Harvard students in the early 2000s, the military was for other people—there wasn't even ROTC on campus, because it had been banned there since the Vietnam War.

It was something he had been thinking about since that morning he was jolted out of his college dorm bed to see the towers fall on TV. He talks about it with a lofty resignation, as if there had been an error in history's dispatch office, and the mild-mannered boy who was supposed to work at a think tank instead ended up in Afghanistan. "Our generational project had been reassigned," he told me over beers at a South Bend bar. "Under the Clintons, it had been about the internet—now it was about war and peace."

It wasn't an obvious fit for Pete, and people who knew him were surprised when he joined. He sucked at sports, he hated fighting, and he would rather talk about philosophers than shoot a gun. But Pete had always had a sense of history. He thought a lot about previous wartime generations, boys his age who had served in the Civil War and in World War I and World War II. It was something that tugged at him, in the back of his mind, a sort of guilt—or maybe it was idealism, or grandiosity, or, underneath it all, political ambition—that none of his friends seemed to feel. His country was at war, yet he was working for McKinsey, looking at spreadsheets.

The feeling got stronger in 2008, as he traversed Iowa knocking on doors as a volunteer for then senator Barack Obama. People would answer the door and tell him they'd like to caucus but they were packing up for basic training. He'd see kids four or five years younger than him who were preparing to enlist. Nearly every other house had a yellow ribbon on the door. Whole towns in rural Iowa had sent their sons to fight in Iraq and Afghanistan, but Pete could count on one hand the number of Harvard classmates who signed up to serve. It wasn't just Harvard—almost nobody in the Ivy League was lining up to join, and few sons from rich families took it upon themselves to serve in the unpopular, seemingly endless wars in Iraq and Afghanistan.

Pete knew it hadn't always been this way. John F. Kennedy and George H. W. Bush, graduates of Harvard and Yale and scions of rich and powerful families, had both been expected to serve in World War II and had been eager to do so. Pete's own great-uncle had been an Army Air Corps captain who was killed in a plane crash in 1941. Occasionally, Pete thumbed through his flight log, filled with terse and manly descriptions of "awful head winds" and "very good blind dates." He got to thinking about how that generation had thought of military service as the mark of an elite, well-educated man doing his duty for society; in his generation, few elites even considered it. Besides, he still dreamed of one day having a political career. It couldn't have escaped his attention that military service would sound awfully good on the campaign trail.

So after the Obama campaign, Pete went to a recruiting office, and once he filled out all the bubble tests and triplicate forms, he was on his way. All he had to do was show up at a Radisson in Des Plaines, Illinois, without any body piercings, hate symbol tattoos, or pants that showed his underwear.

He was hustled through a bunch of tests (swine flu test, blood test, color blindness test, drug test) and had to perform a series of physical exercises in his underwear in front of a doctor until he was declared medically qualified. To be an officer he had to complete the background check, so the navy traced every international trip, every foreign cousin, every time he had ever smoked pot (not often, but not never). Finally, in September 2009, he was approved to take the oath.

He thought it would be like when Richard Gere got sworn in at the end of *An Officer and a Gentleman*: something dignified and rousing, a few flags, a right hand raised in patriotic salute. Instead, the recruiting lieutenant suggested they meet at a Big Boy diner in Coldwater, Michigan, which turned out to be closed anyway, so they went to a no-name coffee shop next door and she pointed at the line where he should put his signature. "If you really want to raise your right hand, we can do that," she said. That was it. He was a commissioned officer in the US Navy Reserve.

Over the next five years, Pete would stay on top of his Navy Reserve duties even as his civilian life got busier. He left McKinsey and moved back to Indiana to run for state treasurer and lost. After that, he ran for mayor of South Bend and won. Once a month he'd head to base for a weekend of Navy Reserve training, but the rest of his day-to-day life had little to do with the military: he was focused on revitalizing South Bend's economy to make it competitive in the twenty-first century.

But in February 2014, he was deployed to the Afghan Threat Finance Cell, a multiagency intelligence unit dedicated to fighting corruption. He took a leave of absence from the mayor's office and handed off his day-to-day responsibilities to a deputy before he shipped out to the Naval Station Great Lakes, north of Chicago, and then to Camp McCrady, near Columbia, South Carolina. When he first got his uniform, his last name wasn't even spelled right.

But by the time Pete arrived in Afghanistan, one of his fellow officers casually informed him that, sorry, buddy, the war is over. Technically over, that is. It had been eleven years since Bush had stood in front of a "Mission Accomplished" sign on the USS *Abraham Lincoln*, four years since the 2009

Afghanistan surge, three years since Obama had promised to withdraw thirty-three thousand troops from Afghanistan. Yet here was Pete, smoking cigars with the other guys in the intel unit around a fire pit near Bagram Air Base, wondering why the hell he was over here fighting a war that had supposedly ended. What did "over" actually mean? Was "ending" a war even possible in this new type of warfare?

By April he was in Kabul, spending most of his time as a vehicle commander on convoys moving people around the city. He had two goals: try not to run people over and try not to get blown up. Most of the intelligence they had on car bombs pointed to someone driving a white Corolla, which was pretty unhelpful because everybody in Kabul drove a white Corolla. When he'd come back to the base, he'd drink beers with the other guys and try not to say too much. Some of them still talked as if they were in middle school, throwing around homophobic slurs and calling each other "so gay." Pete would just smile and say nothing. Don't Ask, Don't Tell had technically been repealed, but Pete wasn't about to go there. He hadn't even told his parents he was gay.

Three months after Pete arrived, Obama announced plans to withdraw troops from Afghanistan entirely. Instead of making Pete hopeful, it just made him more anxious. It was one thing to die in an ongoing war—but the prospect of dying in a war that was supposed to be over felt more depressing. He thought back to John Kerry's words as the spokesman for Vietnam Veterans Against the War, when he had asked during his Senate testimony, "How do you ask a man to be the last man to die for a mistake?"

As it turned out, Pete's tour was relatively uneventful. But the day after he took off from the Kandahar air base to leave Afghanistan, Pete heard that there had been a suicide bombing back in Kabul that left two Americans dead. When the names were finally released, he realized he knew one of the guys: Major Mike Donahue. They hadn't been particularly close but had once delivered supplies to an Afghan orphanage together. Major Donahue had worn the same kind of gear as Pete, and had driven the same type of vehicle along the same circuitous route.

By the time he made it back to South Bend, something in Pete had shifted.

He had risked rocket attacks and IEDs and car bombs, had wrapped his head around the idea of dying a million different ways, and still there was one thing that really bothered him. Most of his friends and family didn't know about a crucial part of who he was. And because of that secret, if he had been the one who'd been blown up by that suicide car bomb, he would have died without having ever been in love.

PART TWO

✯ ✯ ✯

It's not that you guys actually remind me of myself—it's the fact that you are so much better than I was, in so many ways. You're smarter, you're better organized, and you're more effective. . . . Your journey's just beginning. You're just starting. And whatever good we do over the next four years will pale in comparison to what you guys end up accomplishing for years and years to come.

—BARACK OBAMA, NOVEMBER 7, 2012, HOLDING BACK TEARS AS HE ADDRESSES STAFFERS ON HIS REELECTION CAMPAIGN

CHAPTER 6

The Rocket Ship

I n July 2004, Illinois Senate candidate Barack Obama walked onstage at the Democratic National Convention in Boston and began to describe what he called a "politics of hope." He was a mostly unknown Illinois state senator, lanky and big-eared, running to be the only black member of the US Senate.

"Hope in the face of difficulty. Hope in the face of uncertainty," he said. "The audacity of hope! In the end, that is God's greatest gift to us, the bedrock of this nation. A belief in things not seen. A belief that there are better days ahead."

Eric Lesser was a round-faced college intern for CNN that summer, fresh off his first year at Harvard. His main job at the time was to go down to the convention floor at the end of the night and pick up the placards so that they could decorate the CNN office with signs from all the candidates. But when he got down to the floor after Obama's speech, there was not a single placard left. The delegates had taken them all. That was his first signal that Obama was going to be something big.

When Svante Myrick's grandmother in Earlville saw the speech on TV, she immediately bought him a copy of Obama's memoir, *Dreams from My Father*. Svante read it and thought, "It's a shame that somebody like him could never be president." His high school teacher Mr. Sherry recalled that after Svante watched the 2004 speech, he started talking about how "it's not blue America, it's not red America, it's the United States of America." Sherry said most of the kids in his class barely registered that the Democratic Convention had happened. But after that speech, Svante began to walk with a different swagger.

There were kids like Svante and Eric all over America, smart young people were paying attention to politics for the first time. Quantifying Obama's impact on millennial politics is like quantifying how the internet changed communication, or how the Beatles changed rock and roll. Obama emerged just as the majority of millennials were becoming eligible to vote, at a time when many young people were frustrated with their options in national politics: over their short lifetimes, the presidency had begun to seem like a carousel of Bushes and Clintons. There had been some glimmers of the power of youth enthusiasm—particularly in Howard Dean's 2004 primary campaign—but until Obama, the boomer status quo seemed largely intact. This little-known Illinois senator represented a definitive break from the past. Before Obama, politics was for parents and teachers—after Obama, young people began to think they could shape political outcomes. Before Obama, only white guys could be president—after Obama, young people of color could see themselves reflected in the Oval Office. Before Obama, politics was boring—after Obama, politics was cool.

✸ ✸ ✸

Lauren Underwood first met Obama when she interned in his Senate office in the summer of 2006. She was nineteen years old, on an internship sponsored by the Congressional Black Caucus, the only black girl intern working for Obama that summer. "All of the interns in the office knew someone to get the internship," she wrote in her required Congressional Black Caucus intern journal one week. "Many of them are VERY rich."

Mostly she was answering phones, dealing with mail, preparing things for the senator to autograph. Her weekly dispatches to the CBC vacillated between hyperenthusiastic ("I LOVE my job!") and glum. "I've realized that the staff in my office doesn't love me, which is somewhat disappointing," she wrote. "The interns that they love get to go to cool events that the rest of us miss out on simply because we're not thought of."

Each intern got to staff Obama once, which meant they went to all his meetings with him, helped him work on his talking points for the day, and then physically accompanied him wherever he went. On the day Lauren staffed Obama, she helped him prepare talking points about microbicides for a Gates Foundation event. Microbicides are substances that can be applied inside the vagina or rectum to help prevent the spread of sexually transmitted diseases such as HIV. But Lauren absolutely did not ever want to say the words "vagina" or "rectum" to Senator Barack Obama, so she just stuck to "microbicides" and hoped he didn't ask her to get more specific.

Obama wasn't particularly chitchatty, but when he did talk he would make eye contact and look straight at Lauren, like she was a person he respected. As they walked to the elevator to go to the Gates Foundation event, they made a little small talk. She remembered that walking next to him was like "sharing the sunshine."

✴ ✴ ✴

After that first convention speech, Eric went back to Harvard, where he spent most of his time hobnobbing with other young politicos at the Institute of Politics, including Pete and Elise. Pete was a couple years ahead of him, Elise was a year behind, and they all saw one another at Institute of Politics events, when senators or former cabinet officials came through to visit.

But Eric hadn't been able to forget that Boston convention speech, so when Obama announced in 2007 that he was running for the Democratic presidential nomination, Eric dropped his senior thesis so he could spend his weekends driving to New Hampshire to knock on doors. He just had a gut feeling about this guy. At first, there wasn't even an office; they would find people on meetup.com, knock on some doors, and then all go drinking in Manchester. By the time the campaign set up an office in New Hampshire, Eric was already a familiar face, the guy who was always hanging around asking if there was something he could do. Hillary's campaign contained most of the top minds in establishment Democratic politics; Obama's early campaign had a couple of experienced advisors, but it was mostly a bunch of young people who had sensed that other young people would like this guy. Finally, someone gave Eric a job as deputy director of advance, which meant he helped put together all the events that Obama did in New Hampshire: he worked with the field organizers to make sure there was a crowd, and checked that all the logistics were in order so that nothing would go wrong at the event. In the early days, he would sometimes drive Obama around, or grab his lunch for him (the senator preferred plain foods, like grilled fish or chicken and brown rice, and steamed broccoli or steamed spinach). Later, once Obama was driven by Secret Service, Eric would drive the staff van. After graduation he moved to Manchester to live in what he calls a campaign "flophouse," where visiting staffers and volunteers were always crashing on the floor.

Back in Michigan, Haley Stevens had spent 2006 knocking on doors for the Michigan Democratic Party with stacks of papers and a clipboard, trying to organize canvassers to help reelect Governor Jennifer Granholm. She hadn't thought about Hillary Clinton very much at all. But she loved politics, and she wanted to support women, so when someone told her the Clinton campaign was looking for interns, Haley signed up. People noticed that she was the first one at work in the morning and the last one to leave at night, so in March 2007, Clinton's policy director, Neera Tanden, hired her as an assistant in the research department. One time, someone urgently demanded to know the price of milk at a Piggly Wiggly grocery store in Iowa, so Haley picked up the phone and called Piggly Wiggly. Milk, she announced, cost $2.19. Neera was impressed, and Haley was promoted: she would be in charge of the briefing book, the all-important book of information that would be stuffed into Hillary Clinton's brain before every public appearance. If Hillary Clinton seemed overprepared, it's because it was Haley's job to keep her that way.

There were two types of people who worked on the 2008 Hillary Clinton campaign: people who were die-hard Clinton fans, and people who just picked Hillary as their horse in this particular race. Haley was in the second group. But working on this campaign had a way of making even the mercenaries into evangelists: in order to run against a candidate as appealing as Barack Obama, you had to convince yourself that there were real contrasts between the candidates, and those contrasts got you out of bed in the morning.

For the rest of 2007, the Clinton campaign felt like a slow march to victory. The schedule would come out, Haley would scramble to make the briefing book, Hillary would read it, Hillary would spout facts that came from the book, rinse and repeat. Hillary dutifully visited Iowa thirty-five times that year. They went on a ninety-nine-county "Hill-a-copter" tour. They spent more than $95,000 on catering for caucus night. The campaign gave away snow shovels to precinct captains, as if there was anyone in Iowa who didn't already have a snow shovel.

Meanwhile, Obama was spending his time in Iowa cultivating a network of young people who could vote in the Iowa caucuses if they turned eighteen by November 4, 2008. The campaign quickly realized that the locations of high schools and colleges around the state could make the difference between Obama winning and losing. Each caucus was like a mini-election, and they were usually won by single digits— so if Obama could get just a handful of high school students to attend their local caucuses, they could tip the election. They started off using Facebook to find kids who wanted to organize chapters in their high schools, and then those kids would take the lead and recruit fifteen, twenty, one hundred of their friends to join. High school students, the campaign knew, were a captive audience who talked to one another every day: if you could get a few of them excited, it was easy to mobilize the rest. These kids—nicknamed "Barack stars"—would pack campaign offices on Friday nights, where they'd get free pizza and stickers while they made phone calls for Obama.

There were at least 175 student chapters of the Obama campaign in Iowa alone. Before every event, he would make time to meet with high school students in the area, giving them the same status as local elected officials or donors. He made a point of skipping an AARP event to go campaign at an Usher concert—and made sure to let young people know about it. He targeted his ad money toward student voters, and student-to-student phone banks reached tens of thousands of cell phones and dorm phones in the days before the caucus. Later, Obama's national youth vote director, Hans Riemer, told me that "the Iowa class of 2008 elected Barack Obama president."

Young people from all over the country flocked to Iowa to knock on doors for Obama. By then, Pete Buttigieg was working at McKinsey in Chicago and questioning his life choices. He and a few friends from college went to canvass for Obama in south-central Iowa around New Year's. It was so cold he felt the hair in his nostrils freeze, but the towns they visited reminded him of South Bend, which made him feel a little homesick. Their coats weren't warm enough for the cold, and their car wasn't big enough to maneuver in the snow. Once, they got stuck in a snowdrift and tried to use their clipboards to dig out the tires before ultimately knocking on an old lady's door to ask for help. That Iowa trip marked only a small involvement in Obama's campaign, but it was a turning point in Pete's life; while he canvassed, he noticed how many rural families had sent their kids off to war, which got him thinking about whether he should enlist.

The Obama campaign relied on high school kids organizing on school nights, and college kids mobilizing their families over Christmas break, and young adults like Pete spending their holidays on freezing Iowa highways. *TIME* columnist Joe Klein wrote that these young people "reminded me, in classic, solipsistic boomer fashion, of my own generation of the remarkable political activists who went down to Mississippi to register black voters and marched against another war. . . . The end of their time—our time—in the driver's seat may have begun in Iowa."

On caucus night, January 3, 2008, youth turnout in Iowa more than doubled from 2004, when Howard Dean fielded his own student army. Those young people favored Obama by four to one. Voters under twenty-five delivered seventeen thousand votes to Obama—and he won by just twenty thousand. When Obama took the stage after his surprise victory and said, "They said this day would never come," Eric, watching from the couch in his Manchester flophouse, thought, "Holy shit."

The next morning, Eric met Obama on a freezing cold tarmac in Portsmouth, New Hampshire, at the crack of dawn. They did an event at Nashua High School South, and the crowd was so big that Obama was literally trapped inside the school because every exit was blocked. So Obama staffers stayed in one of the side gyms and played basketball until the crowd dispersed. Eric remembers that campaigning in New Hampshire after Obama won Iowa was like "being shot out of a rocket ship."

Obama went into the final days before the New Hampshire primary with a ten-point lead. But when he turned to Hillary in a debate and said, "You're likable enough," and Hillary won sympathy for getting teary on the trail, the race tightened. On primary night, Clinton pulled off a razor-thin win in New Hampshire, although Obama had won the youngest voters in the state by three to one. The Obama team was shocked and despondent, and the chattering class said she was now the frontrunner again. Eric did advance for Obama's election night event, and at first they weren't sure if they were going to have to rip up the whole plan. But Obama decided to give the same speech in defeat that he would have in victory—the famous "Yes We Can" speech.

"In the unlikely story that is America, there has never been anything false about hope," he said to the youthful crowd in the gym at Nashua High School South. "When we have faced down impossible odds, when we've been told we're not ready, or we shouldn't try, or we can't, generations of Americans have responded with a simple creed that sums up the spirit of a people: yes, we can."

For the rest of the primaries, the youth vote kept building Obama's momentum. Reporters began describing a "youth quake" that was shaking the party. In Michigan, where Obama's name wasn't on the ballot because of some dispute with the state's primary scheduling rules, nearly fifty thousand people under thirty voted "uncommitted" as a sign of support. Obama won young voters three to one in South Carolina, which helped offset Clinton's lead with seniors and gave him a pivotal victory there. The campaign was posting constantly on Facebook and putting speech clips up on YouTube, where young voters could share them with their friends. College students "dorm-stormed" their campuses, making sure that every student on every floor was registered to vote. Teenagers urged their parents to support Obama, sometimes with powerful results. Eighteen-year-old Maddie Esposito told her mother she would never speak to her again if she didn't get behind Obama: her mother is Claire McCaskill, a then-powerful Missouri senator whose endorsement helped Obama pick up the crucial swing state. Senator Ted Kennedy and his niece Caroline Kennedy both said their critical decision to endorse Obama (and say he reminded them of JFK) was inspired by enthusiasm among the younger generation of Kennedys.

Obama put generational change at the center of his message. He kept saying that the campaign was about "the past versus the future," which

simultaneously mobilized young people and lashed his opponent to the status quo. Many millennials who were eligible to vote for the first time were
ready for some fresh blood in the White House; some hadn't even been born
when the last president not named Bush or Clinton left office nearly twenty
years before. Obama's beguiling futurism made Clinton seem like the candidate of the past, a cruel irony for the first woman to have a serious shot at the
presidency.

In April 2008, at the height of the Pennsylvania primary, Eric organized
an impromptu Passover seder in whatever crappy hotel they were staying in
that night. They used Maxwell House Haggadahs that his cousin had grabbed
from the University of Pennsylvania Hillel. They were just about to start when
Obama stuck his head in and said, "Hey, guys, is this where the seder is?" They
wouldn't normally have done the whole Haggadah, but since Obama was
there, they amped up the religiosity a bit. Obama kept asking questions, like,
"What's the tradition in your family?" And finally Eric answered, "Respect-
fully, sir, we've never gone this far—we're normally eating by now."

At the end of the seder, everybody lifted their glass and said, "Next year
in Jerusalem," except Obama, who said, "Next year in the White House."

✳ ✳ ✳

After New Hampshire, Eric hustled his way up through the Obama campaign and was finally promoted to "ground logistics coordinator," which basically meant he was a baggage handler. It was like being the equipment
manager for the Red Sox, or the parent hauling the bags on a family vacation.
He kept track of everyone's black suitcases, everyone's BlackBerry chargers,
and all the logistical things that needed to be dealt with to get the campaign
from one place to another. Over the course of the campaign, Eric traveled
about two hundred thousand miles with Obama, visiting forty-eight states,
on the site at every debate and in the wings at every speech. In March 2008,
the campaign hit a rough patch amid press reports about controversial remarks made by Obama's former pastor, the Reverend Jeremiah Wright—the
same speech Lauren sat through as a child after 9/11. To save his campaign,
Obama gave a speech at the National Constitution Center in Philadelphia
that would become known as "the race speech." It did more than denounce

Wright and stabilize the campaign; Obama used the speech to connect his presidential bid to the nation's capacity for change, and the aspirations of American youth.

"This union may never be perfect, but generation after generation has shown that it can always be perfected," he said. "And today, whenever I find myself feeling doubtful or cynical about this possibility, what gives me the most hope is the next generation—the young people whose attitudes and beliefs and openness to change have already made history in this election."

As the words floated through the Constitution Center, Eric was outside, his button-down shirt soaked in sweat, unloading an enormous U-Haul full of nearly identical black suitcases.

On June 7, 2008, Hillary withdrew from the campaign, telling her cheering supporters that she was proud to have put "eighteen million cracks" in the glass ceiling. A few weeks later, Haley emailed Hillary's top aide Huma Abedin that she would be leaving before the convention to try to help Obama win. "I love you guys," she said, "but I really want to finish this off."

✳ ✳ ✳

Haley got a job working for vice presidential nominee Joe Biden doing the same thing she did for Hillary: finding the relevant facts, assembling them in the book, making sure Biden had it when he needed it. But the job was easier: Biden wasn't as much of a stickler for facts and citations as Hillary was, so he used the book a lot less. He wasn't the type of candidate who would memorize everything in the book and then quiz her on it. And because he was running for VP instead of the top job, there was a little less scrutiny.

But still, she was on the rocket ship, and as the Democratic Convention opened in July, it became clear that Obama's youth appeal was a full-on phenomenon. There were more Obama delegates under thirty-six in Denver than at any convention in memory—including some who wouldn't be old enough to legally vote until later in that year.

By then, the Obama campaign had fully mastered how to use digital organizing and social media to reach young voters. "I think it is very significant that he was the first post-boomer candidate for president," Marc Andreessen, cofounder of Netscape and a major tech investor, told *The New York Times*.

"He was the first politician I dealt with who understood that the technology was a given and that it could be used in new ways." A Pew study later found that roughly three-quarters of Americans under twenty-five used the internet to participate in the 2008 campaign. If Kennedy won the 1960 election because of television, Obama won in 2008 because of the internet.

Obama eclipsed Howard Dean's 2004 record to build the largest political email list in history, which helped him raise a record-breaking $750 million from nearly four million donors, many of them small contributors. His inexpensive YouTube videos were watched for more than 14.5 million hours—it would cost $47 million to buy that much airtime on TV news. Most important, his campaign was the first to see the power of Facebook to turn online fans into real-life organizers: by his 2012 reelection campaign, Obama was connected to 98 percent of Facebook users in the United States (more than the total number of voters), which allowed the campaign to target the specific voters they needed to win reelection. By the end of 2012, six hundred thousand Obama supporters had contacted 3.5 million of their Facebook friends in battleground states—and one million of those took some real-world action as a result, such as registering to vote.

On Election Day, two-thirds of voters under thirty voted for Obama, more than double John McCain's share of the youth vote. On that unseasonably warm night in Chicago, as Obama prepared to deliver his victory speech in Grant Park, Eric was in the press filing center, helping reporters get the right power cords and fixing Wi-Fi issues and running around with snacks. Haley was in the front row, close to the bulletproof glass protecting the president-elect and his family.

Obama's historic speech that night gave special credit to the young people who had helped him get elected. "Our campaign was not hatched in the halls of Washington," he said. "It grew strength from the young people who rejected the myth of their generation's apathy, who left their homes and their families for jobs that offered little pay and less sleep."

Campuses across the country erupted in celebration. Jubilant students flooded the streets, blocking traffic and climbing lampposts. At the University of Michigan, they chanted, "Yes, we did!" and waved large American flags as a campus band played the national anthem—a far cry from the bitter and often anti-American campus protests of their parents' generation. For boomers, youth movements had been largely antigovernment and outside the system: they marched in protest against Johnson and Nixon and Jim Crow and Vietnam. But to millennials, Obama's election was evidence that a youth movement could be constructive, and that, organized correctly, young people could help put a president in the Oval Office. At Cornell, the crowd lifted Svante Myrick up on their shoulders—he had already been elected to city council at this point, even though he was still a student—and gave him a bullhorn to speak. "We believed that we could change the world," he shouted, "and we made history!"

Eric and Haley and Svante didn't know it yet, but the Obama presidency would be a transformational moment not just for them, but for their entire generation. Over the course of eight years, the president—*their* president—would deliver for them on affordable health care, college loans, marriage equality, and climate change, all issues that would become especially important to millennials in the years to come. By 2018, polls showed that millennials overwhelmingly thought Barack Obama was the best president of their lifetime.

But before he could get to all that, Obama had a bigger problem on his hands: the American economy was on the brink of collapse.

CHAPTER 7

The Crash

At some ungodly hour in the morning on March 30, 2007, a few months before she joined the Hillary Clinton campaign, Haley Stevens—then twenty-three—signed into her blog and started to type. With her typical dramatic flair, she named her blog post "The Second Coming."

"We are embarking upon another Great Depression," she wrote. "It's written all over the news, but just not in explicit language." She listed her reasons: "sophomoric" President Bush, massive income inequality, MTV shows about enormous houses and elaborate sweet sixteens, a "Gilded Age" pop culture where "people are just famous for being wealthy." The Real Housewives were new to the scene, and Britney Spears, Lindsay Lohan, and Paris Hilton were all in various stages of very public mental breakdowns. But nobody was paying attention to what was really happening, Haley wrote, which was that "the Great Depression II is already upon us in places like Michigan."

A little over a year later, in the summer of 2008, Haley showed up to work for her first day on Biden's vice presidential campaign. They hadn't set up her desk yet, and someone told her to go kill some time near the Chicago HQ, so she wandered into Saks on Michigan Avenue. On the fifth or sixth floor, she saw a crowd of gowns, as if all the mannequins were going to the Oscars. Gowns made of lace, gowns with sequins, gowns with huge satin bows, made by designers with Italian names. They looked as though they cost $5,000 to $6,000 apiece, the kinds of dresses Haley would normally be afraid to touch.

But when Haley looked closer at the tags, she saw that the gowns were 80 or 90 percent off, a fraction of the original price. Every gown in the Saks Fifth Avenue on the Magnificent Mile in the biggest city in the Midwest was being sold for pennies on the dollar. She found a $3,000 yellow-and-cream dress that fit her like a glove and bought it, on impulse, for $500.

When she hung her heavily discounted ballgown next to her Ann Taylor suit, Haley realized that something was very wrong with the economy.

Two months later, on September 15, 2008, Lehman Brothers filed for bankruptcy. The stock market dropped 4.4 percent, the largest single-day decline since 9/11, and two weeks later tumbled again, with $1.2 trillion in market value vanishing overnight. The auto industry—long a driver of the US economy—was suddenly on the brink of collapse, and threatened to bring much of the midwestern economy down with it. By the time the hemorrhaging ended in 2010, roughly nine million people had lost their jobs and health insurance, and two million families had lost their homes.

✳ ✳ ✳

The Ocasio-Cortez family lived in a cramped ranch house in Yorktown Heights with two bedrooms, a sunroom converted into a third bedroom, and one bathroom. Whenever the family had a little extra money, Sergio would make improvements on the house: some new cabinets here, a couple of repairs there. He built a loft for Alexandria's bed so that she'd have room for a desk underneath, and painted a mural of jungle leaves and vines in the corner of her room. Her father, Alexandria once said, "knew my soul better than anyone on this planet."

Sergio loved *The Great Gatsby*, that vision of American life where a self-made man could create a dream house. He hung art deco prints on the walls and built a pergola streamed with grapevines so that his wife, Blanca, could sit in the shade. He'd read all the building codes, so he knew to build it with compacted gravel so that it didn't violate zoning restrictions. Sergio had spent his life designing buildings for other people, but in 2007, he was finally successful enough to think about renovating his own house. He took out a home equity loan to cover a basic renovation: replacing the drafty windows and adding new siding to the house. Right after he took out the loan, his cancer came back.

A couple of years earlier, Sergio had come down with a bad cough, but the doctor had said he was fine and sent him home. Later, he was diagnosed with a rare form of lung cancer. When the family found the scans from that first visit to the doctor, they realized that the mass must have been there from the very beginning, but it had been left to grow for almost a year before it was diagnosed.

At first, the treatment worked, and Sergio went into remission. But in late 2007, just as Alexandria was starting at Boston University, the cancer returned. She had won an internship in Senator Ted Kennedy's office that summer, but she wanted to be home with her dad. Sergio insisted she take the job, and Alexandria spent that summer with a phone to her ear, either calling her father or taking constituent calls in the senator's office. She was one of the only interns who spoke fluent Spanish, so she took the calls about immigration: people whose relatives had been arrested by ICE, people looking for help with their citizenship applications, people looking to get on the right side of the law. She would listen to their stories and pass them along to the senator's staff, but there was nothing she could tell them that would help. Ted Kennedy was the Lion of the Senate, but when it came to individual immigration cases, there was little he could do.

Alexandria went back to school for sophomore year, and in the first week of the semester her mother called her in the middle of economics class and told her to come back down to Yorktown Heights. As soon as she met her brother and mother at the hospital, she could tell her father wasn't doing well. Near the end of their conversation she felt something different from Sergio, a certain finality. She turned to leave and he made a noise, and she turned around again in the door frame, and he said, "Hey, make me proud." To Gabriel, he said, "I love you." Gabriel thought their father knew it was the last thing he would say to both of them, so he said the things they needed to hear on repeat the rest of their lives. Alexandria went back to school, and two days later Blanca called her to come home again, fast. She got there as fast as she could, but she arrived thirty minutes after he died.

Alexandria was back at school a week after Sergio's death, but she was lost. Without her dad, she didn't know up from down. The whole family was spiraling: not only had they lost a husband and father; they had lost their breadwinner just as the entire economic system was melting down around them. And they had to pay off his home equity loan on top of the now-impossible mortgage. Blanca had always cleaned houses, but now she started picking up extra work as a school bus driver. The house was in his name, and Sergio had left no will, so Blanca had to fight her way through the Westchester County Surrogate's Court to recoup his assets, while her court-appointed lawyer made a profit helping her navigate the bureaucracy.

Meanwhile, fifteen-year-old Gabriel was becoming an expert on loopholes in foreclosure law. Once, he saw a lady outside taking pictures of their house. He said, "Can I help you?" and when she didn't answer and scurried to her car, he realized she was an asset manager from the bank. Gabriel had read somewhere that if there's a dog on the property, the asset managers have to mark the house as a risk, and the bank would have to pay them hazard pay to assess the property. Little things like that could slow down a foreclosure process. He started leaving their Great Dane, Domino, out on the porch.

The recession screwed everybody, but people Haley and Alexandria's age got extra screwed. Before the recession, college graduates might have been saddled with student loan debt, but at least they could get a job. After the recession, not so much. More than 50 percent of the class of 2007 had job offers lined up—less than 20 percent of the class of 2009 did. And high unemployment at the time of graduation led to drops in starting salaries that would leave workers behind for decades. The young college graduates who entered the job market at the height of the Great Recession quickly realized that their degrees were like almost everything else in 2009 America: worth less than they paid for them.

Millennials were already off to a dubious financial start, given the sheer amount of educational debt they carried. But the recession made it clear that the "good-paying job" that was assumed to be the logical reward of a college education—the gold sticker at the end of class—was a fiction. Maybe those jobs had always been fictional, maybe they had just evaporated when the economy collapsed, or maybe those cubicles were now filled with recently fired boomers—but whatever the reason, the youngest and newest members of the professional workforce got a raw deal. Young people were roughly twice as likely to be unemployed as adults overall. Unemployment for people in their early twenties spiked to nearly 20 percent, and was especially high for those without high school diplomas. For young African Americans, it was more than 30 percent.

Millennials with college degrees did much better than those without them, but even graduates of good colleges had trouble finding work that paid them enough to manage their loans. Underemployment became a significant social problem, even among the highly educated. They scraped together unpaid internships, gig work, and freelance assignments, and many of them ended up moving back in with their parents to make ends meet.

By 2012, when the economy was inching its way back toward stability, the class of 2009 had already been left behind. Many employers preferred the fresh college graduates over ones who graduated three years earlier and might expect higher wages for the same work. Nobody gets to press pause on their life just because they graduated into an economic crisis.

College debt and the recession fed each other. Graduating with debt into a terrible job market made it much harder to begin paying off the loans—and millennials had taken on at least 300 percent more student debt than their parents. But high unemployment also made young people more likely to go to graduate school, thinking that an extra degree would give them a competitive edge in a job market that was already saturated with overeducated, underemployed workers. In the absence of a "real job," going to graduate school seemed better than driving for Uber or working at Starbucks. So unemployment led to more education, which led to more debt but not necessarily more employment—a perverse cycle that ultimately meant that young workers were paying to train themselves for jobs they would not have.

As bad as this was, it was worse for the roughly 55 percent of millennials who didn't have a postsecondary degree. By the early 2000s, that diploma was a prerequisite for almost any truly good job. By 2014, the poverty rate among young people with only a high school diploma had tripled since 1979: more than one in five of them lived in poverty.

All this led to a generation of young people who had worse jobs, lower income, and more debt than recent generations did at their age. By 2013, there were more than twice as many young men earning poverty wages as thirty-five years earlier. Between 1989 and 2011, the percentage of young graduates with jobs who got health insurance from their employer was cut in half.

Young people always feel as if they're poor, and other generations have had similar economic tales of woe. But the numbers show that millennials actually do earn less and have less wealth than boomers and Gen Xers did when they were their age. By 2014, the full-time earnings of a millennial were 10 percent lower in constant dollars than a comparable boomer male breadwinner's had been when he was young. The average total net worth of a millennial household in 2016 was 20 percent less than the average boomer's had been at their age. One study found that nearly a decade after the recession, households led by people born in the 1980s—millennials—still had 34 percent less wealth than older generations had at their age, and were the only generation to fail to bounce back between 2010 and 2016.

Those financial inequalities were compounded by race. White families had more wealth going into the financial crisis, so they had more cushion for when times got tough. For many black and Hispanic families, the recession completely wiped out their savings. The median wealth of middle-income black families fell 47 percent since 2007, while middle-class Hispanic families lost 55 percent of their wealth. All their gains in the 1990s—and then some—were obliterated. Many white millennials were lampooned for taking money from their parents (like Hannah Horvath in the HBO series *Girls*), but for nonwhite millennials, this was rarely an option. White parents were more likely to be able to help pay their kids' college tuition, offset their expenses as they got on their feet, or help them out if they lost a job. For black millennials, the financial support often went in the other direction: much of their savings went to helping older family members who also got screwed in the crisis. Black families' retirement accounts shrank 35 percent during the recession, while white families' grew by 9 percent, partly because white families were more likely to have other sources of income. Black millennials didn't just have to pay their bills and pay their student loans—they also had to help their parents retire in dignity. White families bounced back from the recession, but many black families couldn't—which is one of the main reasons why the racial wealth gap continues to persist, even ten years after the recession.

✳ ✳ ✳

Most of the stereotypes you've probably heard about millennials can be either wholly or partly explained by the Great Recession. Their economic disadvantage is like an invisible postscript to every flippant generalization about the young.

Yes, millennials moved in with their parents in record numbers after college—because they graduated into an economy where jobs paid too little and housing cost too much.

They couldn't seem to stick to one job—because few of the jobs available to them paid well enough to cover rent and make their student loan payments, and besides, many thought, why be loyal to an employer who pays minimum wage and doesn't offer benefits?

They didn't buy houses or cars or diamonds, and they waited longer to get married and have kids—mostly because they lacked the financial stability to start a family.

The recession had shifted the financial calculus for an entire generation of American workers. It changed the kinds of jobs they got (often precarious, part-time ones), what kinds of benefits they got (usually none), and what kind of schedule they kept (erratic and flexible).

And unlike boomers and Gen Xers, who had the benefit of at least a few decades of twentieth-century-style employment, millennials may spend almost their entire careers in the gig economy. Their careers will be defined by a lack of definition. They are less likely to have the protection of unions (union membership has halved since 1983), less likely to have a set nine-to-five schedule (40 percent of young workers get their schedules just a few days in advance), and less likely to stay at one company for long enough to build a track record of good work. Not to mention the fact that rapid advances in technology in the early twenty-first century made it increasingly likely that automation would take over most low-wage, unskilled jobs.

All that changed how millennials spent what little money they had. When big purchases such as homes and cars were out of the question, many millennials figured they might as well spend their money on things like specialty cronuts and fancy coffees. They tended to prefer experiences over possessions. And a generation steeped in social networks became increasingly comfortable renting things instead of owning them: millennials rented rides (with Uber and Lyft), rented clothes (through Rent The Runway), and rented labor (through TaskRabbit). They also began to look to the gig economy for side hustles to supplement their meager incomes. By 2018, more than 40 percent of eighteen- to thirty-four-year-olds worked as freelancers. For almost half of the largest generation of workers, the traditional work structure that had defined twentieth-century professional life just wasn't available anymore.

A freelance life meant being constantly on, all the time. It meant working two or three jobs to make ends meet—partly to pay off those student loans, partly to pay that health insurance premium, and partly because technology made it possible to work all the time, from anywhere. If you could be working, then you should be working, and thanks to the internet, you always could be working.

The recession also changed millennials' attitudes toward risk. They became less likely to start businesses, apply for credit cards, or invest in the stock market, partly because they were terrified of having the rug pulled out from under them again. They were saving a lot by historical standards—a good thing in a country that had grown too comfortable with endless, irresponsible consumption—but not making smart investments such as buying stock or property. Those "safe" bets no longer seemed so safe.

But at least millennials would be able to count on Social Security when they're old, right? Nah. In 1950, when their great-grandparents retired, there were seventeen American workers supporting each retiree—when millennials retire, there will be just two. That means that costs will quickly exceed revenue, and the Social Security Trust Fund is expected to be depleted by 2035, when millennials are in their forties and fifties. It will almost certainly be replenished, but by the time the government collects enough taxes to make up for the shortfall for boomers and Gen X, millennial retirees will be lucky to get back a fraction of what they paid in.

✳ ✳ ✳

Haley would call her mother in Michigan and hear about all the neighbors who were losing their jobs. Thanks to Blanca's extra shifts as a bus driver and Gabriel's ingenuity, the Ocasio-Cortez family ended up keeping the house— just barely—and were able to sell it a few years later so that Blanca could move to Florida. Every Father's Day, Svante Myrick's mom would give each of the boys a card with ten dollars and a condom inside. After the crash, she gave them five dollars instead. "Due to recession, $10 is now $5," she wrote. "Condom is the same size."

People their age were beginning to learn that the necessities that were once provided by the private sector (a stable income, health insurance, the ability to buy a home) and the protections once provided by the public sector (justice for bad actors, crackdown on corporate corruption, equality under the law) were no longer guaranteed. The system had become a precarious framework of emboldened corporations and feeble regulations. Young people realized they would have to look to the government to address the failures of the private sector, but they would also have to build a government that was up to the task.

There were only two ways out of this. You could either try to fix the system, or you could try to break it.

CHAPTER 8

Fix the System

Haley Stevens wasn't sure what to do. Applying for a job in the Obama administration wasn't like applying to college—you had to know what you wanted, then you had to figure out who had already been tapped to oversee it, then figure out a way to get that person to hire you. It wasn't as if she could Google "how to help the new president navigate an economic crisis."

One night, on her way to a holiday party in Washington, DC, Haley got into her new Jeep Liberty and reached over to buckle her seat belt. Her fingers touched the seat leather and suddenly, a conversation from months ago surfaced in her memory. Her auto dealer had called her in July to ask if she wanted to trade in her old car for a new lease. His voice sounded tense, and he was talking very fast, telling her he could get her a good deal if she signed now. The guy had been her mom's car dealer for years. The longer Haley talked to him, the more desperate he seemed. He told her that the industry had taken huge hits because nobody was buying new cars anymore and that he might go under. She had forgotten all about it until now.

Suddenly, it all seemed so obvious. What could be more important to the American economy than cars? What could be more important to *Michigan* than cars? When she got to the party, she found her old boss Neera Tanden and asked her for a favor.

Neera sent Haley's resume to Steve Rattner, a politically connected New

York investment banker (and former *New York Times* reporter) who had recently been tapped by Obama, Treasury Secretary Tim Geithner, and chief economic advisor Larry Summers to help the Treasury Department save the auto industry. Rattner, who had no experience in the auto industry but managed Michael Bloomberg's billions of dollars in investments and knew his way around corporate boardrooms, was immediately nicknamed the "car czar," which he despised. About three minutes into the interview, Rattner hired Haley to be his chief of staff on the newly created Auto Task Force, to help him manage what would ultimately be the largest government intervention in American industry since World War II.

On her first day, Haley walked up the steps to the 185-year-old building that is printed on the back of the ten-dollar bill. The inside was all gleaming chessboard floors and marble walls and chandeliers. But there was nothing glamorous about Haley's months at the Treasury Department. It felt like trying to put out a house fire with a tiny cup of water. They had a nearly impossible job: to save the US auto industry without a complete government takeover.

Over the previous decade, Detroit had gone through its own version of the housing bubble: easy financing allowed more people to buy bigger cars and trucks, artificially inflating demand while flooding the market with gas-guzzling but durable vehicles that wouldn't have to be replaced anytime soon. By the time the financial crisis hit, there were far more cars in American driveways than licensed drivers. Which meant that when the market crashed and household budgets tightened, buying a new car became an unaffordable luxury. Plus, the companies were badly mismanaged, saddled with bloated labor costs, huge health care bills, and CEOs who liked flying everywhere on private jets.

George W. Bush didn't want to be the president who let the auto industry fail and put thousands of people out of work, so in 2008 he signed off on $17.4 billion in bailout money to help tide over Chrysler and GM until after the election. In 2009, it became Obama's problem.

Obama's economists agreed that GM was too big to fail—with 225,000 current employees, 500,000 retirees, and almost 18,000 suppliers and dealers, letting GM liquidate would trigger a colossal economic disaster. Chrysler was significantly smaller but just as endangered, and the Auto Task Force was torn about whether to let it go under. Some warned that Chrysler couldn't be saved, and that letting it fail would mean less competition for GM and Ford. The Obama administration wanted to look tough on big business, and to show taxpayers that they wouldn't be swayed by corporate sob stories.

But Haley knew that allowing Chrysler to liquidate would mean complete disaster for Michigan. That's because a car isn't just a car: it's a delicate arrangement of thirty thousand parts that are made in different places by different people and yet assembled with perfect precision into the object that had come to represent America's obsession with status and mobility. First you had the dealerships—the slick-talking guy who sold the car to the young couple looking to upgrade to a minivan. The dealerships placed orders with the OEMs, "original equipment manufacturers," such as Ford and GM and Chrysler. The OEMs built the cars, but they relied on hundreds of other companies to make lighting systems and brake pads and wiring, and those companies relied on even more subcontracting suppliers to make plastic, aluminum, and rubber. It didn't always work like a neat pyramid: each of those suppliers was also supplying parts and materials to other industries—appliances, dishwashers, washing machines, industrial equipment, you name it. The OEMs weren't just car companies: they were anchoring an entire manufacturing and wholesale ecosystem. For every automaker job, there were two supplier jobs—which meant that roughly 650,000 jobs were at risk if the auto industry collapsed.

And this wasn't just about numbers—this was about *cars*. The auto industry had a symbolism to it that the financial industry did not. Cars gave America Jack Kerouac, drive-in movies, McDonald's, suburbs, talk radio, Greased Lightning. For an entire state—Haley's state—cars were a way of life. Detroit—the Motor City—was built with auto money, for auto workers, designed to be navigated on four wheels, not two feet. If the auto industry died, an entire region of America would die with it.

By early 2009, things in Michigan were looking bad. Auto sales continued to plummet—GM was down 49 percent, Ford was down 40 percent, Chrysler was down 55 percent—and all three big companies were running out of cash. There were rumors of auto dealers committing suicide. Haley's neighbors were radiating despair.

But many of the finance guys were reluctant to back a total bailout. Mitt Romney—the former Bain Capital exec and future presidential candidate—wrote an op-ed in *The New York Times* titled LET DETROIT GO BANKRUPT (by the 2012 election, that hadn't aged well). Many of Obama's top economic advisors were wary of full-scale government intervention, worried that if the government took over too much of the industry, Washington would own the problem.

Some of the people on the task force had never worked in government. They didn't know how to do things like make a phone call to Congress, or how to set up their computer, or how to send a memo to the president. Haley was the person to ask. She knew who to talk to at the White House, and which staffers were responsible for what, and who needed to be in which meetings. When people called the Treasury Department desperate for information on the auto rescue, those calls went to Haley. Sometimes she'd be on the phone with terrified, crying dealers and suppliers until midnight, eating old Cheerios straight from the box.

Haley's most important moment on the auto rescue came one morning when the team was debating whether to liquidate Chrysler. Gene Sperling, senior advisor to Treasury Secretary Geithner, was arguing that letting Chrysler go under would devastate the economy in the Midwest, and Obama would get the blame. Austan Goolsbee, a member of the Council of Economic Advisers, was saying that liquidating Chrysler could help the other two big automakers get stronger. He argued that business would flow to Ford and GM if Chrysler went under, which would make those companies more likely to survive the crisis and maybe hire more workers.

Haley didn't usually speak up—she wasn't the kind of person who would talk in meetings just to hear the sound of her own voice. When you're younger, and a woman, she figured, they kind of expect you to just shut up and do your job. She knew she was there to make the trains run on time, to get sandwiches for meetings and set up PowerPoint presentations and make sure everyone had a computer at their desk, not to offer an opinion to a collection of the most respected economists in the country. But suddenly her mouth was open and she was talking. "We can't do that," she said. All the heads turned in the room. "That wouldn't be a rescue."

She wasn't an economist, she knew, but she grew up in Rochester Hills, right near where Chrysler has its headquarters. They were talking about jobs as if they were numbers, abstract data points that could be reassigned to different companies. But if a fifty-two-year-old guy got laid off from Chrysler, he wasn't going anywhere. Even if GM did start hiring, it wouldn't hire a bunch of middle-aged guys who had just been fired from Chrysler. Once Humpty Dumpty fell, she said, you couldn't put it back together again.

The men nodded. Her point was taken. They moved on.

Ultimately, the Auto Task Force decided to save Chrysler. The federal government took over GM and Chrysler and shepherded them through managed bankruptcies in mid-2009. By the end of the year, GM and Chrysler were no longer on the verge of meltdown—by 2013, both had paid back their loans to the federal government and been weaned off taxpayer dollars. In 2014, Fiat bought Chrysler; by the end of the year, the bailout had helped create more than 500,000 new jobs.

The Auto Task Force shut down, and Haley got another job in the Obama administration, helping to set up the Office of Recovery for Automotive Communities and Workers, which cut through the red tape to make sure recovery dollars actually went to the people who had been laid off. The economy stumbled back, but at least the auto industry—and Michigan—was safe.

Eric Lesser was one of the first people to walk through the doors of the White House after Obama's inauguration. After hauling bags throughout the campaign, he had been tapped to be the special assistant to David Axelrod, who was now senior advisor to the president. That meant that almost everything that would eventually reach the president himself—whether it was about health care reform or the auto rescue or House Minority Leader John Boehner's mood that week—went through Eric in one form or another. Haley's frantic late-night emails about the Auto Task Force often landed in his inbox.

Every morning at seven thirty, he'd give David Axelrod the "ADB": Axelrod Daily Briefing. For the rest of the day, he'd be on Axelrod's tail, making sure he was on time for meetings, deciding how much brown sugar he could have in his oatmeal, replacing his lost glasses with a stash he kept at his desk, fixing his stained shirt with the tonic water he kept on hand for that exact reason. He and Axelrod became such an odd-couple duo that they even had a comedic nickname: Ax & Lesser.

Eric spent all day sitting in a tiny entryway outside Axelrod's office, which was right in the thick of things. When the restless president got up from his desk in the Oval to roam over to see his top advisor, he often popped his head into Eric's cubby to say hello. Eric was like the Forrest Gump of the early Obama administration: always in the background, an extra in every scene. He'd chat with the First Lady, or bump into the chairman of the Joint Chiefs of Staff in the hallway, or watch from his tiny perch as Secretary of State Hillary Clinton went into the Oval for meetings with Obama. The seder he'd hosted during the 2008 campaign inspired the Obamas to host the first-ever White House seder, which quickly became a presidential tradition.

Less than two weeks after Obama took office, as they were debating the Troubled Asset Relief Program (TARP), Axelrod advised Obama to leverage the bank bailouts to force big banks to stop giving exorbitant bonuses to executives. Obama sided with Larry Summers and Tim Geithner and chose not to use the bailouts as a cudgel to improve corporate behavior. Worried about restoring the investor confidence that was critical for recovery, Obama opted to lecture the CEOs about their bonuses without compelling them to forgo them. In retrospect, this was a mistake: if Obama had used TARP more aggressively to reform the economy as well as heal it, he might have avoided some of the populist uprising that followed the recession. The taxpayers got all the TARP bailout money back with interest, but this mattered little to progressive activists, who were furious at Obama's perceived leniency toward Wall Street. "You could pull [Goldman Sachs CEO] Lloyd Blankfein into a dark alley and slit his throat and it would satisfy them for about two days, and then the bloodlust would rise again," Bill Clinton told Geithner in 2009.

After Obama stanched the bleeding in the financial sector and rescued the auto industry, he turned to health care. When his advisors tried to suggest a reduced plan that could attract bipartisan support, Obama walked out of his own office to dramatize his objection to their timidity; he wanted to fulfill his campaign promises to rein in predatory insurance companies, "bend the cost curve" in the health care industry, and move toward universal coverage, not just make a bad system a little better. But the politics were nasty, and it took the Senate many months longer than expected to pass its plan, while House Democrats squabbled over a public option and other provisions. Republicans, meanwhile, proved so obstructionist that the White House couldn't afford to lose a single Democratic vote, which essentially gave conservative Senate Democrats veto power over the bill.

For months, members of Congress trotted past Eric's tiny office to meet with the president and Axelrod about health care. Obama knew that if he didn't get a health care bill done by the end of 2009, the window for action would close. And in December, Senator Joe Lieberman—who had gone from Al Gore's affable running mate to a grouchy Democrat who often voted with Republicans—announced that he wouldn't support any bill that included Medicare expansion. The White House had no choice: without sixty votes in the Senate, they would get no bill passed at all. They watered down the bill and, after weeks of painful wrangling, the Affordable Care Act passed the Senate on Christmas Eve 2009, with sixty Democrats and zero Republicans. Everyone agreed the bill was imperfect, but at least it made it through. Now the challenge would be reconciliation: to get the House and Senate to agree on a version of the bill that could pass both chambers.

But Senator Ted Kennedy had died in 2009, and Massachusetts was holding a special election for his seat in January 2010. By then, the public was furious at how the health care reform process had unfolded. After all that partisan wrangling, voters were beginning to think the whole thing was a fiasco. And so, three weeks after the Senate passed the Affordable Care Act, Massachusetts voters elected Republican Scott Brown to what had been a safe Democratic seat. The surprise upset was partly fueled by rage at the Affordable Care Act, and partly because Democrat Martha Coakley had committed Massachusetts political suicide by insulting die-hard Boston sports fans. No matter the reason, the outcome was the same: with only fifty-nine

Democrats in the Senate, Obama had lost his chance at a progressive House-Senate compromise. The only way to salvage the bill was for the House to swallow the Senate's more conservative bill whole, which it did only after heroic arm-twisting by Speaker Nancy Pelosi.

Eric saw the ACA as an example of Obama's enduring belief that it was better to get something than nothing. If the president had held out for a public option, Eric knew, he likely would have walked away empty-handed. The Affordable Care Act was a huge win for the public: it prohibited insurance companies from applying lifetime caps on coverage or discriminating against people with preexisting conditions, which helped cut medical bankruptcies in half; greatly expanded Medicaid so millions more low-income people could get coverage; and allowed young people to stay on their parents' health insurance until they were twenty-six (which was especially helpful to under-employed millennials for whom employer-sponsored health insurance seemed like an impossible luxury).

The bill also mandated that everyone buy health insurance or pay a penalty, which forced many young healthy people to dig into their (empty) pockets to buy insurance they would have ordinarily skipped. Republicans were sure this provision would so infuriate young voters that they would flock to the GOP, but this never happened. Instead, most millennials disliked the bill not because it was too liberal but because it was too conservative—over the next ten years, millennials would become the loudest voices demanding single-payer health care, an evolution that would shape the politics of the 2020 campaign.

Eric didn't think the bill was perfect, but he knew it was good. And sitting outside Obama's office, he'd learned how the game was played. He was there for the strikeouts, like when Treasury Secretary Tim Geithner fumbled the rollout of Obama's bank rescue plan. He was there for the home runs, like when the Auto Task Force saved hundreds of thousands of jobs in the Midwest. And he understood the importance of the smaller victories: the singles, doubles, and triples that made up the bulk of Obama's achievements.

Over the next three years, the Affordable Care Act would be challenged in the courts, and Republicans would find nearly every excuse they could to sue the government over the new law. But once it cleared the courts, it was time to implement the Affordable Care Act on the state level. That's where Lauren Underwood came in.

✸ ✸ ✸

Lauren got a job at the Department of Health and Human Services in 2010 as a career employee in the office of the executive secretary. She was on the team responsible for assembling anything that required Secretary of Health and Human Services Kathleen Sebelius's signature or approval, which meant coordinating all the documents for major regulations, policy initiatives, and guidance. It was complicated, and it was draining, and the ACA was under attack from all directions, but Lauren was emotionally invested in the work: the dreary administrative tasks felt as urgently important as anything she'd done in nursing school.

Secretary Sebelius, the former governor of Kansas, wasn't easy—she was a petite woman, very direct, and she didn't suffer fools. Lauren respected her, but was also a little intimidated by her, and it didn't help that Sebelius was always in the hot seat. Anytime anything went wrong with the ACA, Sebelius—not the White House—always seemed to get the blame, whether it was her fault or not.

The whole team felt protective of the boss; one false move and the knives would be out. Once Republicans took back the House in 2010 and ramped up oversight on the department, the stakes ratcheted even higher. They had to be perfect, with zero leaks. Young people in DC liked to hand out their business cards to impress each other at bars, and for the first six months Lauren liked to hand out her card at happy hours and watch people's eyes widen when they saw DEPARTMENT OF HEALTH AND HUMAN SERVICES in embossed lettering under her name. But then she realized that any time anybody emailed her it would be in the public record, which meant it could be subpoenaed. Anything that leaked about the ACA implementation could move the markets. She stopped handing out her business cards. When people talked about the ACA, she would say nothing or change the subject. When people asked where she worked, she'd say she was a nurse, which was technically true.

It was stressful, and it was confusing, and every day Lauren felt like she was swimming in a vast bureaucracy. She could tell there were problems in the institutional culture: staffers at HHS and the Centers for Medicare and Medicaid Services were slow to bring difficulties to the higher levels, which meant that it took longer for things to get solved. The bungled rollout of Healthcare.gov meant the enrollment system was full of exasperating glitches and errors that frustrated users and emboldened opponents. But when the Supreme Court upheld the individual mandate in the ACA in June of 2012, Lauren closed the door to her office and danced to Rihanna.

In 2014, she got hired as a political appointee. Before, she had been a career employee—now she was actually part of the Obama administration. "I was a fan of the team, and I helped the team, but joining the team was just different," she said. "I could wear the T-shirt." Lauren was extra proud to be working for the administration on Obama's signature health policy, because she knew that the Affordable Care Act was the only way someone like her could even get affordable health insurance in the first place.

When Lauren was in third grade, a new wave pool opened in the next town, but Lauren didn't know how to swim. So her mom signed her up for swim classes, and in the final class, the kids were supposed to learn how to tread water. All the other swim lessons had been in the shallow end of the pool, but this one was in the deep end. When she eased herself into the water and stuck her leg down and couldn't feel the bottom, she got scared. All the other kids seemed to be getting the hang of it, but Lauren went from scared to terrified, then from terrified to hysterical. Her heart started racing and she was thrashing and crying and swallowing water, so they pulled her out of the pool and sat her on the side and told her to breathe. She was crying because she was anxious and she was anxious because she was crying, and she had worked herself up so much that the adults figured if they just let her sit and breathe for a while, she would calm down. Eventually she stopped crying and she started breathing OK, but her heart rate never slowed down. Almost an hour after she'd been pulled from the pool, her heart was still racing.

They took her to the emergency room, and she was eventually diagnosed with supraventricular tachycardia, a condition that prevents her heart rate from slowing down the way it's supposed to. Her condition wasn't deadly—it mostly meant she had to watch her exercise and couldn't have caffeine. But it was still a preexisting condition, which meant that until the ACA, insurance companies would have been able to deny Lauren coverage or increase her rates because of it.

She thought about this a lot, in her four years working to help implement the ACA. Without this law, she might be uninsurable. The experience gave her a sense of what was possible in government and what wasn't, and what was required to make something as big as the ACA rollout work. She learned how slowly things could move in Washington: a "quick" response was a month; a slow response was nine. She learned about good management and bad management, good organization and bad organization, how agencies work together and how they don't. She learned what was broken, and what could be fixed.

✸ ✸ ✸

The Obama White House was full of millennials like Haley and Eric and Lauren: bright young staffers learning the Washington ropes, inspired by a president who believed that America was flawed but perfectable. They would carry these lessons with them throughout their careers, and many would go on to populate the political landscape of the post-Obama era.

Six years after Eric Lesser first walked into the West Wing, he was elected to the Massachusetts State Senate. Former NFL linebacker Colin Allred (b. 1983) worked as a special assistant in the General Counsel's office in Obama's Department of Housing and Urban Development—in 2018, he flipped a Texas House seat for Democrats. Andy Kim (b. 1982) was a Rhodes Scholar who served on the Iraq desk on Obama's National Security Council—in 2018, he won a New Jersey congressional seat from a Republican who had tried to dismantle the ACA. Some of Obama's brightest young staffers—Jon Favreau, Tommy Vietor, and Jon Lovett—created Crooked Media and launched *Pod Save America*, which has helped define millennial political attitudes in the Trump years.

They were data-driven and results-oriented. They operated in the realm of the possible. Their goal was to make the system work better, to use the levers of power to develop inspired but workable progressive policy proposals and—crucially—to actually get them over the finish line. They had no patience for Democrats willing to go down in flames for pie-in-the-sky ideas that had little chance of ever being implemented. They didn't make the perfect the enemy of the good.

Obama, Eric says, modeled a style of leadership that was about taking over systems and fixing them from within, a disciplined approach that required keeping your eye on the ball and taking small wins where you could. "You weren't part of the establishment," he said. "But you weren't trying to burn it all down."

But many other people their age didn't believe that the system could be fixed at all. They thought the realm of the possible was a bullshit constraint, a justification for compromise and failure of imagination. The system was too flawed to be fixed, they believed, and electoral politics was too corrupt to bring real change. To them, there was only one way forward: fuck the system.

CHAPTER 9

Fuck the System

In downtown Manhattan, far away from the Treasury Department's gleaming checkerboard floors, another group of young people was building its own response to the financial crisis. More than two years after Obama bailed out the banks and saved the auto industry, activists began to gather in the heart of the financial district to demonstrate their anger. They had various grievances—their crushing debt burden, the influence of money in politics, the impunity of the bankers who had caused the crisis—but most of all, they were furious at the system itself.

The first people to arrive at Zuccotti Park on September 17, 2011, sat under the trees and ate peanut butter and jelly sandwiches. By that afternoon, almost a thousand people had joined them in the three-quarter-acre pocket park. Some were gray-bearded left-wing professors or homeless people, but most were college students or recent grads or dropouts, all sleeping on the same patch of black pavement across the street from Bank of America. While "Occupy Wall Street" was not specifically a youth movement, it was fueled by young people's rage at the financial hand they'd been dealt. One study found that roughly 40 percent of the active participants in Occupy in Zuccotti Park were under thirty, and another found that nearly two-thirds of visitors to Occupy's website were under thirty-four. Older people were more skeptical of Occupy, but roughly two in five Americans under thirty supported the movement.

The internet allowed Occupy's message to spread to exactly the people who needed to hear it. The phrase "We are the 99%" articulated a sense of mass collective solidarity that went viral almost immediately. Tumblr became a bulletin board of financial despair as young people began posting pictures of themselves online holding handwritten summaries of their debt on a page called "We Are the 99 Percent."

"I am a 21 year old college student. I have over $20,000 in student loans and more to go. The best job I can get pays me $7.50 an hour. I've been concerned that I may have a serious medical condition but am terrified of going to the doctor without health insurance."

"I can't find my future. I looked in college: I found debt. I looked at my parents: I found debt and heartbreak. I looked at my friends: I found grief and sorrow. . . . I'm taking my future back. I am the 99%."

"I am 21. I had believed in the American Dream. . . . DHL laid off my mother after 28 years. . . . My mom called my grandmother and asked to borrow rent. . . . I am the 99%."

If they couldn't make it to Zuccotti Park, they set up satellite protests in more than 750 cities around the world. If they couldn't make it to one of those, they vented their rage online. Corporations, they believed, were like parasites on democracy. The protesters were furious that Obama had accepted so much Wall Street money for his campaign, and they didn't think it was a coincidence that he had bailed out the banks in 2009 without any real consequences for the bankers whose recklessness had caused the meltdown. They condemned the Supreme Court's 2010 *Citizens United* decision that allowed unlimited money to flow into the political process. Their manifesto, entitled "Declaration of the Occupation of New York City," began with the assertion that "corporations, which place profit over people, self-interest over justice, and oppression over equality, run our governments." It went on to list grievances ranging from mass foreclosures to taxpayer bailouts to student debt.

The Occupiers stayed in Zuccotti Park for almost two months. They had their own rules, their own makeshift "kitchen," a sanitation department, and even their own newspaper: *The Occupied Wall Street Journal*. Ben Cohen and Jerry Greenfield, founders of Ben & Jerry's, handed out free ice cream. The occupation drew famous visitors from Susan Sarandon to Kanye West. The park smelled like people who hadn't showered, like homeless people, like people who would sometimes piss in doorways because the few neighborhood bathrooms were overrun. Micro-neighborhoods gradually formed: the eastern, uphill part of the park was full of college-educated organizers creating systems for distributing books, food, and clothing, while the western, downhill side had more of a street anarchist vibe, with drummers and weed circles and a guy who had three rats living in his parka. They had no leader, no plan, and little organizing structure, but every night at 7:00 p.m. they would have a general assembly underneath the big red statue by the stairs. They couldn't get a permit to use speakers or a bullhorn, but they didn't need to, because they had "the people's mic." Any speaker could announce they had something to say (by saying "mic check") and their words would be amplified by the crowd around them, allowing further concentric circles to hear what the speaker was saying. If the crowd agreed with the speaker, they'd hold their hands up and wiggle their fingers. If they disagreed, they could cross their arms.

You can't understand the youth movements of the 2010s without understanding the people's mic. It's basically the in-person version of a Twitter thread that is retweeted by everyone who hears it.

For example: At one Zuccotti Park general assembly, a guy with a beard stood up and said, "Mic check!" Everyone within earshot answered, "Mic check!"

"Right now," he said.

"Right now," they repeated.

"A group of bold progressives."

"A group of bold progressives," they said.

"Has generously brought."

"Has generously brought."

"A massive stack of signatories."

"A massive stack of signatories."

"To help us move our money."

"To help us move our money."

"Out of shit banks like those." He pointed at Bank of America.

"Out of shit banks like those."

There were no great speeches made here, no sentences worthy of inscribing on the side of a building or reciting in a second-grade classroom. This wasn't an orator addressing a crowd—it was the voice of the crowd itself, sometimes halting, rarely eloquent, but a collective voice nonetheless. The sentences were short and digestible to maximize the efficiency, and they took on the quality of a call-and-response musical refrain, a kind of singsong solidarity.

Mass power was their message ("We are the 99%") but it was also their method. One sign even spelled it out: WE'RE HERE, WE'RE UNCLEAR, GET USED TO IT. Occupiers felt no need to sharpen their collective demands to a single concrete point, because any one demand might exclude hundreds of other priorities. There was no single objective but dozens, hundreds, or none, depending on whom you asked. Occupy Seattle held votes on its website over demands such as "end corporate personhood" and "universal education," but a nationwide, officially sanctioned list of demands never emerged, partly because there was never a unifying governing body authorized to decide what Occupy stood for and what it didn't—which was just the way the activists wanted it.

The press couldn't understand this. Even progressive journalists, worried that an inspiring movement was hobbling itself, struggled to pin down exactly what the protesters wanted and how they planned to get it. Nobody had the answers to those questions. *The New York Times* ran a headline about WALL STREET OCCUPIERS, PROTESTING TILL WHENEVER. But to the Occupiers, specific demands were irrelevant. This was about expressing incoherent rage at the financial system and rejecting the social hierarchies that the movement was trying—in its unfocused way—to eliminate. Occupy remained leaderless because leaderlessness—a horizontal power structure, a rejection of the very idea of consolidation of power—was kind of the point.

Winter came. People who had warm apartments got tired of sleeping in tents and went home. The spontaneous networks that made Zuccotti Park into a self-contained economy of need began to crumble. While the cable news networks packed up their equipment, the movement seemed to dissolve nearly as quickly as it formed. It had changed almost nothing, critics said.

They were wrong. Occupy Wall Street didn't directly dismantle the financial system, but it did sow the seeds that would flower into the revived progressive movement of the next decade. The movement told a story of American politics that would become the defining narrative for the next generation of progressives: Occupy identified a central problem (income inequality), pointed at the culprits (big corporations), and described how those culprits had controlled the political system (with campaign donations legalized through *Citizens United*). It also gave language to a vague feeling that the vast majority of hardworking Americans were being screwed by a greedy elite: "We are the 99%" would become the rallying cry of the many against the few. Without Occupy, Elizabeth Warren would probably not be a force to be reckoned with in the Senate, Bernie Sanders would not have been a major presidential contender, and Alexandria Ocasio-Cortez likely wouldn't be in Congress. Many of the people who ended up working for progressive candidates over the next decade had camped out in Zuccotti Park that fall.

"There's this common idea that Occupy disappeared—but it just dispersed," says Jake DeGroot, a theater lighting designer who occupied Zuccotti Park before he joined the Democratic Socialists of America. He would later play a key role in Alexandria's 2018 congressional campaign. "Folks in my generation rightly identify economic inequality as the crux of the problem, the central locus from which all other problems flow."

Aside from laying the foundations for a revival of American progressivism, Occupy also demonstrated how the internet—and the sense of radical democratization that went with it—would transform protest movements in the early twenty-first century. Social media would become an entirely new arena for mass protest, a digital version of the streets, where activists could organize themselves and their ideas with many leaders and few rules. Occupy would be the first social movement of the twenty-first century that used the cacophony of internet voices—not a few great leaders—to create, define, and sustain itself.

✷ ✷ ✷

And then, five months after the Occupiers first pitched their tents in Zuccotti Park, a bright-eyed seventeen-year-old named Trayvon Martin was shot to death in Sanford, Florida, while walking back from a convenience store with a bag of Skittles.

Martin's killer, George Zimmerman, was ultimately acquitted of murder under Florida's "stand your ground" laws. After the trial, protesters took to the streets in dozens of US cities. Some wore empty Skittles bags over their mouths. Obama, in a rare public comment on the issue, said, "Trayvon Martin could have been me thirty-five years ago."

On the day Zimmerman was acquitted, thirty-two-year-old Oakland activist Alicia Garza wrote a post on Facebook that she called "a love letter to Black people." She thought of her brother, Joey, who was almost young enough to be Trayvon's age. "I continue to be surprised at how little Black lives matter," she wrote. "Black people. I love you. I love us. Our lives matter."

Garza's post was shared by her friend and fellow activist Patrisse Cullors, whom she had met on a dance floor in Providence, Rhode Island, in 2005. Cullors reposted it with the hashtag #blacklivesmatter. Cullors and Garza reached out to a third young activist, Opal Tometi, who set up the #blacklivesmatter Twitter and Tumblr accounts. The hashtag began to go viral. Twitter was to Black Lives Matter what Tumblr had been to Occupy— the living manifesto of the movement. Some observers critiqued Black Lives Matter for not having a specific set of demands or a foundational document, but in the age of social media, the rules had changed: "Twitter is our text," Cullors told me in 2015.

The movement was an expression of rage: for Trayvon Martin, and later for Michael Brown and Eric Garner and every other unarmed black man killed in America. But it was also about rage at what scholar Michelle Alexander called "the New Jim Crow," a system of mass incarceration that disproportionately targeted black people, overwhelmingly young black men. By 2015, more than 9 percent of black men between twenty and thirty-four were incarcerated, compared to less than 2 percent of white men the same age.

Even as crime rates stayed low in American cities, the school-to-prison pipeline extended across the country. Young black children were often treated as criminals from their first days of class, and the 1990s "zero tolerance" school behavior policies led to a spike in suspensions and expulsions, which disproportionately targeted children of color. According to the ACLU, black students were suspended or expelled three times more than white students, and more than 30 percent of kids arrested in school were black. Those young teens were often fed directly into the criminal justice system. All this had been happening for decades: Black Lives Matter just gave people a vocabulary to describe it.

Until 2013, movements for racial justice in the United States tended to coalesce around small groups of black men, or what *The New Yorker*'s Jelani Cobb called "the great-black-man theory of history." But Black Lives Matter activists were more interested in what they called a "leaderful" movement, like Occupy Wall Street, where no single person called the shots. There was such a distaste for what Garza called "the model of the black preacher leading people to the promised land" that when Rev. Jesse Jackson tried to address protesters after the shooting of Michael Brown in Ferguson, Missouri, he was booed.

"Organizations that are led by one person are very vulnerable," Garza told me. "If there are many leaders, you can't compromise a movement and you can't kill it. If there's one leader, it's very easy to neutralize."

First through Occupy and then through Black Lives Matter, millennials were beginning to seek political change through movements rather than through individuals. So each police killing created new organizers, marchers, and leaders. Some were propelled to leadership by documenting the harm done to young black men by law enforcement; others saw the photos and videos posted online and rushed to join the movement. A new kind of dispersed power structure emerged on social media, as established institutions such as the NAACP proved ill-equipped to respond to each new crisis. They were built to address older concerns, within older systems. "I think what we saw was that young black people were creating their own vehicles," said Garza.

"This is the new civil rights movement," high school student Lotoya Francis told me at his first Black Lives Matter protest in 2016, in New York, two years after Brown's death. "I wanted to be a part of it." And like most racial justice protests in US history, the overwhelming majority of people who showed up were young: by 2016, 58 percent of millennials approved of Black Lives Matter. A later survey found significant breakdowns by race, with white and Hispanic millennials significantly less supportive of the movement than their black peers. Roughly half of white millennials took a "both sides" approach to racial justice activists and alt-right groups, just one of many indications that even though millennials are more racially tolerant than their predecessors, they still face significant hurdles to true equality.

Even though the movement was mostly led by black people under forty, distinctions emerged within that cohort, especially when it came to deciding whether to work within the system or outside of it. Organizers in their late thirties grew up in the era of Rodney King and Amadou Diallo, but also in a period of relative black prosperity. Activists in their twenties and early thirties never directly experienced that prosperity: many saw the response to Hurricane Katrina in 2005 and the daily degradations of black life in America as evidence that government didn't care about black people and never would. "There's cynicism around whether it's enough to have black people at the table making decisions," said Garza, who is in her late thirties. Activists who are younger, she said, "don't believe in the table."

Black people had experienced racist violence for all of American history—but now they had phones in their pockets that could shoot video, and social media platforms that could spread those videos without anyone asking traditional media gatekeepers for permission. Before social media, law enforcement and the white American public had often disregarded, downplayed, or flat-out disbelieved accusations of mistreatment. But the new ability to record and distribute videos of racist police violence provided incontrovertible proof. As the videos and photos spread across the internet, a massive and nimble new racial justice movement grew around them, one that wasn't beholden to particular organizations or specific leaders, and that could rapidly respond to new incidents as they arose. Social media not only enabled the easy spread of information around police killings; it also allowed people to quickly organize to protest them. And, just as Occupy did with income inequality, Black Lives Matter gave a new and compelling framework to describe the systemic racism that had persisted for half a century after the civil rights movement. The movement repudiated the notion that a black president in the Oval Office meant the end of racial injustice in the United States; on the contrary, the fact that so many black men were still routinely killed by police while Obama sat in the White House proved that racial injustice was systemic, beyond the power of an individual to solve, and therefore the solutions would have to be systemic too.

Once these activists established a vocabulary for the public to understand the context of police violence, reports of young black men killed by law enforcement appeared more often in the press. Unfortunately, the new awareness was a double-edged sword: not only were black people still subjected to police violence, but now they felt a new and terrible burden to document the tragedies in real time. In October 2014, seventeen-year-old Laquan McDonald was shot sixteen times in fifteen seconds by Chicago police officers, who recorded the killing on their dash cam. A month later, twelve-year-old Tamir Rice was shot by a Cleveland police officer for waving a toy gun at a playground. In April 2015, Freddie Gray died after his spinal cord was injured while in Baltimore police custody. That July, Sandra Bland was found hanged while in police custody in Texas after being arrested for a minor traffic violation. A year later, in July 2016, Alton Sterling was pinned down and shot six times in the back and chest by Baton Rouge police officers. A day later, Philando Castile was shot by a Minnesota cop, and his girlfriend posted the killing on Facebook Live. And then, in September 2016 in Charlotte, North Carolina, the killing that would change everything for Braxton Winston: forty-three-year-old father Keith Lamont Scott was shot by police in broad daylight as he was getting out of his SUV.

✳ ✳ ✳

Throughout the summer of 2012, Braxton Winston, then twenty-nine, did what he always did, which was build stuff. Important people were scheduled to give speeches at the Time Warner Cable Arena in Charlotte, North Carolina, and they needed something to stand on. He built the frame, tightened the screws, leveled the platforms, helped cover them with blue carpet. That September, at the Democratic National Convention, President Barack Obama stood on the stage Braxton had built and accepted his party's nomination with a passionate argument for why America's first black president should be reelected to a second term.

"Those of us who carry on this party's legacy should remember that not every problem can be remedied with another government program or dictate from Washington," he said. "But know this, America: Our problems can be solved." The audience roared. "Our challenges can be met." He paused again to let the people scream their adoration. "The path we offer may be harder, but it leads to a better place, and I'm asking you to choose that future." Inside the arena, Braxton held his five-year-old son, Braxton III, and had someone take a picture with Obama in the background. He had been at so many events in that arena, but he had never felt the air change the way he did that day. So many people were waving signs that he felt wind on his face.

Braxton was a stagehand. He was used to the rhythms of assembly and production: loading in, putting your back into it, building the platform, watching people step onto it, hearing the building shake and knowing the structure will hold, waiting until the crowds have left to load out. He'd done big conventions, speeches, raves, you name it. He wore his dreadlocks pulled back in a loose ponytail and favored T-shirts with progressive quotes on them.

He would never forget the day he brought his son to see the first black president, a hero to black America, give a speech from a stage he had built. But as Obama's presidency lumbered forward, many young people began to see him as a hero in the Greek sense of the word: powerful, yet fallible. His greatest power was in his rhetoric, but he was often circumscribed by the systems in which he operated. Obama could save a failing economy, but he couldn't solve income inequality or close the growing gap between rich and poor. He could provide a powerful example to black people, but he couldn't cure systemic racism, and he couldn't keep black kids from being shot in the street. Some young people began to think that if this was the best Barack

Obama could do within the system, then there must be something very wrong with the system.

Even though Braxton idolized Obama, he thought he had a "rose-colored view" of government. He was disappointed in Obama's "unwillingness to put his finger on the scale" when it came to Ferguson. By the end of his second term, Braxton was angry. "There was going to be nobody else to come and save us," he said. "I'm going to have to figure it out by myself."

And so the president who was supposed to usher in a post-racial harmony instead presided over a period of growing social unrest. When a great leader like Obama couldn't conquer the entrenched systems of economic and racial inequality, "leaderless" movements rose instead. Both Occupy and Black Lives Matter were about problems that disproportionately affected young people: it was young people whose futures were decimated by the financial crisis, and it was young black people who were most likely to experience police violence. And both movements rose in response to systemic problems that were beyond the power of a single man to fix. The movements were most effective in their abilities to project thousands of voices saying the same thing all at once: "We are the 99%." "No justice! No peace!" And later, after years of youth-led protests about campus sexual assault finally spread into the world of adult professional women: "Me too."

The new "leaderful" movements appealed to a generation raised to believe that everybody was a leader and nobody was a follower. ("Anybody anywhere can be in charge, and for millennials, that's so attractive," says Jess Morales Rocketto. "Everyone's a winner. You're a special snowflake.") And the movements mirrored the social networks that supported them: vast, borderless, with few rules and little definition, yet capable of metabolizing ideas into the national consciousness with remarkable ease. Mainstream media outlets wanted to find a figurehead, someone to give the movements a single human form, but that person didn't exist. No longer would individuals—orators, senators, even presidents—be the sole unit of American political power. If the twentieth century was ruled by Great Men, these activists wanted the twenty-first to be ruled by mass movements with decentralized authority, if there was any authority at all. Power would no longer be drawn in portraiture—instead, it would be pixilated.

✳ ✳ ✳

Leaderless movements were not exclusive to young people, or to the left. The Tea Party, which flourished from 2009 to 2011, was the most electorally effective movement of this period, even if it didn't have the rhetorical power of Occupy or Black Lives Matter. Every action has an equal and opposite reaction, and the Tea Party was the backlash to the election of Barack Obama: furious conservatives who resented the social and racial progress that Obama represented. The Tea Partiers were overwhelmingly white, mostly male, and skewed much older. They believed America's best years were behind them. Their movement was characterized by fears of generational change, fiscal austerity (by some explanations, "Tea" stands for "taxed enough already"), and a loathing of Barack Obama: when asked why they hated Obama, their top answer was "just don't like him." About 30 percent of the Tea Party believed the racist lie that Obama wasn't born in the United States, despite irrefutable evidence to the contrary. Their movement, largely funded by the archconservative Koch brothers, was relentlessly focused on winning legislative votes and important elections, and was enormously successful at it.

During the rise of the Tea Party, Ezra Levin and Leah Greenberg were young Democratic congressional staffers trying to make their way on Capitol Hill. Ezra worked for Rep. Lloyd Doggett of Texas, and Leah worked for Rep. Tom Perriello of Virginia. They were in their twenties, both small-boned and slender, the type of congressional aides who could be easily mistaken for interns. They met and quickly fell for each other, but throughout the summer and fall of 2009, the landlines in their offices never stopped ringing long enough for them to go on a date. Every time Ezra picked up the phone, he heard an angry old person on the other end trying to stop the Affordable Care Act. They called with oddly specific requests, like, "Will Congressman Doggett vote 'no' on the motion to recommit?" and then Ezra would hang up the phone and it would ring again with another person asking about the motion to recommit. Ezra began to wonder how they all knew the same obscure details of congressional procedure, how they all coordinated their "asks," how they built such a disciplined protest movement and targeted it so effectively at the legislative process.

In August, Ezra's boss, Representative Doggett, made the mistake of showing up at a grocery store in his district to explain to his constituents why he was voting for the Affordable Care Act. He was met with a mob of furious conservatives chanting "Just say no!" and holding signs with his face drawn with devil horns. He was relatively lucky—other Democratic congressmen were burned in effigy or presented with nooses. Leah was once at a Virginia event for her boss, Representative Perriello, and was almost knocked to the ground by an angry crush of constituents.

Neither of them had ever seen so many people who were so angry and so effective at translating that anger into specific political action. It was alarming, but it was also impressive. They didn't know that these furious senior citizens were teaching them the most important political lesson of their lives, one that would ultimately help them save the health care bill that Obama had worked so hard to pass.

✳ ✳ ✳

One day in September 2016, Braxton stopped for gas on the way home from coaching his kid's middle school football team and checked his phone. He saw that police had shot a black man, Keith Lamont Scott, just seven minutes from the gas station where he was filling up his car. He decided to go check it out.

Growing up in Brooklyn, Braxton had been vaguely aware of the Crown Heights riots as a kid, but he had never seen a police shooting up close. When he got to the apartment complex parking lot, someone told him the victim had been there waiting for his kids to get off the school bus. A couple hundred people had gathered by then, so he took out his phone and turned on his Facebook Live.

There's a white truck surrounded by police tape, and officers standing around taking notes. Suddenly, a high-pitched scream. "That's my daddy's car! That's my daddy's car!" Braxton steps forward, pushes through the crowd, holding his phone. It's a young woman, braids pulled back, screaming. Someone is trying to hold her and calm her down but then she is on the ground crying, still saying over and over again, "That's my daddy's car!" When they pull her away she is sobbing on somebody's shoulder.

The cops called for reinforcements, and the reinforcements came in black riot gear with masks and batons. Braxton knew a lot of cops from working at the arena, but he couldn't recognize anybody because of their masks. His phone died. He took off his shirt. He stood in front of a line of police officers in riot gear and raised his fist. At some point someone took a picture. Braxton got teargassed and got hit in the head with a rock. When he arrived home that night, he couldn't pick up his baby daughter because his dreadlocks had so much tear gas in them.

The next morning, he woke up to see his image was all over the internet: Braxton, shirtless, alone in defiance against the police. He didn't like it. "It represented the worst night of my life," he told me later. His photo was in news articles that were shared all over Facebook. People he hadn't talked to since college were texting him about it.

That night, he was back in the streets, with the crowd in front of the Omni Hotel in downtown Charlotte. Again he took out his phone; again he turned on Facebook Live.

White vans, and cops with riot masks. People chanting, "No justice, no peace." Suddenly, people start screaming. There's a popping sound. The camera shakes. People who were marching away from Braxton run toward him instead.

Braxton starts to cough. He sees a single police officer rush out the doors of the Omni Hotel, pointing and firing everywhere. He's in this officer's line of vision, and people on Braxton's left and right seem like they're dodging rubber bullets, and Braxton turns to run away, but he tries to keep his phone pointed backward, toward the people running.

Suddenly, there's a big bang, maybe a tear gas canister. He walks toward a group of people clustered around something. He gets closer and it's a body on the ground. Someone is yelling, "Oh shit! Oh shit! Oh shit!" He sees a guy grab his head, take his hand away, and look at the blood on his hand. He starts to fall and is caught by another guy, who lays him on the ground. People crowd around him. Braxton sees his arm underneath the crush of bodies. A woman is screaming, "They shot him in the head, they shot him in the head." Some white women are kneeling down around the guy on the ground. More rubber bullets. There is a very bright light coming from somewhere; people are kneeling and standing and approaching with their phones and screaming. Somebody shouts, "Respect, respect, no recording, no recording." Braxton keeps recording.

The crowd gets stronger, and the wave of people moves Braxton and his camera farther away from the body on the ground. A woman starts to cry. Braxton climbs onto something so he can see better, and from where he is standing it looks like a hurricane of people swirling around whoever is lying on the ground. Another woman starts to shout, "No justice, no peace!" Somebody asks Braxton what happened and he says, "They shot him in the head, man, not ten feet away from me." For a second the video is dark, he's caught in somebody's shadow, and then the phone emerges into the eye of the hurricane and there's a bloodstain on the pavement, a big one, with rivers of blood running into each other like spray-painted graffiti. A man is crouching over the blood, waving his hands over it, not touching it. It's as if he's protecting it, trying to keep anybody from stepping on it, trying to preserve a crime scene in the middle of a crowd.

Later, the police would say that they weren't even shooting rubber bullets that night, and that the dead man, Justin Carr, had been shot with a real bullet by another black man. Braxton thought that was bullshit. You would have to have a death wish to do something like that, to shoot a guy point-blank while surrounded by police officers in riot gear, Braxton thought. You'd have to be the stupidest criminal alive.

Braxton went out into the streets every day for the next five days, until he was arrested. The cops approached him with plastic cuffs, detained him for twenty minutes, searched his bag and found his gas mask, which he wasn't supposed to have. He was arrested under an "extraordinary events ordinance," which had been put in place before the 2012 DNC to crack down on anticipated Occupy protests. He was held for ten hours and released on $500 bail.

When he got out, he had to refocus. He had kids—he couldn't just be getting arrested all the time. He realized that he had been trying so hard to hold the police accountable, but he didn't know how city government worked. He had no idea who was actually responsible for regulating the Charlotte police department—he didn't even know what a city manager was. He decided it was time for him to find out how the system worked from the inside.

Over the decade that followed, the two sides—the ones who wanted to fix the system and the ones who wanted to fuck the system—would circle each other warily, mirroring each other's movements. The people who wanted to fix the system would slowly acknowledge the ways that the system was irreversibly fucked, and the people who wanted to fuck the system would come to realize that they would have to work within it in order to get anything fixed.

THE BIG ONE

Everyone said this was the Big One.

Halloween was canceled. The UN and the New York Stock Exchange were closed. By 9:30 p.m. on October 29, 9-1-1 was receiving ten thousand calls per hour. By 10:00 p.m., Ground Zero was submerged, the subways had flooded, and the Hudson River was pouring into the Hugh L. Carey Tunnel between Brooklyn and Manhattan. New York University's medical center lost power, and doctors and nurses evacuated vulnerable patients by flashlight. Cars floated out of underground parking garages. By midnight the East Village had flooded, a ConEd facility had exploded, and almost all of Lower Manhattan had lost power. In Westchester County, an eleven-year-old boy and his friend were both killed when a tree collapsed into the living room.

On Staten Island, Glenda Moore's house lost power, and her husband (a sanitation worker who had been called into duty to help with the storm) told her to find a safer place to stay. Glenda, a thirty-nine-year-old black woman, packed two-year-old Brandon and four-year-old Connor into their blue SUV and tried to make it through the floodwaters to her sister's house. The waters stalled the car's engine and a wave pushed them off the road. She got out and dragged Brandon and Connor to a small tree near a big yellow house, where they clung to the branches for hours before she finally decided to go up to the house to ask for help.

Glenda told police she knocked on the door, and a white man peeked out but he wouldn't let her in. She went around back with her sons and threw a flowerpot through his window trying to get inside, but couldn't break in. Another wave came and swept away her sons. Their bodies were found a quarter mile away.

Later, the man—a guy named Alan who wouldn't give his last name—said he thought a "man" was trying to break into his house, and that the boys' deaths weren't his fault. "You know, it's one of those things," he said.

At least 147 people died because of Hurricane Sandy. The storm caused $65 billion in damage. Eventually, the federal government spent $766 million to rebuild homes in flood zones in the Rockaways and New Jersey and Staten Island. People began to move on. They figured storms like that come around only once every seven hundred years or so.

CHAPTER 10

The Locals

I n 2008, millennials stepped into the political arena to vote for Barack Obama, and then most of them stepped right back out. Obama's presidency did not coincide with a surge of young people running for office or entering the political sphere: in fact, the opposite happened. Many young people figured that Obama had Washington under control, and that if they wanted to "make the world a better place," they should go into teaching or work at a startup or nonprofit. Obama seemed so powerful, so transformative, that many of his young supporters assumed he had some kind of magic wand that could miraculously fix the problems he described. They put him into the White House: fixing the country was his problem now.

Many also assumed that Obama's star power would be enough to buoy the fortunes of the Democratic Party, but again the party was a victim of its own success: his broad popularity actually created a sense of complacency that hurt down-ballot Democrats. While Obama was focused on reviving the economy, fixing health care, and restoring America's reputation overseas, the feeding and watering of the state and local chapters of the Democratic Party was low on his list of priorities. And Obama's electrifying popularity with young people set an impossible standard for future Democratic candidates. Young voters had gotten used to the idea that they should be truly excited about the candidate on the ballot—and if they weren't, they wouldn't vote at all. That led to dismal youth turnout in midterms when Obama wasn't on the ticket.

That Democratic complacency, combined with the Tea Party surge on the right, helped Republicans reclaim control of the House of Representatives in 2010. Democrats fared even worse on the state and local levels, where the Koch brothers and other conservative groups helped Republicans pick up six governorships and a historic 675 state legislative seats. The GOP's timing was brilliant: the 2010 census let them use their victory to gerrymander the state legislative districts in ways that sharply tilted the playing field toward Republicans in several states.

The Democrats wouldn't bounce back for more than a decade. Over the course of Obama's presidency, they lost more than 950 state legislative seats. Those seats weren't just important for maintaining Democratic presence in statehouses—they were also the lowest rungs on the political ladder, where many young leaders start their careers. The wipeout on the state level left the Democratic team with a star hitter in the White House but nobody on the bench.

Political scientist Shauna L. Shames surveyed dozens of Ivy League law students and graduate students in political science during the second half of Obama's presidency—exactly the type of people who would have once had political ambitions—and found that only a fraction were seriously considering running for office. They told Shames it just wasn't worth it: the costs were too high and rewards were too low, and they hated the idea of constantly asking for money. By the early 2010s, running for the House of Representatives cost about $1.5 million—roughly double what it cost when boomers were first entering political office in the mid-1980s (adjusted for inflation)—and the average state legislative campaign cost $88,000. If most millennials couldn't afford a down payment on a home, how could they possibly scrape together that kind of money?

Of course, there were significant exceptions. Some young people were inspired by Obama's example, and they stepped up to run even while most of their peers were avoiding electoral politics. In the ten years that followed Obama's 2008 election, black millennials in particular emerged as compelling candidates on the state and local level. From Svante Myrick in Ithaca to

Michael Tubbs in Stockton to Braxton Winston in Charlotte, young black leaders across the country were meeting Obama's challenge to "create the change we seek." By 2019, ten years after Obama's inauguration, black millennials sat in the mayor's office in Compton, California; Jackson, Mississippi; Little Rock, Arkansas; Richmond, Virginia; and Birmingham and Montgomery, Alabama.

These young Obama acolytes—including white candidates like Eric Lesser and Pete Buttigieg—ran mostly on the local level, often for city council or mayor of small cities away from the national spotlight, trying out strategies and policy ideas that would hint at what millennial leadership would look like on the national level. They focused on the local issues voters care about most—schools, parks, and economic development—but with a youthful flavor. They updated green infrastructure to prepare cities for climate change, and reformed police departments to reduce fatal shootings. They fought for affordable housing and used technology to update municipal government. Most of all, they demonstrated a willingness to think big about civic possibilities. Government, they thought, wasn't the problem: government could be the solution.

✵ ✵ ✵

Svante Myrick had read all of Obama's books and watched all his speeches by the time he moved to the college town of Ithaca, New York (population 30,000). He had moved there to attend Cornell University, where he quickly became a Big Man on Campus. Svante first found a job working as an assistant to Ithaca Common Council member Gayraud Townsend, who had himself been elected to the council as a college student. When Townsend's term expired, he encouraged Svante—still a junior—to run for his seat. But Svante was torn, because a friend of a friend had offered to help him get an internship in Obama's Senate office. "I was like, 'What would Obama do?'" Svante said. "I think Obama would run for city council." He figured that Obama would be in the Senate for forty years. By the time Obama was elected president a year later, Svante was a twenty-one-year-old college senior serving on Ithaca's Common Council.

At the time, Svante was renting a big house full of guys in Ithaca. They

called it the "Hall of Justice," because it was all public-service types who
lived there: a city council member, a county legislator, two PhD students, and
Svante. They helped him put up posters and played beer pong after campaigning. They called him "the Mayor," ironically at first, because he was
always hogging the remote and pulling rank on house-wide decisions. The
nickname stuck when—after a vigorous campaign that relied on black voters
and decent turnout from Cornell faculty and students—he was actually elected
mayor of Ithaca at age twenty-four.

As soon as he took office as the city's youngest ever and first black mayor,
Svante had more in common with the college students who lived in Ithaca
than the older people who had typically run the city. Svante didn't have a car
and he didn't need the prime parking space reserved for the mayor—so he
turned it into a tiny park, where residents could come and sit on a bench
and talk with him. He biked everywhere and stopped to talk to constituents
whenever they flagged him down. He used Facebook to crowdsource public
funding to bring back the Fourth of July fireworks.

Like many other millennial mayors, Svante prioritized density: he
wanted to make Ithaca more walkable and livable for people who didn't
have cars. To help do that, he'd have to revamp the Ithaca Commons, the
three-block central plaza that was the locus of urban life. The plaza had
become dysfunctional; when it was built in 1974, the city laid the underground gas, power, and water lines in such a way that they couldn't be re-
paired without shutting down businesses. Fixing the Commons required
major internal surgery, not just a face-lift, so Svante made what he called
a "J-curve decision"—short-term financial pain for long-term civic gain—
and decided to revamp the entire Commons. That meant moving and replacing utility lines among other infrastructure improvements and beautification
efforts. It was a two-year project that triggered a lot of grumbling from business owners about the kid mayor, but in the end, the new Ithaca Commons
was more beautiful, more prosperous for retail, and better for the town
overall.

"I think the decision to do it was a youthful one," he said later. "Because
I was naive about how easy it would be, and because I was like, 'What's two
years of pain if we can get this right for a hundred years?'"

He also had to make controversial decisions about policing. There was always a part of Svante that was afraid of the police, ever since his mom had given him and his brothers "the Talk" when they were teenagers. She told them that police officers would be jumpy around them because they were black, and that if they were ever pulled over, they should take their wallets out and put them on the dashboard and keep their hands where the cops could see them. Sometimes, when he was in a different city, he could feel the cops watching him. He realized they didn't know he was a mayor; to them, he was just another young black guy on the street.

But as mayor, his job included negotiating with the police force and swearing in new officers. Svante appointed a black police chief, required all cops to have implicit bias training, and added body cameras and a civilian review board. He directed the city police department to make marijuana enforcement the lowest-priority drug offense, effectively decriminalizing weed in Ithaca. He also added two steps at the end of the police admission test: a psychiatric exam and a polygraph test. Svante said the new evaluations ended up revealing past crimes, drug use, or desire to use a gun in a real-life situation, which disqualified 75 percent of applicants who would have otherwise been hired. This helped Ithaca weed out bad recruits and avoid letting dangerous officers onto the force.

Affordable housing was one of his biggest challenges. Svante had spent time in a homeless shelter, he had watched his mom struggle to make rent, and he was a twenty-four-year-old with four roommates. So he had little patience for the NIMBYism ("Not In My Back Yard") of homeowners who flooded community meetings to oppose building more affordable housing in their neighborhoods. NIMBYism, Svante thought, was the biggest reason for the affordable housing crisis in Ithaca and around the country. Otherwise progressive people—people who had Greenpeace stickers on their hybrid cars—would create "firestorms" to protect their property values, he said. Their demands sounded reasonable: they'd say things like "We don't want to change the character of the neighborhood," or "Quality of life is important to us," or "It's the traffic!" In truth, he thought, they just didn't want poor people moving next door.

Svante suspected it was easier for him to fight the NIMBYs because he wasn't of their world. "I wasn't going to these people's cocktail parties—I wasn't invited to them," Svante said. "I didn't have the same level of connection. Our kids hadn't gone to school together."

Still, rents in Ithaca continued to increase under his watch, and as the city became more dense, it also became more gentrified. Left-wing housing advocates still didn't like that developers had a seat at the table, and some longtime low-income residents wondered why the city was spending money on a fountain on the Commons that it could have spent elsewhere. But Svante made some real progress: over the course of his tenure, Ithaca added more than 1,100 new affordable housing units, according to internal municipal documents, more than the total number built in the twenty years before he took office.

In the twenty-first century, affordable housing became a nationwide crisis, but one that was dealt with mostly on the municipal level. Some young mayors, many of them renters themselves, made that challenge central to their agendas. Quinton Lucas (b. 1984) had been chair of the City Council Housing Committee before he was elected mayor of Kansas City, Missouri, in 2019, partly with the help of affordable housing advocates. He spent his first night as mayor sleeping on the couch of a tenant.

Jacob Frey (b. 1981) made housing a central focus of his run for mayor of Minneapolis. He called housing a "full-blown crisis for millennials." Because they were marrying later, having fewer kids, and trying to reduce their carbon footprint, millennials wanted to live someplace dense and walkable, with public transportation: boomers' exurban McMansions held little appeal for them. Once he was elected, Frey eliminated single-family exclusive zoning in Minneapolis, allowing more duplexes and triplexes to be built as part of a $40 million affordable housing plan for the city.

"This is not the American dream of the 1950s, where the whole goal was that white picket fence out in the suburbs with a forty-five-minute commute to work," Frey told me. Millennials "want to sleep at home, but they want to live in a great city and experience diversity and activity around them. That's a big change."

* * *

Since Keith Lamont Scott's death in 2016, Braxton Winston had decided that if he really wanted anything to change in the police department, he would have to run for office himself. So he ran for an at-large seat on the Charlotte City Council and got the second-highest number of votes for any at-large seat. By the time Braxton arrived on the city council in 2017, six of the eleven seats were held by people under forty, and Charlotte had become the first major city in America to have a majority-millennial city council.

The city council felt a little like a freshman dorm: everyone was roughly the same age, in the same place, but had pretty much nothing else in common on a personal level. Justin Harlow was a young dentist who liked wearing bow ties. Larken Egleston favored plaid shirts and worked in marketing for a liquor distributor. Dimple Ajmera was the child of Indian immigrants and had a degree in public accounting. Matt Newton sported a 1950s haircut and a copy of *Profiles in Courage* in his office. Tariq Bokhari—the only Republican under forty on the council—worked out of a tech coworking space. For all their personal differences, the young city council members immediately agreed that Charlotte needed more transparency. So the first thing they did was livestream the city council meetings so that constitu ents could watch from home. Larken and Tariq soon started a podcast, a sort of left-right debate that they modeled as a municipal version of *Pod Save America*.

Charlotte was growing quickly and attracting new business, but with growth came gentrification and income inequality. A 2014 report had ranked Charlotte dead last among the top fifty cities in America for economic mobility. Kids who were born poor in Charlotte were likely to stay poor, and the massive influx of new business into the city was only gentrifying it even faster. Housing costs were reaching crisis levels: rents had climbed 45 percent since 2010.

The 2016 shooting of Keith Lamont Scott put a spotlight on racial and social inequality in Charlotte. So the new city council took the "dive in headfirst" approach and tried everything at once. The council's plan had three parts: they planned to build new housing units, preserve existing affordable homes, and keep people from getting displaced. They embraced a new pilot program—developed by Harvard economist Raj Chetty and funded by Harvard's Opportunity Insights Institute and UNC Charlotte—to help low-income families move to higher-opportunity neighborhoods. The reformers had good intentions, but progress was slow. The Charlotte City Council had promised to build five thousand affordable housing units in three years, but by 2019, almost half still hadn't been built.

As the city council was debating affordable housing, the police shootings that brought Braxton into public office continued. In March 2019, a Charlotte police officer shot and killed a young man named Danquirs Franklin in front of a Burger King in broad daylight, after he apparently refused to drop his gun.

Braxton was less than a mile away from the Burger King when it happened, and he went over to see for himself what was going on. He was there to stand in solidarity with his community, just as he had three years earlier. But this time, he wasn't there as an activist—he was a representative of the city. "This is us now," Braxton thought. The police department was "not 'them' anymore—I'm part of this." Instead of confronting police officers, he was giving out his business card to anybody who wanted to follow up with city hall about what had happened. "I don't like to criticize if I don't have a path forward," he said. "I can't say, 'You should do'—I have to figure out what we are going to do."

Three days after Franklin's death, Braxton wrote an op-ed in *The Charlotte Observer*: "Unfortunately, once again, this citizen was delivered to the morgue instead of a jail to await trial."

In the weeks that followed, Braxton advocated for increased investment in crisis intervention training for Charlotte police, including how to respond to someone who is mentally ill. He wanted additional money for training cops in first aid, so that if they hurt someone, they could start helping them immediately. The cops had called for a medic after Franklin was shot, but they hadn't tried to treat the wounds themselves. He had lain bleeding on the ground in front of them. Braxton voted against authorizing the Charlotte police to spend over half a million dollars on night vision goggles and a projectile launcher that could fire 40mm rubber bullets. "I have been at the receiving end of those forty-millimeter rounds," Braxton said. "I can tell you that they are painful, that they are used against peaceful, nonviolent protesters, and it is not something I think we need to expand." And when the police department tried to release only a fraction of the officer's body cam footage, Braxton spoke up from the city council, calling it a "flagrant skewing of the evidence in this case." The full tape was eventually released.

Braxton knew he couldn't fix everything. He couldn't bring Danquirs Franklin back, or Keith Lamont Scott back, and he couldn't cure systemic racism in Charlotte with a single seat on the city council. But he was learning how to find the pressure points in the system and how to use the budget to shape policy. He realized that the city government was full of people who wanted to do the right thing, if only the city council gave them permission. That was the biggest surprise for him: that the system, with enough effort, could be made to work.

✳ ✳ ✳

Michael Tubbs was learning a similar lesson in Stockton, California. As a young mayor of a city with more than three hundred thousand people, Tubbs had spent his entire political career looking for ways to use city government to cure the systemic violence and poverty that plagued the city. During his sophomore year in college, his twenty-one-year-old cousin was murdered at a Halloween party. His senior year, seventy-one people were killed in Stockton—more per capita than Chicago or Afghanistan. People began to call Stockton the "murder capital of the country."

Born to a seventeen-year-old mother and an incarcerated father, Michael was raised by a trio of women he calls his "squad"—his mother, his aunt, and his grandmother—who kept him on a tight leash so that he could work hard in school. He was chubby-faced and tall, with a wide smile and an easy way about him, and like every other smart kid in Stockton, California, Michael's goal was to grow up and get out.

But when Michael got to Stanford, he realized that the kids he met there were no smarter than the kids he knew at home. These were the elite who would be making policy, he realized, yet none of them had ever been on welfare, so how could they know what poverty really meant? In 2010 he scored an internship in the Obama White House, assigned to the team coordinating with mayors and city councils. Later he would often repeat what Michelle Obama said when she addressed the interns: every day you walk through these doors, she said, you bring your community with you.

After graduation in 2012, most of his Stanford classmates were moving to Silicon Valley to work for Google or Facebook, but Michael went home to Stockton to run for city council. At first, his campaign was just his mom, cousins, and old friends from high school knocking on doors. He'd show up to talk to kids whose families had been affected by the violence in Stockton, and you could hear the Obama affect creeping into his voice. "Throughout history, when anything was going to be done, it was young people who did it," Michael told a group of high school kids. "Old people like me can do our part, but it's really going to be young people like you who can move the city forward." He was twenty-two.

That November, he became the youngest person elected to the Stockton City Council. Four years later, on the same night Trump won the presidency, Michael became the youngest mayor of an American city with more than one hundred thousand people. He was twenty-six.

Michael redid the mayor's office with pictures of Frederick Douglass and Muhammad Ali and had his favorite J. Cole line ("Anything's possible, you gotta dream like you've never seen obstacles") painted on the wall. He belted out *Hamilton* in his car on the way to meetings. When his interns arrived, they were sorted into Hogwarts houses: Slytherin, Hufflepuff, Ravenclaw, Gryffindor. Michael, of course, was a Gryffindor. Over the doorway to his office, he has two words inscribed on the wall: "Fret not."

He adopted Obama's cool, inspirational rhythm, his words rising in the middle of the sentence and then trailing off at the end. He did things in the Obama way: a coalition of politics, business, and tech, all under the mantle of "hope and change."

Michael's major initiatives tended to take a bold, holistic approach to city problems. He tried to implement what he calls "cradle-to-grave" services to help elevate poor kids out of poverty. He created the South Stockton Promise Zone, an effort to coordinate city and community organizations to help lift the kids in South Stockton—mostly black, poor kids—by facilitating regular collaboration between the cops, teachers, and mental health professionals who work in that community. (He often prefaces meetings by saying, "I know you've probably been doing this for longer than I've been alive, but can you help me understand why this is the process?") It ended up becoming an elaborate form of community policing.

Michael quickly built a relationship with the police chief, Eric Jones, and they made an unlikely duo: a twentysomething black city council member and a fortysomething white police chief texting each other in the middle of the night. He and Jones brought the Advance Peace program to Stockton, which offers counseling, job training, and stipends to the young men most likely to commit violence—essentially incentivizing them to not fire their guns. By 2018, homicides had dropped 40 percent, although they later crept back up significantly, an example of how entrenched the violence had become.

Soon, they were having regular lunches and Michael was teaching Chief Jones how to eat edamame and how much sriracha to put on his poke bowl. With Michael's encouragement, Chief Jones retrained Stockton police in de-escalation of force and rewrote the protocol around shooting into cars. "My perception of cops was like every other black kid in an urban community," Michael says. "He was the first officer I had a conversation with."

Michael implemented the first basic income pilot program in the nation, guaranteeing $500 monthly checks to a select group of residents for eighteen months to test whether simple cash transfers could alleviate poverty. While democratic socialists were writing long op-eds demanding universal basic income, Michael was actually testing how it could work. He started the Student Success and Leadership Academy, a group of about eight hundred kids who clean up parks during the summer; the program simultaneously keeps the city's parks nice and gives the kids something to do when school is out. But Michael knew they would still be left behind without more education. So he snagged a $20 million grant to create the Stockton Scholars program, which aimed to triple the number of Stockton kids who go to college.

Michael recognized that the slow pace of government could be difficult for millennials who grew up accustomed to the instant gratification that comes with a computer in their pocket. "Government is not designed to move fast," he said. "For young people who want to be disruptive, government will be very frustrating." Tech entrepreneurs could "move fast and break things" because the stakes were lower. "If you prototype something and it fails, it's just an internal conversation in your office," he said. "If I prototype water delivery or trash, it touches everyone, especially the most vulnerable. So there has to be some caution."

✳ ✳ ✳

Eric Lesser was familiar with just how slow government could go. He had left the White House in 2011, gone to law school, gotten married, and then gone home to Western Massachusetts, to run for office. In 2014, he won a seat in the Massachusetts State Senate and became one of the only millennials in the statehouse. As soon as he got there, he turned on his laptop and realized that there was no Wi-Fi. "Every Starbucks in the world has Wi-Fi," he said. "But the Massachusetts statehouse didn't."

He represented a semi-rural district that was more conservative than the rest of the state. His constituents had been left behind, not just culturally and economically, but literally: their grown children had moved away in search of economic opportunity, mostly because their student loan debt kept them tied to higher-paying jobs in big cities. Eric began to realize that the student loan crisis was directly connected to the hollowing out of America's rural and suburban areas: young people who owed hundreds of dollars a month in loan payments couldn't afford to move back to Western Massachusetts to start a business, or take an entry-level job at a local company, or live on savings to take care of their parents. That's why Eric tried to address the crisis on the state level, by introducing a student loan bill of rights to help protect against predatory lenders—but it languished in committee.

Eric's great white whale was the trans-state railroad. He wanted to build a rail line connecting Springfield and Boston so that people who lived in Western Massachusetts could easily commute to the city without spending hours in heavy traffic. He thought this was a no-brainer for the state: good for the economy, good for the environment, a way to help young people stay near their families while commuting to well-paying jobs. He argued it could improve both housing affordability in Boston and economic development in the western part of the state.

Eric ran straight at it, "Leslie Knope–style," he says, but he had no idea how hard it would be. It would take him years just to get a feasibility study. In 2014, he was elected on the promise of building a rail line. In 2015, he got a feasibility study included in the Senate budget, but the House blocked it. In 2016, he used what he calls "Obama tactics"—bringing together different public and private sector interests groups to support it—and got it past both chambers of the state legislature, but Republican governor Charlie Baker vetoed it under pressure from the owner of a bus line. In 2017, the Senate approved it, but the House blocked it again. In 2018, Baker—who was up for reelection—suddenly had a change of heart. All those years of pushing just to get the state to do a feasibility study—just a study!—examining what it would take to build a rail line. By 2019, Eric had gotten the state to lay out six different east-west passenger rail scenarios, but there was still no money attached. He had a long way to go.

But he remembered from his Obama days that politics isn't usually about the home runs in the early innings: it's about singles, doubles, advancing the runner. If he could stay in the game, maybe that rail line homer would come one day.

＊ ＊ ＊

The despair Eric saw in Western Massachusetts was eating away at industrial regions all across America. Places that had once been vital to the American economy had been decimated by the financial crisis, and felt left out of the recovery. In 2011, *Newsweek* put South Bend, Indiana, on its list of "dying American cities," pointing out that the economy had stalled since the Studebaker plant closed in the late 1960s, and that the population of young people had dropped by 2.5 percent.

Pete Buttigieg had originally moved back to Indiana in 2009 to challenge the archconservative state treasurer who had (unsuccessfully) sued to stop Obama's Chrysler bailout that would eventually save thousands of Indiana jobs. Pete thought it was insane that a statewide elected official was fighting *against* saving jobs in the state. He was a twenty-seven-year-old management consultant with a funny name, but he ran hard, crisscrossed the state talking to farmers and eating kielbasa and bratwurst. He lost big.

But he had made enough of an impression that people started suggesting that maybe Pete should run for mayor of South Bend instead. He was a fresh face, not loyal to any of the dueling factions of city politics. He had a background in management consulting, which could help the city with its economic development. And he was young and well-educated, at a time when most young and well-educated kids who grew up in South Bend were fleeing as fast as they could. He worried that his age could be a liability, but it turned out to be an asset: some of his strongest support came from senior citizens who thought the city needed a fresh pair of eyes. He was elected mayor in 2011.

Pete dragged the processes of municipal government into the twenty-first century, embracing technological solutions to many of the city's problems. Like most millennials, Pete saw technology as an obvious way to increase efficiency and transparency, and he quickly worked to update the city's outdated, paper-based bureaucracy. Before he took office, the mayor would get crime stats by fax—he put a stop to that immediately. He set up a 311 system that allowed residents to report potholes and other public nuisances in real time. Pete brought in new investors and together they built a data center and other offices in the old Studebaker plant. This Obama-esque embrace of technocratic solutions to entrenched problems seemed to work: he cut unemployment in half in six years.

The more he worked on economic development, the more he realized that well-meaning liberals who urged aging manufacturing workers to "learn to code" or "get a nursing degree" were missing a crucial understanding of the meaning of work. Work wasn't just a job or a paycheck: it was an identity. You couldn't say, "You're broken, let me fix you," to a worker who had lost his job. Instead, you had to offer ways to allow that person to keep his or her sense of self, but in a modern, technological world. You couldn't tell an auto worker to learn to code so they could work for Snapchat—but you could tell him computer science was important because all the latest cars contained digital technology. For many of the aging white workers in the industrial Midwest, Pete came to understand, their economic anxiety *was* identity politics—because to them, their jobs were their identity.

He quickly realized that as mayor, success was hard to quantify and failure was easy to spot: either the potholes got fixed or they didn't, the snow got plowed or not. One of his biggest priorities was revitalizing South Bend's sagging downtown. He implemented what he called a "road diet," slimming streets down from four lanes to two, and added sidewalks, bike lanes, trees, and little flowers to make downtown more walkable. He arranged liquor licenses for some downtown businesses, wrangled renovations of hotels and restaurants, and added a "First Fridays" festival. He realized that more downtown condos would attract both young people and empty nesters, so he helped turn some old buildings into apartments. He rebuilt a community center in one of the poorest black neighborhoods in South Bend, which now features three basketball courts, a bike repair shop, and a music studio for kids who need a place to go hang out after school. For South Bend's 150th anniversary in 2015, Pete commissioned an artist to install an interactive light sculpture illuminating the St. Joseph River, inviting people to walk along the banks and watch the light show. And after six years of Mayor Pete, South Bend was no longer "dying"—it was growing with purpose and cautious optimism.

He also made some big mistakes. While South Bend's economic development revitalized the downtown, many low-income black residents on the west side of the city felt ignored or left behind. One of his big local initiatives — tearing down or repairing one thousand vacant homes in one thousand days—helped neighborhood revitalization in the mostly white downtown, but ended up having unintended consequences in black communities, where many black families lost investment properties or unoccupied homes that had sentimental value. And Pete fired the popular black police chief after he came under FBI investigation for allegedly taping South Bend police officers using racist language, which caused a major backlash. Perhaps most important, he failed at his goal of diversifying the South Bend police department. When a white South Bend officer shot a black man named Eric Logan in June 2019, Pete—who was by then running for president—faced widespread criticism for letting the department stay so white on his watch. It became clear that as much as he had tried to address systemic racism in South Bend, he didn't try hard enough.

Black residents in South Bend seemed to have a mixed opinion of him.

Some rightly pointed out that the black community hadn't shared equally in the economic development Pete brought to the city, and that his push for more growth had caused gentrification that left black communities behind. Nobody thought racial inequality in South Bend had been fixed. But some black South Bend residents told me they thought Pete was a good listener, and that when presented with problems with his policies, he was willing to adjust his plans to find a solution. He governed from a sense of practicality, not ideology, which meant he was usually comfortable adjusting his course when he faltered and admitting when he'd been wrong. As a mayor of a small city, that worked great. As a national political figure, it was a tougher sell.

✳ ✳ ✳

Somewhere along the line, Pete had decided that he could be with men or he could have a public life, but he couldn't have both. He was in his thirties, had watched most of his friends get married and have kids, and he just always assumed that door was closed to him. Most nights he went home after work and watched *The Wire* or *Family Guy* alone with a Sam Adams beer.

All that changed after he got back from Afghanistan. He decided it was time to get serious about his personal life. But as Pete started slowly coming out to family and friends over the course of 2015, things in Indiana were changing fast. In March, the Republican-controlled state legislature had passed the Religious Freedom Restoration Act, which allowed local businesses to discriminate against same-sex couples, and Governor Mike Pence signed it into law. Corporations threatened to leave Indiana in protest, and athletes and artists boycotted the state. The pressure worked: a week later, the legislature amended the bill to protect the LGBTQ community. In June, the Supreme Court ruled that same-sex marriage was protected by the Fourteenth Amendment in all fifty states. Over the course of three months, gay couples had gone from being targeted in Indiana to being embraced nationwide.

As the country was reckoning with equal rights for same-sex couples, Pete decided it was time to tell his constituents the truth. "I was well into adulthood before I was prepared to acknowledge the simple fact that I am gay," he wrote in an op-ed in the *South Bend Tribune*, less than two weeks before the Supreme Court verdict was reached. "It took years of struggle and growth for me to recognize that it's just a fact of life, like having brown hair, and part of who I am." It was a risky move: he was running for reelection in a state where many were still hostile to the idea of same-sex marriage. But Pete was surprised by the overwhelmingly positive reaction: people mostly loved it, or else they just didn't care, and he easily won reelection. A few older constituents asked him if he had a "special friend." He didn't.

Next, he had to actually find someone. So he did what everyone else his age did—he downloaded Hinge. To avoid the awkwardness of dating a constituent, Pete set a wide radius on his Hinge location settings, and after a few swipes he matched with Chasten Glezman, a substitute teacher in Chicago who was working on a master's at DePaul University, ninety-five miles away. They started FaceTiming, sitting alone with their beers, staring into their screens, almost a hundred miles apart.

One day, Chasten drove to South Bend to meet Pete for coffee. But he hit some traffic, so coffee turned into drinks, and it took forever for them to get to the bar because people kept coming up to Pete to say hello, and when they finally got there the bartender said, "Mayor, it's on the house," and turned to Chasten and said, "That will be eight dollars." Then drinks turned into dinner, and then Pete took out two baseball tickets he had bought, just in case things went well.

After the game, as they walked by the river, Pete felt Chasten touch his hand. Later, Pete would say it was the most thrilling moment of his life. Three years later, in 2018, they got married on Gay Pride weekend and livestreamed their wedding on YouTube. Six months after that, Pete was preparing to run for president.

THOUGHTS & PRAYERS

DECEMBER 14, 2012
NEWTOWN, CONNECTICUT

We are following some breaking news right now out of Newtown. State police have confirmed there is a shooting at a school in Newtown: Sandy Hook Elementary School. . . . Reports say the number of dead is closer to thirty than to twenty, and sadly, most of them are children. . . . "One of my students would say things like 'It's OK, I know karate, so I'll lead the way out.'" . . . "We got in a line and we had to close our eyes. We all put our hands on other people's shoulders." . . . **IN STATE WITH 'ASSAULT WEAPONS' BAN, LANZA'S RIFLE STILL LEGAL:** Adam Lanza blasted through the glass doors of the Sandy Hook Elementary School clutching a military-style Bushmaster rifle with 30 rounds in the clip and hundreds more at the ready. But under Connecticut's firearms laws, considered strong by national standards, the lethal weapon that Lanza employed was perfectly legal. . . . **'THESE TRAGEDIES MUST END,' OBAMA SAYS:** *"In the coming weeks I'll use whatever power this office holds"* in an effort *"aimed at preventing more tragedies like this."* . . . **@SpeakerBoehner:** Our thoughts and prayers are with the families and victims of the Sandy Hook elementary school tragedy #prayfornewtown . . . **@TedCruz:** Thoughts and prayers are with the victims and families of all those impacted by today's tragic shooting in Newtown, CT . . . **@SenJohnMcCain:** my thoughts and prayers—and those of all #Arizonians—are w/ the victims and families affected by today's senseless tragedy in #newtown . . . **OBAMA CALLS FOR ASSAULT WEAPONS BAN, BACKGROUND CHECKS:** President Obama unveiled the most sweeping set of gun-control proposals in two decades on Wednesday, a package that includes universal background checks on all gun buyers and a renewed ban on "military-style" assault weapons. . . . **@NRA:** Law-abiding gun owners will not accept blame for the acts of violent or deranged criminals! . . . **McCONNELL VOWS TO BLOCK GUN CONTROL MEASURES:** *"Know that I will be doing everything in my power as Senate Republican leader, fighting tooth and nail, to protect your Second Amendment rights."* . . . **SENATE BLOCKS DRIVE FOR GUN CONTROL:** President Obama called it a "shameful day for Washington." . . .

CHAPTER II

The Young Grand Old Party

Elise Stefanik could feel the young people sliding away from her party. In the months leading up to Obama's 2008 election, she was working in a small office in the Bush White House, doing a similar job to the one Eric Lesser would later do for Obama. She was working late in the West Wing on election night, and went home to watch the returns on TV. Everyone could see that the Obama campaign was electrifying young people in a way that hadn't happened for a generation. The problem for the GOP was that all of that enthusiasm was happening on the Democratic side.

But Elise wasn't ready for her party to give up on young people. So when it came time for Obama to run for reelection, she joined the 2012 Mitt Romney campaign, where she helped prepare Rep. Paul Ryan for his debates. Ryan, many conservatives thought, was poised to be the Republican JFK: a blue-eyed Boy Scout with a full head of hair who rolled up his sleeves and looked photogenic in front of whiteboards full of numbers. If anybody could reboot the Republican image with young people, it was Paul Ryan.

Everyone on the Romney campaign had been sure that the Obama fever would break, that Romney-Ryan would win, and that the country would return to old-fashioned free-market conservatism. Internal polls showed him winning Florida, Colorado, New Hampshire, and Virginia, and he was feeling good about Ohio. Romney spent Election Day shaking hands and thanking volunteers working a phone bank in Richmond, Ohio, then stopped for lunch at a Wendy's before heading back to his Boston HQ. He was so confident in his impending victory that he had written a 1,118-word victory speech but hadn't drafted a concession speech.

When he lost, Elise was devastated. Not only had Romney and Ryan failed to take the White House, but they had lost specifically because her party had fallen short with people like her: young unmarried professional women, who voted overwhelmingly for Obama. It was clear that Republicans were still relying on older, whiter, male voters—a rapidly expiring demographic—and that if they didn't change fast they might lose a whole generation of support. Elise genuinely loved her party, but it felt as if nothing was changing. The communication strategy in 2012 seemed unchanged from 1992, when she was a kid.

She wasn't the only one doing some soul-searching. The Republican National Committee published an "autopsy" analyzing what went wrong in the 2012 election and concluded that the GOP needed to be more inclusive and welcoming, and do better with Hispanic voters and women. One of their biggest problems, the report assessed, was young people: Obama beat Romney with voters under thirty by more than twenty points.

"The RNC must recognize that today's young voters will be voters for the next 50-plus years," the authors wrote. "For many of the youngest voters and new 2016 voters, their perception of the two parties was born during the Barack Obama era, and that perception will help determine their worldview moving forward." The Koch Brothers also saw the writing on the wall: they started Generation Opportunity, a well-funded but largely unsuccessful attempt to woo young voters to the GOP, which included creepy ads showing Uncle Sam playing gynecologist in a bid to urge young people to opt out of the ACA.

Four years later, that 2013 GOP report would read like a relic of a different era. Donald Trump won the 2016 election by running 180 degrees in the opposite direction: he demonized immigrants, insulted women, and ignored college campuses, and got elected anyway. But even though the autopsy failed to predict Trump's rise, it was right in the long term: the GOP had only a few years to attract the young voters it would need to build a sustainable majority. If Republicans wanted to cut into the Democrats' overwhelming youth advantage, they'd have to act fast.

It used to be that young people mostly voted like their parents and grandparents, influenced by the same social or economic factors as the rest of their family. But over the last two decades, an unprecedented political gulf has emerged between young and old, with more and more young people identifying as liberal or progressive and fewer calling themselves conservatives. That doesn't necessarily translate into more allegiance with the Democratic Party—millennials are generally skeptical of both political parties, and they're much more likely to call themselves Independents than older generations ever did. But even if they scoffed at the official party labels, they had clearly picked a side: by 2018, only 12 percent of millennials identified as consistently or mostly conservative; 57 percent said they were consistently or mostly liberal, and they voted for Democrats by roughly two to one.

The GOP didn't have much to offer millennials, and didn't seem to care. Republicans tended to do well with married people; millennials were marrying later than ever. Republicans were strong with evangelicals and other religious voters; millennials were widely rejecting organized religion. Republicans were more popular with white voters; millennials were the most racially diverse voting bloc in history. On nearly every predictor of social conservatism—marriage, religion, and race—young voters were headed one way and the GOP was headed another.

Beyond values, the GOP seemed hopelessly out of touch with most young people's policy priorities. Republicans plunged the United States into two disastrous foreign wars: millennials resisted military intervention abroad. Republicans opposed same-sex marriage: millennials overwhelmingly supported it. Republicans blocked environmental legislation and dabbled in climate change denial: most millennials acknowledge climate change as an existential threat. Young conservatives could be found on every college campus in every state, but they were quickly learning what it felt like to be a member of a minority group.

Conservative pollster Kristen Soltis Anderson, one of the nation's smartest interpreters of young Republican behavior, argues that the GOP's problem with young people dates back to the George W. Bush era. In her prescient 2015 book, *The Selfie Vote: Where Millennials Are Leading America (and How Republicans Can Keep Up)*, she wrote that after Bush's disastrous handling of Hurricane Katrina, Republicans won less than 40 percent of voters under thirty in the 2006 midterms—one of the worst turnouts for any age cohort in decades and the first sign of a growing generation gap. Two years later, in 2008, and then again in 2012, young people voted for Obama by two to one, a historic margin that Soltis Anderson writes "highlighted a generational political divide never before seen in modern American politics." After eight years of Obama—a cool, youthful president who played basketball and hung out with Beyoncé and understood the realities of climate change—most young people were voting for Democrats.

"The problem with the Grand Old Party was right in the name," she wrote. "It was *old*."

It's widely assumed that young people have always leaned liberal and grow more conservative as they age, raise families, and accumulate wealth. Winston Churchill supposedly once said, "If you're not a liberal at twenty, you have no heart; if you're not a conservative at forty, you have no brain."

This sounds right—but the data tell a different story. Life events like having kids or buying a home can lead to slight shifts in attitudes about property taxes or education policy, but overall political values are highly determined by what happens in the world during the first few years of political awareness. A landmark 1987 study by Keith R. Billingsley and Clyde Tucker found that, contrary to the conventional wisdom that people simply get more conservative as they age, "each generation seems to display its own political behavior as a result of experiences during early adulthood."

Nearly thirty years later, Columbia political scientist Andrew Gelman and data scientist Yair Ghitza built on this research in their 2014 study of longitudinal data on voter behavior. They found that while variables such as religion, geography, or parental political influence remain important, shared experiences between ages fourteen and twenty-four have a significant impact on lifelong political attitudes. "It's much more about cohort than age," Gelman told me. "One way of understanding these up and down trend lines over the decades is asking: What happened when people were young?" (It's worth noting that Gelman and Ghitza were studying data specifically on white voters, since longitudinal data on voters of color tended to be less reliable in the mid-twentieth century, when widespread discrimination prevented many black Americans from voting.)

Political attitudes, in other words, are formed in early adulthood, usually in response to whoever is currently in the White House. Popular presidents attract young people to their party; unpopular presidents repel them. And once young people pick a side, they usually stay there. For example, a Pew study of twenty-five thousand people after the 2012 election found that people who turned eighteen when Nixon was president tended to vote for Obama, while people who turned eighteen during the Reagan years tended to vote for Mitt Romney.

Gelman and Ghitza found that even people who were of roughly similar age could have radically different politics based on the political climate in their late adolescence and early adulthood. So if you were born in 1942 and came of age during the Eisenhower years, an era of relative peace and productivity under a Republican president, then, by 2012, you'd be seventy and leaning slightly Republican. If you were born just eight years later in 1950, you came of age during the Nixon scandals, so by 2012, you'd be sixty-two and leaning toward Democrats. That eight-year difference probably didn't mean much in terms of personal life: both seventy-year-olds and sixty-two-year-olds have likely become parents, bought property, built careers, and had other life experiences that might be expected to shift their politics to the right. The difference is that one cohort developed its political identity at a time of prosperity under a Republican president, while the other did so at a time of scandal.

Of course, demographics aren't destiny, and overconfident Democrats have been predicting for years that increasing racial diversity alone will obliterate the GOP's power. That won't happen, at least not right away. In every state and county, senior voter turnout dwarfs youth turnout by vast margins. And since the 2010 census, Republicans have routinely used gerrymandering (which Democrats have also used when they control state legislatures) and voter suppression techniques (such as elaborate voter ID laws) to stymie younger, nonwhite, urban voters and increase the power of older, whiter, rural ones. The dominance of white baby boomer Republicans in state legislatures means that even when younger people do vote, their power is often diluted. These strategies have helped the GOP hold on to power, even with a looming generational showdown on the horizon.

Still, none of this looks good for Republicans in the long term. The oldest millennials, born in 1981, turned eighteen in 1999, just after Bill Clinton's sex scandal, which may explain why Gelman and Ghitza found that people born in the early 1980s leaned slightly toward Republicans. But after that, the trend lines all point toward Democrats. Even if you were born just four years later, in 1984, you'd have turned eighteen around the time George W. Bush was leading the country into the Iraq War. If you were born four years after that, in 1988, then you probably cast your first-ever presidential vote for Barack Obama. If you were among the youngest millennials, born in 1996, you probably joined the vast majority of young people who voted against Donald Trump in their first presidential election.

✳ ✳ ✳

That meant someone like Elise was rarely in the majority. As an undergrad participating in Harvard's Institute of Politics, she was often on the defensive. She was a year ahead of Eric Lesser and two years behind Pete Buttigieg, and they would all run into each other at the IOP pizza parties and panel events. She and Pete didn't know each other well, but they had coffee once (campus gossips said it was a date, but Pete and Elise both say it was purely friendly.) Eric Lesser remembered that Elise's ideas at the IOP "were always getting challenged," in a way that actually made her more formidable. "For conservatives, especially on campuses like Harvard, their arguments become even stronger and sharper because they're constantly forced to be challenged in a way that I'm not sure progressives are," he said. "I think she's used to being in a room where she's got to be really on top of things." After graduation, she shot straight up the GOP ladder, first in the Bush White House on the Domestic Policy Council Staff and in the Chief of Staff's office, then the Romney campaign.

For Elise, Romney's loss was a make-or-break moment. She had read Sheryl Sandberg's *Lean In* and knew that women had to put themselves forward or risk getting left behind. "Either I was going to take a total step back and do something completely separate from politics, or I can try to be part of the solution," she told me years later. "And instead of complaining about our lack of ability to reach out to young women, I can try to do something about it."

So Elise moved to Willsboro, New York, where her family had vacationed when she was growing up, near where New York runs into Canada. She spent the summer of 2013 driving her F-150 truck around the rural upstate New York district—one of the largest on the East Coast—asking local Republican leaders for their blessing. The twenty-first district was enormous—it made up nearly 30 percent of New York State. Sometimes she would drive five hours just to meet with a handful of people. People there had voted for Bush, then twice for Obama, and they had been represented by a Democrat in Congress for years. The district included pockets of rural poverty where people—usually white, often older—struggled to buy a full tank of gas and felt ignored by the Democrats in Washington.

It seemed at first like a crazy idea. She was a twenty-nine-year-old who worked at her parents' plywood company: she had no way to raise the hundreds of thousands of dollars it would take to unseat a sitting Democrat. People did a double take when she introduced herself; sometimes she would be asked about her outfit, or why she wasn't married, or whether she was planning to have kids. But she remembered the advice her mentor Paul Ryan had given her and scores of others trying to cut it in a profession where anything you say can and will be used against you: "You have one mouth and two ears; use them in that ratio."

She started to rack up big endorsements: first Ryan, then Mitt Romney endorsed her in the primary. The incumbent Democrat retired, making it a race for an open seat. She was running a fairly typical Republican campaign, focusing on ending Obamacare, reforming the tax code, and creating jobs—but she was a young woman up against a self-funded millionaire who had already run twice for the seat. Republican donors flocked to her cause. She got funding from the Koch brothers and significant backing from the free-spending libertarian Paul Singer, and Karl Rove's American

Crossroads PAC spent $800,000 pummeling her primary opponent as a "perennial loser" on TV. She won the June primary, then zoomed into the 2014 general election on a wave of enthusiasm and national media. Party bigwigs including Speaker John Boehner and House Majority Leader Kevin McCarthy did events for her. Fox News talking heads began to tout her as a "fresh face" in the GOP.

She ended her closing statement in the debate with "I hope to bring new ideas, and a new generation of leadership with fresh energy and independent approaches." She won.

Elise delivered her acceptance speech wearing a blue jacket, a red manicure, and white pearls. At thirty, she was then the youngest woman ever elected to Congress. She said her victory would "add an additional crack to the glass ceiling for future generations of women." Then she thanked her opponents with a bipartisan generosity that would be hard to find just two years later. "No matter their party, our democratic process is strengthened by those individuals willing to put forth their ideas, and with the courage to put their name on the ballot," she said.

When Elise first arrived on Capitol Hill in 2015 she was sometimes mistaken for an intern or a spouse. Someone tried to give her a pager, and she said, "I don't need this pager—I have an iPhone." It was her first hint of just how outdated Congress would be.

But Elise figured things were looking up for young Republicans. The money was flowing, Obamamania was fading, and the GOP was angling to position itself as the party of the future. Elise was close with Paul Ryan, who had cachet in the caucus and was a natural pick for Speaker of the House when John Boehner dropped the gavel. The Tea Party Republicans who had helped the GOP take the House in 2010 were mostly middle-aged white guys, but the Republican caucus was still, on average, a few years younger than the Democrats, and they had term limits in leadership that allowed for more turnover within their ranks. Besides, Elise was happy to see that after the 2014 election, her party was becoming younger and more diverse, with newly elected young Republicans such as Haitian-American Mia Love from Utah (the first black woman Republican elected to Congress) and Carlos Curbelo from Florida, whose parents were Cuban exiles. Elise and Carlos became friends almost immediately: they were both young, moderate, forward-thinking, and a little out of place in a GOP that seemed full of old white men.

Carlos Curbelo (b. 1980) was slim and boyish, with a full head of black hair and a dimple on his chin. A young Latino dad from Florida who sought solutions on immigration, he was sometimes called the next Marco Rubio. He had a habit of talking very slowly and clearly, as if to a person who can't hear well: as the only child of aging Cuban exiles, Carlos had grown up surrounded by old ladies. He spent his after-school hours shuttling between his grandmothers and their sisters, watching telenovelas and listening to Cuban radio while he ate his after-school snack of rice and bistec de palomilla. His mother's relatives would tell him about the Cuban Revolution, about how things were bad politically under Batista but under the Communists things were worse. After the revolution, they told him, they lost their basic rights and freedoms, and people were being executed for their political beliefs. Carlos's grandfather on his father's side had been a political prisoner for twelve years—he had been accused of being a "dangerous person" because he had been a career military officer before the Revolution. Carlos's father explained to him that Americans weren't like that. American politics, he said, wasn't about violence or imprisonment or locking up your political opponents. America, he explained, was about a contest of ideas.

Elise and Carlos were similarly moderate on social issues like marriage equality and immigration, but fiscally conservative, and they both wanted to move the party toward millennial sensibilities. They cosponsored a bill that would increase flexibility for federal student aid and allow students to get year-round Pell Grants (it failed initially but was later passed in an appropriations bill). Carlos worked with the Obama White House to help get accreditation for nontraditional higher education programs, such as coding boot camps. Whenever the old guard of the GOP would say something ridiculous in a meeting, Elise and Carlos would look at each other and smile. Carlos says they'd sometimes go on double dates, and he and his wife would give Elise and her boyfriend advice about marriage (when they finally tied the knot in 2017, Carlos was there). Sometimes Carlos would tease Elise because whenever he'd text her to come out for drinks, she'd usually reply that she was already in bed with a book.

Elise routinely criticized Obama's "failed policies," but there was one big area where she and Carlos and their fellow young Republicans diverged from their older GOP colleagues and aligned more closely with Democrats: climate change.

* * *

Millennial concerns about climate change transcended party loyalty. Almost everyone under forty agrees that the planet is changing and humans have to act to fix it—they differ only on how best to do it.

Young Republicans are much more concerned than older Republicans about the environment. According to a 2018 Pew study, millennial Republicans are twice as likely as boomer Republicans to understand that the Earth is warming mostly due to human activity. Roughly 60 percent of millennial Republicans think the government is doing too little to protect animal habitats and water quality, and half say the government is doing too little to reduce the effects of climate change. (Less than a third of boomer Republicans agree.) Vast majorities of young Republicans favor expanding the use of wind and solar energy, and they're much less likely than older Republicans to support expanding coal mining and oil and gas drilling. Unlike older generations, who had the luxury of debating the science or ignoring problems that seemed far in the future, most millennials of both parties grew up knowing that some of the worst effects of climate change would happen within their lifetimes. By the time they were adults, the science was unanimous, and the forest fires, floods, and hurricanes had already begun. Their parents and grandparents could afford to put the problem on the back burner; millennials couldn't. Carlos believed that sea-level rise was an "existential threat." The Florida Keys—which some scientists predicted would be largely underwater in thirty years—were in his district.

So when Elise got to Congress, she and her fellow young Republicans were some of the loudest voices advocating for conservative solutions to climate change. Carlos cofounded the Climate Solutions Caucus in early 2016, a bipartisan group created to push for real progress on climate change, and Elise was an enthusiastic early member. Over the next three years, nearly every Republican under the age of forty-five was in the caucus, no matter how conservative: members included conservative stalwarts such as Utah's Mia Love, Wisconsin's Mike Gallagher, Florida's Brian Mast and Matt Gaetz, Illinois's Adam Kinzinger, and New York's Lee Zeldin. "If you look at the sort of members in the Republican caucus who have been willing to vote to just say basic things like 'Climate change is happening, it's a national security threat,' it tends to be the younger members," said Rep. Mike Gallagher, himself a millennial.

Elise introduced a House resolution in 2017 to commit to addressing climate change, saying that it was "a conservative principle to protect, conserve, and be good stewards of our environment," and concluding that "if left unaddressed, the consequences of a changing climate have the potential to adversely impact all Americans." She was joined by Carlos and several of the other younger Republicans in the Climate Solutions Caucus, including Rep. Mia Love and Rep. Brian Mast. The resolution was more of an aspirational gesture than a piece of legislation—it was a generalized commitment to doing something—but it was one of the first public acknowledgements of climate change to come from congressional Republicans in almost a decade. (Representative Chris Gibson had introduced a resolution recognizing human impact on climate change in 2015, which Elise and Carlos also supported.) Later, Elise and Carlos would be two of the loudest Republican critics of Trump's decision to withdraw from the Paris Agreement on climate change.

Of course, the Climate Solutions Caucus didn't actually . . . do anything. Carlos points out that Climate Solutions Caucus members helped block some anticlimate amendments in a defense budget. But zero significant pieces of legislation came out of the caucus, and worse, it gave members political cover to vote for fossil-fuel-friendly bills such as the Keystone XL pipeline (which both Carlos and Elise supported.) Hardcore environmentalists saw gestures like the Climate Solutions Caucus and Elise's resolution as empty handwaving to excuse inaction: they were dismissed as "climate peacocks," who produced press releases and not much else.

But compared to the rest of the party, the young moderates in the Climate

Solutions Caucus might as well have been dreadlocked tree huggers. The GOP was still firmly the party of climate change deniers, and boomer Republicans either didn't believe the science or didn't want to. It didn't help that many were accepting massive donations from fossil fuel companies or else afraid of a primary challenger who would. The year the Climate Solutions Caucus was founded, 53 percent of House Republicans and 70 percent of Senate Republicans denied or questioned the science behind climate change. Ten of the eleven Republicans on the Senate's Environment and Public Works Committee (chaired by top climate change denier Sen. James Inhofe, b. 1934) had said that climate change was not happening or humans hadn't caused it. Inhofe, who represents oil-and-gas-friendly Oklahoma, himself had taken almost $2 million in campaign contributions from the oil and gas industry and wrote a climate change denial book called *The Greatest Hoax*. In 2015, the eighty-year-old senator brought a snowball onto the Senate floor to stick it to the "eggheads."

So even if the Climate Solutions Caucus and Elise's climate resolution didn't do much, at least they established that young Republicans actually understood the science. This was one issue, they thought, where they could build common ground with the next generation of Democrats.

Climate was the biggest area of overlap—but actually there were many areas where young Republicans like Elise and Carlos seemed to agree more with their peers than with their party.

On most social issues—with the significant exception of abortion—young Republicans tilt to the left of their party. Pew found that more than 60 percent of young Republicans favor allowing people in same-sex relationships to marry, compared to less than a quarter of Republicans who were senior citizens. In the years since the Supreme Court affirmed same-sex couples' right to marry, most young conservatives have given up on the issue. The Republican leaders who continued to try to curb LGBTQ rights were from older generations, while younger Republicans simply ignored gay marriage or even supported it. By 2014, nearly half of millennial evangelicals said they supported same-sex marriage.

On marijuana and immigration, too, younger Republicans are signifi-cantly more liberal than older ones. According to Pew, almost two-thirds of millennial Republicans favored marijuana legalization, compared to just 38 percent of boomer Republicans. And 58 percent of millennial Republicans say immigrants strengthen the country, compared to about a third of Gen X Republicans and much smaller shares of older generations. (Carlos, in a Hail Mary, sponsored his own version of the DREAM Act, shielding young un-documented immigrants from deportation. It failed.)

A Pew study from 2014 laid out this mind-set pretty well. Of the young voters who leaned conservative, most fell into a category Pew described as "Young Outsiders." They had a higher opinion of Obama than traditional Republicans, even if they disliked both parties. They tended to agree with traditional Republicans that the government was wasteful and inefficient and that the state couldn't afford to do much to help the needy, but they were more likely than other Republicans to say that environmental regulations are worth the cost, that homosexuality should be accepted and that mari-juana should be legal. According to Pew, the "Young Outsiders" significantly outnumbered young conservatives with typically right-wing views. That study came out the same year Elise was elected to Congress.

In other words, young moderate conservatives were shaping up to have a strong libertarian streak. They were done fighting the religious right's cul-ture war over family values, and they didn't see why the government should have a role in deciding who could get married or who could smoke weed. "This is a live-and-let-live generation," Carlos said. "We don't seek to impose our moral codes on others. We encourage people to take responsibility for their own actions, and whatever it is they like to do and enjoy, go ahead and do it as long as it doesn't infringe upon the rights of anyone else."

So young Republicans like Elise and Carlos were walking a tightrope between their generational attitudes and the values of the GOP. And in a period of massive Republican obstructionism against Barack Obama, the millennial GOP members of Congress seemed at first just a little less obstruc-tionist than their older colleagues. Despite a few loud Gen Xers, most of the Tea Party member of Congress elected in the Obama years were in their late fifties, and they went straight to work channeling the grievances of their white boomer base, which meant blocking Obama at every possible move.

Elise and Carlos and their cohort, by contrast, tended to avoid the brink-manship of their older colleagues. One of the first bills Elise ever sponsored repealed a badly enforced Obamacare requirement that employers automat-ically enroll new employees into their company's health care plan—Obama signed it into law as part of a budget agreement in 2015. "Older elected offi-cials have basically aged during so much gridlock and partisan fighting," Elise said. "I just think my generation doesn't want to see the extreme parti-sanship. We want to see a government that is effective and accountable."

In their first term in Congress, Elise and Carlos were both ranked in the top fifty most bipartisan members of Congress, according to a nonpartisan index out of Georgetown University, along with a handful of other young Republicans. By their second term, they were both in the top twenty. They had big plans: "We wanted to solve immigration, we wanted to address stu-dent debt, we wanted to reduce fiscal debt, we wanted to address climate change in a serious and thoughtful way," Carlos said. "A lot of us were hope-ful we would get a president like Jeb Bush or Marco Rubio who could help us achieve all those things."

The future of the GOP, many thought, would be full of young Republi-cans like Elise and Carlos. They would work with Democrats to enact free-market solutions to environmental problems. They would solve immigration and fix student debt. They would calmly explain their economic policy in well-reasoned Facebook posts, and all the comments would be respectful and productive. Their Republican Party would be tech-friendly and data-driven, tolerant and welcoming, generous yet responsible. Marco Rubio or Jeb Bush would win the White House back from the Democrats; women would embrace a conservative version of feminism; Latinos would realize that the GOP was their natural home; young people would see Republicans were actually cool, after all.

For the young moderates of the GOP, things were looking up.

PART THREE

★ ★ ★

It's time for us to come home.

—ALEXANDRIA OCASIO-CORTEZ

CHAPTER 12

House of Glass, 2016

By 2016, Alexandria Ocasio-Cortez's life was defined by a few key numbers. She was almost five years out of college, with about $25,000 of debt and an Affordable Care Act health care plan with a $7,000 deductible. She had moved to the Bronx to start a project to close the literacy gap, and ended up commuting to Manhattan to work at a Union Square bar and restaurant called The Coffee Shop to pay the bills. If there was a big event in Union Square, she could clear $400 in tips, but on a normal day it was about $200 for a nine-hour shift, and other days were so empty that she barely cracked $60.

Her best friend at work was Maria Swisher, a tall redhead from Missouri who was trying to make it in experimental theater. Maria had a sense of serenity that came from years of doing trust exercises in black box theaters, and they became friends immediately. At the start of every nine-hour shift, they'd come in and get the cash drawer and count the money, and then the coffee guys would sneakily make them espresso, and then people would start coming in. They had some odd regulars: one guy who had written an incomprehensible book that he gave to the whole staff, a CEO who liked to debate them about libertarianism, an older Irish man who gave them wine from a vineyard he owned.

But between her rent and her student debt and her health insurance premiums, the money she made in tips wasn't making ends meet. So when Bernie Sanders started making speeches in 2015 about a living wage, Medicare for All, and free college, Alexandria was an instant convert. She volunteered at Bernie's Bronx field office in between her shifts at work, organizing routes for canvassers and managing people who were knocking doors. She had done grassroots organizing before, but it had always been for a cause, never for an election. This was the first time she had ever put in the work for a candidate, because this was the first time a candidate had ever talked about systemic inequality in a way that made sense in her life. For millennials like her, the Sanders campaign created a framework for understanding their financial plight, a way to think of their problems as systemic failings rather than individual struggles.

It was a movement that was spreading fast among young people across the country. After years of Obama's tacit cease-fire with Wall Street, Bernie's attacks on corporate America felt like a breath of fresh air. They liked that he didn't take money from big corporations, that he promised free college and universal health care, and that he didn't sound as if he had been cooked up in a lab by a team of marketing consultants. Hillary seemed too scripted, as though she was trying to say what she thought people wanted to hear—and besides, she did take money from corporations, big PACs, and super-rich donors. To many young people, Hillary felt like the candidate of their parents' generation: she represented a brand of compromise and moderation that they thought soothed the comfortably wealthy but failed to deliver real economic results. She was solidly part of the establishment—and after Occupy and Black Lives Matter, it was clear that many young people thought the establishment had failed.

So Bernie crushed Hillary Clinton by seventy points among young voters in Iowa. In New Hampshire, Bernie won 83 percent of voters under thirty and 78 percent of first-time voters. By April 2016, Bernie had a net favorability of nearly forty points with voters between eighteen and twenty-four, while Hillary Clinton was underwater by more than twenty points. Even at Hillary Clinton's alma mater, the all-women Wellesley College, the college kids were feeling the Bern. He was the most popular politician in America among the under-thirty set. By March, Bernie Sanders had won more young voters than Trump and Clinton combined.

In April, shortly before the New York primary, Alexandria and Maria waited in lines snaking around the block to get into a Bernie Sanders rally in Washington Square Park. People were packed into the park, overflowing onto the streets, and a whiff of marijuana hung in the air. The mood was electrifying. Maria remembers it as one of the first moments when she thought something like a progressive revolution could really happen, and she and Alexandria worked even harder for Bernie than they had before. But soon, progressives hit a wall: New York had strict and inconvenient voting laws in 2016, and Independents who wanted to vote in the Democratic primary had to have switched their registration more than six months earlier, which meant a substantial part of Bernie's base wasn't eligible to vote for him.

Hillary Clinton ended up winning the New York primary, and then the nomination. As the general election wore on, Alexandria and Maria were torn. Neither of them were excited about Hillary, Maria remembers, and both were anxious about whether she could win. Maria in particular was worried about Hillary's unpopularity in her home state of Missouri: she told Alexandria, "I don't know if New Yorkers know how likely it is that she might not get elected." When business was slow, they stood behind the bar and debated whether it was ethical to vote third party. Ultimately, Maria said, they both decided that they were privileged to be able to vote at all, and that going third party would be throwing away their votes. "The people who washed the dishes in the back of the restaurant needed Hillary to win," Maria told me later. "So we better suck it up."

✳ ✳ ✳

Something didn't feel right. It was a few days before the election, and Hillary was supposed to be crushing Trump. Many pundits said it would be an easy win, and almost all the polls had her ahead. But Haley Stevens had spent the last week of the campaign knocking on doors for Hillary in Ohio and the mood felt off. Voters seemed a little muted, a little reluctant. She would get people at their doors who twisted their mouths when she asked if she could count on their support. Maybe Hillary was the lesser of two evils, people would say. There was just something they didn't like about her.

Haley wasn't on staff for Hillary this time, but she had volunteered in the last few weeks to help out her old colleagues. And if Hillary did win, Haley wanted to be at her New York victory party on election night. So she got a cheap flight on Southwest Airlines and when she landed for the layover in St. Louis, her computer was dead and her charger was fried and she couldn't do anything but sit in the airport Chili's and wait for her connecting flight. Chili's was playing the football game. She said, "Guys, it's Election Day—can we turn on CNN?" The guys at the bar shrugged and kept the game on. Another bad sign.

Election Day was gorgeous, crisp and clear, and the line outside the Javits Center stretched for more than ten blocks down the west side of Manhattan. It was full of women wearing pantsuits, or dressed as suffragettes, or waving American flags with their young daughters. Haley began to feel a little better. Groups of girlfriends had gathered to celebrate the last few hours of the patriarchy. In hours, they thought, a woman would finally be elected president of the United States.

The Javits Center, the largest event space in Manhattan, glittered like an enormous prism. It was decked out in wall-to-wall Americana for the tentatively scheduled historic programming. The ceiling was made of glass, which would have made for lovely symbolism had Hillary Clinton won. Nobody mentioned that the glass ceiling was reinforced with steel beams.

✽ ✽ ✽

Elise Stefanik knew exactly what was going to happen. Her upstate New York district was peppered with Trump signs, most of them handmade. She spent September and October crisscrossing her district campaigning for reelection, and saw only two Hillary Clinton signs the whole time.

She couldn't understand why the media was pretending that Hillary Clinton's win was inevitable. All you had to do was look outside the window in St. Lawrence County to see which way the wind was blowing.

Elise wasn't Trump's biggest booster. Throughout the primary, she vowed to support the eventual Republican nominee, but she never got too vocal about Trump in particular. Sure, she toed the party line like any good freshman House Republican was expected to do, but she developed an approach that amounted to ignoring the elephant in the room: she did the bare minimum to support him and also the bare minimum to condemn him. After Trump attacked the Khan family, whose son was killed in Iraq, she said, "There is no excuse to be attacking Gold Star families." After the *Access Hollywood* tape came out, Elise said that Trump's "inappropriate, offensive comments are just wrong, no matter when he said them or whatever the context." She criticized his foreign policy, saying that she opposed "his statements regarding NATO, his statements regarding Putin." But, she added, "we also need to look at Hillary Clinton's failed ethics record." Besides, it wasn't as if Republicans had a monopoly on sexism: one union leader who supported Elise's Democratic opponent had taken to calling her "Elsie the cow."

Her friend Carlos Curbelo was far more outspoken. He said he wouldn't vote for Trump, no matter what. "That is not a political decision," he told a local TV station. "That is a moral decision." In the end, he voted third party, and he wasn't alone: many young conservatives who had supported Romney in 2012 couldn't bring themselves to support Trump. One study found that a third of voters under forty who supported Romney in 2012 either stayed home, voted for Clinton, or voted third party.

But Elise couldn't go that far. Because no matter how much she disagreed with Trump on decency, or respect for women, or foreign policy, she couldn't cast a vote for Hillary Clinton. She couldn't even consider doing it. It was never going to happen.

Many Democrats assumed that women like Elise—well-educated feminist conservatives who were appalled by sexual assault—would pick Clinton over Trump after the *Access Hollywood* tape was released. This assumption vastly underestimated just how deeply many conservatives loathed Hillary Clinton, not just for her politics, but for her connection to Bill Clinton, whom many Republicans considered to be a corrupt pervert who tarnished the Oval Office. Whether this judgment was fair or not was beside the point: it was visceral and immutable, and nothing would change their minds. To understand the depth of this loathing, it helps to turn the tables: Imagine, for a moment, that after the Trump presidency, Ivanka Trump served as a senator, then as secretary of the Treasury, and then ran to be the first woman president in 2036. Would Democratic women vote for her? Absolutely not.

Still, the election put Elise in a tough position. She had made a point of advocating for more women in political office: now a woman was running for president and she wasn't supporting her. Whenever she was asked about it, she had a careful dodge. When a *Washington Post* reporter wondered what a Clinton win would mean for women, Elise was curt: "I think the more women we have running for office the better," she said. "I'm supporting the Republican nominee."

✳ ✳ ✳

Leah Greenberg and Ezra Levin had been married almost two years and had already written all the thank-you notes for wedding gifts they were ever going to write.

They had spent the days before the election persuading about fifteen friends to go from DC to Philadelphia to knock on doors for Clinton, and on election night they had their friends over to watch the returns on a big projector in their living room. They lived in a small cream-colored row house in Columbia Heights, with a white picket fence and a Black Lives Matter sign in the window. Leah had kept an extra "I Voted" sticker as a memento of the time she voted for the first woman president. The screen was projected onto the wall near the framed front page of *The Washington Post* from the day the Affordable Care Act was passed, which also happened to be the day Leah and Ezra started dating. They had flirted for months as young congressional staffers—Leah worked for Rep. Tom Perriello of Virginia, Ezra worked for Rep. Lloyd Doggett of Texas—as they helped their bosses work to pass health care reform and handled the onslaught of Tea Party rage. But it wasn't until the ACA cleared the House that they could admit that this little flirtation might actually be "a thing."

Overall, the mood was good. They served leftover Halloween candy and popped the champagne early. Some people were worried Democrats wouldn't take the Senate, but everybody was sure they were celebrating a presidential win. They were all young DC creatures who knew how to read exit polls, who texted with strategists, who followed the right reporters on Twitter. Nobody said so, but they all knew that at least their short-term professional ambitions depended—to one degree or another—on the outcome of this election.

No one fretted. The snacks were tasty and the booze was good.

✴ ✴ ✴

Svante was on Team Hillary, even though Ithaca was Bernie-land. He canvassed for her in Pennsylvania and Connecticut and upstate New York. He defended her to crunchy progressives who thought she was too moderate. He defended her to rural farmers who thought she was too Washington. He defended her so often and so loudly that he sometimes forgot to ask himself why he was having to defend her so much in the first place.

Svante genuinely liked Hillary. When she ran for New York Senate in 2000 and visited Earlville, he saw her speak and thought she was just another white lady making big promises. But then she came back and gave them an update on the things she had promised. And she came back again. New Yorkers learned to trust and respect her. She was reelected in a landslide in 2006.

Sure, people seemed a little reluctant, even in a state she represented in the Senate, but Svante thought that was probably just post-Obama grumps. He was so positive that she would win that he drove four hours down to the city for election night and headed to the Javits Center.

The first person he saw was his old friend Andrew Gillum. He knew Andrew from the Young Elected Officials Network—Andrew ran it and Svante would soon be running it. In four months, Andrew—not yet forty—would launch a closely watched race for governor of Florida, but that night he was still mayor of Tallahassee. Andrew said he was nervous. He didn't like the feeling in Florida. They went to get drinks, but the bar was so packed with people that you could barely move, and they saw DeRay Mckesson there, one of the most visible activists in Black Lives Matter. DeRay was nervous too.

Svante remembered that when he had been canvassing for Hillary in a black barbershop in Harrisburg, Pennsylvania, one of the barbers had said, "But what about her emails?" That wasn't a good question to hear from a black barber. Andrew said that in Florida he was seeing people who had never voted before getting ready to vote, and they were mostly Trumpy people.

But no, Svante thought. This was hers! America was the greatest country in the world, a country where Barack Hussein Obama could be elected president, a country where twenty-six-year-old Svante Myrick could be elected mayor of Ithaca, New York. Svante believed in Americans, and he knew that Americans would do the right thing and elect the woman who worked harder than anyone in politics. Not only that, Svante had decided long ago that Republicans would never win another presidential election. They were too racist, and the country was too diverse, he thought. They could have won in 2012, but they blew it. Their time was done.

The night was inching onward, it was getting dark outside, the Empire State Building was lit up red, white, and blue. Big screens around the hall were playing CNN, where pundits were saying, "Let's wait and see," in a thousand variations.

CNN analysts poked at maps on screens that turned states red or blue according to various "projections." Andrew and DeRay were getting jittery. They were in the bowels of the Javits Center, the area reserved for family and friends, and the mood had soured. Ohio was taking too long to come in, and there was a sudden chill in the area. The latest exit polls had Ohio leaning toward Trump, 51–44. "Don't worry!" Svante told them, clapping them on the back. Everyone was being such a downer! On the greatest night in American politics!

A staffer they knew walked by, and she didn't look happy. Andrew stopped her. "How's it going?" he asked.

"I don't know," she said, but it sounded like she knew.

"Svante is very confident," Andrew said. "He thinks we're gonna be fine."

"Unless you know something we don't know, it's not going to be fine," she said, and disappeared.

Svante didn't believe her. "What a negative Nancy!" he told Andrew and DeRay. "A gloomy Gus!" They didn't laugh.

✳ ✳ ✳

Around 9:00 p.m. at Leah and Ezra's, the champagne was almost gone and the party was divided between people who were getting their information from TV and people who were getting their information from Twitter, and the Twitter people looked worried.

Suddenly it occurred to Leah that she had thought it would be over by now. Everyone around her was still laughing and toasting, but Leah was about a half an hour ahead of them, realizing that Hillary was not winning the way she should have been, the way all the people who "knew" about politics said she would.

Leah and Ezra were believers. They worked the system and revered their mentors: they even asked Rep. Tom Perriello to officiate their wedding. But over the next three hours, something about their understanding of the world began to crumble. That morning, they had woken up in an orderly nation, managed by informed adults who were in charge. That night, they went to sleep deeply skeptical about the wisdom of those supposedly responsible adults. Even if the grownups had been in charge, it was clear they had failed.

The minutes started moving more slowly. Most of the states that CNN had colored yellow for "too close to call" one by one began to turn red.

* * *

Dan Crenshaw didn't think Trump could win. By then he was out of the military, studying to get his master's of public administration from Harvard's Kennedy School of Government. In the military, he had been surrounded by guys who were mostly conservative: here, almost everyone was liberal or progressive.

Whenever he would reveal he was conservative, there would be a ripple in the conversation. People would stammer, their faces would tighten up just a little, and then they'd swallow and smile to prove that they still liked him even though he was clearly a bad person. After a few months, Dan began to think it was funny to watch people's faces change as they rearranged their features into what they thought was a pleasant demonstration of magnanimous tolerance. There would always be a barrier with these people, he thought. "I saw what the elite future of the Democratic Party really thought of conservatives," he told me later.

Dan took mostly classes in economics or national security, where there wasn't a lot of room for "obvious bias." He knew other conservatives who took classes on morals or ethics and were pulling their hair out. But even in the more numbers-based classes, he saw how clueless liberals were about conservative principles. One left-leaning economist had described a carbon dividend policy to him, explaining that it was "great for conservatives" because it didn't add to government revenue. Dan was shocked. "You think that's what I care about?" he remembers saying. "What I care about is the government is taking my money, creating a whole new bureaucracy to figure out how to redistribute it, and then picking winners and losers." Harvard taught him that conservatives knew how liberals thought, but that liberals had no idea how conservatives thought.

Dan hadn't been a Trump guy in the primaries: he'd wanted a candidate with a mixture of Marco Rubio's charisma, Ted Cruz's conservative principles, Jeb Bush's executive experience. But he was living in California then, and by the time the primary came around, Trump had already sewn up the nomination. Dan wasn't staunchly anti-Trump: he liked some of what Trump said, and not other things. He had once called Trump's proposed Muslim ban "insane" and "hateful" on Facebook. But he despised never-Trump Republicans—he thought they just wanted to get attention and approval from the left. Dan thought of himself as trying to call balls and strikes: celebrate what was good about their nominee, and criticize what was bad.

He spent election night with a group of classmates at John Harvard's Ale House in Harvard Square, watching the election returns on the big TVs that normally played Patriots games. Dan thought Trump had a better shot than his classmates did, but he had resigned himself to Hillary winning the election. He wasn't happy with the idea of a Clinton presidency, but figured it was a done deal.

As the returns came in on the big TVs in the brick-lined basement of John Harvard's, everyone around Dan started to freak out. Dan described it as a "sky is falling" moment: people started talking about the economy collapsing and minorities being rounded up off the street. Democrats at other tables were crying.

At first, Dan was surprised by the results, and then the surprise turned into amusement. It wasn't that he necessarily loved Trump or thought he would be such a spectacular president. But people around him were in hysterics, a ridiculous overreaction. And there was a part of him that enjoyed watching those smug Harvard faces melt into panic. The faces of the same people who had been so satisfied with themselves around him, so *tolerant* of a *real conservative* in their midst, suddenly stripped of their careful masks and reduced to true horror. "You guys have been bashing us for so long," Dan thought. "And look what happened." He began to smile.

✳ ✳ ✳

As the night wore on, Haley went into a kind of "fortitudinal denial," she called it later. By 9:30 p.m., people on the floor of the Javits Center were crying. Haley turned to her friends and said, "No crying." They were standing right next to the stage. "It's fine," she told them. "We just have to stay the course." All around them, people were whispering into cell phones and leaning on each other's shoulders. It felt like that part of *Titanic* when the boat slowly tilts vertically into the air but hasn't split in half yet. At a certain point, Haley turned to her friend. "If she doesn't win," she said, "I'm gonna run."

The building was freezing, the bone-deep chill of a poorly heated glass building in early November. Svante had given up trying to cheer anybody up. There wasn't much to do anyway except wait, and they waited for hours. Ohio turned red, then North Carolina, then Florida. It was getting late, past midnight, and the CNN talking heads were just stringing words together at that point. Somebody turned off the news on the Jumbotrons in the Javits Center, so that the people in the main hall wouldn't freak out. They started playing Hillary ads instead. There was a buzz in the air of people trying to convince each other of the "narrow path to victory."

The networks called Pennsylvania for Trump at 1:35 a.m.

Suddenly, Svante's vision narrowed. It was like one of those Spike Lee movies where they put a camera on a track and the actor zooms along and everyone else is a blur. He had a sense that he was floating through a crowd of people. Just two weeks earlier, they had been talking about the "midwestern firewall"; they even suspected Hillary could win Arizona or Georgia. Now Utah, Ohio, Pennsylvania, Florida—all gone.

A half hour later, John Podesta came out and said that they were still counting the votes, which is what you say when you haven't counted enough votes to win yet. He said that Hillary wouldn't be speaking tonight, which is what you say when you've got a concession call to make.

Meanwhile, Elise had won her reelection campaign early in the night. She was calm and collected, just like she always was, her hair curled into Kate Middleton waves as she gave interviews to local news stations about continuing to advocate for small businesses and veterans. "I will work with whoever the next president is," she told NBC 5. "I'm willing to work with anyone, regardless of their party affiliation, as long as they have good ideas and a willingness to bring them to the table." Trump ended up winning her district by thirteen points—she had won by forty-five.

Back in Leah and Ezra's living room, the crowd was sad drunk. When people got their coats and tried to leave, Leah begged them to stay. If the house emptied out and they dumped out the snack bowls and collected beer cans and turned off the projector, then that would mean that the night was over and this had happened. If people stayed, maybe there would be a miracle. Everyone left.

✳ ✳ ✳

The next morning, Haley and Svante and Leah and Ezra woke up in a new country. It was slowly becoming clear what had happened: white voters— especially older white voters—had overwhelmingly voted for Trump. White working-class voters in the Rust Belt had demolished Hillary's so-called midwestern firewall, and despite Hillary's feminist messaging and Trump's grabby hands, even white women had broken slightly for Trump. Trump won with majorities of voters over forty-five, who vote in high numbers. Hillary won voters younger than forty-five by double digits, but the turnout among them was not nearly as heavy, and concentrated in all the wrong places. Hillary ended up winning the popular vote by nearly three million votes but fell well short in the Electoral College.

The nation would spend the next six months debating why Trump won, and all the explanations were partially right. He had ridden a surge of white grievance that he'd helped stoke during Obama's presidency. Hillary had put resources into Arizona and didn't visit Wisconsin. Too many people voted third party in Michigan, and too many young Bernie types sat out the general election. The white working class felt that Trump stood up for them. Hillary's baggage was too heavy and her gender too unsettling. The media didn't know how to cover a presidential candidate with so little regard for the truth. Russians used social media to meddle in American democracy. The hundreds of stories about emails were confusing but they stuck to Hillary. People were sick of the Clintons and ready for a change. All of it mattered.

Another explanation: the country was changing too much, too fast, and many older white people longed for simpler times when, in their sepia-toned imaginations, America had been "great." Globalism had diluted the sense of national identity that they remembered from the twentieth century. It was the same thing that happened during Brexit five months earlier: seniors had voted for the United Kingdom to leave the European Union, while younger people overwhelmingly voted to remain. Trump, like Brexit, was part of a backlash against a globalism that many young people had already embraced.

That popularity with older white voters was enough to help Trump win the election. Later, when the analytics geeks dove into the numbers, the age breakdown became clearer. Young voters between eighteen and twenty-nine were the only group that increased turnout since 2012 (by just over one point), but they still didn't match the turnout rate of their parents and grandparents: roughly 46 percent of eligible voters under thirty cast a ballot in 2016, compared to more than 70 percent of eligible voters over sixty-five. Clinton won solid majorities of young voters, including most young people of color and young unmarried women, but roughly a third of young people voted for Trump, and those who did tended to resemble Trump's base overall: they were mostly white and male.

The early punditry described Trump's victory as the result of an anti-elitist backlash from the working class. Alexandria was one of many people who took to Facebook to publish long, anguished posts trying to describe what had happened. Her take was that Trump—like Sanders—had tapped into a deep populist rage at elites. "Like it or not, you will have to listen to the clear message working Americans sent last night," she wrote. "If you truly love others, you will go beyond the fight against racism—for that is an effort to change a man's attitude. By fighting for economic justice, you seek to change his life. That is the path forward."

The next few days confirmed Dan's suspicions that the supposedly smartest economists and political thinkers in the country didn't understand conservatives at all. Larry Summers, former Treasury secretary and former president of Harvard, gave a lecture predicting that the economy would soon tank (in fact, the stock market soared over the first two years of Trump's presidency). Another economist, Doug Elmendorf, dean of Harvard's Kennedy School of Government, sent out a school-wide email announcing a "community gathering" for people "experiencing strong emotions regarding the election."

Dan saw this campus-wide despair as evidence that his left-wing teachers and classmates were just as biased as he had suspected. He'd assumed an elite institution was supposed to be about actual analysis, asking, "What's the difference between the left and the right?" Instead, he thought, everyone around him was coming from an assumption that Trump was a threat to democracy, and nothing could change their minds. "They operate out of a premise and they don't question that premise: it's not debatable," he said. Every question, he thought, came from a place of bias: "Given that everyone on the right is bad, what do we do about it?" The cultural clash was beginning to feel like a war, and if there was one thing Dan was good at, it was war.

After everything that happened, Haley had to go back to Columbus to get her car, which meant she had to fly back through St. Louis and visit that same damn Chili's on another four-hour layover. This time, she didn't have to ask anyone to put the news on, because it was all about President-elect Trump. She sat next to a guy from Colorado. "I didn't even vote," he told her, and shrugged.

When she finally got home, she started making phone calls and looking at precinct data. She had already decided that she would run for Congress.

✳ ✳ ✳

The morning after the election, Ezra wrote an email to about twenty-five people, and the first word was "Fuck."

"We need some organization or plan in place when Trump begins collecting the SSNs of Muslims, or starts targeting kids that applied for DACA, or decides to use executive branch tools to undermine the press," he wrote. "And we need to think about what it means to fight for a Democratic Party that doesn't fail us."

About twenty people showed up at their house that Saturday to talk. Versions of this meeting were happening all over the country—people reaching out to their friends and neighbors to figure out what to do next. But in Leah and Ezra's living room, the mood was particularly grim. The people in their circle weren't alienated outsiders; they believed in the establishment (even if they didn't call it that) and had worked for institutions—Congress, federal agencies, liberal think tanks—that viewed government as a force for good in American life. Obama had forged a diverse coalition that over an eight-year period had built a new political paradigm for the country; that edifice had suddenly collapsed. "There was a sense that there were adults in charge," Ezra recalls. "And what became clear that night was that there weren't any adults in charge, and the structures that should have been in place to prevent this disaster just weren't there."

After that first meeting, Leah and Ezra dove into the online frenzy of resistance organizing. They joined Facebook groups and Google Hangouts and email chains. People were sending around Google Docs with advice on everything from hiding from government surveillance to aiding Muslims to fighting fascism. Across the country, unable to sleep, idealistic Americans— many of them young—were staying up late into the night writing feverish Facebook posts about tactics and solidarity and resistance.

Over Thanksgiving, Leah and Ezra met up with an old friend who was managing a Facebook group called Dumbledore's Army, a shout-out to every millennial's favorite wizard. She said the group was hitting a wall, because everyone seemed to be writing postcards to House Speaker Paul Ryan demanding that he not certify the election, and calling electors telling them to vote for the popular vote winner. That was clearly not going to happen.

Then came a lightbulb moment. Leah and Ezra actually knew how to do something useful: influence Congress. Ezra remembered when activists chased Lloyd Doggett out of an Austin supermarket; Leah remembered being lifted off her feet by a crowd of furious Tea Partiers protesting Tom Perriello. They had taken the phone calls, they had worked the rallies, they knew what kind of constituent activism worked and what got ignored. They had watched a conservative grassroots movement almost stop Obama's health care reform in its tracks. They knew what to do (call your representative, be specific about what you want, say "thank you" when they vote your way) and what not to do (call senators or House members who don't represent you, make vague requests). Leah suggested they make a how-to guide for influencing representatives. Suddenly, they could see a path forward.

They started the guide on the Wednesday before Thanksgiving, and by Sunday night they had a draft. The only thing they needed was a name. They tried to find something rooted in American history that would evoke patriotic values. They wanted to re-create the magic of the Tea Party, which was so resonant of a particular American revolutionary mood. Something like "the Great Society" or "Four Freedoms," but simpler.

Leah wanted a name that would make people feel as if they were all part of the same thing at the same time. She began to mumble the Pledge of Allegiance under her breath. As soon as she said the word, Ezra stopped her: "Oh my God, that's it."

Indivisible.

CHAPTER 13

The Pilgrimage of Alexandria Ocasio-Cortez

Many of the people who came to Standing Rock repeated the same legend. Someone—maybe Crazy Horse—had made a prophecy a long time ago—probably in the late 1870s—when the Lakota were fighting the white man. The "who" and "when" parts of the story were always fuzzy, but the prophecy was always the same: the "black snake" of darkness and discord was going to infect the land, seeping into the fires and air and water, spreading conflict and violence, and threatening the reciprocal relationship between humans and the earth. But the second part of the prophecy predicted that in seven generations, the young people—"the tip of the spear"—would rise up and kill the black snake, and restore order and harmony.

Like many folktales, this one can be neither entirely proven nor disproven. What mattered was that in 2016, roughly seven generations after Crazy Horse's death in 1877, many of the people who traveled to the Standing Rock Indian Reservation believed the legend to be true.

In April 2016, months before the election of Donald Trump, a small Lakota Sioux youth group moved into a few teepees at the northern end of the Standing Rock Indian Reservation, near the Cannonball River in North Dakota. They had started out as a support group called the One Mind Youth Movement, trying to keep Native kids off drugs and alcohol and curb the epidemic of teenage suicides on the reservation. At first, they had joined the fight against the construction of the Keystone XL pipeline that would go under the Cheyenne River, but after the Obama State Department nixed the Keystone plans, they turned their attention to the 1,172-mile Dakota Access Pipeline, scheduled to run from northwest North Dakota to central Illinois. The pipeline company, Energy Transfer Partners, wanted to pump half a million barrels of oil a day underneath the Missouri River, which could threaten the drinking water for the Standing Rock reservation and destroy sacred Lakota burial sites. Elders spoke of the pipeline as the "black snake" of the prophecy. After the Standing Rock Sioux tribe put out a call for solidarity, One Mind Youth moved their teepees to the reservation, lit a sacred fire, and ate some bologna sandwiches at their new "prayer camp."

Soon, they were joined by activists from the Indigenous Environmental Network, which had fought the Keystone XL pipeline, and within months a few tribal elders joined the camp, bringing the traditional Council Lodge teepee. Chief Arvol Looking Horse, the spiritual leader of the Lakota Sioux, gave the young organizers a priceless gift: a 300-year old pipe (known as a *chanupa*), one of the most significant objects in the Lakota religion. It represented a vote of confidence, a transfer of power from the old to the young. At that point, the organizers gave themselves a new name: the International Indigenous Youth Council.

People began pouring in from around the country to serve as "water protectors" and resist the construction of the Dakota Access Pipeline. Dozens of visitors to Standing Rock turned into thousands. They arrived through the summer and fall of 2016, living in tents, eating communal food, and engaging in nonviolent protest and meditation. The protesters survived several confrontations with local police officers and private security forces, who shot tear gas and rubber bullets to try to get them off the land. The 2016 election came and went, and still the water protectors stayed on, undeterred in their spiritual resistance. About a month after Trump was elected, Alexandria Ocasio-Cortez went to join them.

✳ ✳ ✳

In the weeks after Trump's election, New York was in a deep funk. The subway was full of people wincing at news alerts on their phones; coffee shops were full of depressed conversations about what had gone wrong and why they hadn't seen it coming. New Yorkers woke up the morning after the election feeling as if they lived on an island in a foreign country. Alexandria felt drawn to Standing Rock, almost as if she was being called on a spiritual journey.

When Alexandria first contacted an organizer at Standing Rock and asked how she could help, she figured she could fundraise in New York City, or raise awareness among her friends. But the organizer told her that there was actually an urgent need for women to physically come to Standing Rock. In Oceti Sakowin tradition, women served as "water protectors"—the men's role was protecting the protectors. Without enough women in prayer, they believed, the spiritual resistance would lose its power. Alexandria didn't need to be asked twice. She wasn't about to move there to be a full-time water protector (she wasn't *that* spontaneous), but she figured it was at least worth a road trip to deliver some supplies and spend a few days praying in solidarity.

So she teamed up with her bartending buddy Maria Swisher and Maria's friend Josh, a photographer with a dark beard who would prove to be chivalrous at things like de-icing the windows. They had started a GoFundMe page to raise money to buy firewood, wood-burning stoves, sleeping bags, and cots for the water protectors struggling through the sub-zero winter in North Dakota. The plan was to drive the supplies to Standing Rock while livestreaming their road trip on Facebook so their friends could follow along and donate to the cause. "If you want to help us fund the trip, you can Venmo us," Alexandria said into the camera with a wink. She proved to be surprisingly good at this form of online fundraising: they asked for a few hundred dollars, and reached their GoFundMe goal in a single day.

It was Alexandria's idea to try Facebook Live. She and Maria had been brainstorming during downtime at work about what to do after Trump's election, and they decided they needed to get out of their bubble. They wanted to hear from people outside New York to get a sense of how this could have happened: a road trip to Standing Rock, they figured, could bring them some answers.

As soon as they drove Maria's borrowed 1998 Subaru onto the George Washington Bridge and out of Manhattan, they started streaming. The plan was to drive through New Jersey and Pennsylvania and head to Cleveland, Ohio, where they would crash with one of Alexandria's friends from college. They called their livestream "the Road to Standing Rock." It would live for years on Alexandria's personal Facebook page, undiscovered by the press even as she became one of the most famous women in America.

Maria did most of the driving at first, and her main goal was not dying. She told their dozens of viewers that she almost ran over a pedestrian in the beginning but swerved just in time. It wasn't that Maria almost killed him, Alexandria said, more like she "reminded him that he was alive." Meanwhile, Alexandria said that all her friends had been texting her to make sure she wasn't the one driving, because apparently everyone thought she was a terrible driver. "Rude!" she said.

After Ohio, they were going up to Flint, Michigan, then Indiana and then Minneapolis, and then they would leave Minneapolis and get to Standing Rock with enough sunlight to set up camp. It would take them three days, two nights, and countless snack runs. "How many Red Bulls does it take to get three millennials to an Indian reservation?" Alexandria asked their followers.

The whole trip had the feel of a college bull session. They talked about media narratives around racism. They talked about whether Bernie would have won. They talked about how unfair it was that white homeowners could block new housing that could damage their property values but that the Lakota Sioux couldn't block an oil pipeline that could cause massive environmental pollution and poison their drinking water. Alexandria was beginning to learn how to think on camera, how to have conversations with people in the comments, how to bring her viewers along for the ride and deliver her opinions in stream-of-consciousness lectures that were at once natural and informative. It was the birth of a social media persona that would define her later political career, and it also meant they got lost a lot. "Every time we turn on the Facebook Live, we make a wrong turn!" Alexandria said. "We're working on it, people."

Somewhere between New Jersey and Cleveland, they started talking about why they thought the media was incentivized to cover the most sensational angle of every story. "CNN has made me so mad this year, *New York*

Times, so disappointing, the institutions that we're supposed to rely on," Alexandria said. "I think a lot of Americans are really angry at the fact that the media just sold out to Hillary Clinton.

"I voted for her," she continued, "but we have a problem in this country with elitism." She was starting to say that Hillary was "immensely qualified, immensely intelligent," but she got interrupted because Maria wasn't sure if she was in the right lane or not. Josh told her to just keep going straight. Maria got off at the exit, which was the wrong exit. Josh, it turned out, was not great at giving directions.

"I think a lot of people were frustrated that the media was trying to make the news, and trying to determine the candidates instead of reporting on them," Alexandria continued while Maria tried to find their way back to the route. "I think people got really frustrated at that."

"The bias was so obvious," Josh said.

Alexandria nodded. "We saw that in the exit polling, no matter who you voted for, everyone in the exit polls was dissatisfied with their options," she said. "But I do think that Bernie Sanders did speak to a demographic of people that may have wanted to be a little more constructive in their political movements and actions—but when that was no longer an option, they decided to be destructive."

Maria said that during the primary, everyone was focused on whether Bernie was electable enough to carry the South, but what they should have been worried about was whether Hillary could carry the Rust Belt. "There are places that went for Obama that didn't go for Hillary," Maria said. "Maybe misogyny was stronger than racism in the United States."

"I think that's so dumb, when people say, 'Oh, this country is more sexist than it is racist,'" Alexandria replied. She pointed out that Hillary didn't make a single visit to the United Auto Workers in Michigan—of course the unions weren't going to organize for her if she didn't show up to see them.

"Democrats have also been spoiled by Barack Obama because he had one of the strongest organizing campaigns that we've ever seen, and I think that's what it takes," she continued. "It takes that ground game."

They stopped at a Quick Mart to buy coffee, and did the whole transaction by themselves because there were electronic kiosks instead of human cashiers. "They replaced all the cashiers with two people, so what would have been five people employed is now two," Alexandria said when they got back into the car. "What do we do about technology eliminating jobs? What should be done?" AI could replace everyone from administrative assistants to programmers. Nobody's job was really safe. "We can't always be just relying on our elected leadership for answers," she said. "We need to look to ourselves for answers."

✳ ✳ ✳

Day two began with Alexandria in the driver's seat. They had gotten up at what she called "the butt crack of dawn" to make it to Flint, Michigan, which had already become known as ground zero for environmental racism. State-appointed emergency managers of the mostly black city had switched the municipal water source from Lake Huron to the Flint River, which contained so much chloride that it made lead pipes rust. People immediately thought the water seemed weird. It was oddly colored—sometimes brown, sometimes blue, sometimes green—and smelled like gasoline. People began getting rashes, hair fell out in the shower, and kids' skin began flowering with horrible splotches. Parents showed up at city council meetings to complain that they were bathing their kids in poisoned water, but nobody was listening. City officials insisted everything was fine, and the mayor even gulped a glass of water on television to prove it was drinkable. But doctors kept recording kids getting sick, and researchers found that instances of lead poisoning in kids under five had doubled since the water switch.

"I was really asking a lot of questions, trying to figure out, like, why did this breakdown happen? And where did it start? Were local politicians bought out? Was it the state? Is it a bureaucratic thing?" Alexandria told her Facebook Live audience, which had grown to a couple hundred viewers. "And it seems as though, like, when you connect some of these disparate thoughts, it all does come back down to the influence of money in politics."

It reminded her of why they were doing this in the first place. "You're always going to hear the same narrative about public protest," she said. "You're always going to hear, 'Protesters are rabble-rousers, they're troublemakers, protest doesn't do anything, it's ineffective.'" Alexandria thought that narrative was missing the point. "Protest galvanizes public sentiment, and when public sentiment is galvanized to a certain extent, then that turns into public pressure, and then when public pressure is applied to a certain extent, then we get policy change," she said. "That is how protest works." This was her theory of change, in a nutshell.

That's why she was so annoyed that people kept asking her why she was going to Standing Rock. "This isn't your issue," they'd say to her, but what they really meant was "This is someone else's problem." As if they couldn't understand why she would care enough to physically drive from New York to North Dakota to be in solidarity with a tribe she didn't belong to, on land she'd never seen. "It goes back to this fundamental value, I think, where we are one," she says. "We are one nation, and what happens to some of us happens to all of us."

Josh, who was the navigation czar of the road trip, interrupted to tell her which exit to take. Ahead of them on the road, they saw a vehicle with a bumper sticker that said "Not a Liberal." It didn't say "Proud Republican" or "Make America Great Again" or "Trump"—it just said "Not a Liberal."

Alexandria continued. "When children's water is being contaminated in Flint, it is my business," she said. "And when people's lives are in danger because their sovereignty is at risk, it is my business, because a threat to you is a threat to me. And to close my eyes in the face of my neighbor's injustice only opens the door to my injustice."

She was so distracted by conviction that she missed the exit. "That was us," Josh said.

"Fuck," she said quietly.

Her mother piped up in the comments: "Hey, watch it."

✳ ✳ ✳

Missed exits aside, Alexandria was surprised at how spiritual the whole trip was. They felt as if there was a motion behind them, a force, a momentum of some kind. The feeling was so powerful that Maria had been overcome at a rest stop and began to cry.

On the surface, Standing Rock was a battle between the corporations and the people who owned the land. But to Alexandria, it went deeper than that: it was a moral struggle, a spiritual confrontation, a standoff between the present and the future.

On the fourth day, they arrived at Standing Rock. They were driving down a road flanked with flags from all the different tribes who were there. The stars were the brightest Alexandria had ever seen.

When they got to camp it was dark and somebody was playing the flute. Everybody made eye contact with them, and strangers gave them long hugs. It was the most intimate mass gathering that Alexandria and Maria had ever been to. They were given a tent and a wood-burning stove and zero-degree sleeping bags. The organizers asked if they needed any clothes or food, and after all that, they thanked them for coming. Alexandria's socks got soaked through, and somebody offered her a fresh pair. There were boxes filled with donations: headlamps, portable batteries, and food were all piled up together next to a sign that said PLEASE TAKE CARE OF ONE ANOTHER AND TAKE WHAT YOU NEED.

There was no money or trade or bartering. Camp was totally clean, even though nobody was in charge of trash. To Alexandria, it was almost like a utopia: she saw how others treated her, and she aspired to pay it forward. It reminded her of a show she had seen at MoMA once, by a performance artist named Marina Abramović who would sit in a chair and stare directly at whoever was in the chair opposite her. People sat there and stared back, or tried to talk, or cried. The point was that it was a direct connection unmediated by technology or pleasantries. That was the way people looked at each other at camp. Alexandria and Maria went to a few camp meetings, and they visited a sweat lodge once, but mostly they tried to exist in solidarity with the tribes and try to lend their spiritual support.

Every morning the camp woke up before dawn so they could get together to watch the sunrise. There was a guy who would go around with a microphone, like Robin Williams in *Good Morning, Vietnam*, and his job was to deliver a cheery wake-up call to the camp.

"Good morning, all you no-DAPL-onians," he said in his low, singsong voice. "Remember why you're here."

He drew out his words into a tuneless song. "You're heeeeeere for a reeeeeeason!"

They only stayed for a few days: Alexandria had to leave to spend Christmas with her boyfriend's family. On the drive out of the reservation, Alexandria got a call from an unknown number. Just after the election, her brother had sat in his car during a rainstorm and typed a letter on his phone nominating her to run for office with an upstart organization called Brand New Congress. She knew he'd submitted her name, but she never thought anything would come of it. But when she picked up the phone in Maria's borrowed Subaru, a voice on the other end of the line told her that they wanted to help her run for the House of Representatives in New York's fourteenth district.

✳ ✳ ✳

Even before the election, young people all over the country were beginning to mobilize in new ways around climate change. In 2016, as it became clear that Bernie Sanders would lose the Democratic primary, a handful of young organizers who had protested the Keystone XL pipeline and agitated for fossil fuel divestment met to plot their next move. They were sick of just protesting to stop pipelines and get colleges to divest from fossil fuels—Bernie's campaign had taught them that the real targets were big fossil fuel donors and the politicians who take their money. They called themselves the Sunrise Movement, and their goal was insanely ambitious: to build a "youth army" of climate activists to punish politicians who take money from so-called fossil fuel billionaires, and to elect leaders committed to bold action on climate change instead.

After Trump won, their mission became even more urgent. "Trump's victory has blown over the barriers between young people and political engagement, pointing towards the possibility of a sea change at every level of government," wrote the Sunrise cofounders. The group developed its strategy over the course of 2017, with an eye toward the 2018 elections.

They were young and cheerful and loved to sing, like eco-activist von Trapps. Previous iterations of the environmental movement had focused on doom-and-gloom predictions, with an emphasis on dutiful personal behavior: turn off your lights, eat less meat, use less gas. The Sunrise organizers thought that none of this would be enough. In order to slow climate change, they explained, the United States had to radically shift its entire energy system away from fossil fuels, and that would require a political revolution. "We are living through one of the most epic worldwide changes in human history, and the outcome is still uncertain," said a perky female voice in their announcement video. "It all depends on one question: Will the young people of the world quietly watch as everything unravels around us, or will we decide to unite and set humanity on a better course?" They had reason to be dramatic: in 2018, the UN's Intergovernmental Panel on Climate Change (IPCC) released a report that warned that "there is no historical precedent" for the economic transformation needed to prevent global temperatures from rising to catastrophic levels; just half a degree, they warned, could cost millions of lives.

Sunrise wasn't alone. Young people all over the world were realizing that the adults weren't going to make their governments address climate change—so they would have to do it themselves. In 2018, a few months after the release of the IPCC report, a soft-spoken fifteen-year-old Swedish girl with Asperger's syndrome named Greta Thunberg gave an electrifying speech at the annual United Nations climate talks in Poland that excoriated adult leaders for failing to act boldly to prevent climate catastrophe. "You say you love your children above all else," she told a room full of world leaders, her two long braids hanging over her shoulders. "And yet you are stealing their future in front of their very eyes." Weeks later, kids all over the world went on strike to demand climate action. Belgian students skipped school every Thursday, and by the end of February they had sparked large demonstrations in Brussels, which led to the resignation of one of the Belgian environment ministers. The next year, Greta came to the United States, sailing across the ocean on an emissions-free sailboat to address the UN's Climate Action Summit. The kids were waiting for her. Roughly four million young people skipped school and poured into the streets to protest adults leaders' inaction on climate change in what would be called the Global Climate Strike: up to 250,000 kids flooded the streets of New York City, carrying signs with slogans like WE VOTE NEXT. "You are failing us," Greta said, stone-faced to world leaders at the UN. "But the young people are starting to understand your betrayal."

Sunrise gatherings featured activists singing the old labor ballad "Which Side Are You on?" to spook lawmakers, and young people telling stories of wildfires and catastrophic hurricanes threatening their homes and family livelihoods. Alexandria hadn't formally joined the Sunrise Movement, but she had just experienced her own version of this "aha" moment. Her journey to Standing Rock, she told me later, was the first time she realized just how much power was concentrated in the hands of fossil fuel companies. That long, caffeinated drive from Flint to Standing Rock connected "a lot of different dots." She realized that the black families drinking poisoned water in Flint and the indigenous activists shivering in North Dakota were not separate from the rising sea levels threatening Puerto Rico or Miami: they were all part of a broader national crisis, which was that the big money was on one side and environmental justice was on the other.

"When you actually see an issue up close, it truly changes the urgency and the intensity with which you see that problem," she said. "For some folks they may have a relative that got addicted to opioids; for other people it may be because their house got foreclosed on in 2008. And for me it was my experience at Standing Rock."

Sunrise quickly settled on a goal: in order to transform the American economy in twelve years to avoid the catastrophe described in the IPCC report, the US government needed to put millions of people to work installing solar panels, planting trees, and renovating homes and businesses to make them carbon-neutral. Their plan—which at that point was more of a wish list—would create millions of jobs, update crumbling infrastructure, wean the United States off fossil fuels, and ensure a "just transition" for communities affected by the massive new changes.

They called it the Green New Deal.

THE BIG ONE

Everyone said this was the Big One.

When Hurricane Harvey dumped twenty five inches of rainwater on Houston, Texas, the water had nowhere to go. Houston's lax zoning laws allowed developers to build wherever they wanted, including on marshland that would have absorbed rainwater. Roads turned into rivers, parking lots became lakes, the water reached the bottom of the highway signs, furniture floated through living rooms. A three-year-old girl was rescued after she was found clinging to her dead mother's body; a man drowned after he drove around a road barricade into a flooded underpass; four kids and their great-grandparents drowned in a submerged van. Houstonians fled to shelters and then the shelters flooded too. Some who had fled Katrina twelve years earlier and relocated to Houston found themselves in shelters again. People took refuge in the George R. Brown Convention Center, which quickly began to look like a refugee camp, full of donated shoes, blankets, granola bars. Inside, it smelled like feet and tater tots and unwashed hair, like a high school locker room and cafeteria mixed together. When the waters receded, people found black mold in their now uninhabitable homes.

Across the region, at least one hundred people died, thousands lost their homes, and the damage cost about $180 billion, the costliest hurricane on record. A few months after the storm, the state unveiled a $61 billion plan to "future-proof" Houston by building new reservoirs, buying out houses in low-lying areas, and building a sixty-mile "coastal spine" of sea walls, levees, and floating gates to protect the Houston area. But they would have to fight other states for federal funding, and the year wasn't over: by the end of 2017, hurricanes would cause more than $300 billion in damage in the US and its territories.

CHAPTER 14

"Senator, We Run Ads"

When Donald Trump took office, he was the oldest first-term president in history. He was elected overwhelmingly by older, whiter voters, and he appointed high-level officials who were older and whiter than their predecessors—the average age in his original cabinet was sixty-two, higher than Obama's and Bush's. Half of his original cabinet was born before the invention of color TV. Staffers at the Commerce Department said there was only a small window of time every day when Secretary of Commerce Wilbur Ross (b. 1937, before the invention of the ballpoint pen) was able to "focus and pay attention and not fall asleep."

Trump and his allies quickly went about implementing policies that appealed to his graying base but that would leave young people to deal with the long-term consequences. His 2017 tax cuts helped create a $1 trillion deficit that millennials would have to pay down in the future. He rolled back protections for LGBTQ people, alienating the roughly one in five millennials who identify as something other than straight and cisgender. Even the small appointments spelled disaster for young Americans. In the endlessly frustrating labyrinth of student debt loan forgiveness, the Consumer Financial Protection Bureau (CFPB)—created by Elizabeth Warren in 2010—was the main government entity that was helping student loan borrowers fight predatory lenders. But in 2017, Trump appointed Mick Mulvaney (who had once called the CFPB a "sick, sad joke") to run the agency, and six months later he fired the entire advisory board and attempted to gut the bureau. One official who had been the student loan watchdog at the CFPB resigned with a scathing letter saying that the new leadership "turned its back on young people and their financial futures." (Mulvaney would eventually become Trump's acting White House chief of staff.)

In a particularly cruel attack on young people, Trump's then attorney general Jeff Sessions gleefully announced in 2017 that the government was unilaterally eliminating Obama's Deferred Action for Childhood Arrivals program (DACA), which shielded young immigrants from deportation. Sessions—who was born in Alabama in 1946, had a carefree childhood under Jim Crow, and had never gone to school with a black student until college—already had a reputation for outdated, racist views: in 1986, his nomination to the US District Court had failed, partly because of reports he had once called a black colleague "boy" (an allegation he denied) and because Coretta Scott King wrote a letter accusing him of using his role as US Attorney in a "shabby attempt to intimidate and frighten elderly black voters." Eliminating DACA was a highlight of his years-long crusade against immigration, one that could ruin the lives of nearly seven hundred thousand millennials living and working in the United States. (The DACA rollback was later stuck in limbo in the courts, but young immigrants were used as a political football throughout the Trump administration.)

Trump's views on climate change confirmed his total disregard for future generations. On June 1, 2017, he announced plans to withdraw from the Paris Agreement on climate change, making the United States the only major nation in the world to reject the landmark international accords. On Capitol Hill, twenty-two Republican senators—average age sixty-seven (including four octogenarians)—supported his decision to withdraw. These Republicans had taken a combined $10 million in donations from the fossil fuel industry over the past three election cycles.

Rejecting the Paris Agreement was just the beginning of Trump's assault on the environment. Trump saw the Environmental Protection Agency as part of the so-called deep state, and he appointed Scott Pruitt, an advocate of the fossil fuel industry who says climate change could be good for the planet, to roll back much of the progress made by the Obama administration and its predecessors. Several of Trump's top advisors who viewed climate change as a problem (including his first secretary of state, former ExxonMobil CEO Rex Tillerson) were ultimately sidelined or fired partly because of their slowness to implement his anti-environmental agenda. He rolled back Obama's Clean Power Plan, which would have forced coal-fired power plants to close, and nixed Obama's requirement that federal infrastructure projects take climate change and rising sea levels into account. His administration refused to sign an international commitment to protect the Arctic unless the statement was stripped of any climate change language. In the first twenty-three months of Trump's presidency, his administration took at least 114 executive actions—more than one a week—to weaken environmental regulations.

Trump may have been able to get away with this partly because he was surrounded by people who knew they wouldn't live to see the worst of climate change. His Republican-led Congress was one of the oldest in history, with an average age of fifty-seven in the House and sixty-one in the Senate— up almost ten years since the 1980s. It wasn't just Republicans: Democrats also had a serious age problem. In the aftermath of Trump's election, the party was led by Nancy Pelosi in the House (b. 1940) and Chuck Schumer in the Senate (b. 1950), and congressional Democrats were on average slightly older than Republicans in the House. In 2018, eighty-four-year-old senator Dianne Feinstein (b. 1933, years before the chocolate chip cookie was invented) ran for reelection and won, putting her on track to be a nonagenarian senator—a year later, she was caught on video lecturing school kids from the Sunrise Movement that "there's no way to pay for" a Green New Deal, telling them, "I've been doing this for thirty years—I know what I'm doing." Republicans were in fact slightly less calcified: the GOP had passed a rule in the 1990s that placed term limits on committee chairmanships, so younger Republicans had more opportunities for advancement within the party, which helped young conservatives like Paul Ryan become Speaker of the House at forty-five.

The oldsters in Washington weren't just bad on climate change—they were fundamentally out of touch with the ways American society had changed since the twentieth century. This became most obvious when lawmakers who had grown up before the invention of the handheld calculator tried to regulate big tech. In April 2018, when thirty-three-year-old Mark Zuckerberg testified before the Senate's Commerce and Judiciary Committees about Facebook's handling of personal data and the Russian attempts to influence US elections, the lawmakers at the hearing were an average age of sixty-two, and most of the chairs and ranking members were over seventy. Senator Orrin Hatch (b. 1934, thirty years before audiocassettes were first sold in the United States) asked him, "How do you sustain a business model in which users don't pay for your service?" Zuckerberg, clearly surprised at Hatch's total ignorance of Facebook's business model, replied: "Senator, we run ads."

That wasn't a one-off gaffe. In December 2018, Google CEO Sundar Pichai testified before the House Judiciary Committee to answer questions about Google's data collection practices. "I have a seven-year-old granddaughter who picked up her phone before the election," said Rep. Steve King (b. 1949, he was older than the Hula-Hoop). "And she's playing a little game, the kind of game a kid would play, and up on there pops a picture of her grandfather, and I'm not going to say into the record what kind of language was used around that picture of her grandfather, but I'd ask you: How does that show up on a seven-year-old's iPhone who's playing a kids' game?"

"Congressman," said Pichai, "the iPhone is made by a different company." These gaffes didn't just reveal that the septuagenarians in Congress were out of touch with the rest of the country: it showed that they fundamentally didn't understand the forces that were reshaping twenty-first-century American society. Facebook and Google weren't just trendy startups for posting pictures and playing games. They were massive conglomerates with the power to reshape the American political and social landscape. Facebook had already proven its power to manipulate American democracy—that's why Mark Zuckerberg was there in the first place. If the leaders in Congress were too old to understand how Facebook worked, they were too old to provide effective leadership in twenty-first-century America.

Many young people saw these viral moments as evidence of a fundamental disconnect between the gerontocracy on Capitol Hill and what was happening in the rest of the country. By then, tens of thousands had joined what had already become a national resistance movement. Trump was the main impetus, but many young people were beginning to see a wider problem: if this was what the country's old leaders were doing, they figured, then maybe it was time for some new ones.

✳ ✳ ✳

"The Resistance," as it was quickly named, was immediate. Less than twenty-four hours after Trump's inauguration, more than four million people took to the streets for the Women's March, now considered the largest single-day protest in US history. The crowd in DC drew at least twice as many people as Trump's inauguration. One out of every one hundred Americans showed up to a march: if you took the total number of people serving in the armed forces and tripled it, that was the size of the nationwide Women's March. From above, Washington was filled with so many pink "pussy hats" that it looked as if the city was blooming.

Lauren Underwood was somewhere in the crowd in DC, shivering in the gridlock as a crowd too big to move flooded the capital. Svante Myrick was one of ten thousand people who showed up to the Ithaca Women's March, roughly a third of the city's population. Mayor Pete Buttigieg, who was weighing a run for DNC chair, skipped a donor retreat in order to speak at the march in South Bend, where more than one thousand pink-hatted women took to the streets. "A woman's place is in the house all right, like the state-house," he said, standing coatless in a blue shirt in front of a sea of pink. "And the House of Representatives. And there will be a woman in that White House soon enough."

Alexandria Ocasio-Cortez drove down to DC with Maria in the same 1998 Subaru they used to drive to Standing Rock. They livestreamed their trip from New York to DC on Facebook Live as a sequel to their Standing Rock journey (Alexandria called it season two, episode one) and as soon as they got on the road, they realized that everyone else on the highway was going to the same place. "Guys," Alexandria said into the camera, "it's almost one o'clock in the morning and the gas stations are so full." She rolled down her window and yelled at the car next to her, "Yo, you guys going to the Women's March?" They cheered.

"We're at a really unique place in history, and when I think about things that I want to tell my kids that I did, I'm, like, proud," she said. "This is the essence of what democracy should be about."

Alexandria wore her cream-colored coat and her late father's watch. She and Maria had planned to march with the Standing Rock delegation, but as soon as they got off the Metro, they could tell this was not like any other protest they'd ever seen—they were many blocks away from the National Museum of the American Indian, which was where they were supposed to meet the rest of the Standing Rock crew, and already the streets were so full of people it was hard to move forward.

Their live feed kept cutting out because there were so many millions of cell phones in the same place. Alexandria held her phone high on a selfie stick as she and Maria stood in a crowd of people chanting, "The people! United! Will never be defeated!" There were so many people that it wasn't a march anymore, more like millions of people just standing in place, united by their rage.

It was an event of mass catharsis. Women who had spent the previous two months screaming at their televisions could now look around and see that millions of other women had done the same. In St. Paul, Minnesota, State Rep. Ilhan Omar took the stage that morning wearing a purple leopard-print hijab. Ilhan—a thirty-four-year-old refugee from Somalia who had been elected to the state legislature as the first-ever Somali-American lawmaker the same night Trump won the presidency—addressed the nearly one hundred thousand people gathered in front of the state capitol in St. Paul. "I'm here because I am a woman," she started. "But I'm also here because I am a black woman. And I'm here because I'm a Muslim woman . . . I am here for women who are queer, I am here for transgender women, I am here for immigrant women, I am here for refugees." This was the language of intersectionality—a concept of interlocking identities that was first coined by the scholar Kimberlé Crenshaw that had been planted on college campuses, taken root at Occupy, grown buds throughout Black Lives Matter, and now flowered in full at the Women's March.

The march wasn't exactly leaderless. But the national cochairs, Tamika Mallory, Linda Sarsour, Bob Bland, and Carmen Perez—all in their thirties as they planned the march—had gotten most of their organizing experience in the various racial justice organizations that had formed alongside Black Lives Matter. So the Women's March used a distributed organizing structure that allowed local leaders to plan "sister marches" in their own communities, an early example of the way the anti-Trump resistance would emphasize ground-up organizing. (This would create problems down the road, as the Women's March organization became plagued by infighting, but in January 2017 the cohesion was on display.)

Women marched in nearly every major city in America. They jammed the streets of New York and Los Angeles. Five people marched in a cancer ward of a California hospital. In tiny Unalakleet, Alaska, thirty-eight people marched in a minus-forty-degree windchill. Gloria Steinem, who had been mobilizing feminists for half a century, said she had never seen anything like it. "This is the other side of the downside," she said in her speech.

The next day, before they got back in their Subaru to return to New York, Alexandria and Maria went to the Jefferson Memorial. Trump hadn't even been president for two days, and already it seemed as if the winds were changing. As they looked across the Mall toward the Washington Monument, Alexandria said she felt a surge of hope. She was still a private citizen, but she was already beginning to work with Brand New Congress to mount a congressional bid: she, like the rest of the country, was on the verge of transformation.

They walked inside the Jefferson Memorial, past the bronze statue of the nation's third president, livestreaming their visit on Facebook. The video was a mixture of patriotic earnestness and internet-speak, without the heavy dose of politics that would blanket her social media feed in just a few months. Alexandria said that even though Lincoln was her "all-time bae," Jefferson was one of her favorite presidents as a writer and philosopher. They knew he owned slaves, but Alexandria said she loved his voracious curiosity about the world. She and Maria stood under the rotunda and read the passage from the Declaration of Independence, written in big letters on the southwest wall. Jefferson had been just thirty-three when he wrote it, only a couple of years older than they were. "'We hold these truths to be self-evident,'" she read aloud from the writing on the wall to Maria. "If you spoke like that at a Republican debate or a Democratic debate, people would think, 'What a dork.'"

They turned to the southeast wall. "'Laws and institutions must go hand in hand with the progress of the human mind,'" she read. "'We might as well require a man to wear still the coat which fitted him when a boy as civilized society to remain ever under the regimen of their barbarous ancestors.'"

This was what was so remarkable about Jefferson, she said. Two hundred years ago he had written a document that established the values of the United States, and inherent in those values was the idea of generational change, or as he called it, the "sovereignty of the living generation." He was wise enough to know the limits of his wisdom, and had the perspective to realize that the future should not be bridled by the past. She was clearly still waffling between Sandy the bartender and Alexandria the congressional candidate, because no New York City Democrat would so openly praise the slaveholding Virginian the way she did next. "Jefferson was a progressive," she told her followers. "That goes beyond party."

Then, just as quickly, her candidate side was back. "The theme yesterday was 'one for all and all for one,'" Alexandria said. "We're not going to pick and choose our issues and say, 'We're going to march but we don't know how we feel about immigration or we don't know how we feel about health care.' No. If I stand with you, any issue that affects you affects me."

Somebody in the comments asked whether she thought bartenders would be good at running for office, and she and Maria laughed. Of course they would, she said. Bartenders have to talk to people all the time, even people they don't agree with. You can't just run away into your Facebook echo chamber—your livelihood depends on those tips. "Bartenders are better listeners," Alexandria said. Four months later, she would file her documents with the Federal Election Commission for her first congressional bid.

✳ ✳ ✳

Everybody agreed that the Women's March was the beginning of the Resistance, but nobody realized how broad and effective that Resistance would become. The news coverage largely focused on the sheer size of the march, illustrated with pictures on TV of what looked like swarms of pink ants devouring DC. But what would come next? "Without a clear path from march to power," wrote Micah White, one of the original organizers of Occupy, "the protest is destined to be an ineffective feelgood spectacle adorned with pink pussy hats."

But that massive swarm of ants quickly organized itself into a sophisticated colony. Different people in different parts of the country did different things—donated or organized or put themselves on the ballot—but almost everyone did something. The strangers who had met for the first time on the buses to the Women's March became coconspirators planning their next steps on the bus ride home. When they got back to their communities, many started or joined local resistance groups: at first just a few women meeting for coffee, then a few more women writing postcards, then a few more women calling their congresspeople. Some women even looked at the reality-show president and his congressional enablers and began to wonder if they should run for office themselves.

After the Women's March, the movement accelerated in response to Trump's outrages. First, just a week after the inauguration, Trump signed an executive order banning travel from seven majority-Muslim countries. Hours after the so-called Muslim ban was announced, twenty-four-year-old Tara Raghuveer, then working for the National Partnership for New Americans, urged activists to get to New York's JFK Airport. She was joined by young immigration lawyers like Camille Mackler and immigrant activist groups like Make the Road New York as the protest grew spontaneously on social media. Within hours, demonstrations against the Muslim ban had sprouted in dozens of major international airports across the country.

Leah Greenberg, who was still building Indivisible, raced to Dulles Airport ("Cannot believe I'm willingly going to Dulles," she tweeted), where she stood in a crowd of what felt like a thousand people singing "This Land Is Your Land." Pete Buttigieg was in Texas at the time, so he headed to the Houston airport to join dozens of people at Terminal E with signs saying things like BAN THE POTUS and GIVE ME YOUR TIRED, YOUR POOR, YOUR HUDDLED MASSES YEARNING TO BREATHE FREE. He knelt and took a picture with a little girl who had a sign that said BOO DONALD TRUMP in jagged handwriting she had clearly done herself,

Trump's election had suddenly changed the moral calculus for a genera-tion of young progressives, and apathy was no longer cool. People showed up to block the airports and build mass physical opposition to Trump's execu-tive order, but it was also about performing resistance as much as practicing it. The Women's March and the airport protests were full of signs and hats and T-shirts that seemed tailor-made for Instagram, like the toddler who wore a sign to the Women's March that said I LOVE NAPS BUT I STAY WOKE. It was a new form of prepackaged protest, designed to be both physical and digital at the same time. People saw photos on Instagram of their friends protesting, and they went to be part of the resistance, too.

By then, Jess Morales Rocketto had transformed from a Hillary cam-paign staffer to a full-on anti-Trump resistance machine. During the Muslim ban protests, her Twitter feed became a de facto dispatch hub, directing ac-tivists to the different airport protests and thanking elected representatives who had shown up in support. ("Send thank yous to @petebuttigieg for head-ing out to the airport tonight!" she tweeted after Pete showed up in Hous-ton.) For Jess, it would be the first of many spontaneous anti-Trump protests she would help organize over the next four years. After Trump's Department of Homeland Security began separating migrant children from their fami-lies, she organized Families Belong Together, a coalition of 250 groups de-manding an end to family separations. She stormed Senate offices to protest the appointment of Judge Brett Kavanaugh to the Supreme Court after he had been credibly accused of sexual assault. (He denied the allegations and made it onto the bench.) By the 2018 midterms, Jess was organizing domestic workers to get out the vote in Georgia.

Activists have always tended to be young—it's a combination of politi-cal naivete, youthful energy, and more free time to organize and wave signs. But in the Trump resistance, people of all ages swarmed the airports, marched in the streets, called their representatives, and met for local meet-ings. In fact, many of the most enthusiastic resisters were middle-aged moms, who did the lion's share of ground organizing in suburban swing districts. This would be a cross-generational movement for change, but like so many movements in history, most of the national leaders would be under forty.

For the first few months, there was a protest nearly every weekend: first the Muslim ban protests, then Day Without Immigrants (to protest Trump's plan to deport undocumented immigrants), then the Tax March (to pressure him to release his taxes) and the March for Science (to protest the Trump administration's assault on climate science). But it was becoming clear that marching wouldn't be enough. To actually take on the Trump administration, the Resistance would have to up its game.

✳ ✳ ✳

Within three months of Trump's election, Leah Greenberg and Ezra Levin's Indivisible Guide had been downloaded nearly a million times. In the same way that Tumblr enabled Occupy and Twitter enabled Black Lives Matter, Indivisible owes its success to Google Docs: before Google, it would have been impossible to distribute such a sophisticated set of instructions to so many people so quickly. Groups were forming all over the country to use their guide to build a Tea Party–style resistance against Trump. By the end of 2017, nearly six thousand groups had sprouted around the country, roughly two in every congressional district. While some took different names, or affiliated more closely with other networks, a substantial proportion of local resistance groups were taking their cues from the Indivisible Guide.

Leah and Ezra developed an explicitly hands-off approach to the organization. They used the national network as a way to give the local groups resources but not orders. Local chapters could call themselves Indivisible groups if they wanted, but they didn't have to. Non-Indivisible groups could download their guide for free online. Leah called this a "more-the-merrier, all-of-the-above approach." Unlike the Tea Party, Indivisible had no specific ideological leaning. Some Indivisible groups in liberal areas were ultra-progressive, others in Republican-held districts were moderate, but they all shared the same goal: to force their representatives to hold Trump accountable, and punish them if they didn't. Ultimately, Indivisible would become a highly effective blend of the tech-enabled leaderless movements modeled by Occupy and Black Lives Matter, and the hyperpractical, nuts-and-bolts electoral tactics adopted by the Tea Party. The strategy was simple: make specific asks of local members of Congress, force them to answer questions, and try to humiliate them in the local press if they didn't.

Leah and Ezra and their team were all millennials, but their vision had intergenerational appeal. Most of the rank-and-file Indivisible members were middle-aged white women, often in the suburbs, the stereotypical "resistance moms." According to research by Harvard sociologist Theda Skocpol, who cowrote a book about the Tea Party and spent 2017 and 2018 studying local resistance groups, Indivisible grew bigger and faster than the Tea Party did: the Tea Party had only about 900 to 1,500 local groups at its height, while Indivisible had thousands. Skocpol found that the median age of an Indivisible member was around fifty, that Indivisible groups were roughly 70 percent female (unlike the Tea Party, whose leadership skewed male), and that groups were mostly made up of retired teachers, professors, or health care workers. These middle-aged ladies had flooded congressional offices with phone calls to oppose Trump's Muslim ban. But that would turn out to be a practice run for Indivisible's biggest battle of 2017.

Shortly after Trump took office, he and the Republican Congress attempted to do what the GOP had been promising for years: repeal and replace Obamacare. It didn't help their cause that the "replace" part of the promise was empty: for all the rhetoric, the GOP never offered a plan that would include coverage of everyone who was covered by the Affordable Care Act. But the Republicans were hell-bent on repeal, and it looked for months as if they would achieve it.

Until Indivisible stepped up. Local groups confronted their senators and representatives at every town hall, forcing them to explain why they would vote to kill a law that might be flawed but was helping millions afford health care. When Republicans stopped showing up to town halls, Indivisible groups held their own, with empty chairs or cardboard cutouts of members of Congress too cowardly to meet their constituents. They called them in the morning to talk to staffers and at night to fill up their voicemails: one Colorado Indivisible group urged protesters to make their representatives "feel like they are walking into a political buzzsaw." Protesters in deep-red districts confronted stunned Republicans with chants of "Do your job!" and "You work for us!" They staged sit-ins in Senate offices, often with disabled constituents or seriously ill kids. They brought cardboard gravestones to "die-ins" in front of Republican offices in twenty-one states. One aging New Jersey lawmaker, Rep. Rodney Frelinghuysen, was heckled so mercilessly that he gave up his chairmanship of the powerful House Appropriations Committee and chose to retire rather than face reelection in his hostile district. When members ignored the thousands of letters sent to their offices, Indivisible sent potatoes instead. "The women are in my grill no matter where I go," GOP Rep. Dave Brat complained. "We're getting hammered." Members of Congress started canceling town halls and refusing to appear in public for fear of meeting their angry constituents.

After weeks of demands from local Indivisible activists and the League of Women Voters, Republican Illinois representative Randy Hultgren finally agreed to appear at a town hall in his district. Hultgren, stocky and bespectacled with salt-and-pepper hair and a jovial smile, was already reeling under the pressure. As soon as the ACA repeal had come up, Indivisible protesters had swamped his phone lines and practically camped out in his district office. Finally, speaking at a theater in St. Charles, Hultgren told his constituents that he was "committed to voting no" on any version of the GOP health care repeal that didn't protect people with preexisting conditions. Sitting in the audience with her mom, Lauren Underwood exhaled. At least he would vote against a bill that would keep her from getting health insurance, she thought. Without the ACA's protections, she knew her preexisting condition could make her insurance prohibitively expensive. She thought her representative would keep his word.

The House GOP health care plan would allow insurance companies to jack up prices for people with preexisting conditions and resume other predatory practices outlawed by the ACA, but ultimately Rep. Randy Hultgren broke his promise and voted for it anyway. The Republican-led House passed the ACA repeal despite the intense local resistance, but it set the stage for a showdown in the Senate.

After Trump celebrated the House passage of Obamacare repeal, Indivisible groups kept up the pressure. They coordinated protests at the offices of Maine senator Susan Collins, Alaska senator Lisa Murkowski, and Arizona senator John McCain—the three votes they would need to prevent Obamacare repeal in the Senate. The 62 Indivisible groups in Maine, 16 in Alaska, and 141 in Arizona coordinated with disability rights groups like National ADAPT and women's health groups like Planned Parenthood to relentlessly pressure their senators to vote against the bill. In the end, Collins and Murkowski came out against the ACA repeal and in a dramatic moment on the Senate floor, a cancer-stricken Sen. John McCain doomed the GOP health plan like an emperor condemning a wounded gladiator, shocking his party with a thumbs-down vote.

The Indivisible resistance didn't single-handedly kill the GOP's repeal of Obamacare—that honor belonged to Collins, Murkowski, and McCain. But the publicity around the historic vote galvanized hundreds of local organizers to redouble their efforts on the House side. Their groups grew smarter and stronger as the months went on, and they never let their members of Congress forget that vote. House GOP incumbents would now be hounded by hecklers as they ran for reelection. By the time the midterms rolled around, Indivisible groups were focused and furious, and ready to work for any Democratic nominee in their districts.

In some ways, the 2016 election and the resistance that followed were liberating for young organizers. Many saw Trump's election as confirmation of what they had already secretly suspected: that many twentieth-century political assumptions no longer held true, and that decades of conventional wisdom about elections conveyed earnestly by pundits and consultants could be chucked out the window with Hillary's "midwestern firewall." The established political organizations were weighed down by decades of what Jess Morales Rocketto called "cruff" (a mashup of "crud" and "stuff")—baggage that might have helped them win elections in 1992 or even 2008 but was close to useless two decades into the twenty-first century. They had outdated habits like investing in mailers instead of a digital strategy, or failing to buy enough cell phone numbers even though most young voters and voters of color don't have landlines, or polling too often during the day, which skewed the results toward older, retired voters.

The ethos of disruption that had already pervaded the business world had finally arrived in mainstream politics. "Internet startup culture is so built into our generation," Jess said. "Everybody believes the hype that you can start it if you work hard enough, and if it fails, it's not the end of the world."

And so young people started their own organizations. Some worked outside the system, staging mass protests and coordinating street pressure on elected officials. Others played an inside game, recruiting and training exciting new candidates to run for office. It was like a truckload of construction workers descending on an old, creaky house—some ripped up the floorboards; others built shiny new additions.

To do it, they used tools that had already been sharpened by Republicans over the previous ten years. Indivisible had borrowed from the Tea Party's tactics, but that was just the beginning. For the first time in a generation, national Democrats began focusing their energy on state and local races, as the Koch brothers and other Republicans had done for years.

Catherine Vaughan, a gravel-voiced former management consultant who had worked as a field organizer for Clinton, was thirty when she started Flippable, which targeted state legislative seats to help Democrats flip statehouses blue. Just as Leah and Ezra were trying to co-opt the Tea Party's activism, Vaughan was mimicking GOP mastermind Karl Rove's 2010 statehouse strategy. Rove's plan, known as REDMAP, was to invest $30 million in statehouse races to win control of state legislatures just before the 2011–2012 redistricting, so that states could gerrymander districts to favor Republican candidates for the rest of the decade. Rove announced his master plan in a 2010 column in *The Wall Street Journal*, subtitled "He who controls redistricting can control Congress." The plan was widely successful: by 2016, the GOP controlled two-thirds of the nation's state legislature chambers, even in places that leaned Democratic. Vaughan's goal was to undo the Republican damage and win back those state legislatures for Democrats in time for the 2021–2022 redistricting. It was an exercise in long-term political thinking. "People are focused on a single cycle, but we're playing the long game," Catherine told me. "If we don't flip these statehouses and state senates, we could lose the opportunity to have a Democratic House for a decade."

Other millennial organizers were driving the party to the left by mimicking the Republicans' tendency to slay their moderates. Former Bernie Sanders staffers Saikat Chakrabarti and Corbin Trent started Brand New Congress, aimed at replacing every member of Congress with working-class progressives: this was the group that called Alexandria as she drove back from Standing Rock. They soon joined forces with the Justice Democrats, which had a more specific goal: to mount progressive primary challengers to moderate Democrats who took money from big corporations, including fossil fuel companies. Just as Tea Partiers had slammed "RINOs" (Republicans In Name Only), Justice Democrats vowed to target what they called "corporate Democrats." Both groups were run by young people (Justice Democrats executive director Alexandra Rojas was just twenty-two), and they mostly endorsed young progressive people of color.

Over the next two years, the anti-Trump resistance would forge an uneasy alliance between the young organizers who had come up in protest movements and the more experienced politicos who had cut their teeth on electoral work. For the first time in their careers, many of the young activists began thinking about elections, and many of the DC political creatures started engaging in activism. Five years earlier, the bedraggled tent-dwellers at Occupy and the frenzied workaholics in Washington, DC, had almost nothing in common: they spoke different languages and existed in different universes. In the beginning of the Trump era, they would start to sing the same song.

✳ ✳ ✳

Amanda Litman had thought her life pretty much couldn't get any worse after she spent election night puking out of a cab. She had run Hillary Clinton's email program, and she was one of the last people out of the Javits Center before she asked the cab driver to stop so she could retch in the predawn hours of Trump's America. Two months later, she twisted her knee and became essentially homebound for weeks. So while everyone she knew marched in the Women's March, she was horizontal on her couch in Brooklyn with her loyal mutt, Sadie.

Amanda was twenty-six, sarcastic but kind, prone to blinking slowly under her bangs at idiotic men who tried to explain politics to her, but she broke into an easy grin whenever anyone mentioned dogs or state legislatures. Just after the election, she had received a few Facebook messages from people she vaguely knew asking if there were any organizations set up to help young people run for office—as far as she knew, there weren't. She spent her recuperation scrolling through her anguished Facebook feed. At one point, she saw that a Democratic operative she admired posted something like "The grown-ups have failed you, nobody is going to ask you to take over, just do it." This was a guy she had thought was an adult in the room, saying there were no adults in the room. She remembered her friend who wanted to run for office but didn't know where to start. She remembered the hollowed-out state party apparatuses that had lain dormant in the Obama era, and began to wonder why there wasn't an organization devoted to helping young progressives run for state and local office to build a Democratic pipeline.

She emailed her friend Jess Morales Rocketto about the idea, and Jess connected her to her husband, Ross Morales Rocketto, who had been thinking about this for years. Together, Amanda and Ross started Run for Something to help young progressives run for school board or state legislature. They launched on Inauguration Day, thinking they could meet with each candidate one-on-one to help them craft a campaign plan. Over the first three days, eight hundred people signed up. By the end of the week, they had more than a thousand.

Most of the people who end up founding big political organizations come up through traditional campaign channels: field, media, finance. Amanda and Ross were some of the first founders to come up on the digital side, and it showed. Amanda's background in email organizing and Ross's experience running texting programs meant they didn't even bother telling candidates to waste money on snail mail. They ran the organization out of their apartments, and nearly all their communication with their candidates was digital: they did it all on Google Docs, video calls, and chat rooms. There were chat rooms that discussed everything from how to handle childcare for young children to what to wear to run for office. (One young candidate for the Texas state legislature, Erin Zwiener, ended up wearing the same blazer she had worn to Model UN in high school.)

The Virginia state elections in 2017 were Run for Something's first test. The first big statewide election of the Trump era would signal whether all those women who marched in Washington were willing to show up to vote, especially in an off-year election that wasn't even a congressional midterm. "Protests were good, calls to Congress were good, stopping legislation was good," said Amanda, "but this was proof of whether it could translate into an electoral success."

Run for Something ran ten millennial candidates for the Virginia House of Delegates, in districts spread across rural areas and well-to-do suburbs. Amanda and Ross had a theory: that local, down-ballot candidates would essentially act as super-canvassers for whoever was at the top of the ticket (in this case, Democratic gubernatorial candidate Ralph Northam). The idea was that young, energetic local candidates would probably get to know their voters better than a gubernatorial candidate ever could. They'd sit in their living rooms, pet their dogs, talk to their kids. And when Election Day came around, voters would come out to vote for that interesting young person who kept knocking on their door—and while they were in the booth, they'd cast a vote for whoever was at the top of the ticket.

Amanda and Ross called this the "reverse-coattails" theory. It was the opposite of long-standing conventional wisdom, which usually relied on the top of the ticket to drag in the obscure down-ballot candidates. It also made intuitive sense: statewide candidates couldn't possibly meet everyone in every district—but young local candidates could.

When Virginia Democrats won big on election night, it was played as a big night for women. But the results also showed young voters awakening from their slumber. Youth turnout doubled from 2009—and 69 percent of young voters went for Northam, which gave him the margin he needed to be elected governor. (Boomers, not surprisingly, voted for the Republican candidate, Ed Gillespie.)

Amanda and Ross ran seventy-two millennial candidates in state races across fourteen states, and almost half of them won their seats. Of the fifteen seats Democrats flipped in the Virginia House of Delegates, eight were won by millennials. They were people like Danica Roem (the first openly transgender person elected to a state legislature), and Chris Hurst (who had lost his girlfriend Alison Parker, a TV news reporter, in a gruesome on-air shooting, then beat an NRA-backed incumbent), and Jennifer Carroll Foy (who gave birth to premature twins during her campaign and won anyway).

And young people in other states were beginning to pay attention.

CHAPTER 15

Millennial Red

I n 1952, a cartoon turtle in a bow tie and a tiny helmet began to appear in American classrooms. Bert the Turtle was the federal government's friendly ambassador reminding schoolkids to "duck and cover" in the event of a nuclear attack by the Soviet Union. These kids—the young baby boomers—rehearsed hiding under their desks with their arms over their heads to protect themselves from an atomic blast launched by America's Communist nemesis. The fight against communism would be part of the boomers' formative experiences: from the McCarthyism of the 1950s to the Vietnam War of the 1960s and '70s to the fall of the Berlin Wall in 1989.

Even the millions of boomers who opposed the excesses of McCarthyism and the Vietnam War grew up to think, with considerable justification, that capitalist economies created more wealth for their countries than socialist ones. When many socialist countries in the developing world shifted to more market-based systems in the 1990s, many boomers saw it as vindication: boomer historian Francis Fukuyama called this shift "the end of history" and characterized it as a decisive victory for free-market capitalism and liberal democracy. Even those over fifty who didn't conflate socialism with communism were leery of what a more socialist America might do to their income.

But Alexandria Ocasio-Cortez didn't have memories of the Berlin Wall falling the year she was born, and she was a child when Eastern European, African, and Asian countries converted from socialism to capitalism to improve their standards of living. She never ducked under her desk to hide from a Soviet missile, because millennials were taught how to hide from mass shooters instead.

Kids her age had read about the perils of socialism in history books: the Stalinist purges and mass starvation, the Cultural Revolution in China, and the desire of even Communist regimes like those in China and Vietnam to shed their command-and-control economies. But they also heard more than many of their parents did about examples of socialist policies succeeding, such as universal health care in Canada, subsidized college in the UK, and free childcare in Sweden. Many millennials began to believe that the horrors of Soviet communism and Maoism were more a function of long-standing despotic traditions in those countries than socialist economic models. In Europe, Canada, and even the United States, where everything from Social Security and Medicare to farm subsidies and bank bailouts were inherently socialistic, democratically elected governments had peacefully implemented socialist ideas without anybody ending up in a gulag. And after everything that had happened in the United States over the last two decades—stagnant wages, widening income inequality, crushing tuition bills, soaring prescription drug costs, predatory lending, obscene CEO pay, rapacious fossil fuel companies, the stranglehold of corporate donations on American politics, and a devastating financial crisis caused by deregulated banks—many young people (and plenty of people of all ages) had come to think that unfettered capitalism, not creeping socialism, was the source of the problem.

So in the summer of 2017, Alexandria went to her first meeting of the Democratic Socialists of America (DSA), mostly because she kept seeing DSA activists at events for other causes she cared about, such as Hurricane Maria recovery and Black Lives Matter. She learned that much of the DSA, like her, didn't believe in nationalizing industry or inhibiting entrepreneurship, only that people's basic needs—health care, education, housing—shouldn't be tied to corporate profit. And, like most Democrats, she thought that many of the justifications for unfettered capitalism were flawed: tax cuts for corporations didn't translate into more jobs or higher wages; they just allowed corporations to hire more lobbyists to wrestle more tax cuts. "We've never seen a form of this late-stage, hypercapitalist, trickle-down, give-corporations-everything-and-you'll-be-taken-care-of strategy work for everyday people," she told me. "In fact, we've seen it get worse because of the corrupting role of money in politics.

"We saw the gambling with Wall Street lead to one of the greatest economic periods of instability since the Great Depression, and the recovery has not been meaningful for us," she continued. "Spoiler alert: the gig economy is about not giving people full-time jobs. And when you don't have full-time jobs, you don't have the insurance in the same way that people had. So it should be no secret why millennials want to decouple your insurance status from your employment status." For her, democratic socialism was about ensuring Medicare for All, mandating a living wage, and creating a Green New Deal with a jobs guarantee to put people to work.

As early as 2010, young Americans like Alexandria were already much more skeptical of capitalism than their parents—43 percent of eighteen- to twenty-nine-year-olds thought "socialism" had a positive connotation, about twenty points higher than their parents and thirty points higher than their grandparents.

In other words: capitalism itself may be falling victim to the free marketplace of ideas. If it were a company, it would be in trouble: by the Trump era, capitalism had both a product problem and a branding problem, at least in some corners of the country. It hadn't kept up with the times, its customers were dissatisfied, and its marketing was stale. Entrepreneurs would call that "ripe for disruption."

The product problem was that many young people thought that capitalism just wasn't working for them. They had worse jobs, lower pay, and less stability than their parents. In the 1940s, 90 percent of children would earn at least a little more than their parents—by the time millennials were growing up, fewer than half would achieve that baseline American dream. They found it difficult to afford the staples of capitalist achievement (houses, cars), and some could barely scrape by with the basic human necessities (medical care, education). The free market as advertised was supposed to ensure that ordinary hardworking people could have those things, for a reasonable price—for many young people, it felt like false advertising.

The branding problem was that capitalism and socialism had different connotations depending on when you were born. To boomers, capitalism connoted hardworking entrepreneurs hiring new workers, and big money on Wall Street if you had the right pedigree; to millennials, it conjured images of oil executives cutting checks to politicians to stop environmental legislation. To boomers, socialism meant Russian gulags or Venezuelan famine; to millennials, it meant Nordic-style universal health coverage and subsidized day care. Years of exploitation and income inequality had hurt the capitalist brand with young people, while visions of successful health care and education systems in other countries had made socialism and its cousins more appealing. It was the ultimate generational Rorschach test.

* * *

Boomers think socialism is a relic, and they're right that the word can be politically toxic. To millions of older voters, "socialism" smells of a discredited past, which is not good news for self-described socialists trying to win in swing districts. But the Cold War is not the whole story: In fact, the renewed enthusiasm for socialism is entirely consistent with historical patterns of political responses to major economic dislocation. At nearly every moment when huge technological advances have changed the nature of work (check) or created sky-high income inequality (check) or economic downturns that have resulted in mass hardship (check), Americans have turned to socialist ideas to strengthen the social safety net.

The American socialist movement began in the early twentieth century, with labor leaders demanding better worker protections, a minimum wage, and the abolition of child labor—all ideas that would eventually be accepted by both major parties. It was a time of vast economic inequality, when a railroad tycoon had a toilet seat covered in 23-karat gold while millions of families worked 80-hour weeks in dangerous factories. "If the people who were making policies were smart," said Michael Carter, a shaggy-haired

DSA member who worked for Bernie Sanders and later served as deputy campaign manager for Alexandria Ocasio-Cortez, "they might realize that taking us to levels of inequality not seen since the Gilded Age might take us to similar politics of the Gilded Age."

After the stock market crashed in 1929, America was once again at a moment of massive inequality—and again responded with efforts to strengthen the social safety net. Three years into the Great Depression, Franklin Delano Roosevelt embarked on a series of government interventions in the economy designed to protect Americans from the ravages of the free market: the New Deal. He reorganized the banks through the Emergency Banking Act, put three million men to work planting an astonishing three billion trees in the Civilian Conservation Corps, and created millions more temporary government jobs through the Works Progress Administration and other new agencies. He regulated Wall Street for the first time by establishing the Securities and Exchange Commission and legalized collective bargaining— the key to union power—through the National Labor Relations Act. He created universal pensions (also known as Social Security) and ensured federal government protections for orphans and the disabled. Even though the New Deal perpetuated racial inequalities (people of color were largely excluded from the newly created jobs and the easy access to homeownership that would come after the war), it was still the largest expansion of the social safety net in American history. FDR called the New Deal "bold, persistent experimentation." His critics called it "socialist."

Beginning an eighty-five-year tradition of Republican attacks, one Republican member of Congress called the New Deal "undisguised state socialism," while another said that Roosevelt was "a socialist, not a Democrat." These attacks angered the highly pragmatic FDR, who, when asked his political philosophy, answered, "I'm a Christian and a Democrat. That's all." Former New York governor Al Smith, a Democrat, gave a speech smearing the New Deal as Communist and un-American. "Get the platform of the Democratic Party, and get the platform of the Socialist Party, and lay them down on your dining room table, side by side, and get a heavy lead pencil and scratch out the word 'Democratic' and scratch out the word 'Socialist,'" he told a crowd at the American Liberty League Dinner in 1936. "There can be only one atmosphere of government, the clear, pure, fresh air of a free America or the foul breath of Communistic Russia."

Despite the vast expansion of social protections in the New Deal, most actual socialists thought it didn't go far enough. Like Occupy activists eighty years later, they wanted the president to dismantle the system entirely, not just reform it. And FDR opposed the creation of public sector unions, arguing they would require state governments to essentially negotiate against themselves. But FDR also fought for programs that would be considered radically left even by today's standards. He wanted cradle-to-grave Social Security for all Americans—essentially a universal basic income—but never proposed it because he thought it was politically impossible. In 1942, five months after the United States entered World War II, he asked Congress to increase the top marginal tax rate to a level that would virtually eliminate great wealth. "Discrepancies between low personal incomes and very high personal incomes should be lessened," he said. "I therefore believe that in time of this grave national danger, when all excess income should go to win the war, no American citizen ought to have a net income, after he has paid his taxes, of more than $25,000 a year." (That's roughly $400,000 in 2019 dollars.)

But part of Roosevelt's genius was realizing that ideology was irrelevant for most mainstream American voters. He didn't care about the semantics, as long as the New Deal worked. When asked about the political philosophy behind the Tennessee Valley Authority, he said, "It's neither fish nor fowl, but whatever it is, it will taste awfully good to the people of the Tennessee Valley." Almost nine decades later, Pete Buttigieg would have a similar answer when asked about whether the Democrats should embrace socialist ideas. "For years, socialism has been used as a kill switch to just stop an idea from being talked about, but if you're from my generation, the real interest is: Is an idea good or not?" he said on *Morning Joe* in February 2019. "We don't care whether it reads to some conservatives as more socialist or not—we care about whether it works."

The New Deal exacerbated the racial wealth gap by enshrining redlining as federal policy, which barred people of color from accessing the homes (and opportunities to build generational wealth) that were newly available to white families. But the government programs and the subsequent government-funded mobilization for World War II created a stable middle class of white parents who raised boomers in an era of relative income equality and unprecedented prosperity. FDR's allegedly "socialist" tax policies sustained American growth for a generation. The top marginal tax rate topped 90 percent throughout the 1950s, then was cut to 70 percent in the 1960s and 1970s. While most wealthy Americans found loopholes to shrink their effective tax rates, the basic structure worked well: it paid for social welfare programs and ambitious infrastructure projects, such as the interstate highway system, while lessening income inequality in what was then the greatest economic expansion in world history. The top marginal tax rate didn't fall below 50 percent until the late 1980s, when Ronald Reagan slashed it to 28 percent.

But thanks to deregulation and privatization in the 1980s and 1990s, income inequality today is back where it was before the Great Depression. According to historian Jill Lepore, in 1928 the top 1 percent of American families earned 24 percent of all income, but income inequality shrank significantly in the 1940s—by 1944, the middle class had grown and the top 1 percent earned only about 11 percent of the total. But by 2011, Gilded Age income gaps had returned: the top 1 percent were again earning 24 percent of all income, giving the United States the highest inequality of any Western democracy.

At the same time, the economy changed faster than the people who worked in it. The nature of work was morphing so quickly in the early twenty-first century that many people felt the benefits and protections of stable employment being ripped out from under them. Just as workers in the late nineteenth century had to navigate the new factory exploitations of the industrial economy, workers in the early twenty-first century had to adjust to unpredictable gig work in a digital economy.

"Moments of great change, the industrial or the digital revolution, are times when you see an interest in socialism rise," says John Nichols, author of The S Word: A Short History of an American Tradition. "If you don't get your health benefits from your work because your work has been so redefined that you're a freelancer, then you're really going to be saying: Where does my health care come from?"

That was exactly what many young people were wondering. How would they get health insurance when so many of the jobs they could get didn't offer employer-sponsored plans? How would they afford college when the government no longer subsidized higher education the way it once did? Those were exactly the questions Bernie Sanders wanted to answer.

✴ ✴ ✴

Millennials had been socialist-curious for a while, but Bernie Sanders's 2016 presidential campaign was an ideological turning point for many left-leaning young people. Sanders offered universal solutions that seemed to match the scope of the problems young people faced. Health care is too expensive? Medicare for All. Student debt weighing you down? Free college. Can't make ends meet? Raise the minimum wage to fifteen dollars an hour. As Obama's vision of a unified America was increasingly seeming like fantasy, Bernie seemed to be speaking truth to power when he drew battle lines and pointed at a real enemy: the "millionaires and billionaires" who benefited from a "rigged system" that allowed dark money to flow into political coffers. (Never mind that by the time Sanders was delivering this message again in his 2020 campaign, he had become a millionaire himself thanks to his bestselling book.) Obama had talked about "us"; Bernie pointed at "them." He called BS on the system that young people knew was broken, and he told them who to blame for it.

It was an argument that appealed to well-educated, downwardly mobile millennials who felt they had done everything right but were still getting left behind. "There are a lot of people who are deeply invested in telling us that there's nothing we can do, that we have no way to change the economy to better reflect human needs, that all we can do is tinker around the edges with tax rates and this and that instead of actually imagining a future that is up to the challenges that we face," says Michael Carter, the democratic socialist who organized for progressive candidates like Sanders and Alexandria. "A lot of the attraction is the imagination. We're a generation that was told we can be anything we want to be, that we're able to change the world. Meanwhile, all the baby boomers are like, 'We're not gonna change anything and we want all the money still, and just chill out.'"

Even though Bernie Sanders lost both the 2016 and 2020 primaries, his campaign served as a crash course in democratic socialism for an entire generation of young voters. Just as Hillary's loss spurred a defiant horde of liberal women to avenge her defeat, Bernie's campaign converted thousands of millennials to the gospel of socialism. After Trump won, the DSA more than quadrupled its membership to thirty-five thousand—less than the capacity of Fenway Park, but still a sign of vitality on the progressive left.

The socialist craze was a cultural movement as well as a political one. In hipster Brooklyn, the moral clarity of socialism seemed fresh and electric, while Obama-style technocratic moderation began to seem dumpy and outdated. Trump's election had made mainstream Democrats seem not only ineffective, but deeply uncool. When boomers tried to lecture millennials about Chairman Mao or the dysfunction of Eastern European postwar economies, it only reinforced how much they were stuck in the politics of the past. The more the establishment denigrated socialism, the more young progressives embraced it. In leftist online circles, "neoliberal" was thrown around with the force of a sick burn. Usernames flanked by red rose emojis—the signifier of socialist sympathies—became more and more common on social media and dating apps. *New York* magazine even ran a cover story called "When Did Everyone Become a Socialist?"

According to John Della Volpe of Harvard's Institute of Politics, by 2018 only 43 percent of eighteen- to twenty-nine-year-olds said they supported capitalism, while 39 percent said they supported democratic socialism. And even if they didn't quite embrace the label, many young people were embracing socialist ideas: the poll found strong majority support for Medicare for All, a federal jobs guarantee, and tuition-free public college. Gallup found that young people's approval of capitalism had dropped twenty-three points between 2010 and 2018. By 2019, democratic socialism had so deeply pervaded millennial attitudes that even young Republicans acknowledged its appeal. In one 2019 poll, roughly 30 percent of Republicans under thirty-five (and 75 percent of young Democrats) said they thought the word "socialism" had a positive connotation, and that there was an unfairness in the economic system that favored the wealthy. These were young people who were *still calling themselves Republicans in 2019*.

Establishment liberals were appalled by the youthful lurch to the left, while Republicans were thrilled. Experienced Democrats worried—with good reason—that embracing socialism would alienate moderate and conservative boomers in swing districts who bristled at the idea of a socialist revolution that might take away more of their money. Medicare for All sounded good, those Democrats noted, but 150,000,000 Americans got employer-based health insurance and many millions of them wanted to keep it. (Those Democrats preferred a public option, which Pete would eventually refer to as "Medicare for All Who Want It.") When an NYU student asked Nancy Pelosi in 2017 whether there was room for Democrats to move left on economic issues, she replied curtly, "We're capitalists." Two years later, she sharpened her criticism. "I do reject socialism," she told *60 Minutes*. "That is not the view of the Democratic Party."

Republicans, of course, had a field day. Socialism quickly became the de facto attack line on Fox News, with Sean Hannity airing monologues about the "radical far-left Democratic Party and the dangers of socialism" and Tucker Carlson devoting whole segments to ridiculing democratic socialists. As his 2020 reelection bid approached, Trump painted the Democrats as the party of socialists. In his 2019 State of the Union, he vowed that "America will never be a socialist country." Speaking to the Conservative Political Action Conference in 2019, Trump said, "We believe in the American dream, not the socialist nightmare."

But for a generation who hadn't grown up with the Soviet threat, that attack line had lost its bite. The GOP had been crying wolf about socialism for so long—most recently calling Obama a socialist for trying to expand health care access, even though his plan was based off one from a conservative think tank—that they inadvertently linked the term with policies that were overwhelmingly popular with young people. "I think the right did us a service calling Obama a socialist for eight years," Saikat Chakrabarti, one of Alexandria's earliest allies, told *The New Yorker*. "It inoculated us. But people focus on the labels when they are not sure what they mean. What people call socialism these days is Eisenhower Republicanism!"

✳ ✳ ✳

Meanwhile, socialist candidates were beginning to inch forward on the local level. Chokwe Antar Lumumba, son of the late civil rights lawyer Chokwe Lumumba, was elected mayor of Jackson, Mississippi in 2017 to deliver on his father's promise of a black socialist utopia in the South. He vowed to make Jackson "the most radical city on the planet," with a "dignity economy" that included guaranteed basic income to some public housing residents. In the Virginia statehouse elections in 2017, thirty-year-old socialist Lee Carter ousted the well-funded Republican majority whip with the help of the Democratic Socialists of America. Young socialists won city council seats in Rock Island, Illinois, and in South Fulton, Georgia.

As the 2018 midterms approached, more socialist candidates began to join the fray on the state level. Democratic Socialists ran smart campaigns for state legislature across the country (they'd win statehouse seats in New York, Maine, Pennsylvania, and Maryland). And Rhodes Scholar and former Detroit health commissioner Abdul El-Sayed ran a closely watched primary campaign for governor of Michigan.

Abdul, a thirty-three-year old physician with a gift for oration and a sharp sense of style, was endorsed by the Democratic Socialists of America and Bernie Sanders. His grassroots campaign was based on the assumption that Sanders's surprise victory in the Michigan primary in 2016 hinted at a groundswell of socialist support in the Rust Belt. He thought about democracy the way a doctor would think about a sick patient, and he wasn't satisfied with a patient who was only slightly less sick. "Outcomes aren't measured by good or bad," he told me. "They're measured against the outcomes you could have had." Cancer in remission against cancer cured. Patchwork climate regulations against a Green New Deal. The Affordable Care Act against Medicare for All. This was how a lot of young socialists thought about politics: halfway solutions didn't count as solutions at all.

Abdul was a genuine political talent: he drew big crowds, inspired fevered devotion among young activists, and rarely gave the same speech twice. He had the stamina to campaign with Detroit-area Muslims till 1:00 a.m. during Ramadan, sipping avocado smoothies and posting photos of them on

Instagram. He thought he could win the primary not by responding to the little issues (his opponent Gretchen Whitmer's slogan was the uninspiring 'Fix the Damn Roads'), but by reshaping the debate altogether. "Great politicians don't respond to issues," he said. "They create them."

Meanwhile, Democratic Socialists were running for Congress everywhere from Michigan to Kansas to Hawaii. And in the Bronx, Alexandria was challenging Rep. Joe Crowley in New York's fourteenth district.

THE BIG ONE

Everyone said this was the Big One.

FEMA resources were depleted. Journalists were exhausted from covering Harvey. The public had had their fill. But when Maria hit Puerto Rico, it made Harvey seem like a thunderstorm. Maria was the most terrifying storm in ninety years, a category 4 hurricane squatted directly on top of the island, pelting it with 155 mph winds and two feet of rain. It hacked the island to pieces like a jackhammer. The entire island lost power, and not just temporarily—the energy grid was essentially destroyed. Homes looked as if they had been bulldozed. Cell service was out: even the governor of the territory couldn't get through to his family members. At least sixty-four people died in the storm, but that was just the people they counted immediately after the hurricane left the island. When President Trump visited, he downplayed the disaster, saying it wasn't a "real catastrophe, like Katrina," and then threw rolls of paper towels to survivors. People went without clean water, electricity, and medical care for months. The blue tarps covering thousands of homes became the symbol of Puerto Rican resilience. A year after the storm, the true death toll emerged: more than 4,600 American citizens had died because of Hurricane Maria, almost as many as 9/11 and Hurricane Katrina combined.

CHAPTER 16

The Pink Wave

O n April 1, 2017, about four months after she got that first call from Brand New Congress on her way home from Standing Rock, Alexandria Ocasio-Cortez posted an Instagram video to share some big news. "Hey, everyone, I have a super crazy announcement," she said to her iPhone camera, wearing a gray tank top that looked as if it could be pajamas. "I'm just going to share it on Instagram stories first, because it can go away, right? (This story, like many others, was also shared to her personal Facebook, where I was able to find it years later.)

"So basically, I've been nominated to run for office through Brand New Congress," she said. She would be running in the Democratic primary against fifty-six-year-old Rep. Joe Crowley, a powerful member of the Democratic leadership who had served in Congress for almost two decades and had not faced a primary challenger in fourteen years. Besides being in Congress, Crowley was the head of the Queens Democratic Party, the last of the old Tammany Hall–style machines; it had 150 years of experience in retail politics and still controlled many of the political levers in the borough. Alexandria, by contrast, was at square one. "I will be flying to Kentucky later today and spending this weekend in training, and I wanted to document this process for you guys in case there's anyone out there that's thinking of running for office either this year or next year."

She was running on an updated version of Bernie Sanders's progressive platform: Medicare for All, a fifteen-dollar minimum wage, a Green New Deal. But unlike Sanders, she was an open book: her personal narrative was as much a part of her campaign as her ideological goals and she put almost everything on Instagram. She knew that the most important thing was to make the voters see her as human, and the way to make them see her as human was to give them a peek inside her life. She thought of the 2018 media ecosystem almost like *Infinite Jest*: if politicians got boring, then entertainers would become politicians. She had to keep the people entertained.

Her district included parts of Astoria—sometimes known as "Actoria" because of all the actors who live there—and several of her staffers had come from the theater world. That gave her early campaign the feel of an improv theater production in which she was the star. She intuitively understood that campaigns are about narrative as much as policy, and that people needed to be told a story in order to understand an idea. Her story—a young bartender taking on the most powerful politician in Queens—resembled David and Goliath.

From the start, Alexandria was beating the drum of generational change. "Previous gens have used millennials like a credit card: leaving nonstop war, an eroding planet, and education profiteering to fix ourselves," she tweeted in February of 2018. "The same officials who got us into this mess aren't going to get us out. It's time to elect a new generation to office."

"The average age of a House Democrat has skyrocketed to 65," she tweeted in March, "It's time to hand over the keys." When Mark Zuckerberg had to explain Facebook's business model to aging senators, she tweeted that millennials would be better equipped to handle issues like privacy, election security, and deepfakes. "It's a HUGE problem that our leadership isn't digitally competent," she wrote. "How can they prep us for the future?"

The diversity of Queens and the Bronx offered Alexandria an opening, and her timing was exquisite. This race would be all about the primary, since a Democratic victory was assured in this solid blue district. New Yorkers were furious about Trump and wanted fresh blood in Washington, and many were excited about the progressive ideas in Sanders's platform. That offered an advantage to a fresh progressive outsider, though no one gave her much of a chance at the time. For months, reporters barely covered the race. Why bother? Crowley was a shoo-in. Most political insiders failed to notice that his primary opponent had rare political talent.

Her campaign structure was very informal, almost communal. Most congressional campaigns trust volunteers only to knock on doors or stuff envelopes, but Alexandria didn't have enough money to pay a large staff, so she had to rely on enthusiastic volunteers for everything from fundraising to data. The idea was that if your day job was working with data, then you could do data on the campaign. If your day job involved communications, you could do communications on the campaign. By the time they moved into an office in Queens, they had an unofficial system: everybody sat under a Post-it that labeled their job, and as people switched jobs they would move the Post-its around. Former Bernie Sanders staffer and democratic socialist Michael Carter came on in early 2018 as a fundraiser—by the summer, he was deputy campaign manager.

The strategy was to focus on digital and field operations while downplaying paid communications and fundraising. They bought no TV ads, and they didn't spend time or energy schmoozing with big donors since they weren't going to be getting big corporate money, anyway. More than 60 percent of their donations were under $200. Joe Crowley, meanwhile, was sending glossy campaign mailers (Alexandria called them "Victoria's Secret catalogues") with big pictures of his face and promises to "deliver" for Queens and the Bronx. "'Deliver' is insider talk," Alexandria said, referring to the style of retail politics that had given Crowley his clout. "'Deliver' means 'pork.'"

Without polls, Alexandria had no firm idea of how she was doing, but it felt pretty good on the street. When she finally got on TV to debate Crowley, she went on the offensive. She attacked his donations from luxury real estate developers, his lack of participation in the community, and the fact that he didn't even send his kids to school in the district. "If a person loves our community, they would choose to raise their family here," she said in the debate. "They would choose to send their kids to our schools; they would choose to drink our water and breathe our air."

She spent days on street corners speaking into a bullhorn in Spanish, standing and walking so much that she got holes in her white sneakers. That was OK, because a shot of her changing from high heels into sneakers on a subway platform made her first ad go viral, which helped her campaign raise a much-needed $200,000—two-thirds of her campaign budget. Eight weeks before the primary, the Democratic Socialists of America endorsed her, joining Sunrise and other young progressives groups to bolster her field organization.

"After ten years of failed leadership, we have lost a thousand Democratic seats nationwide. We have lost the House, we have lost the Senate, we have lost the presidency," she said at one debate with Crowley, raising her hand in the air like a preacher, already competent in the sort of rousing oration that would become her calling card. Crowley sat there like a marshmallow. "It would be a profound mistake if we believe that the same leadership getting us into this mess is going to get us out."

Crowley raked in $3 million, but he was so confident of winning that he spent only a portion on the primary, with two-thirds earmarked for the general election. He pulled in high-profile endorsements and campaigned in senior centers that somehow weren't open to politicians when Alexandria tried to visit. The Crowley organization—years in the making—seemed to have its tentacles everywhere. When her campaign finally got enough money to do a poll, it showed Alexandria about thirty-five points behind.

A week before the election, Crowley dodged a second debate and sent a Latina former city councilwoman in his place. This struck Alexandria as bizarre and many voters as patronizing, and generated a *New York Times* editorial critical of Crowley. In an unorthodox move, she went to Texas the week before the primary to show solidarity with young immigrants separated from their families at the border, which played well in a progressive district that was sympathetic to undocumented migrants.

By primary night, Alexandria wanted to lock herself in a closet. She knew she had done everything she could, but she felt a sense of dread. She hadn't checked any of the early returns, because she didn't want to see anything or know anything. On the way to her watch party at an old billiards hall in the Bronx, her mother's phone chirped and she made her put it on mute. The car was silent for a second, until she looked out the window and said, "Oh my God, oh my God," and put her hands on her temples. She turned to her boyfriend, Riley, and whispered, "I saw press running to our party."

When they arrived, she paused. Riley gave her a big hug and told her they had done the best they could do. "I don't know if I want to go in," she told him as they walked to the door. "I'm scared." Then she saw a TV through the window with a chyron that showed her name. She started running inside. Security stopped her at first, until she said, "That's me on the poster," and then they let her through. When she got inside she looked back up at the TV and saw the margin—fourteen points—and the number of precincts reporting, and then she screamed and covered her mouth with her hand.

✳ ✳ ✳

A few weeks after Trump was elected, Lauren had gone to something called the Arena, a PAC started by Obama alums who wanted to recruit and train the next generation of leaders. Haley was there too, and they met and exchanged phone numbers. Lauren sat next to a woman named Sarah Feldmann, a small business and nonprofit consultant who was so upset by the 2016 election that she flew alone to the Arena meeting just to see if she could find a campaign to help. Lauren came away from the Arena with a sense that young people were going to save America.

She wasn't sure what she would do next, but she saw that some of the districts on the Democratic Congressional Campaign Committee's list of targets were near Naperville. She thought she could help out whoever decided to run. So after the Women's March, she decided to move home and live in her parent's guest room until she could get a place of her own.

It is hard to overstate the whiteness of Naperville. In 2018, it was 77 percent white and 15 percent Asian—black families like Lauren's made up less than 5 percent of the population. One Naperville man wrote a viral Facebook post about how in his entire life in Naperville he'd never had a black doctor or a black dentist, or been pulled over by a black police officer. There are thirteen golf courses in a seven-mile radius.

But Naperville was home to Lauren, and she was enmeshed in the community. She had gone to the local high school and had spent years in the local Girl Scout troop. It had occasionally occurred to her to run for office—her ultimate dream was to be a senator, and she had gone to a couple of candidate training programs—but she didn't think she would be doing it so soon.

But in April, Lauren watched with disgust as Rep. Randy Hultgren promised to vote against any bill that would jeopardize coverage for preexisting conditions and then, two weeks later, voted for the GOP health care bill that did exactly that. His vote would flush all the work Lauren had done for years, and her own health insurance with it, after he looked his constituents in the face and promised he wouldn't. She watched Trump hold a celebratory press conference in the Rose Garden, surrounded by old white men giving one another high fives and clapping one another on the backs. That was it. She was in.

She had no idea where to start, but the idea kept bubbling up in her mind. So a few weeks later, Lauren and Sarah met for a BBQ lunch at Green Street Smoked Meats in Chicago. Lauren told Sarah that she wanted to run but she didn't even know how to do any of the first fifteen things she was supposed to do to run for office. Sarah reached into her purse, pulled out a notebook, and began to take notes. That was the first time Lauren's campaign existed outside her own head. Sarah said, "What do you need?" and from then on, they were a team.

Later, Lauren would say that she and Sarah willed the campaign into existence in time for their launch on August 9, 2017. They built a Squarespace website and Lauren started finding pictures to post on it. They made a logo. They made lists of local officials to call. They wrote the script for her announcement video: "I'm running for Congress because I believe that this moment in history needs strong, courageous leaders to step forward," she said. It looked amateurish, because it was: her delivery was wooden, the lines were cliché, the camera work was a little shaky.

"She didn't really know what she was doing; I didn't know what I was doing," Sarah said later. "There was something exciting about the idea that just a regular person could do this thing."

They ran their campaign on instinct and grit. They brought in a couple of campaign staffers who had more experience, who "knew how things worked," but they weren't a good fit. They decided that skills learned from other industries—planning, execution, empathy, discipline—were basically all they needed to run a campaign.

The established power brokers largely ignored them at first. The DCCC (the Democratic party's congressional arm) and Emily's List (which helps pro-choice Democratic women candidates) kept asking about their fundraising numbers, but their fundraising numbers weren't very good, because Lauren and Sarah decided to spend most of their time at picnics and house parties instead of raising money. They were told they had to be spending eight hours a day in "call time"—calling people asking for money—but Lauren didn't even know who she would be calling. She didn't have rich friends! Someone told them they had to do a nine-piece mail program and that they had to spend 80 percent of their budget on communications. They decided instead to spend that money on field organizers, because people kept showing up to their office asking to volunteer and they had nobody to organize them. "We had less reverence of structure and order and the way things are supposed to be," Sarah said. "We were thinking, 'There's a different way to do things.'"

The campaign was all about field organizing. Lauren reached out early to the local resistance groups to get their support, so that when angry women asked one another what they could do to fight Trump, the answer would be "Go knock on doors for Lauren Underwood." She slowly built a base of field organizers who spent hours calling and knocking on doors on her behalf. Haley Stevens texted her the day before the primary to wish her luck. "ONE MORE DAY," she wrote. "You are shining and crushing it."

In 2014, only about eight thousand people had voted in the Democratic primary in the fourteenth district—in 2018, more than fifty-one thousand people did. Lauren beat her six white male opponents with 57 percent of the vote, but she knew that was just the beginning: the real test would be the general election against Randy Hultgren.

✳ ✳ ✳

By the time Haley Stevens finally got home from New York after her dismal night at the Javits Center, she had a new plan. She immediately began looking up precinct data for Michigan's eleventh district and started making phone calls. Just before Thanksgiving, she wrote an email to her mother, Maria.

She asked to borrow the car, made plans for the holiday, and then got down to business. "On another front," she wrote, "I would like to take some time this holiday season to discuss with you an idea I have started to explore.

"I am weighing whether I should return to Michigan (Oakland Co) to run for office in the year 2018," she wrote. She was thinking of challenging Rep. Dave Trott for his congressional seat, a "Trump supporter" who had "profited greatly from the foreclosure crisis."

"Why am I motivated to do this?" she wrote to the woman who raised her. "1) To be the real and accessible voice for the people of this district 2) To champion economic development and job growth in advanced industries for the region 3) To continue to fight for women and families." These three bullet points would evolve into her stump speech. Even with her closest confidant, she was a politician to the core.

"Since Hillary's bruising loss, this is what has kept me going," she continued. "And it is what her campaign has asked us to do and even what Donald Trump's bizarre election has shown: IF HE CAN DO IT, WHY CANT I??

"I am giving myself until mid-January to make this decision," she continued. "If I go forward, I will need to make a few changes starting with changing my residency (Q1) and then beginning to transition my time back to Michigan (Q2/3)." She would spend the holidays "soul searching," and asked Maria for her advice but also asked her to keep the news to herself. "This is a private and internal matter for now," she said.

Maria was so enthusiastic about the idea that she became the campaign treasurer. By February 17, less than a month after the Women's March, Haley had signed the papers to create an exploratory committee to run for Congress.

She started going around to local meet and greets. She would say things like "We must lead the way into 2050" and "We must capture our future destiny." She would meet with people all over the district and look intensely into their faces as they told her their concerns, pursing her lips and narrowing her eyes, and she'd take notes of those conversations in little notebooks and then go home and type them up into a big file.

She never got too ideological. She said "health care for all" instead of Medicare for All—she wanted to fix and update the Affordable Care Act, not revamp the entire system. She talked about an "innovation agenda" instead of a jobs guarantee. And she tried not to talk about Trump too much. Instead, any question in her district could be answered with a reinvestment in

Michigan manufacturing. Any problem would be solved with more manufacturing jobs. She loved to talk to the builders, the tinkerers, the people who
made things. When she'd go around to people's houses to canvass, she'd always look at what car was in a driveway, and if it was a GM or Chrysler model,
she'd exclaim, "Great car!" and tell whoever answered the door about her
role in the rescue of the auto industry.

Meanwhile, the Republican incumbent, Dave Trott, was on the defensive. Activists with the local Indivisible group were calling his office demanding he vote against the GOP health care bill. He kept avoiding public
town halls—people began calling him "Chicken Trott"—and when he did
finally show up to face his constituents they chanted, "Shame on you!" and
held up pictures of their sick kids. He voted for the GOP health care plan
anyway, signing his own political death warrant even as the bill failed in the
Senate. By September, he had decided he wouldn't run for reelection. Michigan's eleventh district was now an open seat.

Haley spent the next eleven months shaking hands. She'd go to community events like Greek festivals and church picnics and work the crowd,
slowly making her way through a scrum, telling people about her time on the
Auto Task Force and listening to their concerns. This was a suburban district
that voted for Trump, full of middle-aged men in golf shirts and moms wearing fun prints. Most of the people who lived here worked in the auto industry,
but they weren't factory workers; these were the mid-level managers, the
guys who worked in sales or accounting. The district was mostly white and
upper middle class and tended to swing Republican. That meant Haley had
to be careful in her approach. She couldn't go in with a barn burner: she
talked a lot about economic policy, the manufacturing industry, and bringing
jobs back to Michigan. Over and over, she detailed the auto rescue and how
she'd helped save two hundred thousand Michigan jobs. This was a little
inflated—after all, she had been a twenty-five-year-old aide who had occasionally spoken up in meetings but whose main responsibilities included facilitating meetings and setting up computers and occasionally delivering
sandwiches. But she was right that it was a small team that had achieved big
results, and she had been on it from the very beginning.

The day before the primary, Hillary Clinton recorded a robocall in support of Haley, whom she called "a fresh, new Michigan leader." Even though Clinton had lost Michigan, it was a breakthrough moment in the campaign, because millions of women still supported her. "I've seen Haley in action, and we can count on her to protect the gains we've made with Obamacare," Hillary said. "Please vote for Haley Stevens on Tuesday."

That day, Haley was canvassing wearing a blue top and black pants and an orange wrist purse, all very Ann Taylor Michigan chic. She went from door to door in the pouring rain, ringing doorbells and introducing herself when people answered, leaving a handwritten note when they didn't. The notes said, "Would love to have your vote tomorrow! Oh, and Hillary endorsed!"

Beyond touting the Auto Task Force, she would compliment their dogs, their porches, their gardens. She dropped "gollys" and "gotchas" and "nice to meetchas" and it didn't sound too forced, because that's how Haley actually talked. The dark circles under her eyes had gone from gray to purple.

"I'm a woman in manufacturing," she would say. "I'm a local girl trying to make a difference for us." "It's time to stand up for Michigan again in our economy," she'd say. "Great car, by the way!" She gave out her personal cell phone number. If it was a Republican or a moderate at the door, she just asked them to give her a shot—they could vote her out if they didn't like her. Her campaign manager held an umbrella over her head as she trotted down well-kept suburban blocks.

The men grunted that they would consider it, but many of the women who answered the doors were all in. One woman came out of her house in a caftan, saying she was already planning on voting for her. "If there's a man and a woman on the ballot," she said, "I want the woman."

At another house, a woman burst out of the screen door as soon as Haley rang the bell. She had just gotten the robocall from Hillary Clinton—"Nobody endorses in primaries unless they're really huge!"—and she told Haley she was voting for women up and down the Michigan ballot, from governor to state representative, because "all the blue women are coming to fix the stuff the men broke."

On the morning of the primary, the weather had cleared. Maria cast her ballot at Holy Name Church in Birmingham, Michigan, and fought a sense of déjà vu. The last time she had voted at this precinct was two years earlier, when she and her sister put up a Hillary Clinton doll in their driveway, just before Trump won the state and then the election. This time, she was taking pictures in that same driveway with her thirty-five-year-old daughter, a candidate for the US House of Representatives. "I voted for all women," she said. "It's the year of the female."

Lauren had already won her primary, but that morning she texted Haley. "This will be obvious to you but it wasn't to me . . . so just in case . . . in preparation for your BIG WIN TONIGHT (!!!) make sure you can accept all the congratulatory phone calls and clear out your voicemail early," she wrote. "I was completely overwhelmed and missed a bunch of congressional calls (vm was full for Steny Hoyer)." She added a facepalm emoji.

Once the polls closed, Haley put her phone away. She didn't want to stare at a clock or wait for the phone to ring. So while the rest of the staff was glued to Twitter, Haley and her mom and aunt played Scrabble.

Haley was always a mediocre Scrabble player: she tended to hoard her good letters until she had a perfect big word, and she sucked at the little details like the two-letter words. That night, she was especially bad: she could feel the tension in the room, and sometimes she saw her mom peek at her phone when it wasn't her turn. Haley tried to focus on her letters, but her letters were crappy. She played worse than ever.

By midnight, the race hadn't been called. All the other candidates had dropped out, and the primary was between her and Michigan state representative Tim Greimel. Still, she was pretty sure she was going to win. She kept thinking about all those women who had come out of their houses in their flip-flops and told her they were voting for only women this year. She stopped by her election night party, even though the results weren't in yet, and then she went home and lay in bed and stared at the ceiling. Then it was morning. She had slept about an hour.

She woke up and remembered that some of her friends who had flown in to canvass for her were coming over for breakfast. But she didn't have any food in her fridge or gas in her car. She wanted to serve bagels and lox, and if you serve bagels and lox, then you also have to have onions and capers, so at 8:30 a.m. she was standing in the canned foods section of the grocery store, staring at jars of olives and wondering if the capers would be near the olives, when her cell phone rang. It was Tim Greimel, conceding the primary.

She called her mother to tell her the news. "You may have won," Maria said, "but you lost at Scrabble."

***

All those women who came out to vote for Haley spelled doom for somebody like Abdul El-Sayed. Abdul was sure that Michigan was ready to elect a "true progressive" governor who supported Medicare for All, a fifteen-dollar minimum wage, and a Green New Deal—after all, he said over and over again, Michiganders had voted for Bernie Sanders over Hillary Clinton in the 2016 primary. His campaign strategy was rooted in positioning himself as the Bernie of the race while subtly aligning his opponent Gretchen Whitmer—longtime Democratic leader of the Michigan State Senate—with Hillary Clinton. He was endorsed by Justice Democrats, the same group that endorsed Alexandria.

The parallels were obvious. Abdul had support from DSA activists, the Sunrise Movement, Alexandria (who had become a Democratic superstar since her surprise primary win), and even Bernie Sanders himself. Whitmer had support from Emily's List and the Michigan Democratic establishment, and had deep ties to corporations such as Blue Cross Blue Shield. Abdul had hordes of young progressives working for his campaign; Whitmer had solid support from suburban moms. Abdul hoped his 2018 campaign could finish what Sanders started in 2016. Ever since Trump's election, progressives had been loudly insisting that Sanders would have won key swing states: Abdul's race seemed to be the biggest test of that assertion.

But on primary day, those suburban Michigan women who told Haley they were voting for women "up and down the ticket" voted overwhelmingly for Gretchen Whitmer. It turned out the progressive wave in Michigan—and in the rest of the battleground districts—wasn't quite as strong as activists had thought.

The progressives who did win tended to be women, often women of color: Democratic socialist Rashida Tlaib won her congressional primary in a deep-blue Detroit district and went on to join Alexandria as one of two newly elected socialists in the House of Representatives. Other candidates endorsed by the progressive Justice Democrats such as Ilhan Omar in Minnesota and Ayanna Pressley in Massachusetts also won their primaries in solid Democratic districts and joined them in Congress.

But while Bernie-endorsed candidates did well in safely blue areas, his candidates fared poorly in swing districts. Bernie stuck his neck out for candidates in battleground races in Kansas, Illinois, Pennsylvania, and Wisconsin, and one by one they failed. The DSA had better luck in state legislatures: three of their candidates won seats in the Pennsylvania statehouse, two won in Maryland, and another in Maine. In a much-touted victory, democratic socialist Julia Salazar was elected to the New York State Senate thanks to a surge of door-knocking by her comrades. The DSA put out a statement calling the victories "the rebirth of the American socialist movement after generations in retreat," which, given how many of their candidates lost, seemed a bit overblown. When *The New York Times* asked Bernie Sanders about the progressives' losses in Iowa and Pennsylvania, he said, "It's not a baseball game."

The midterms illustrated how far the progressive movement had come since Bernie's campaign in 2016, and also how far it still had to go. Boomers in the Midwest still shuddered at the thought of a socialist America, and the Democrats who flipped Republican seats in 2018 tended to be moderate women running in suburban conservative districts, like Haley and Lauren. More "establishment" Democratic women beat Sanders-style socialists in primaries all across the Midwest, and many of them went on to flip Republican-held seats. This was the crux of an emerging problem for Democrats: socialism was reshaping the political debate among millennials, but its adherents failed to prove that their message could actually turn red seats into blue ones. The progressives had thoroughly changed the conversation—but they hadn't yet put points on the board.

✳ ✳ ✳

Max Rose wasn't interested in debating the nuances of progressive doctrine; he was interested in flipping a seat. After he got back from Afghanistan, he'd worked for Brooklyn District Attorney Kenneth Thompson to help run a program to resolve low-level warrants, and then worked as chief of staff for a nonprofit health provider. By 2018, he was running for a Republican-held House seat that represented parts of Brooklyn and Staten Island—the only GOP seat in New York City. You used to be able to see the Twin Towers from parts of the district, but by 2018 the view was of the Freedom Tower, which stood there like a big shiny peg leg, a sturdy symbol of something that had been lost. Almost every other house had an American flag; Max figured Staten Island probably had the highest flag-to-people ratio in the entire city. This was convenient because Max was good at talking about American exceptionalism, "I don't want us to look like fucking France," he said. "I am not a socialist, and I don't want us to go down the road that those nations have gone down." He called himself "an old-school Democrat, without the racism."

The campaign reminded Max of being deployed. You had to be careful where you stepped: if you made one mistake, you were fucked. And Staten Island was populist but not particularly liberal, which meant that Max had to walk a delicate line: he had to have bold ideas, but they couldn't seem too radical. He had to be proactive without necessarily being "progressive." Socialism, in this area, was political cyanide.

The district, which included Staten Island and some nonhipster parts of Brooklyn, had more registered Democrats than Republicans, but it tended to skew conservative, partly as a reaction to the rest of New York City. So Max ran right down the middle, saying that both Democrats and Republicans had failed Staten Island. He wasn't running against the incumbent, Dan Donovan—he was running against everyone in charge, on both sides. He criticized Trump and Donovan, but he also slammed Nancy Pelosi and Democratic New York mayor Bill de Blasio. "The Republicans, the Democrats, all the politicians in DC are more interested in winning an argument than solving a problem," he said in a campaign ad. "They've had their shot. Now it's our turn."

He was solidly anti-establishment, but not necessarily "progressive" in the way that Justice Democrats defined it. He was skeptical of the whole "true progressive" thing: he knew it was a litmus test, but he didn't know whether it was a policy distinction or a cultural distinction. The policy part was tricky for him, because it veered too close to socialism for his taste. But he didn't like the cultural aspect of it either. Who decides what "progressive" means, anyway? "I'm unfairly tagged as a fucking centrist," he said. He granted he was probably more moderate than people like Alexandria. But a centrist? No way. "Centrist" was wishy-washy, like a guy who couldn't make up his mind. Max preferred "no bullshit."

He thought it didn't make sense to talk about a "politics for the working people" when not all working people were the same. "Working people" in the Bronx might be house cleaners or waitresses who leaned left, but "working people" in Staten Island were cops and firefighters who leaned right. "Blue collar," in his district, wasn't about income as much as it was about culture. "It's a question of whether you like the show *Blue Bloods* or not," he says.

Instead of wading into fights about the hot-button progressive issues, Max focused on ideas that fell outside the center-versus-left debate that the rest of the party seemed to be having on Twitter. He talked less about social safety nets and more about building things and solving problems. "I want to see the Interstate Highway Act of this generation," he said. "The Apollo project for battery technology.

"If we don't have a battery for the twenty-first century," he added, "everything else is fucking semantics."

He spent his days canvassing the district, talking about the opioid epidemic ravaging the island, transportation infrastructure, and building a sea wall to prepare for another superstorm. He drilled home the fact that his opponent had taken money from the company that makes OxyContin.

Later, Max would say that he knew all along that he would win, but he couldn't have known for sure. NY-11 was a swing district, the type of Obama-Trump district that Democrats needed to win in order to stay viable nationwide. Neighborhood change helped the campaign: Staten Island and Bay Ridge had once been full of hardcore conservatives, but over the last several years young families and artists who had been priced out of fancier parts of Brooklyn made their way to the district. People whose votes might have been lost in the din of progressive Brooklyn precincts made all the difference in NY-11, where his team attracted enough volunteers to knock on 575,000 doors, more than some gubernatorial campaigns.

He was talking to voters until he called it a day at eight forty-five, a little before the polls closed. He went to the watch party at the Vanderbilt restaurant. He smoked a couple of cigarettes, had a glass of scotch, and won the election.

✻ ✻ ✻

Roughly a thousand people came to the Kane County Fairgrounds for Lauren Underwood's election night party. Lauren thought it was wild that all those people had come just to see her. Her staff wanted her to stay secluded in a private holding room until the results were released, but she knew that it was going to take a while for anybody to know anything that night. So she went into the big room wearing her blue two-piece suit and smiled her big smile, trying not to look at her phone or think about the county tallies that were coming in. She hopped from person to person, waving and taking pictures and smiling and saying "thank you," trying to avoid looking at the big screen with the talking heads and the blue-and-red graphics.

Lauren had a good feeling about the race. Her organizers were seeing levels of volunteer enthusiasm that were more similar to a presidential campaign than a congressional election: sometimes three hundred people would show up to volunteer in a single day. Volunteers were knocking on doors and hearing from Trump voters who had voted Republican for years but planned to vote for Lauren. Mostly, voters were telling them they were furious about how Randy Hultgren had ignored his constituents and voted with the Republicans to jeopardize their health care. One voter told Lauren's organizers that she would never vote for a man again.

But that night, the networks were taking too long to call her race. They called Sean Casten's race, in the district next door. Then they called Betsy Dirksen Londrigan's race, also in Illinois. Lauren's staff up in the holding area were seeing exit poll numbers that looked good, but Lauren was with her supporters, so she knew only what she saw on the news. She saw an alert on her phone that the fourteenth district had 90 percent reporting, but they still didn't call the race. That was when she started getting nervous. If they had 90 percent of the votes, why wouldn't they call it? It meant she lost—she knew it.

Suddenly she didn't want to be in a room full of strangers. She was surrounded by hundreds of people who would see her cry if she lost: every local news station, every local newspaper, and everybody's phone was pointed straight at her. She found her parents and said, "We need to go." They hurried out the door and into the elevator and went up to the floor where her staff was waiting in a conference room.

She was thinking about why she probably lost the election. After she appeared in an ad wearing scrubs and greeting patients, Hultgren and the right-wing blogs questioned whether she was actually a real nurse: one blog ran with the headline FOR CONGRESSIONAL HOPEFUL UNDERWOOD, NURSING IS JUST PART OF THE ACT. The piece said that Underwood had misrepresented herself because she didn't actually practice nursing. The attack wasn't unfounded; they had shot the ad at her dentist's office, and Lauren had worn blue scrubs and held a stethoscope as if that were what she normally wore to work, when actually she had mostly worked in the health policy space. She was a nurse—she had a bachelor's degree in nursing and a master's of science in nursing and a master's of public health from Johns Hopkins, and was a licensed registered nurse in Illinois, DC, and Maryland—but she didn't treat patients. The right was using the ad to paint her as a liar, and to say she wasn't a real nurse at all. If she lost the election, she thought as the elevator crept upward, it would be because of this.

The elevator doors opened, and she walked out silently, her parents trailing behind her. She opened the door to the conference room where her staff was waiting and suddenly she was surrounded by people who were cheering and jumping around. In the ninety seconds it took her to come up in the elevator, CNN had flashed her face on the screen and declared her the winner. She had won seven out of seven counties in Illinois's fourteenth district. Her cell phone rang; it was Randy Hultgren, conceding the race.

* * *

Haley approached the general election the same way she'd approached the primary: knock on people's doors, compliment their cars, and tell them about her plans to bring manufacturing jobs back to Michigan. Haley probably said "woman in manufacturing" and "good manufacturing jobs" and "regional economy" about a hundred times a day.

There was going to be a big election night party in the ballroom of the Townsend Hotel in Birmingham, Michigan. It was a fancy hotel where auto executives liked to stay, all gold accents and crystal chandeliers, one of the premiere wedding venues in the area. Just like primary night, Haley didn't want to watch with everyone. She planned to spend the night in a suite with her mom playing Monopoly (her lucky piece was the boot), but they ended up playing Scrabble again instead.

The results took a while to come in. Too long, actually. Haley had been solidly up in the polls for weeks before the election, so the results should have come in sooner than they did. But finally, a little after 10:00 p.m., they flashed her face on the screen and declared her the winner. She came out, grinning in a green blazer, absolutely ready for this.

"I am Michigan's first millennial federal representative," she said, before quoting Martin Luther King Jr. and John F. Kennedy. "I am the daughter of a fabulous mother"—the crowd cheered—"whose fortitude, talent, and success encouraged my own path. Thank you, to my amazing mother.

"Make no mistake about it," she said, her arms thrown wide with her index fingers pointed upward. "We are the defenders of our democracy!"

✳ ✳ ✳

There were Haleys and Laurens and Alexandrias all over the country, first-time women candidates running and winning races. The wave of pink pussy hats that had stormed the National Mall in January 2017 had eventually dispersed around the country, taking their anger with them. In 2015 Emily's List—which recruits and funds pro-choice women Democrats—had received about nine hundred inquiries about running for office; during the year following Trump's election, more than twenty-six thousand women reached out about running, nearly a thirtyfold increase. Emily's List grew so fast they had to knock down a wall in their office to make room for all the extra staff they had to hire. The number of Democratic women challenging incumbents in the House of Representatives jumped 350 percent since 2016. And once they decided to run, these women candidates did well: 53 percent of women Democrats won their primaries, compared to 34 percent of men.

On election night, women and millennials won big. Newly elected women picked up thirty-six seats in the House that night—bringing the total number of women in Congress to a record high—and twenty millennials were elected to Congress for the first time. Most of that energy was concentrated on the Democratic side. Of the thirty-six new women elected to Congress in 2018, all but one were Democrats. And Democrats made up fourteen of the twenty new millennials joining the House of Representatives. They would join the most female, youngest, and most racially diverse House of Representatives in history.

Women voters and young voters decided the election in Democrats' favor. According to FiveThirtyEight, women voters chose Democrats by twenty-three points, the largest gender gap in a midterm election in a generation. And record high youth turnout was key to Democratic victory. The three youngest generations—Gen X, millennial, and Generation Z—cast sixty-two million votes in 2018, outpacing the boomers and older generations. Millennials had the highest jump—one estimate found their turnout nearly doubled between 2014 and 2018—and those new young voters supported Democrats by two to one. Nearly 70 percent of eighteen- to twenty-nine-year-olds and almost 60 percent of thirty- to forty-four-year-olds voted for Democrats, while voters forty-five and over were evenly split between the parties, according to Pew. More than 90 percent of young black voters and 82 percent of young Hispanic voters chose the Democrats. Young voters were decisive in electing a Democratic governor in Wisconsin, and Democratic senators from Nevada and Montana.

Trump had been a wake-up call for millennial voters. And now they were finally showing up.

✳ ✳ ✳

Elise Stefanik had been warning about this for months. Between the blue wave, the so-called pink wave, and the youth wave, Republicans were left with a congressional minority that was even older, whiter, and more male than it had been in years. After the midterms, Democrats had eighty-nine women in the House, while Republicans had dropped from twenty-three women to thirteen. By the end of the thumping, women held only 3 percent of House Republican seats (compared to 20 percent of Democratic seats) and

9 percent of Republican state legislature seats (Democrats had more than twice as many). By the time all the votes were counted, women representation among House Republicans hit a twenty-five-year low.

It seemed as if Elise was one of the only people in the Republican Party who thought this was a big problem. As the first female head of recruitment for the National Republican Congressional Committee (the NRCC), Elise had recruited more than a hundred Republican women to run for Congress in 2018. She thought they were smart and capable and would have been great nominees. But the party wasn't giving them enough resources, and they kept getting picked off in the primaries by white men, so by the general election, the vast majority of Republicans on the ballot were men.

After the election, Elise went to a forum for her colleagues running for party leadership positions. She stood up and waved her hand around the room full of white men. "Look around," she said. "This is not reflective of the American public." She asked both the candidates for minority leader what they were going to do to recruit more women candidates, and neither one of them had a good answer for her.

She circulated a letter urging House Republicans to pay attention. "We fell short across multiple demographics, including women, who represent a growing segment of America's voting population," she wrote.

But none of the leadership seemed alarmed. Emphasizing gender seemed to hit too close to the "identity politics" that conservatives had spent the last decade maligning. So when Elise said she was stepping away from the NRCC to build a new PAC to help women Republicans win primaries, and the NRCC chair said it would be a "mistake," Elise had had enough.

"NEWSFLASH," she tweeted, adding red siren light emojis, "I wasn't asking for permission."

THOUGHTS & PRAYERS

@TheCaptainAidan: My school is being shot up and I'm locked inside. I'm fucking scared right now . . . Good evening, it began as an ordinary school day, and it was almost over when gunfire erupted this afternoon. This deadly mass shooting happened in Parkland, Florida. . . . **@ohstephany_:** Today I started my school day freaking out about a gov test I had. I ended my school day freaking out about if my friends are alive or not . . . **@Melody_Ball:** my little brother just sent me this video of the swat team evacuating his classroom at stoneman douglas . . . **@Sarahchadwickk:** you truly don't understand how horrifying this is until you're in the school when it happens and when your friends and teachers are the ones that are shot . . . **SEETHING PARKLAND LEGISLATOR: 'YOU KNOW WHAT IS GOING TO HAPPEN AFTER THIS? NOTHING.'** . . . **@realDonaldTrump:** My prayers and condolences to the families of the victims of the terrible Florida shooting . . . **@chaddiebaddie:** I don't want your condolences you fucking piece of shit, my friends and teachers were shot. Do something instead of sending prayers . . . **PARKLAND STUDENT: MY GENERATION WON'T STAND FOR THIS** . . . "They say that tougher gun laws do not decrease gun violence: we call BS," said Emma González. "They say a good guy with a gun stops a bad guy with a gun: we call BS." . . . **RUBIO: GUN LAWS WOULDN'T HAVE PREVENTED PARKLAND** . . . **@Sarahchadwickk:** We should change the names of AR-15s to "Marco Rubio" because they are so easy to buy . . . **STUDENTS LEAD HUGE RALLIES FOR GUN CONTROL ACROSS THE U.S.:** For many of the young people, the Washington rally, called March for Our Lives, was their first act of protest and the beginning of a political awakening. . . . **AFTER PARKLAND, STATES PASS 50 NEW GUN LAWS:** States across the country, including 14 with Republican governors, enacted 50 new laws restricting access to guns . . . **PARKLAND SHOOTING SURVIVORS RELEASE AMBITIOUS GUN CONTROL PLAN.** . . . **@davidhogg111:** Policymakers have failed, so survivors are stepping up. . . .

CHAPTER 17

Defend, Distance, Defect, or Defeat

efore Trump, things had been looking sunny for the up-and-comers in the Republican Party. Obamamania was dying down, the economy was ramping up, and the GOP seemed poised to make a rational appeal to business-minded young people about free markets and lower taxes. Plus, they had exciting fresh faces to help them rebrand the party. "While the Democrats have Joe Biden and Hillary Clinton, we have leaders like Marco Rubio, Paul Ryan, Kelly Ayotte, and Bobby Jindal, among many others," party leaders wrote in the 2013 GOP autopsy. "We also have a youthful RNC Chairman, Reince Priebus." (Baby-faced forty-one-year-old Priebus had helped commission this report.)

Then Trump happened. The 2016 election worked like napalm on the GOP's bench of up-and-coming talent: Trump humiliated Rubio in the 2016 primary, fired Priebus as his chief of staff by tweet after just six months, frustrated Ryan into an early retirement, and Ayotte lost her Senate seat. More broadly, his surprise win made the 2013 RNC autopsy look like a joke. The committee had warned that the Republican Party would have to embrace Latinos, women, and young people if it was going to survive. Three years later, Trump called Mexicans "rapists," referred to women as "fat pigs" and "dogs," and won the presidency anyway.

But Trump's victory didn't prove that the party autopsy was wrong—just that its timing was off. The world was in fact changing in all the ways party elders said it would: the share of the Hispanic vote was growing, women were becoming a more important political coalition, and young voters were shaping up to be a sleeping giant. Trump wasn't the vanguard of a new Republican wave: he was the last gasp of the old one.

His election may have thrilled the older white working-class voters and graying evangelicals who put him into the White House, but millennial conservatives were ambivalent. Six months into Trump's presidency, only 12 percent of millennials said they were "consistently" or "mostly" conservative, compared to nearly 60 percent who said they were "consistently" or "mostly" liberal (the rest were in the middle). One 2018 poll found that 57 percent of Republicans in their twenties and thirties wanted another Republican to challenge Trump for the nomination in 2020—among Republicans under twenty-five, an overwhelming 82 percent wanted a primary challenger to Trump.

Two years into Trump's presidency, more than three-quarters of Republican senior citizens approved of his performance, but less than half of millennial Republicans did. Young conservatives were the only GOP group to give him a double-digit disapproval rating.

Trump caused a generational schism within the Republican Party. Older conservatives were sick of arguing for morality and losing. They remembered when liberals stuck by Ted Kennedy after he left a woman to drown, and when Democrats defended Bill Clinton even when he was caught philandering with a White House intern. They had lost almost all the moral battles they waged against popular Democratic politicians, and even when they ran presidential candidates with spotless moral character (such as Bob Dole or Mitt Romney), they lost anyway. They were ready for a political jackhammer, morals be damned: millennial conservative thinker Ben Shapiro wrote that older conservatives knew Trump was a bull in a china shop, but "he's *our* bull in *their* china shop." Younger conservatives were less scarred by the morality wars of the 1990s, and they had more political battles ahead of them, so they were less willing to sacrifice long-term high ground for short-term political wins. Older Republicans saw Trump as payback for the past— younger ones saw him as a liability for the future. Or, as Shapiro put it, "Older conservatives judge Trump on his politics; younger conservatives judge Trump on his values."

Young conservatives were more bothered by Trump's meanness, by his ideological inconsistencies, and by his character flaws. "It became harder and harder for me to confidently say, 'I'm a Republican,'" one young conservative told journalist Eliza Gray. "Because every day he's saying something that reflects badly on my party."

So his election put the rising generation of young Republican leaders—many of whom agreed with their peers on marriage equality and climate change—in a tough spot. They were young and ambitious in a GOP gerontocracy, outliers in a party that was becoming increasingly toxic among millennials. They had only four options: they could defend Trump and flunk a major character test of their generation, they could distance themselves from the president and hope not to get caught in the crossfire, they could publicly defect from the party in search of moral high ground, or they could loudly criticize him and risk defeat.

✳ ✳ ✳

Dan Crenshaw was a defender. After a stint as a legislative assistant on the Hill, he took the advice of John Noonan, a fellow veteran who had served as Jeb Bush's advisor on national security, and jumped into a 2018 House race in Texas when GOP representative Ted Poe retired. Dan made the runoff in the primary, despite a bruising super PAC attack over some 2015 comments he made criticizing Trump's "hateful" and "insane rhetoric" toward Muslims, and won with a mere 155 votes to spare. He went on to win the general election, becoming one of only a handful of millennial Republicans elected in a year that saw a massive influx of young Democratic women. Thanks to his war-hero background and media savvy, Dan was quickly anointed one of the young standard-bearers of the Republican Party. But his Houston-area district included affluent suburbs full of older, Trump-loving Republicans, so he had to be careful to stay in the president's corner.

Dan had won his race in a conservative area by campaigning on entitlement reform, even though his consultants told him it was the so-called "third rail" of politics. He framed fiscal responsibility as a generational issue. "If we don't tackle certain problems like our debt crisis, then the millennials are the ones that have to pay for it," he said. He didn't get much applause when he spoke to the older Tea Party voters in the conservative parts of his district; he had better luck when he went out to Houston bars on Saturday nights and talked to everyone there—including Independents and Democrats—until they got a sense of what he was about.

"Young people liked the solutions, the technocratic language, the facts and figures in the policy," said Brendan Steinhauser, a GOP consultant who worked with Dan since before his primary. "Whereas some of our older voters are kind of like the guys in *South Park* going, 'They took our jobs!'"

In many ways, Dan had little in common with Trump. For one, he had honorably served five tours of duty as a Navy SEAL, and he had an eye patch, two Bronze Stars, a Purple Heart, and a Navy Commendation Medal with valor to show for it. He posted cute Instagrams with his wife, Tara, who had supported him through his hospitalization and his many deployments. At thirty-four, he seemed to recognize the need to appeal to young people, even if he didn't necessarily align with most of his fellow millennials on issues such as immigration.

But he shared the president's star power and his mastery of social media. Dan's prodigious Instagram posts—of everything from his workouts to his votes on Capitol Hill—drew some comparisons to Alexandria Ocasio-Cortez. And, like Trump, he seemed to intuit how to use the mainstream media to his advantage. After *SNL* comedian Pete Davidson mocked Dan's eye patch (he said he looked like a "hit man in a porno"), Dan agreed to go on *SNL* to accept Davidson's apology. After making fun of Davidson's blue hair ("He looks like if the meth from *Breaking Bad* was a person") and teasing him with a song by his ex-girlfriend Ariana Grande, Dan got down to business: "There's a lot of lessons to learn here, not just that the left and right can still agree on some things, but also this: Americans can forgive one another." He ended the segment by honoring Davidson's father, a firefighter who died saving lives on 9/11.

The moment was political gold, and quickly established Dan as the right's voice of reason against what many considered to be rampant left-wing political correctness. If the battle over civility and free speech was the new culture war, then Dan was the conservative Achilles.

He seized the moment by writing a *Washington Post* op-ed about the dangers of what he called "outrage culture." "It seems like every not-so-carefully-worded public misstep must be punished to the fullest extent, replete with soapbox lectures and demands for apologies," he wrote. "Anyone who doesn't show the expected level of outrage will be labeled a coward or an apologist for bad behavior. I get the feeling that regular, hard-working, generally unoffended Americans sigh with exhaustion."

Some young Republicans built their entire careers around complete devotion to Trump. Rep. Matt Gaetz (b. 1982) was subjected to an ethics investigation into whether he tried to intimidate former Trump fixer Michael Cohen before his explosive public testimony against his old boss. ("Do your wife & father-in-law know about your girlfriends?" Gaetz tweeted. "I wonder if she'll remain faithful when you're in prison. She's about to learn a lot.") He brought a Holocaust skeptic to the State of the Union, hired a speechwriter with ties to white nationalists, tried to expel the parents of slain schoolkids from a gun safety hearing, and went on MSNBC to defend Trump when he called Haiti a "shithole country." Unsurprisingly, he was often described as Trump's protégé. But even Gaetz had a millennial agenda: ending the 9/11 wars and legalizing marijuana were two of his biggest priorities in Congress.

Dan was a little more subtle about it. His position as the affable warrior against the sanctimonious left tapped into one of the only areas in which Republicans seemed to be gaining ground with young people. The "outrage culture" on the left was very real, especially on college campuses, and Independent and conservative-leaning young people were constantly finding themselves accused of "hate speech" and "microaggressions" by their left-leaning classmates. In the Trump era, the thrill of rejecting the overzealous "social justice warriors" (also known as "owning the libs") seemed to be one of the only things driving young people *toward* the Republican Party. Wide majorities of Americans said they thought the country was getting too "politically correct," and in one Harvard poll, nearly half of young voters said they thought political correctness was at least partly responsible for America's problems. Young conservatives often felt especially maligned: "They say we're white supremacists, racist, misogynistic, and we have internalized misogyny," one young member of the College Republicans at the University of North Carolina told *Vanity Fair*. "Name-calling is the first place they go."

Young conservatives were united by opposition to the anti-Trump left more than by loyalty to the president himself. Even those who disliked Trump said they resented the sanctimonious left even more. Reporting from the Young Women's Leadership Summit, hosted by the conservative group Turning Point USA, *New York Times* reporter Astead Herndon observed that "more than any political ideology, the women at the summit appeared united by their criticism of recent social movements." To them, he wrote, "there was nothing worse than being labeled racist, sexist or homophobic by 'the left,' because liberal name-calling was worse than any sin that could precede it." (Of course, Turning Point USA did its own fair share of de-platforming, hosting a "Professor Watchlist" of left-leaning academics for conservatives to boycott.)

That's why young conservatives loved Dan: he attacked the outraged mob of "woke police" that seemed to be always attacking them, but unlike Trump, he wasn't always digging them into an even deeper hole. He was likable and reasonable and hadn't bragged about sexually assaulting anyone. He tried to be funny without being mean. He liked to talk in interviews about how it was important to "treat each other like human beings." When Pete Davidson posted an alarming pseudo-suicidal message on Instagram a few weeks after the SNL appearance, Dan called him to check in. He had all the political priorities of Donald Trump without the nasty streak. People started calling him the "future of the GOP," and soon he was hosting conferences for conservative students in the Houston area, complete with logos featuring his distinctive eye patch.

Dan's position as the anti-anti-Trump was extremely convenient: it spoke to legitimate widespread frustration with liberal political correctness, while also excusing him from the responsibility of condemning Trump for anything he said. His whole brand was tied up in not joining social justice pile-ons—and he used that as a convenient excuse to avoid condemning the president for nearly anything he did, no matter how outrageous.

"Let's not forget that both Romney and McCain were supposedly racist Nazis," he told me. When I pushed back that they didn't embrace the white nationalist subculture to the same extent, Dan said, "No, but it doesn't matter. We know conservatives were getting called that, no matter what. At a certain point, it broke the conservatives. We're like: we just want somebody who will go in there like a bull in a china shop and fight back."

It also allowed him to defend Trump without being painted as a loyalist. "I support the president on pretty much everything, but there's a couple things I disagree with," he told Ben Shapiro. "I'd grade him pretty high." He had criticized the president on a few of his less conservative policies, such as his plan for new tariffs on Mexico. He slammed Trump's impetuous withdrawal of US troops from Syria, cosponsored a bipartisan resolution opposing the withdrawal, and went on Fox News to say it would create "chaos." He told me he didn't like Trump's "unpresidential demeanor," but "it doesn't emotionally trigger me" because he's able to "compartmentalize" and be "ultra-objective." He avoided mentioning Trump in his speeches—he talked about Reagan instead.

But Dan and Trump were totally aligned on most of the big issues, particularly immigration. He said the president was "absolutely right on the border issue." Dan gave numerous interviews explaining why a border wall was a commonsense solution to stop five hundred thousand migrants from crossing the border every year, and posted a sympathetic video of a "ride-along" with Border Patrol as they discussed the best ways to apprehend illegal immigrants. When images of kids in cages at the border caused widespread outrage on the left, he said they were "trying to stand on their moral high horse." On climate change, he said in a Facebook Live that he wanted to listen to what the "science says on both sides," but he subsequently clarified that he understood that manmade emissions play a part in climate change. (He didn't support the Green New Deal, but he had his own climate change legislation the LEADING Act that incentivized research for carbon capture technology and natural gas.) If he ever spoke out about the president's denigration of nonwhite Americans, he didn't do it very loudly. He defended Trump's meetings with Kim Jong Un and Vladimir Putin. According to an analysis by FiveThirtyEight, Dan voted with Trump 94 percent of the time in the first nine months of his term: he broke with the administration's priorities only three times.

When Gaetz defended Trump, it seemed like a pit bull defending its master. But Dan had built enough cultural clout that when he defended Trump, it resonated as authentic. Was Trump ignorant and cruel and blind to the lessons of history? Yes. Was Dan willing to give him political cover, anyway? Also yes.

When he went on *The View*, he was asked how he supported the president, given his character. "I support his policy agenda. I don't have to support every character flaw that he has," he said. "We can have multiple ideas in our head at the same time." He bulldozed exactly the lane many young Republicans were looking for: permission to support Trump's policies without defending his behavior. "I can't focus on every single little thing," he told me. "He's getting slammed for it in the media, so why do I have to pile on?"

So when Trump said something racist, Dan tended to ignore it or dismiss the controversy as evidence of outrage culture, neatly deflecting the blame from the president to his critics. When Trump tweeted in July of 2019 that four of his Democratic colleagues—all women of color—should "go back" to the "crime infested places from which they came" Dan joined most Republicans to vote against the Democrats' resolution to condemn Trump's comments, calling it "juvenile politics." It wasn't the first time Dan defended the president's racism, his vulgarity, and his undermining of American democracy—and it was far from the last.

Still, at least one early ally worried that even with this delicate dance, Dan was firmly aligned with the president in a way that could cause him problems in the future. "I do worry about the taint of Trump rubbing off on him," says his old advisor Steinhauser. "Democrats are going to come in and say, 'Sorry, Dan Crenshaw, you've been carrying water for Donald Trump.'"

When he explained his positions on Instagram, he took on the tone of a smarter older brother who was trying to explain the ways of the world. To fans, it sounded like real talk—to critics, it sounded like mansplaining. "I don't like what the president said on Twitter, I really don't, but this resolution goes way beyond that," he said in an Instagram story explaining his vote not to condemn Trump's comments. "It doesn't capture the intent of what he was saying, and it actually includes way more condemnation than his comments have anything to do with . . . The reality is this entire thing is exhausting." The next day, when Trump supporters at a North Carolina rally chanted, "Send her back!" about his Somali-American colleague, Rep. Ilhan Omar, Dan said nothing.

Later, I asked him whether the president's comments were racist. "I do think the word 'racist' is thrown around way too loosely, to the point where it's totally lost the meaning," he said. "Are there times where he at least could be interpreted as going over the line? Yeah, of course." But "I fundamentally do not believe" he's racist, Dan added. "His long history and career in public life doesn't indicate it."

What about the allegations of racial discrimination at his family's real estate business? Or the ad he took out demanding the execution of the Central Park Five? Or when he called some largely black and brown nations "shithole" countries?

"Well, I don't think any of those examples you just gave me were racist examples, either," he said. "Just because you're calling a country a shithole country, again, how is that racist? You're saying, well, it's majority minority people there. Again, how is that racist? What is racism?"

I asked him to define what "racism" means.

"Taking an action or saying something or treating somebody differently solely because of an immutable characteristic that is the color of their skin," he said. "None of those cases were because of that. Simple as that."

Conversations with Dan often went in circles like this. Nearly every indictment of Trump triggered an exoneration, designed to dismiss or belittle whoever had criticized the president in the first place, but in a way that had a sort of joking nature to it. He defended the president with an eye roll, not a shriek—a sharp contrast to the harsh and ugly rhetoric coming from Trump's inner circle. He liked to "break things down," positioning his perspective as the "objective" one, and he had particular disdain for liberal ideas that he thought were rooted in emotion rather than facts. His insistence on his own rationality positioned his opponents as ridiculous and hysterical.

He was a fighter just like Trump, but he was smarter and more subtle. He was better at exposing his opponents' weaknesses and more disciplined about avoiding self-inflicted wounds. Trump got elected, he said, because conservatives wanted a warrior against the overzealous left. "We're never going to go back from that," he said. "Conservatives are always going to want that now.

"But they don't need it to be Trump," he added. "And they don't need it to be Trump's style." Dan knew better than anybody that there were many ways to fight a war.

✳ ✳ ✳

At first, Elise Stefanik didn't actively defend Trump the way Dan did, but she wasn't about to alienate the party to which she had devoted her entire career. She was in it for the long haul, which meant she had to be careful. Plus, her constituents had voted for Obama twice and then Trump. So for a while, she did what many young Republicans tried to do: she distanced herself from the president as much as she could without pissing him off.

In the beginning, she supported a lot of his legislative agenda but not all of it. She repeatedly called for more investigation into Russian interference in the 2016 campaign, and condemned her fellow Republicans for the "politicization" of the investigation—but after the Mueller report came out, Elise sided with the administration, tweeting that the report concluded "there was no collusion between the Trump campaign and the Russian government." Throughout his first two years in office, she voted with him almost 90 percent of the time.

She criticized him often, but her criticisms had the tone of dutiful scolding rather than outrage. When he banned travel from majority-Muslim countries, she posted on Facebook that she "opposed President Trump's rushed and overly broad Executive Order." A few months into his presidency, she said she didn't think his plans for a border wall were "realistic" and that the president wasn't "exactly right on that." When Trump said he didn't want any more immigrants from "shithole countries," her spokesperson released a statement that said she "believes the President's comments were wrong and contrary to our American ideals." When Trump said he could pardon himself, Elise said she "disagrees with the president's assertion."

Still, her equivocation was frustrating her constituents. After Trump

told four of her fellow young congresswomen to go back to where they came
from, Elise tweeted that his comments were "inappropriate, denigrating, and
wrong," but, like Dan, refused to vote for a House resolution condemning his
comments. Her local paper, the *Post-Star*, ran an editorial calling her out for
failing to have a "moral center."

"We remind Rep. Stefanik that this is New York, and that there is a statue
in the harbor that welcomes the downtrodden and huddled masses yearning
to breathe free," the editorial board wrote. "We suggest she visit soon."

Elise didn't attack Trump's character, or call him a racist, or rail on him
as a danger to democracy. Her criticism, which became increasingly rare,
was typically at a volume that was perfectly calibrated to avoid making news
or antagonizing the president: she expressed her disagreement, stated her
reasoning, and moved on. And she kept her head down and focused on her
district—in 2019, she won a large military designation for Fort Drum, which
would bring jobs and funding to her constituents. Besides, staying in Congress and moving up the ranks in the House was the only political path forward for Elise: as a Republican in New York, she had little chance in the
foreseeable future of winning a Senate or statewide office. She had to keep
her head down and stay the course.

But because she represented a more moderate district in a blue state, she
was able to push back on some of Trump's early agenda. While she backed his
efforts to repeal Obamacare (a litmus test issue in the pre-Trump era), she
opposed his tariffs and voted against his tax plan, mostly because it wouldn't
allow New Yorkers like her constituents to deduct their state and local taxes.
She voted against deep budget cuts to the EPA, opposed Trump's rollback of
the Clean Power Plan, and voted to block him from withdrawing from the
Paris Climate Agreement. She and Carlos Curbelo were among the first Republicans to call for the resignation of EPA director Scott Pruitt after multiple corruption scandals, and cosponsored the Honest Ads Act, which would
combat foreign disinformation like the kind that helped get Trump elected.
After the Trump administration ordered children to be separated from their
parents at the border in 2018, Elise cosponsored the Family Reunification
Act. When Trump forced a government shutdown to demand money for a
border wall, Elise voted with Democrats to reopen the government. By 2019,

Elise was voting with the Trump administration only about half the time. But this was not the way to rise in Trump's GOP.

Walking the Trump tightrope was tricky: every day was a balancing act between her party and her constituents. At a town hall in April 2018, one man wearing a hat that said "I'm a Deplorable" rose in outrage about Nancy Pelosi's criticism of Trump's tax bill. Elise twirled on the tightrope: she slammed Nancy Pelosi as "out of touch," but explained that she voted against the bill because "it penalized high-tax states, and unfortunately we're in a high-tax state." Another man stood and asked why the president hadn't released his income taxes. "I believe the president should have released his taxes," she said. "Everyone running for federal office should release their taxes, which is why I do it."

An older woman with white hair rose to ask Elise what she was going to do as a "check and balance" of Trump. People began to clap, and Elise pursed her lips and closed her eyes as the clapping went on. "I think it's important to respect voters in this district," she said, adding that the voters there chose President Obama twice and then Donald Trump.

"Certainly he tweets too much. I'm stating the obvious. I think most Republicans would probably agree with that," she continued. She took a deep breath. "I get criticism for not supporting the president enough, or for supporting him too much. I have to call it like I see it, as I said, and do the best job I can."

That November, when Republicans around the country were losing their seats to Democratic women, Elise was reelected in a landslide.

✳ ✳ ✳

Despite the efforts of people like Dan Crenshaw and Elise Stefanik, the GOP was still losing with young voters. Trump took a party that was already distasteful to most young people and made it nearly radioactive.

As the Trump presidency dragged on, some young Republicans defected from the GOP altogether. A Pew study found that nearly a quarter of young people who had identified as Republicans in 2015 had left the GOP by 2017. Only about half of Republicans under thirty had stayed loyal to the GOP throughout Trump's rise: 21 percent had left the party and then returned, while 23 percent had permanently defected. By 2018, only 17 percent of millennials identified as solidly Republican. Only 6 percent strongly approved of Trump. These were brutal numbers for anyone concerned about the future of the GOP.

Some prominent young conservative voices expressed anguish over what their party had become under Trump. Meghan McCain, daughter of the late senator John McCain and the main conservative voice on *The View*, lamented Trump's racist behavior: "It's all these old racist dog whistles that have plagued this country for so long," she said.

Other up-and-coming Republicans saw the writing on the wall and left before too much of the Trump stench rubbed off on them. Jeff Flake, the youthful-seeming Arizona senator with a full head of hair and presidential potential, retired in 2018 rather than trying to run a primary as an anti-Trump Republican. Paul Ryan, once the wunderkind of the Republican Party, chose to retire as Speaker of the House in 2018 after passing Trump's massive tax cut; he knew the Democrats would likely win control of the House and was worn out by dealing with Trump. Nick Ayers, once the thirty-four-year-old chief of staff to Mike Pence, was reportedly offered a job as Trump's chief of staff but opted to move back to Georgia instead. Both Ryan and Ayers said they left Washington to "spend more time with their families," but Ayers's name would soon be floated as a possible GOP Senate candidate in Georgia.

But the first Republican congressman to publicly break from his party and stay to fight it out was Justin Amash (b. 1980). Justin was the son of Christian immigrants from Palestine and Syria, a bespectacled young dad in a blue polo shirt, a guy who was so proud of his perfect attendance in Congress that he cried when he missed his first vote on the Hill. Justin believed in the purity of American democracy and the infallibility of the Constitution. His father's family had been driven from Palestine and then resettled by a pastor in Michigan, and his father had drilled into him a particular strain of American exceptionalism: that no matter where you were born, you could become American; that anyone could make it in America if they were willing to work hard enough; that the American system allowed people to build their lives without having to worry about the sectarian violence or religious conflict. It was an ethos of freedom and individualism that grew into libertarianism, a fierce defense of the opportunities America had given the Amash family.

Justin was a Tea Party conservative who had cofounded the House Freedom Caucus: he opposed some of the GOP budget slashes because they weren't deep enough; he wanted to eliminate the ACA completely; he opposed pretty much all environmental regulations and hoped to dismantle the Department of Education. But where he was out of step with his peers on health care and government spending, his libertarianism put him in line with some other millennial priorities—he opposed federal restrictions on marijuana, for example, and condemned Trump's overreach on immigration.

He had bucked his party before. He was against defunding Planned Parenthood and NPR, not because he supported them but because he didn't think the government should be singling out particular organizations to punish. He broke from his party in opposing expanded government surveillance. He was the only House Republican to vote against a resolution expressing support for ICE. When Michael Cohen testified before a House committee, most Republicans simply attacked Cohen for flipping on Trump or used the questioning to defend the president; Amash was one of the only Republicans who interrogated him about his boss, asking, "What is the truth that you know President Trump fears most?"

After reading the Mueller report, Justin was the first Republican to say that Trump had engaged in "impeachable conduct." In a series of tweets in May, Amash said that "Mueller's report reveals that President Trump engaged in specific actions and a pattern of behavior that meet the threshold for impeachment," and that he believed Attorney General William Barr had misrepresented the findings of the report. Later, he would say that some of his GOP colleagues privately agreed with him—but Justin was the only Republican gutsy enough to say so and to point out the moral hypocrisy in his own party (he is also the only millennial elected official in this book who did not grant me an interview).

"We've witnessed members of Congress from both parties shift their views 180 degrees—on the importance of character, on the principles of obstruction of justice—depending on whether they're discussing Bill Clinton or Donald Trump," he tweeted.

Justin quickly became a pariah in Trump's Republican Party. On July 4, 2019, he wrote an op-ed in *The Washington Post* announcing he was leaving the GOP, calling his decision a rejection of partisan politics altogether: "No matter your circumstance," he wrote, "I'm asking you to join me in rejecting the partisan loyalties and rhetoric that divide and dehumanize us."

Afterward, he told reporters he felt liberated. He wouldn't have to listen to leadership anymore, or worry about upsetting powerful Republican allies, or be pressured to fall in line. He didn't have to contort himself to defend things he thought were indefensible. He was free, but he was also in the wilderness. He had resigned from the House Republican Conference and stepped down from the House Oversight Committee before he could be removed.

When he had gone back to his district after calling for Trump's impeachment, his constituents greeted him with a standing ovation. People started asking him if he would consider running for president in 2020. But Justin knew he couldn't survive politically outside the two-party system, and he would never be at home in Trump's GOP. Instead, he decided to give up his seat, announcing he wouldn't run for reelection.

✳ ✳ ✳

Carlos Curbelo was in a tough spot: he was a moderate anti-Trump Republican representing a Democratic-leaning district that included the Miami suburbs and the Florida Keys. His 70 percent Latino district was full of recent immigrants, and his constituents regularly felt the brunt of persistent flooding as hurricanes got stronger with every year of warming. That was part of the reason he had tried to steer his party toward immigration reform and climate change solutions, joining the small but growing cohort of Republicans who hoped to move the ball toward issues that millennials were concerned about. But in the party of Trump, he was drowning: even though he'd been reelected in 2016, his voters had chosen Clinton over Trump by the second highest margin of any Republican-held district in the nation.

While Amash was the first to call for impeachment, Carlos had challenged Trump's immigration and climate policies more loudly than any other Republican. He proposed a carbon tax that would have reduced emissions by a third, putting the United States on track to meet the standards set by the

Paris Climate Agreement—in Trump's GOP, it went nowhere. When Trump announced his "zero tolerance" immigration policy that resulted in family separations at the border, Carlos was one of the few Republicans who visited the detention facilities where children were being held.

But Carlos really went nuclear over DACA. Carlos said he wouldn't vote for government funding at the end of 2017 without a solution that would protect these young Dreamers, and at the 2018 State of the Union, he brought a DACA recipient as his guest. A few months later, he went even further: using a little-used procedural rule called a discharge petition, Carlos gathered signatures of moderate Republicans and Democrats to force a vote on a compromise immigration bill that would give Trump some funding for his border wall but also provide a pathway to citizenship for Dreamers—Elise was one of the first Republicans to sign on. He spent two months muscling bipartisan support: he needed twenty-five Republican votes to override the GOP House leadership and bring the measure to a vote. He got only twenty-three. Although he didn't get the signatures, the maneuver did force Speaker Ryan to allow the House to vote on two compromise immigration bills, including one that Carlos cosponsored that outlined a path to citizenship. It failed to get any Democratic votes and was opposed by the right wing Freedom Caucus, so it didn't pass.

Carlos was still a small-government conservative, so he voted with his party on repealing Obamacare (even though one hundred thousand of his constituents relied on it), and he supported Trump's tax bill. But he was also more outspoken against Trump's personal conduct than most of his fellow Republicans. When Trump belittled a female reporter for "not thinking," Curbelo said, "Why do you have to be such a jerk?"

He thought Trump was to the Republican Party what the sex-abuse scandal was to the Catholic Church—a stain on a great institution, but not a fatal one. He wanted to fight within the ranks to make the party better, to move it away from Trump and his red-hatted mobs. He wanted to heal the GOP, not abandon it. "The party has struggled, and Trump is a manifestation of that," he told me. "But I do know there's a lot of young conservatives who want to fix this and make it their party, not Trump's or the party of older generations."

As the 2018 election approached, he knew that he was hanging on by his fingernails, but he could also see that the Republican Party was at risk of losing an entire generation of voters. "I see the change coming, where we leave behind this legacy of the baby boomer generation of the all-or-none approach, the politics of personal destruction, the politics of humiliation," he told me. "Millennial legislators on both sides of the aisle are the ones who are going to turn the page on this dark chapter of our country's politics."

But those legislators couldn't turn the page if they didn't stay in Congress. And on election night 2018, the young, moderate Republicans came up short. Carlos lost his seat by less than two points.

In his concession speech, Carlos called for peace. "This country, our politics, are in a very bad state," he said. "Americans who disagree with one another think of themselves as enemies." Afterward, Trump said he "felt just fine" that Republicans who criticized him, like "Carlos Que-bella," had lost their seats.

Carlos wasn't too bothered by it. "All it means as far as I'm concerned is that we're even closer to the post-Trump era," he told me after he lost. "And that will be the time when this party can be recast and redefined and look towards this rising millennial generation."

But by the time Elise was sworn in for her third term, most of the rising stars of the moderate, millennial GOP had already fallen. The dice were cast. The GOP was not moving in the direction she and Curbelo may have hoped. So she stepped off the tightrope and into the circus ring. Gone were the outspoken efforts to move the party on climate change and immigration, the feeble criticisms of Trump's behavior. The old Elise, the one who seemed to care about the integrity of the democratic process and the importance of bipartisan collaboration, was finished. Instead, she would transform into one of Trump's most visible attack dogs during his 2020 impeachment trial in the House, and join his reelection campaign as a cochair. Boosted by the fundraising of the MAGA base, she became a top antagonist of the "radical" left, and embraced her role as defender of the president, no matter what he did. "Our support for President Trump is stronger than ever," she said, beaming at the RNC. She had picked her side: she was a Trump Republican now.

CHAPTER 18

Ladies of the House

H er friends had called her Sandy, her campaign staff had called her Alex, and the New York press had called her Ocasio—but by the time Alexandria Ocasio-Cortez arrived on Capitol Hill, she'd adopted a new name for herself: AOC. On the first day of orientation, she swept into the Capitol and immediately posted a video of herself with fellow newly-elected progressives Ayanna Pressley, Ilhan Omar, and Rashida Tlaib. She looked at the camera and sang, "Say hi, everyone, we out here!" It was the political equivalent of picking a table in the cafeteria. She had the spotlight: this was her crew.

Soon they were quote-tweeting one another on Twitter, posting Instagram videos from one another's offices, and hosting joint press conferences. They had a private text chain, and so did their staff. When Fox News flashed a picture of the four of them next to a graphic about the "radical new Democratic ideas" including free college, free health care, abolishing ICE, and a Green New Deal, AOC posted it proudly on Twitter and Instagram. "Oh no!" she wrote. "They discovered our vast conspiracy to take care of children and save the planet."

By then, she was already a celebrity. Alexandria's red lipstick—Stila Stay All Day Liquid Lipstick in Beso—was sold out at Sephora the day after she won her June primary. By July, twice as many people had bought her lipstick as live in the fourteenth district of New York. Overnight, she had gone from being an unknown candidate in a long-shot Democratic primary to being one of the most famous women in politics.

She instantly attracted enormous media attention, some good, some bad. She did the late-night talk show circuit with Stephen Colbert and Trevor Noah. She sat with David Remnick, the editor of *The New Yorker*. She was featured in *Vanity Fair*. She also became the right wing's favorite punching bag overnight. Her face was plastered all over Fox News and trolls flooded her social media with disgusting memes and threats. But she quickly learned to handle the spotlight.

For most freshmen, orientation was about figuring out the secrets of how Congress works—for AOC, it was about bringing her Instagram followers behind the scenes so that they could almost experience it themselves. No freshman member of Congress had ever been quite so open with their constituents about the details of what it's like to arrive on the Hill for the first time.

Whatever you thought of her, AOC's use of social media sharply changed the tone on Capitol Hill, where just months earlier some octogenarian senators had been confused about how Facebook worked. Her Instagram stories made people feel as if they were there with her, as if she was an ordinary person who happened to be elected to Congress. She posted about her commute, her lunch order, even the press-on nails she applied on the Amtrak. But she didn't post about the awkwardness with other Democrats who were wary of her allies' plans to challenge incumbents, or the death threats she got from stalkers, or the tension with party leadership. It gave her the illusion of transparency—but she was still fully in control.

Other freshmen quickly tried to emulate her social media mastery, but few seemed as effortless. All those hours of Facebook Live in Maria's borrowed Subaru had taught AOC how to perform without seeming like she was performing, and how to improvise short stream-of-consciousness political speeches peppered with interesting personal details. "What happens when you actually check in to orientation?" she said into her camera. "You get a swag bag!" It was a black tote bag with the seal of the House of Representatives on it. "What we actually need as elected officials is very high-security data devices, so that's what's inside the bag—a new tablet and a new phone."

"You also get a freshman yearbook. It really is like orientation!" she said next. "And I get a folder with my ID, like a college ID!" She took her phone into the bowels of the Capitol, where members of Congress shuttle back and forth between their offices and the Hill. "There are secret underground tunnels between all of these government buildings," she whispered into her camera.

Her story had familiar undertones: plucked from obscurity, she became world famous overnight and was suddenly whisked off to a historic institution where she and her friends could use their powers to fight for good over evil. When she posted a photo of the Library of Congress, she captioned it: "Welcome to Hogwarts."

✳ ✳ ✳

Lauren flew from Chicago to Washington for freshman orientation in her signature spearmint green coat. As the plane took off from O'Hare, she looked down at Lake Michigan and took a deep breath. The days since the election had been a whirlwind of phone calls and meetings and plans and media interviews, but here, high above the vast lake that crowned her home state, it began to hit her that this was really happening. She, Lauren Underwood, was about to be the youngest black woman ever to serve in Congress.

She landed in DC and went to baggage claim to find her bags, just as she had hundreds of times before, but this time a guy from CBS News recognized her green coat and approached her. That was when she realized that her old life was over. The Lauren Underwood who loved Whitney Houston and kept old shopping bags in her trunk and forgot to take her makeup off before she went to sleep would have to step aside. Now she was Representative-elect Lauren Underwood of the fourteenth district of Illinois.

She took a cab to the Courtyard Marriott where other freshmen were staying and when she got there, she found a line of paparazzi and TV cameras and reporters with microphones outside the only entrance to the hotel. It was like the Oscars, except she wasn't dressed for this and she had all her suitcases with her. So she just walked past and waved and then tried to get into the hotel as fast as possible.

She thought freshman orientation would be kind of like a graduation from the campaign, a big celebration, like, "Wow, you did it!" But by the second day, the party was over. It became clear that almost everybody in the Democratic caucus was running for something except Lauren, and if they weren't running, then they were angling, and if they weren't angling, then they were networking. Some people were reflexive campaigners, pulling their way through packed rooms by shaking one hand after another, looking for people out of the corners of their eyes, spewing meaningless pleasantries. What mattered was that they were talking, they were chatting, they were building relationships—it didn't seem to matter much what they said. Washington had its own special language, a dialect of duplicity. The more people said, the less they meant. Powerful people could spend entire evenings whispering smart nothings in one another's ears, and Lauren hadn't quite learned the vocabulary yet. She knew how to speak campaign-ese ("Can I count on your support?") but this was something new: six hours of back-to-back receptions full of schmoozing, glad-handing, finding something to say just to build a connection.

Washington seemed like a maze of vaguely familiar strangers, people you should know but didn't. Even the Capitol Building itself appeared almost intentionally hostile to newcomers, with hidden bathrooms and incomprehensible signage and nearly unmarked coffee shops in the basement, impossible to find unless you already knew where they were.

That was the gist of it: you didn't know anything unless you already knew it. You couldn't find the coffee shop unless you had already found it; you didn't know the leadership's top aides unless you had already met them. The Way Things Worked was like an elaborate dance, and everyone else seemed to already know the steps.

At least she would get to see all the other women who won. She called them "the Girlfriends": the women who had been texting and cheering one another on since before Election Day. Haley had been sending her emojis since the very beginning. Chrissy Houlahan from Pennsylvania had texted her before the election that she was thinking of her and pulling for her. She knew the other new black women, including Ayanna Pressley and Lucy McBath and Jahana Hayes. They had all been on various text threads and group chats, and they had all gasped when they saw the others had won.

At least, she thought, she wouldn't be alone.

✳ ✳ ✳

As soon as she got to Congress, Haley Stevens was ready to go. She was there to represent the people of Michigan's eleventh district, and she said it over and over, every chance she got. On Haley's first day, Lauren took a photo of her sitting on the floor of the House, looking like a very excited tourist who had wandered into the seats to get a good picture to send to her mom.

But she wasn't naive—she probably knew more about how government worked than most of the other freshmen. Haley already spoke Washington-ese and was fluent in platitudes: she said things like "We have a great class that's been elected from all over the country" and "The power of new members is to represent the voice of their constituents in the nation's capitol." So when she got elected copresident of the freshman class, with fellow millennial Texas representative Colin Allred, nobody was shocked. She was a class president to the bone.

In the wake of AOC's arrival, all the other freshmen were posting Instagram stories as well, but Haley couldn't quite get the tone down. In one of them, she looks straight into the camera on Rep. Lois Frankel's Instagram and says, "There's a lot of women who just got elected and we are ready to get to work for the American public." She was doing the old-fashioned stuff instead—sitting next to Republicans who might share some of her manufacturing interests, hobnobbing with other members from the region who might build coalitions with her.

Over the first few days, most of the members were walking around with their spouses, but many of the other new women in Congress were single like Haley. That was fine by her. "The only thing we're married to is making the government work for the people!" she told me, without a hint of irony.

She applied her enthusiasm to things only a member of Congress could love, with lots of exclamation points captioning fairly boring Instagram posts. She met with the local chamber of commerce! Here was a picture of the Veterans Day event in her district! She was thrilled to spend the day meeting with the Alzheimer's Association and volunteers and the township supervisor of Waterford, Michigan!

When she walked down the halls of the Capitol and her heels clicked on the marble, it sounded like *tick-tock-tick-tock-tick-tock*. Sometimes, while she was walking with other freshmen to a lunch or a meeting, she'd stop and look around at all the new women members of Congress who won districts they weren't supposed to win and think, "They made the impossible possible." This was a paraphrase of Hillary Clinton's Wellesley commencement address in the 1960s, which Haley had so thoroughly internalized that she spoke the words as her own. She called these other women the "never-evers"—the new members of Congress who had never been elected to anything before—and she was filled with a sense of wonder at the fact that they had all managed to get here.

"I can't help but think of the Founders and our relation to them," she told me earnestly. "We are remolding and remaking this government of ours not through constitutional design but rather through newfound collaboration and redefined collegiality." She continued: "A sisterhood."

✳ ✳ ✳

It all reminded Max Rose of the first day of high school. There were popular kids and rumors and cliques and rivalries. As soon as everyone arrived on the Hill, they began to sort themselves into little tribes.

AOC led her squad of four hardcore progressives: Ilhan Omar of Minnesota, Rashida Tlaib of Michigan, and Ayanna Pressley of Massachusetts. There were the Big Six, which included the freshman class copresidents, Haley Stevens and Colin Allred, plus other freshmen such as Lauren Underwood and Katie Hill, who attended party strategy meetings. Then, of course, there were the military and intelligence veterans, or as Max called them, "the Gang of Nine," which included Elissa Slotkin of Michigan, Chrissy Houlahan of Pennsylvania, Jason Crow of Colorado, Mikie Sherrill of New Jersey, Gil Cisneros of California, Jared Golden of Maine, and Elaine Luria and Abigail Spanberger of Virginia. That was his crew.

But it was disorienting to walk around, not knowing your place or who your friends were, or if you had any friends at all. Especially if you were a guy like Max, who knew he was, as he put it, "eminently hateable." You either liked him or you didn't. He barreled into crowds not remembering people's names or half remembering people's names, worried that someone didn't

like him, noticing if someone had given him a weird look, but charging forward anyway. If this group was sitting over there, could he go sit with them,
or would he have to sit alone? He told himself that everyone felt that way—it
wasn't just him. Maybe he would be more popular here than he was in high
school. "Fingers crossed!" he said.

He was surprised by how antiquated the place was. They still used paper
ballots for leadership races. He figured that if you went to any high school in
America they would not be electing their student body president using paper
ballots. All these "bullshit" rules kept them from actually planning for the
future and getting anything done. There were endless cocktail parties full of
schmoozing, people asking for his endorsement for this and that, people
whose names he was supposed to remember but didn't. If Max ate another
mini crab cake he was going to shoot himself.

He was supposed to wear a tie on the floor of Congress, as if it were Ex-
eter or something. It felt like a noose. It clouded his thinking. When I asked
him why he didn't just suck it up and wear one, he said, "Why don't *you* wear
a fuckin' tie?"

✳ ✳ ✳

As soon as they got to Congress, all the freshmen had to find someplace to
live. After eighteen months without a paycheck, Lauren couldn't afford to be
paying for two homes—one in DC and one in her district—so she asked
around to see if any of the other freshmen wanted a roommate. Katie Hill of
California was in a similar situation, so they decided to team up. Katie was
bubbly and exuberant, another millennial Democratic woman who had
flipped a Republican-held district, and she was quickly gaining traction as an
up-and-comer in party leadership. By New Year's they had signed a lease
for a two-bedroom. They went to Ikea and then hauled everything up to their
apartment, carrying big furniture through the halls two by two, with
Katie walking backward down the hall and Lauren walking forward. Katie
posted on Instagram that Lauren was "the best Ikea partner I could imagine—
a true test of roommate compatibility!"

Lauren had gone to the Crate & Barrel outlet and bought a bed, but it
didn't come with any slats for under the mattress. She slept on an air mattress

for the first month of her term until Katie helped her fix the bed. "It took two Congresswomen, two Ikea deliveries, a trip to Home Depot, some Amazon Prime and cut-up cardboard boxes to make it happen," Lauren posted on Instagram. "SOOOoo grateful for my fearless roomie!" (Months later, Katie would be forced to resign from Congress after her estranged husband allegedly released intimate pictures of her with a female campaign staffer, becoming the first millennial lawmaker to resign because of leaked photos.)

Most of the new young members hadn't been getting a paycheck during their campaigns, so by the time they arrived in DC they were living off savings or fumes. Most older congressional candidates had spouses, passive income, or investment accounts to support them throughout their long unpaid campaigns—many millennial candidates didn't. A week after AOC got to Congress, she had less than $7,000 in her savings account. She wouldn't start getting a paycheck until after she was sworn in, so she wasn't sure how she was going to rent an apartment in Washington, DC. She had saved a few thousand dollars from her job at the restaurant, and told *The New York Times* that she and her boyfriend were "squirreling away" to afford something in DC. Republicans and conservative news outlets pounced immediately.

OCASIO-CORTEZ CLAIMS SHE CAN'T AFFORD A DC APARTMENT, BUT RECORDS SHOW SHE HAS AT LEAST $15,000 IN SAVINGS, blared a Fox News headline, citing months-old financial disclosures that showed she had between $15,000 and $50,000 in a checking account. Then a reporter at a conservative outlet tweeted a photo of her, from behind, adding, "That jacket and coat don't look like a girl who struggles," launching thousands of viral memes.

She hadn't even been sworn in yet and she was already the right wing's favorite target. They picked everything apart in an effort to make her seem like a silly little socialist. It wasn't just that she was young and female and Latina, representing three demographics the right has struggled to reach. They were dying to expose some deep lie at the core of her politics. If she was broke, they twisted it to look as if she was a whiny millennial who was irresponsible with money. If she had nice things, they twisted it to look as if she was feigning solidarity with the working class. They seemed to think that any happiness negated her outrage, that if she were really so oppressed, she wouldn't be smiling, or dancing with her friends, or wearing nice clothes.

They tried to twist every small part of her life into evidence of hypocrisy, as if it were impossible to both fight for justice and live with joy.

But most of AOC's fans weren't watching Fox News—they were watching her Instagram. Thousands of people tuned in to watch her eat mac and cheese with a coffee stirrer because she didn't have utensils yet, all while explaining how committee membership works. She made Instant Pot ramen and cookies and black bean soup in her Bronx kitchen, sometimes riffing off the events of the day, sometimes taking questions. She used Instagram like FDR used fireside chats: a way to connect with her followers without going through any intermediary. The difference was that FDR did two or three fireside chats a year, while AOC posted several times a day. As a freshman member of Congress, she had almost zero real political power except the kind that was most important: the ability to craft a narrative.

✳ ✳ ✳

As the freshman members of Congress settled into their new offices, the Sunrise Movement had been making plans. They had already developed their Green New Deal—a massive jobs program to put Americans to work building green infrastructure to help the country reach 100 percent renewable energy in the next twelve years—but now they needed congressional backing. One day in November, right in the middle of freshman orientation, AOC and her fellow democratic socialist member-elect Rashida Tlaib showed up to a Sunrise meeting in a DC church, where AOC climbed onto a folding table and pledged her support.

The next day, Sunrise staged a protest in Nancy Pelosi's office. A couple dozen kids wearing black T-shirts that said 12 YEARS on them sat uninvited on the part of the floor that depicted the seal of the House of Representatives, and held up yellow signs demanding GREEN JOBS FOR ALL. Teenage Sunrise activist Rose Strauss told the story of when her house was almost devoured by wildfire. She described how she had asked an older male politician to address climate change, and he had called her "young and naive." "In that moment, I felt as helpless as I did watching fire race towards my home," she said. "If politicians think that young people are going to stand by while you make decisions that are detrimental to our future, they're the naive ones."

Rose was still talking, but the mood in the room was changing. People were beginning to look toward the door. AOC had arrived, carrying her black coat over one arm, a big tote bag over her shoulder, wearing her signature red lipstick and her hair in a low bun. She had decided to join them at the last minute, the only new member of Congress to join the sit-in in the prospective Speaker's office. It was a risky decision—so risky that Alexandria later said she was so nervous that she almost threw up that morning.

Yet here she was, joining a protest in the office of the woman who would effectively be her boss after the leadership elections. For any other member, it would be political suicide: once she was was reelected Speaker of the House, Pelosi would control which committees AOC would sit on, which of her bills would reach the floor, and who would vote for them. But AOC wasn't necessarily concerned with wrangling votes in the House—she, like Trump, had grasped a central tenet of twenty-first-century politics: if she could tell the best story, she could rule the day. Whether breaking through the noise could be converted into genuine political power was another question.

And so she stepped onto the seal, right at the spot where Rose had just stood, and began to speak. "We do not have a choice," she said. "We have to get to 100 percent renewable energy in ten years. There is no other option. The IPCC let us know that. And so for me as a member, I want to thank you all, because you are giving us as a party the strength to push."

She tried to take a little bit of the sting off Pelosi. "This is not about a person—this is not about a personality," she said. "Should Leader Pelosi become the next Speaker of the House, we need to tell her that we've got her back in pursuing the most progressive energy agenda that this country has ever seen."

As she left, she repeated the same message to reporters: "I, not just as an elected member but as a twenty-nine-year-old woman, am thinking not just about what we're going to accomplish in the next two years but the America that we're going to live in in the next thirty years," she said. "I don't want to see Miami under water, I don't want to see my own district under water, and I know that Leader Pelosi doesn't either."

It would have been more dangerous if it hadn't been such a popular idea.

The idea polled well with nearly everybody: 98 percent of loyal Democrats said they supported it in a December 2018 poll, and 66 percent of loyal Republicans. More than 90 percent of Obama voters who had switched to Trump voters favored something like this. By 2019, several of the Democratic senators who would soon announce campaigns for the presidency in 2020 were supporting the Green New Deal. Only later, when critics slammed the idea as socialist overreach and moderates balked at the price tag, did enthusiasm begin to wane.

Still, it was a bold move for a prefrosh. AOC, who had been in Congress for all of twenty-four hours, was making demands of Nancy Pelosi, who had been serving in Congress since before she was born. It set up the fault lines of a new dynamic: the new young women in Congress would radically expand the range of possibilities for what the Democrats wanted, and what they would do to get it.

✳ ✳ ✳

On the morning of the swearing in, all the freshmen walked onto the House floor and took their seats. Haley wore a blue dress with her metal pearls she had worn on the campaign trail. Lauren wore a pink tweed Chanel-style suit. Ilhan Omar wore a hijab on the House floor after she fought to change House rules that prohibited head coverings. AOC wore a tailored suit in suffragette white. She wore her red lipstick and gold hoops to channel Supreme Court Justice Sonia Sotomayor, who was advised to wear neutral-colored nail polish to her confirmation hearings but wore red anyway. "Next time someone tells Bronx girls to take off their hoops," AOC tweeted, "they can just say they're dressing like a Congresswoman."

The sixty-seven freshman Democrats in the House of Representatives were the youngest, most diverse, and most female in history. More than 60 percent of the seats that Democrats flipped in 2018 were flipped by women, and a fifth of the new freshmen were millennials. In 2018, there had been five millennials in Congress; in January 2019 there were twenty-six. But they were also like any other freshman class: they had different friends, different interests, and different priorities.

There had been surges of new freshmen before; the class elected in 1992 with Bill Clinton's presidential campaign had 110 new members, the largest in five decades. But the class of 2018 more closely resembled the "Watergate Babies" who were elected to Congress in 1974 to clean up Washington after Nixon's scandal.

When the Watergate Babies arrived in Congress with their shaggy hair and wide ties, the median age in the House dropped to below fifty for the first time in decades. They saw themselves as a new generation of leadership storming Washington to demand reforms from an institution that seemed stuck in another era. "We were the children of Vietnam, not children of World War II," Timothy Wirth, who was elected as a congressman from Colorado in 1974, once said. "We were the products of television, not of print. We were the reflections of JFK as President, not FDR." When they arrived in DC, the Watergate Babies dismantled the system of seniority that had allowed all the oldest members to hog committee chairmanships and stymie progressive legislation. They were the first cohort to demand that committee meetings be televised—which had unintended consequences when members began performing for the cameras as well as for the committee. (The grandstanding ended up deepening partisan divisions.)

All this was laid out in John A. Lawrence's perceptive book *The Class of '74: Congress after Watergate and the Roots of Partisanship*. Both Haley and Max kept copies in their office. Just like the Watergate Babies, it was already apparent that the class of 2018 would bring its own distinct style to Congress, but it wasn't yet clear how much would actually change.

Once the campaign high wore off, most of the exciting young freshman Democrats began to splinter into different groups. What had seemed like a distinct generational cohort during the 2018 elections largely melted into the rest of Congress over the course of their first year on the Hill. They ranged from moderate Democrats representing Trump-supporting districts to full-on democratic socialists, which meant that while they often agreed on broad goals, they usually disagreed about the right way to get there. They all wanted the government to do more to address climate change, but they didn't all support the Green New Deal. They all opposed Trump's immigration policies, but they weren't all willing to defund the border over it.

It didn't take long for a reality check to set in. Even under the best of circumstances, House freshmen are on the lowest rungs of the totem pole in DC, and they typically have very little chance of getting bills passed, let alone signed into law. As freshman Democrats with a Republican Senate and Trump in the White House, those chances fell to nearly zero. With the exception of a few renamed post offices and commemorative coins, very few bills made it through the House and Senate and onto Trump's desk, which meant that most of the freshman Democrats weren't getting much done.

Of course, they tried to make their marks where they could. Lauren co-founded the Black Maternal Health Caucus and secured research funding to study disparities in maternal health. Max got rid of a "piece of bureaucratic bullshit" standing in the way of the construction of a crucial Staten Island sea wall that would protect his constituents against the next major hurricane, and secured split tolling on the Verrazano Bridge. Two of Haley's bills—one to strengthen US global leadership in manufacturing, the other to strengthen early childhood STEM education for girls—passed the House.

But from the beginning, the millennial freshmen proved better than their older colleagues at using social media to shape the conversation. Like the Watergate Babies, they fought for more transparency and less entrenched seniority. "We collectively have more attention, more of a public voice, than probably most of the other members at this point," Katie Hill told reporters after she and other freshmen used the hashtag #WheresMitch to hunt for Mitch McConnell when he refused to schedule a vote on a bill that would end a government shutdown. "So how can we use that to our advantage?"

Nobody was better at that than AOC.

✳ ✳ ✳

AOC had run on Medicare for All, a living wage, and a Green New Deal, but none of that was going to happen in 2019 with Mitch McConnell leading the Republican Senate and Donald Trump in the White House. Besides, she had

learned that the House of Representatives wasn't built for quick implementation of bold legislation. "The system of seniority here is something that
doesn't work," she said. Things in Congress moved so slowly, she realized,
that she needed to be thinking about 2025, not 2019, because "by the time
legislation actually gets through, it is five years from now."

So AOC became more of an activist than a legislator. Rather than
wrestle with Republicans for incremental progress on legislation, she focused on broadening the range of possibilities and changing the frame of
the conversation. A few weeks after she got to Congress, she introduced a
resolution for a Green New Deal: the most ambitious climate change policy
proposal to date.

It was supposed to be a slam dunk. She got eighty-nine cosponsors to
sign on to her highly anticipated resolution in February, just weeks after she
was sworn in. It wasn't a full bill; it was just a resolution to "achieve net-zero
greenhouse gas emissions through a fair and just transition for all communities and workers" and "create millions of good, high-wage jobs and ensure
prosperity and economic security for all people of the United States." Some
areas of the resolution (such as renewable energy sources and specific types
of jobs) had been left purposely vague in order to attract cosponsors, but the
point was clear: to establish a broad commitment to fighting climate change
and social inequality at the same time.

But then she botched the rollout. One of her staffers accidentally released
a fact sheet from her office that contained inflammatory details, including
guaranteed jobs even for those "unwilling to work," retrofitting every building in America, and eliminating airplanes and methane emissions from "far-
ting cows." The right immediately had a field day, and the Green New Deal
quickly became a punching bag instead of a win.

It was AOC's first big misstep, one that would give her opponents ammunition and her potential allies pause. Even Max, whose district was pum-
meled by Superstorm Sandy and who was all for bold solutions on climate
change, couldn't get on board, because he thought AOC was using the Green
New Deal to promote a socialist agenda. The resolution, he said, was a "thinly
veiled effort to use climate change as a Trojan horse to advance an economic

system that I don't believe is effective." Haley and Lauren didn't cosponsor it either.

✳ ✳ ✳

But even after the botched rollout, AOC quickly became the face of the progressive wing in the House. She and the Squad embodied the generational and political shifts roiling the Democratic Party.

Speaker Pelosi was a legislative wizard who had mastered the tried-and-true art of persuasive politics and had wrestled the Affordable Care Act into law. Over thirty years in the House and sixteen in party leadership, the mother of five had built her political capital through sheer force of will, and she did things the old-fashioned way, measuring progress by whether she kept the majority and passed strong bills. The Squad represented a young, progressive insurgency with an enormous online presence that was quickly reshaping the conversation among Democrats—but not necessarily flipping seats or winning votes. The media was enthralled: the Squad was diverse and exciting, often unpredictable, and made for a better story than the same old Democrats who had been in charge forever. But some of their colleagues bristled that this group of four freshmen got so much attention, and others who represented swing districts were worried that their far-left views and high visibility might jeopardize Democratic support among moderates.

For the first few months, things were mostly stable between the Squad and Democratic leadership. Pelosi, AOC, and Ilhan Omar even posed together on the cover of *Rolling Stone*. But in the summer of 2019, things started going downhill. A surge of migrants at the border had left immigration detention centers overcrowded, with children living in squalid conditions in poorly run shelters. The Republican Senate had approved $4.6 billion in humanitarian aid to improve conditions at the border, but progressives wanted a bill that would include stronger protections for child migrants and less funding for ICE. In the end, moderate House Democrats voted for the Republican bill, opting to get the urgently needed money to the border fast rather than arguing over the politics of immigration. AOC—who had called the border detention facilities "concentration camps"—slammed the vote as "an abdication of power," and her then chief of staff Saikat Chakrabarti tweeted that centrist Democrats were enabling a "racist system" by blocking an effort to defund ICE as part of the emergency border relief package, and compared them to segregationists. Pelosi's carefully balanced coalition was suddenly in disarray.

The Squad had been causing Pelosi problems for months. First, video surfaced of Rashida Tlaib vowing to "impeach the motherfucker" on the campaign trail, then Ilhan Omar tweeted back-to-back comments about Israel that struck many as anti-Semitic. Aides said Pelosi moved to isolate the Squad in order to protect the more moderate "majority makers" who would be vulnerable in 2020. When *New York Times* columnist Maureen Dowd asked her about the Squad in the aftermath of the immigration showdown, she dismissed their "Twitter world" and said, "They didn't have any following. They're four people and that's how many votes they got."

Pelosi had made dismissive comments before (she'd referred to the Green New Deal as "the Green Dream or whatever"), but this was a shot across the bow. AOC and her chief of staff tweeted criticism of Pelosi (a big no-no for a freshman), and AOC subtly accused her of bias in the press. "When these comments first started, I kind of thought that she was keeping the progressive flank at more of an arm's distance in order to protect more moderate members, which I understood," she told *The Washington Post*, saying that it felt like an "explicit singling out of newly elected women of color." Pelosi had a full-on insurrection on her hands.

But every time the Democrats seemed to be coming apart at the seams, Donald Trump came in to give them a reason to stitch themselves back together. This time, it was a string of racist tweets telling the Squad to "go back" to the "crime infested places from which they came." It was ripped from the birther playbook, suggesting that the congresswomen—all citizens, all women of color—weren't truly American. In fact, all but Ilhan Omar had been born in the United States, and Omar was a refugee who had been a US citizen for years.

The attack enabled Pelosi and the Squad to put aside their bickering. Pelosi immediately came to their defense, calling for a vote to formally condemn Trump's "racist" tweets. "In a family you have your differences," Pelosi said after a private meeting with AOC a few days later, "but you're still a family."

Shortly afterward, Chakrabarti and Corbin Trent—two staffers who had cofounded Justice Democrats and been with AOC since the beginning—left her congressional staff. And in the months that followed, AOC began to subtly change her approach. She started to build bridges with her more moderate colleagues, boosted some of the "majority makers" on Twitter, and seemed to be more careful about blasting other Democrats on social media. She endorsed a handful of progressive primary challengers to conservative Democrats, but, in a sign that she was learning the ways of Washington, she also endorsed her Green New Deal cosponsor Sen. Ed Markey, who had taken money from corporate PACs. Progressive activists grumbled that she seemed to have stepped away from the "burn it down" approach that had fueled her early rise. She told *The New York Times* that she felt like she was walking around with a "scarlet letter," because many members would blame her for their primary challengers, whether she had endorsed them or not. "It's not just about being an activist," she told the *Times*. "It also requires an assessment for a capacity of growth and how to navigate a space like this."

For all their differences, AOC had become Nancy Pelosi's natural heir, not as the Democrats' political leader, but as one of its most public faces. For more than a decade, Republicans ran ads against Democrats in swing districts linking them to Pelosi, who was portrayed as the Wicked Witch of the Democratic Party. By fall of 2019, Republicans had recast their villain.

Within a month of his swearing in, Max Rose drew a Republican challenger who launched her campaign with an attack on "self-described socialist Alexandria Ocasio-Cortez." It was clear that the Republicans wouldn't be running against their actual Democratic opponents—they'd be running against AOC.

CHAPTER 19

The Double Helix

I n early 2017, Pete and Chasten Buttigieg adopted a brown-and-white rescue beagle. Pete named him Truman, because Harry Truman had once
said, "If you want a friend in Washington, get a dog."

"But you live in South Bend," I reminded him, shortly after Truman
came to live in their stately white house with columns and a portico. Pete
replied with a vague smile.

Throughout 2017 and 2018, Pete had been watching and waiting. He was
ready for something new. After two terms as South Bend mayor, he was still
a gay Democrat in Indiana, which meant that he would have a tough time
winning his congressional seat, let alone statewide office. He had run for
DNC chair in 2017 and lost; the race had boiled down to a contest between
the establishment Democrats and the insurgent progressives, and he was
neither. If he was ever going to move out of South Bend city hall, he had to
shoot for something bigger.

By late 2018, Pete was thinking about his future with a typical Obama-
esque logic that attempted to get to what he called the "theory of the case":
What did the country need, what did he offer, and was it a fit?

He figured that the Democratic Party needed generational change, a
way to "reacquaint the coasts and the industrial Midwest," a hopeful economic message, and a way of transcending the fruitless tug-of-war between

the left and the center. He was a millennial from Indiana with a background in economic development and few ideological allegiances. "Most people will develop a theory of the case that's at least a little self-serving," he acknowledged. "But you come out with something that'll tell you whether it's worth a shot, and then your results tell you whether your theory of the case was any good." In other words: he was beta testing his own political future.

Besides, Pete was already getting noticed by liberal tastemakers and some mainstream media. *The Washington Post* had called him "the most interesting mayor you've never heard of," Obama had mentioned him to David Remnick as an up-and-coming Democrat, and in 2016 Frank Bruni of *The New York Times* wondered in a column if Pete could be the "first gay president."

So in 2018 he persuaded his old friend from high school, the placid and practical Mike Schmuhl, to move back to South Bend to form a political action committee. He didn't say he was running for president, but it was an unspoken agreement. He had already been working with Democratic strategist Lis Smith, a communications savant who had been arranging meetings with national reporters for more than a year. Smith was a hardcore New Yorker who liked black leather jackets and five-inch stilettos and saying "fuck" all the time. The folksy midwesterner and the shit-talking New Yorker made an odd couple, but their strategy was smart: they had Pete sit down with as many national reporters as possible, so that by the time he announced his campaign, journalists felt as if they were early to the story.

By early 2019, Pete had formed an exploratory committee. The plan was to go hard on media—all media, no matter how niche—because as soon as people heard what Pete had to say and how he said it, they usually started to like him. He was especially good at long podcast interviews or cable news sit-downs: he came off as thoughtful and interesting, a fresh face in a primary already dominated by familiar names such as Joe Biden and Bernie Sanders.

His campaign began to gain traction in March of 2019, when he called Vice President Mike Pence a "cheerleader of the porn star presidency" during a CNN town hall. In the next twenty-four hours, he raised more than $600,000 from more than twenty-two thousand donors. Over the next two months, Pete would talk to almost any reporter who asked. He and Lis knew that the press needed to be regularly fed, and that a young campaign needed as much free media as it could get, so they took a more-is-more approach to exposure. He did everything: *Pod Save America*, *The Breakfast Club*, *West Wing Weekly* (a podcast for *West Wing* obsessives), *Desus & Mero* (where he drank whiskey out of a paper bag), even *New York* magazine's celebrity shopping column, where he listed all the things he "can't live without" (beef jerky, Moleskine notebooks, nice scotch, and a copy of *Ulysses*).

He began to impress the elite, well-educated, MSNBC-watching liberals who missed Obama and wanted somebody smart and well-spoken who didn't seem like a socialist: Pete, an articulate Rhodes Scholar who spoke seven languages, seemed to fit the bill. He went from total unknown to serious presidential contender in a matter of weeks. Democratic donors have always had a weakness for brainiacs in a way that Republicans have rarely mirrored, and even though he refused corporate PAC money, Pete quickly became a favorite of the Democratic donor class. Mika Brzezinski called him the "Mr. Rogers of the Democratic field."

Still, as a thirty-seven-year-old mayor of a small midwestern city, he was obviously green. "What's the rush?" Stephen Colbert asked him on *The Late Show*. "Why not get a little more salt and pepper in your hair and a little more moss under the soles your feet before you run for president?" In response, Pete launched into the generational argument that underpinned his entire campaign.

"I belong to the school shooting generation. I was in high school when Columbine happened," he said. "We're the generation that provided most of the troops for the conflicts after 9/11, we're the generation that's going to be on the business end of climate change, and if nothing changes economically, we'll be the first generation ever to make less than our parents." He said he thought a lot about 2054, when he'd be Donald Trump's age. "Why not have somebody in there who actually views the condition of the country in that year as a personal issue, not somebody else's problem?" This argument became a key point in his stump speech, and he tried to put a generational spin on nearly every early debate performance.

When Trump said, "Alfred E. Neuman could never be president"—referring to Pete's resemblance to the big-eared mascot of *Mad* magazine—Pete had to Google the reference ("I guess it's a generational thing"). But even as progressive millennials stayed cool to his campaign, legions of well-educated boomers were drawn to Pete. He had the particular quality that journalist Michael Kinsley had noticed in thirty-eight-year-old Al Gore three decades earlier: "An old person's idea of what a young person should be."

Pete became a curiosity because he could speak so many foreign languages (one video of him speaking Norwegian to a reporter went viral early in his campaign), but his most useful linguistic talent was his fluency in the dialect of the industrial Midwest. He positioned himself as a translator: someone who could help the Democratic Party speak to the voters they had lost, a diplomat who could negotiate a new alliance between the progressive coasts and the moderate middle.

Fifteen years after he wrote his *Harvard Crimson* columns about how Democrats needed to reclaim the language of patriotism, his presidential campaign tried to do exactly that. In each of his speeches, he wrote a new thesaurus for Democrats, a way to reframe controversial, scary ideas ("consumer financial protections," "climate policy," "voter suppression") into patriotic, American words ("freedom," "security," "democracy"). He used the vocabulary of midwestern moderates to describe the ideas of coastal progressives. Regulating the financial system created "freedom" from economic exploitation. Information warfare and election hacking were twenty-first-century "security" threats. Regulating campaign finance wasn't about socialism; it was about "democracy." Offering bold solutions to climate change wasn't radical; it was "pragmatic." His gift was finding a friendly synonym.

While his top-tier competitors were running their campaigns on policy proposals and movement building, Pete was running on personality. He talked about big ideas in a calm and reasonable way, making them seem transformative but nonthreatening: he started his campaign calling for abolishing the electoral college and reforming the Supreme Court, which were both major structural changes that didn't conjure up images of tax hikes or massive new government programs (and which were both extremely unlikely to happen.)

But by 2019, the progressive movement had successfully defined "bold" and "radical" as ideological terms: the boldest idea, in their book, was always the one that was furthest to the left. Pete, a master of redefinition, attempted to sidestep this framework: to him, boldness was more about ingenuity than ideology. It was about finding the smartest solution that worked for the most people, not the one that conformed to some preexisting dogma. His health care plan—"Medicare for All Who Want It"—attempted to achieve the main goals of universal coverage without eliminating private health insurance plans that were working for some people. Progressives thought that was bullshit, but some voters seemed sick of the ideological tug-of-war: by November, he was first place in Iowa, positioning himself as the younger, more coherent alternative to seventy-seven-year-old Joe Biden. I even met voters in Iowa who had supported Bernie in 2016 and now planned to vote for Pete.

Still, his campaign would run into some serious problems. Although he was a favorite among Silicon Valley tech bros and moderate midwesterners, he struggled to make inroads with the activist Democratic base: many of the young progressives who might have been excited about generational change thought he was too moderate for their tastes. More important, he failed to attract meaningful support from black and Hispanic voters, not a good place to be in Democratic primaries. His struggle got harder when a black man, Eric Logan, was shot by a white South Bend police officer while Pete was on the campaign trail. Although he immediately returned to South Bend to grieve with the community, the incident highlighted Pete's failure to diversify the local police department and further alienated him from voters of color.

But Pete stayed calm. While Bernie Sanders was running on "political revolution" and Elizabeth Warren branded herself as a "fighter," Pete's campaign had a sense of peace and healing to it. At first, he seldom attacked anybody, except the occasional potshots at Donald Trump or Mike Pence, and while his opponents slammed big corporations and special interests, he drew large crowds talking about redemption rather than retribution. Even though he'd served in the military, Pete never really had the soul of a fighter: he was running on a platform of reconciliation, to be the candidate for the people who were sick of the fighting. He talked about "picking up the pieces" after the Trump presidency. His campaign logo was literally shaped like a bridge.

When he announced his campaign, on a freezing April day in the old Studebaker plant in South Bend, people stood for hours in lines that snaked around the block to hear him speak. Supporters—many of them white working-class auto workers—shivered in the frigid old auto plant and waved tiny American flags to the tune of Barbra Streisand's "Don't Rain on My Parade" as they waited for Pete to emerge.

When he finally spoke, Pete gave a speech that echoed one Barack Obama had given more than a decade earlier. He spoke of the "audacity" of running for president at thirty-seven, he peppered in references to "hope" and "change," and he painted a rousing picture of an American future that was forged more in unity than in division. Just as Obama's experience as a biracial boy raised by loving white grandparents had given him faith in American redemption, Pete rooted his hopeful message in the country's evolution on gay rights. Five years earlier, he had sat silently as his navy buddies shouted homophobic slurs; today, his husband would kiss him onstage as he announced his candidacy for president of the United States.

Pete always said that politics should be about the future, and that any message that was rooted in returning to the past was inherently dishonest. But if he could go back in time, he said, "it would be just twenty years back, to find a teenage boy in the basement of his parents' brick house, thinking long thoughts as he played the same guitar lick over and over again, wondering how he could belong in this world," he said. "To tell him that one rainy April day, before he even turns forty, he'll wake up to headlines about whether he's rising too quickly as he becomes a top-tier contender for the American presidency. And to tell him that on that day he announces his campaign for president, he'll do it with his husband looking on."

The crowd cheered. I saw an older man in a flannel shirt grip his American flag and stare at Pete with tears streaming down his face.

"How can you live that story and not believe that America deserves our optimism, deserves our courage, deserves our hope?" he said. "Don't we live in a country that can overcome the bleakness of this moment? Are you ready to turn the page and write a new chapter in the American story?

"It's cold out, but we've had it with winter," he continued. "You and I have the chance to usher in a new American spring."

✹ ✹ ✹

If Pete was attempting to channel the Obama legacy, AOC was the heiress to Bernie Sanders. She represented the anti-establishment rage that had fueled the millennial left since the financial crisis: the young progressives who slept at Zuccotti Park in 2011 and turned out for Sanders in 2016 and embraced socialism in 2017 found their voice in her. Her story wasn't about healing and redemption; it was about justice and retribution. She wasn't reaching out a hand to her opponents; she was shaking her fist at the bad guys.

She crackled with a ferocious energy as she tweeted thunderbolts at corporations, the Trump administration, Democratic inertia in Congress, right-wing trolls. Some fights got her in trouble: her opposition to Amazon's expansion in New York City irritated many city- and state-elected officials, and eventually the company canceled its planned construction of a new headquarters in Long Island City that would have brought twenty-five thousand jobs to the area.

But every day was another battle, because as an organizer and activist, she had been trained in the art of public political combat. "In activist spaces, you only have so many tools," she told me. "We're not used to winning. So you're fighting and you're protesting and you're organizing, because it always feels like you're fighting against a system that's set up against you." Someone even made a comic book of a superhero-style AOC wielding a cell phone over a dying elephant, called "Alexandria Ocasio-Cortez and the Freshman Force." When Stephen Colbert asked, "How many fucks do you give?" about pissing off the Democratic establishment, she said, "I think it's zero."

In her first months in office, AOC's Democratic colleagues were scared of her vast Twitter following (well over five million by August) and her threat to support Democratic primary challengers against incumbents. (She did ultimately endorse a few challengers, but not as many as her colleagues had feared.) Social media was her weapon of choice. Her well-prepared and pointed questioning in committee testimony quickly went viral, as fans watched Trump officials writhe under her interrogation like a real-life episode of *Law & Order*. She sometimes wrote out her committee questions in pencil, like a script, phrasing them in a way that could create easily tweeted sound bites or sharable video clips.

Like her colleagues, AOC got almost nothing passed—but then again, she wasn't a legislator at heart. Legislation, she quickly learned, was only part of what a member of Congress could do. Instead, she was an activist who happened to wear a congressional pin: her role wasn't to craft elegant policy or twist arms for votes or build durable coalitions, but to expand the parameters of debate. She did what protesters do: she caused a stir, pissed people off, and changed the conversation. Some called it "purity politics," others called it "moral clarity," but for a generation disappointed with bland calls for unity, her antagonism was refreshing.

But eventually, as all young people do, AOC began to mature. She stopped attacking Democrats so much on Twitter. She checked her facts more carefully, and she stopped lashing out at Nancy Pelosi. She learned how the game was played. Unlike Sanders, who had a reputation as a prickly loner, AOC used her emotional intelligence to her political advantage. She worked to build relationships with allies, even when they didn't align 100 percent. Over the course of her first year in office, she learned how to fight smarter, even if she was still a fighter at heart.

But she had already made her mark. Across the country, young women like AOC began making plans to challenge incumbent Democrats who were too cozy with corporate interests. And these young challengers were learning that social media could be their most powerful political tool. After former vice presidential candidate Joe Lieberman told FOX that AOC wasn't the future of the Democratic Party, she tweeted the headline and wrote, "New party, who dis?"

✳ ✳ ✳

By late 2019, it was clear that millennials were abandoning the GOP, and that Pete and AOC represented the two paths forward for the Democrats. He was a peacemaker; she was a warrior. He was a midwesterner trying to reconcile with aging, white rural voters; she was a New Yorker who focused on mobilizing working-class people of color. He was an intellectual pragmatist; she was an ideological activist. He promised redemption; she promised retribution. He was New Testament forgiveness; she was Old Testament justice.

They both found their stride in their ability to repackage old ideas for new audiences. In perhaps one of her best speeches of her early career, AOC gave the keynote address at the 2018 Netroots Nation convention, an annual gathering of progressive activists. She framed the progressive push forward as a return to the New Deal era. She reminded the audience that universal health care, a federal jobs guarantee, and exploration of a basic income were not new ideas.

"It's time to own that our party was the one of the Great Society, of the New Deal, of the Civil Rights Act," she said. "That's our party, that's who we are, and it's time for us to come home."

By the end of 2019, it was clear that Pete and AOC were two of the most talented young politicians in America, mostly because of their rare ability to create and maintain traditional and social media buzz, the oxygen of twenty-first-century American politics. Not that they were friends or even allies. Pete said he thought AOC was "fantastic" and that "her arrival was a really important moment not just for our generation, but for the Congress"—a typical Pete compliment, bland but genuine. But as the presidential campaign heated up and it became clear that Pete was a threat to the progressive left, AOC began to throw him some shade on Twitter. And in October, she endorsed Bernie Sanders, giving his campaign a much-needed boost after he had a heart attack on the campaign trail.

Just as Pete had rooted his campaign in his experience of 9/11, school shootings, and the war on terror, AOC rooted her endorsement in her own experiences as a working-class millennial waitress with student debt. "I didn't have health care, I wasn't being paid a living wage, and I didn't think that I deserved any of those things," she told a crowd of thousands who were cheering and waving blue and white signs on a cloudless October day in Queens. "It wasn't until I heard of a man by the name of Bernie Sanders that I began to question and assert and recognize my inherent value as a human being that deserves health care, housing, education, and a living wage.

"The logic that got us into this mess," she continued, "is not going to get us out."

Pete and AOC may have been on opposite sides of the Democratic primary, but together they would represent the dawn of a new political era—one in which millennials swung the center of political gravity to the left just as boomers had swung it to the right. In the 1980s and '90s, Reagan's conservatism and Clinton's triangulation had defined the contours of the boomer political debate. In the first decades of the twentieth century, millennials' lurch to the left would be defined by the progressive activism of people like AOC and the technocratic pragmatism of people like Pete Buttigieg. They wouldn't like to admit it, but their goals were largely aligned: universal health care, a massive government investment in addressing climate change, a twenty-first-century social safety net, and a reformed democracy. The skirmishes between the Obama pragmatists and the Bernie activists—the ones who wanted to fix the system and the ones who wanted to fight it—would be about the scope and implementation of those goals. The two unlikely young stars were like twin strands of DNA, a double helix that contained the blueprint for the Democratic Party's future.

And that future has already arrived.

EPILOGUE

A fter all that—the wars and the recession and rise of Trump— came the Year of the Plague: 2020. The coronavirus pandemic triggered the second major economic downturn in twelve years, one that destabilized whatever little security millennials had built since 2008. Young people were much more likely to lose their jobs than older people during the pandemic, dealing another major financial blow to an already precarious generation. COVID-19 interrupted all aspects of life just as millennials were beginning to find their footing—weddings were canceled, friendships frayed, the rituals of early adulthood were put on ice. The generation that was already busy trying to slow climate change, address structural racism, and lessen economic inequality was now tasked with helping the nation rebound from the largest pandemic in a century.

But 2020 was also the year that Trump lost the presidency, in no small part because of a generational alignment against him. Despite his popularity with young progressives, Bernie Sanders didn't capture the Democratic nomination, but young voters still did their part to defeat Trump. Youth voter turnout surged past 52 percent in the 2020 general election, and young voters sided with Biden by twenty-five points, a record showing that helped lift Biden over the top in key states. As young voters were making their generation heard at the ballot box, millennial leaders were well into their political ascent, one that was looking like it could take longer than expected.

Pete performed surprisingly well in the 2020 Democratic primary, winning the Iowa caucuses and coming in a close second in New Hampshire—that a no-name gay mayor from Indiana who would have been the youngest president in history bested well-known senators and a former vice president in the first and arguably most important contests of the 2020 primary was a testament to his political skills and the power of his generational message, even if he never captured the full support of his fellow millennials. Biden later tapped Pete to lead his Department of Transportation, which would make him the first openly gay cabinet secretary and set him up as a standard bearer of the young, moderate wing of the Democratic Party.

Alexandria maintained her position as effective leader of the congressional left, becoming a vocal surrogate for Bernie Sanders during the 2020 primary as he once again emerged as the candidate favored by the young. She continued to agitate for progressive goals, but she sharpened her toolbox, working with the Biden team to strengthen their climate policy. By 2020, her model of social media–based political power was growing, with new members of Congress and legislators all over the country modeling themselves after AOC.

Haley emerged as a major voice in Congress urging support for manufacturers making the equipment needed to treat COVID-19—her experience with supply chain management came in handy. Lauren pushed for major COVID-19 relief legislation, got legislation passed to lower the price of insulin, and drew on her experience in public health during the pandemic. Haley won reelection easily; Lauren kept her seat by just a few hundred votes. Both of their political futures were tied to the suburban realignment that helped Biden beat Trump.

But the division and disinformation of 2020 also took down some rising stars. In a surprise upset, Mayor Michael Tubbs lost his bid for reelection as mayor of Stockton, partly because of a widespread disinformation campaign. Max Rose lost his seat to an opponent who tried to tie him to the socialist "Squad," painting him as a "radical" after he showed solidarity with Black Lives Matter activists following George Floyd's death.

Even though Trump lost reelection, the Republican Party was so thoroughly in the grip of Trumpism that even people who probably knew better—like Elise Stefanik and Dan Crenshaw—seemed to embrace the dangerous conspiracy theories that the election had been stolen. Both lent their credibility to the unpatriotic efforts to overturn the results of the 2020 election, including spurious lawsuits and bogus claims of widespread voter fraud. Their complicity in the undermining of American democracy was cynical at best, and seditious at worst; Elise even voted to object to the certification of Pennsylvania's electoral votes, part of a slow-motion Republican coup that would have disastrous consequences. After Trump urged a mob of domestic terrorists to storm the Capitol building on January 6, neither Dan nor Elise joined the braver conservatives who held him accountable for his incitement. These two promising Republicans could have been the vanguard of a newer, modern conservative movement that rejected conspiracy theories and defended the bedrock of the republic. Instead, at the exact moment when they could have stood up for truth, decency, and the rule of law, they lashed themselves to Trump. It is not yet clear whether that decision will haunt their political careers, but this is only the first of many books to note their complicity. It will not be the last.

But they were in the minority. Most people under forty worked for four years to oppose Trump, then did everything they could to vote him out of office. And as millennials organized and ran for office and campaigned for a better future, the generation behind them—Gen Z—was building its own political identity. The oldest members of Gen Z were twenty-three in 2020; the youngest were nearing the end of elementary school. Many of the kids born since 1997 barely remembered 9/11, or the wars, or Obama's 2008 campaign—instead, they were shaped by the terrifying new world ushered in by Donald Trump's presidency. Their formative years were spent under an adult political authority that seemed even more morally bankrupt than it had been during the millennial era: they watched as America caged immigrant children at the border and destroyed the environment; they listened as the president routinely embraced white supremacists and spouted conspiracy theories; and they lost more than a year of their adolescence and young adulthood to the COVID-19 pandemic, a crisis made worse by the Trump administration's staggering incompetence. The vanished memories, interrupted education, and hundreds of thousands of dead Americans made COVID-19 a transformative political moment for this rising generation of voters—one that will shape their political identities in ways that are not yet clear.

Even though most of Gen Z was not yet eligible to vote, they did not leave their futures in the unreliable hands of adults. Growing up in the Trump era gave Gen Z their own urgent priorities. High school activists led the March for Our Lives protests against gun violence in 2018; schoolchildren poured into the streets for the student-led Global Climate Strike in 2019; young Americans flooded American cities to protest racial inequality in the uprisings of 2020. And so, as millennials grasped their first toeholds of elected political power, as they made gains on Congress and presidential contests and even in the US Senate, Gen Z was watching, learning, and getting ready for its moment.

—January 15, 2020

ACKNOWLEDGMENTS

This book is the result of two years of research, reporting, and writing that could not have been possible without a tremendous amount of support. Thank you, first and foremost, to my agents Allison Hunter, Clare Mao, and the team at Janklow & Nesbit who believed in me and my work from the very beginning, and to the team at Viking who heard this idea and immediately understood what kind of book this would be. Thank you especially to my editor, Emily Wunderlich, who helped me wrestle this from vague musings into the book you're holding, and to Nidhi Pugalia, Kristina Fazzalaro, and Gabriel Levinson, who helped make it real.

I am especially grateful for the support of my colleagues at *TIME*. From Susanna Schrobsdorff, who has been my friend and mentor ("friendtor") for nearly seven years, to Ben Goldberger and Karl Vick, who helped shepherd my first story on millennial mayors, to Sam Jacobs and Nancy Gibbs, who first hired me and then gave me a shot at the big leagues, the extraordinary thinkers and mentors at *TIME* have shaped the approach to journalism that informs this project. Thank you to my smart and generous colleagues—Haley Edwards, Alana Abramson, Justin Worland, Belinda Luscombe, Molly Ball, Dan Macsai, and Massimo Calabresi—who provided key advice and support throughout this process; and to Diane Tsai, Francesca Trianni, and

Paul Moakley, the best video and photo collaborators in the business; and to Phil Elliott, for giving me gut checks when I needed them most. I owe special thanks to my editor Alex Altman, for supporting my work on this project even when it was inconvenient, for believing in my stories, and for teaching me to structure my writing and trust my instincts. And this book simply would not exist without the support of Edward Felsenthal, a visionary editor-in-chief and a true friend, who encouraged me to find my voice, boosted me when I was down, and gave me the three greatest gifts any editor can give to a writer: trust, time, and health insurance.

On a more practical level, this book has benefited from the labor of many people who helped me along the way. Jacqui Rossi helped me with research in the early stages, lending her extraordinary brain to some of the main themes of this project, and Alex Lipton spent hours of his weekends helping me get organized. When I spilled water on my computer just as I was about to turn in my first draft, Meredith tech nerds Rodney Mayers and Kevin Kelly saved my work (and taught me how to do automatic backups). Soraya Shockley provided a valuable cultural read, and Mike Blumenthal and Natan Last gave me crucial feedback on key chapters. Madeleine Levinsohn transcribed hours of Facebook Lives and Rohan Naik helped me with research and endnotes. Karen Obrist, my favorite photographer and a true artist, lent her talents to my author photos. Perhaps most important, Barbara Maddux was a journalistic partner whose exhaustive fact-checking allowed me to sleep at night. Barbara is a true hero: any mistakes in this book are my own.

I'd like to thank my friends for still being my friends even after I spent the last two years sitting in my cave staring at my computer instead of hanging out with them, especially those who sent me pickles and chicken dinner and words of encouragement. Thank you also to Mary and Ken Chiusano, who taught their son to vacuum and wash dishes and care for others, who raised the partner I needed to finish this project, and who welcomed me into their family over the course of writing this book.

I would not have made it through without my brother, Tommy, whose instincts never fail, and my sister, Molly, who has superhuman powers of analysis: they made me laugh and kept me sane during this grueling process. Thank you especially to my mother, who taught me how to approach the world psychologically, how to buckle down, and how to find the interesting details in boring stories. And to my father, who taught me almost everything I know about politics, who read every draft of this book, and who once pulled me from the bottom of the pool.

None of this would be possible without my partner in life and work, my husband, Mark Chiusano, who read every chapter until his contact lenses gave out, who offered to transcribe for me when I couldn't do it anymore, who brought me ice cream in my cave, who believed in me when I didn't believe in myself. I am always trying to write as well as he does.

NOTE ON SOURCES

T his book draws on hundreds of interviews conducted over the course of
eighteen months, including dozens of interviews with the characters
themselves and anyone I could find who knew them. I interviewed their
staff, parents, siblings, coworkers, partners, opponents, high school friends,
high school frenemies, college roommates, acquaintances, advisors, and army
buddies wherever possible. Some descriptions of their lives are taken from
their childhood diaries, internship journals, emails to family, and social media
livestreams from both their public and private Facebook accounts. All quoted
dialogue comes from at least one person who was in the room, and all accounts of the characters' internal thoughts are taken from my interviews
with them and validated with the characters themselves or with people who
knew them. Any detail that does not come from my own reporting is cited in
the endnotes. This book was professionally fact-checked to ensure accuracy.

Many of the characters and events in this book also appear in my *TIME*
reporting on the anti-Trump resistance, the 2018 midterms, the 2019 Congress, and the early parts of the 2020 presidential election. Quotes and details that had previously been published in *TIME* are cited accordingly.

In the episodic chapters on school shootings, the text is made up of real
news coverage of the events and from social media responses of victims and

lawmakers. These chapters were formally inspired by George Packer's *The Unwinding*, which was inspired by John Dos Passos's U.S.A. trilogy.

One benefit of writing about the social media generation is that so much of their political and personal lives have been documented with live online video. So this book benefits from both traditional political reporting and social media stalking. For example, Alexandria Ocasio-Cortez's trips to Standing Rock and the Women's March are informed by hours-long Facebook Live videos posted to her personal Facebook page, and accounts of Braxton Winston's activism with Black Lives Matter in Charlotte are taken from live video he posted of those nights.

NOTES

INTRODUCTION

xi **biggest bloc of eligible voters:** "Millennial Life: How Young Adulthood Today Compares with Prior Generations," Pew Research Center, February 14, 2019, pewsocialtrends .org/essay/millennial-life-how-young-adulthood-today-compares-with-prior -generations/.

xiii **by white voters over sixty-five:** "An Examination of the 2016 Electorate, Based on Validated Voters," Pew Research Center, August 9, 2018, people-press.org/2018/08/09 /an-examination-of-the-2016-electorate-based-on-validated-voters/.

xiii **one of the oldest Congresses in history:** "Membership of the 115th Congress: A Profile, Congressional Research Service," December 20, 2018, senate.gov/CRSpubs/b8f6293e -c235-40fd-b895-6474d0f8e809.pdf.

xiv **"is a new people.":** Alexis de Tocqueville, in *Great Ideas of Western Man* (Chicago: Container Corporation of America, 1974).

xiv **historical and social events:** Sofia Aboim and Pedro Vasconcelos. "From Political to Social Generations: A Critical Reappraisal of Mannheim's Classical Approach." *European Journal of Social Theory* 17, no. 2 (May 2014): 165–83. doi:10.1177/1368431013509681.

xiv **"people moving through time.":** William Strauss and Neil Howe, *Generations: The History of America's Future, 1584 to 2069* (New York: William Morrow, 1991).

xiv **shape lifelong political leanings:** Andrew Gelman and Yair Ghitza, "The Great Society, Reagan's Revolution, and Generations of Presidential Voting," Working Paper, Department of Statistics and Political Science, Columbia University, 2014, stat.columbia .edu/~gelman/research/unpublished/cohort_voting_20140605.pdf.

xv **have been about ninety-seven:** Dave Merrill and Yvette Romero, *Bloomberg*, "Millennials Can't Crack Congress," November 10, 2016, bloomberg.com/graphics/2016-millennial -generation-in-congress/.

xv **"Here's the thing about the real world":** Jon Stewart, Commencement Address at William & Mary College, May 20, 2004, youtube.com/watch?v=ajPvjKFFIAo.

xvi **address the student debt crisis:** "Voters Keen on Lowering Student Debt Through Greater Federal Funding," Ipsos/Newsy, May 23, 2019, ipsos.com/en-us/news-polls /voters-keen-on-lowering-student-debt.

xvi **may be coming to an end:** "Gen Z, Millennials and Gen X Outvoted Older Generations in 2018 Midterms," Pew Research Center, May 29, 2019, pewresearch.org/fact-tank /2019/05/29/gen-z-millennials-and-gen-x-outvoted-older-generations-in-2018 -midterms/.

xvi **immigrants and nonwhite Americans:** "Millennials in Adulthood," Pew Research Center, March 7, 2014, pewsocialtrends.org/2014/03/07/millennials-in-adulthood/.

CHAPTER I: ONE SUNNY TUESDAY

5 **"stranglehold on our political vocabulary":** Peter P.M. Buttigieg, *The Harvard Crimson*, "The Struggle for Language," December 8, 2003, thecrimson.com/article/2003/12 /8/the-struggle-for-language-you-heard/.

5 **"Establishing a new vocabulary":** Peter P.M. Buttigieg, *The Harvard Crimson*, "The Liberal Art of Redefinition," May 28, 2004, thecrimson.com/article/2004/5/28/the -liberal-art-of-redefinition-last/.

6 **something to drive by:** Pete Buttigieg, *Shortest Way Home: One Mayor's Challenge and a Model for America's Future* (New York: Liveright, 2019).

6 **screw-up of any kind:** Charlotte Alter, "Mayor Pete Buttigieg's Unlikely, Untested, Unprecedented Presidential Campaign," *TIME*, May 2, 2019, time.com/longform/pete -buttigieg-2020/.

7 **deflect attention from their sexuality:** Andrew Tobias, *The Best Little Boy in the World* (New York: Random House, 1973).

7 **the more they achieved:** John E. Pachankas and Mark L Hatzenbuehler, "The Social Development of Contingent Self-Worth in Sexual Minority Young Men: An Empirical Investigation of the 'Best Little Boy in the World' Hypothesis," *Basic and Applied Social Psychology* 35, no. 2 (March 2013), tandfonline.com/doi/full/10.1080/01973533.2013 .764304.

7 **not the same as capitulation:** Peter Buttigieg, *Bernie Sanders*, John F. Kennedy Presiential Liberary and Museum, 2000, jfklibrary.org/learn/education/profile-in-courage -essay-contest/past-winning-essays/2000-winning-essay-by-peter-buttigieg.

11 **Gloria Estefan superfan:** Elise Stefanik, Instagram story, July 2018.

13 **apple cheeks and sandy hair:** Dan Crenshaw, tweet, February 28, 2018, twitter.com /dancrenshawtx/status/968936595842838528.

24 **microscope for her birthday:** Charlotte Alter, "Change is Closer Than We Think: Inside Alexandria Ocasio-Cortez's Unlikely Rise" *TIME*, March 21, 2019, time.com /longform/alexandria-ocasio-cortez-profile/.

24 **instead of a high school senior:** Andy Newman, Vivian Wang, and Luis Ferré-Sadurní, "Alexandria Ocasio Cortez Emerges as a Political Star," *The New York Times*, June 27, 2018, nytimes.com/2018/06/27/nyregion/alexandria-ocasio-cortez-bio-profile .html.

25 **SAT lessons for Alexandria:** *Knock Down the House*, directed by Rachel Lears (2019; Netflix).

26 **events of their lifetime:** Claudia Deane, Maeve Duggan, and Rich Morin, "Americans Name the 10 Most Significant Events of Their Lifetimes," Pew Research Center, December 15, 2016, people-press.org/2016/12/15/americans-name-the-10-most-significant -historic-events-of-their-lifetimes/.

THOUGHTS & PRAYERS

27 **"another high school: Columbine":** Michael Elizabeth Sakas, "In 1999, Columbine Felt Like a Galvanizing Moment for Gun Control," NPR, *All Things Considered*, April 20, 2018, npr.org/2018/04/20/604070881/19-years-ago-columbine-felt-like-a-galvanizing -moment-for-gun-control.

27 **"gunshots to the chest.":** ABC News Special Report on the Columbine High School shootings, April 20, 1999, youtube.com/watch?v=ejBrRrTJbS4.

27 **"shot her in the neck.":** Mark Obmascik, "Columbine High School Shooting Leaves 15 dead, 28 Hurt," *The Denver Post*, April 21, 1999, denverpost.com/1999/04/21/columbine -high-school-shooting/.

27 **LAW, GUN FOES CLAIM:** "Teen's Easy Purchase Shows Flaws in Law, Gun Foes Claim," *The Denver Post*, June 10, 1999, extras.denverpost.com/news/shot0610c.htm.

27 **"I would like you to write me a letter":** Diane Carman, "Colo. Youths Meet GOP Wall in D.C.," *The Denver Post*, July 15, 1999, extras.denverpost.com/news/shot0715d.htm.

27 **"I'm busy, write me a letter":** Diane Carman, "Teens Talk Guns with D.C.'s Elite," *The Denver Post*, July 16, 1999, extras.denverpost.com/news/shot0716.htm.

27 **HOURS AFTER SCHOOL SHOOTING:** Frank Bruni, "Guns and Schools: The Legislation; Senate Votes Gun Curbs, Hours After School Shooting," *The New York Times*, May 21, 1999, nytimes.com/1999/05/21/us/guns-schools-legislation-senate-votes-gun-curbs-hours-after-school-shooting.html.

27 **DEFEATS GUN CONTROL BILL:** Eric Piain and Juliet Eilperin, "House Defeats Gun Control Bill," *The Washington Post*, June 19, 1999, washingtonpost.com/archive/politics/1999/06/19/house-defeats-gun-control-bill/9b903285-1339-4379-a209-49ffb41af509/.

CHAPTER 2: HARRY POTTER AND THE SPAWN OF THE BOOMERS

29 **than long-term productivity:** Steven Brill, *Tailspin: The People and Forces Behind America's Fifty-Year Fall—and Those Fighting to Reverse It* (New York: Alfred A. Knopf, 2018).

29 **"economic security unmatched in history,":** "*TIME* Man of the Year: The Inheritor," *TIME*, January 6, 1967, content.time.com/time/subscriber/article/0,33009,843150-4,00.html.

30 **soaring income inequality:** Steven V. Roberts, "Making Mark on Politics, Baby Boomers Appear to Rally Around Reagan," *The New York Times*, November 5, 1984, nytimes.com/1984/11/05/us/making-mark-on-politics-baby-boomers-appear-to-rally-around-reagan.html.

30 **"America's reigning political generation":** Peter Beinart, "The Rise of the New New Left," *The Daily Beast*, September 12, 2013, updated July 11, 2017, thedailybeast.com/the-rise-of-the-new-new-left.

31 **is still hard at work:** Bruce Cannon Gibney, *A Generation of Sociopaths* (New York: Hachette, 2017), 130.

31 **doubled since the 1970s:** "Federal Debt: Total Public Debt as Percent of Gross Domestic Product," Federal Reserve Bank of St. Louis, fred.stlouisfed.org/series/GFDEGDQ188S.

31 **"During the years of boomer dominance":** David Brooks, "Your Baby Boomer Report Card," *The New York Times*, August, 8, 2019, nytimes.com/2019/08/08/opinion/baby-boomers-report-card.html.

32 **"In the world that boomers":** Michael Kinsley, "The Least We Can Do," *The Atlantic*, October 15, 2010, theatlantic.com/magazine/archive/2010/10/the-least-we-can-do/308228/.

32 **at any time in history:** "Record Share of New Mothers Are College Educated," Pew Research Center, May 10, 2013, pewsocialtrends.org/2013/05/10/record-share-of-new-mothers-are-college-educated/.

32 **unintended pregnancies declined:** Guttmacher Institute, January 2019 Fact Sheet, "Unintended Pregnancies in the United States," guttmacher.org/fact-sheet/unintended-pregnancy-united-states.

32 **with small children were working:** Elen Galinsky, Kerstin Aumann, James T. Bond, "Times Are Changing: Gender and Generation at Work and at Home," Families and Work Institute, August 2011, familiesandwork.org/downloads/TimesAreChanging.pdf.

32 **had at least three:** "Family Size Among Mothers," Pew Research Center, May 7, 2015, pewsocialtrends.org/2015/05/07/family-size-among-mothers/.

32 **who chose to stay home:** Google Books NGram Viewer, "parenting", books.google.com/ngrams/graph?content=parenting&year_start=1950&year_end=2000&corpus=15&smoothing=0&share=&direct_url=t1%3B%2Cparenting%3B%2Cc0#t1%3B%2Cparenting%3B%2Cc0.

33 **starting in the mid-1990s:** Heidi Shierholz, Natalie Sabadish, and Nicholas Finio, "The Class of 2013," Economic Policy Institute Briefing Paper #360, April 10, 2013, epi.org /files/2013/Class-of-2013-graduates-job-prospects.pdf.

33 **and from organized activities:** Gallup, In Depth: Children, news.gallup.com/poll /1588/children-violence.aspx.

33 **$300 billion worth of time:** Garey Ramey and Valerie A. Ramey, "The Rug Rat Race," Brookings Papers on Economic Activity, Economic Studies Program, *The Brookings Institution* 41, no.1 (Spring 2010): 129–99.

34 **"Believe in yourself" increased sixfold:** Dr. Jean M. Twenge, *Generation Me* (New York: Free Press, 2006), 65.

34 **"belief that you're important.":** Twenge, *Generation Me*, 63.

34 **Gen Xers had in 1988:** Twenge, *Generation Me*, 70.

35 **more time on homework:** Malcolm Harris, *Kids These Days* (New York: Back Bay Books, 2017), 20.

35 **"lean, mean production machines.":** Harris, *Kids These Days*, 76.

36 **record levels of anxiety:** "Stress by Generation," The American Psychological Association, apa.org/news/press/releases/stress/2012/generations.

36 **only 13 percent did:** Nancy Gibbs, "The Growing Backlash Against Overparenting," *TIME*, November 30, 2009.

37 **school-related thefts dropped 82 percent:** David Finkenhor, "Trends in Bullying & Peer Victimization," University of New Hampshire, Crimes Against Children Research Center, August 2014.

37 **zero tolerance policies echoed:** Harris, *Kids These Days*, 36.

37 **at keeping schools safe:** Harris, *Kids These Days*, 36

39 *New York Times* **bestseller list:** Paul Gray, "Wild about Harry Potter," *TIME*, September 20, 1999.

39 **Potter juggernaut, or "Pottered.":** Gray, "The Magic of Potter."

39 **them to the press:** Nancy Gibbs, "The Real Magic of Harry Potter, *TIME*, June 23, 2003.

39 **fastest-selling book ever:** Anthony Gierzynski, *Harry Potter and the Millennials* (Baltimore: Johns Hopkins University Press, 2013).

39 **had actual Quidditch teams:** Gierzynski, *Harry Potter and the Millennials*.

39 **phenomenon was "literally unprecedented.":** Gray, "The Magic of Potter."

39 **"For an entire generation of children":** Gibbs, "The Real Magic of Harry Potter."

40 **superfans of the series:** Gierzynski, *Harry Potter and the Millennials*, 50.

41 **than kids who didn't:** Loris Vezzali, et al., "The Greatest Magic of Harry Potter: Reducing Prejudice," *Journal of Applied Social Psychology,* July 23, 2014, onlinelibrary.wiley .com/doi/full/10.1111/jasp.12279#accessDenialLayout.

41 **Pope Benedict XVI warned:** Nancy Gibbs, "Runners-up: J. K. Rowling," Person of the Year 2017, *TIME*, December 19, 2007, content.time.com/time/specials/2007/personoftheyear /article/0,28804,1690753_1695388_1695436,00.html.

41 **American Library Association's list:** Pat Peters, "Harry Potter and 20 Years of Controversy," American Library Association, *Intellectual Freedom Blog*, August 28, 2017, oif .ala.org/oif/?p=10636.

41 **to an antigenocide hotline:** Gibbs, "Runners-up: J. K. Rowling."

41 **to his daughter Malia:** Julian Kossoff, "Barack Obama Under the Harry Potter Spell," *The Telegraph*, July 19, 2007, telegraph.co.uk/news/worldnews/1557929/Barack-Obama -under-the-Harry-Potter-spell.html.

41 **agency called "Dumbledore's Army":** Jessica Silver-Greenberg and Stacy Cowley, "Consumer Bureau's New Leader Steers a Sudden Reversal," *The New York Times,* December 5, 2017, nytimes.com/2017/12/05/business/cfpb-mick-mulvaney.html.

41 **to block his agenda:** Bess Levin, "Trump's Allies Are Using Harry Potter to Dismantle the Deep State," *Vanity Fair*, December 7, 2017, vanityfair.com/news/2017/12/trumps -allies-are-using-harry-potter-to-dismantle-the-deep-state.

41 **"Like kids versus evil.":** Author's interview with David Hogg, early March 2018.

THE BIG ONE

43 **helicopters ignoring them overhead:** Kirk Johnson, "For Storm Survivors, a Mosaic of Impressions," *The New York Times*, September 11, 2005, nytimes.com/2005/09/11/us /nationalspecial/for-storm-survivors-a-mosaic-of-impressions.html.

43 **coffins dislodged from graves:** Carlos Barria, "Hurricane Katrina: Scenes of Destruction 10 Years On—In Pictures," *The Guardian*, August 28, 2015, theguardian.com/artanddesign /gallery/2015/aug/28/hurricane-katrina-scenes-overlaid-in-pictures.

43 **walkway to their death:** Nat Scott, "Refuge of Last Resort," *USA Today*, August 24, 2015, ftw.usatoday.com/2015/08/refuge-of-last-resort-five-days-inside-the-superdome -for-hurricane-katrina.

43 **schools were forced to close:** Irwin E. Redlener and Gabrielle Schang, "Responding to a Humanitarian Crisis in Louisiana and Mississippi: Urgent Need for a Health Care 'Marshall Plan,'" Columbia University, Mailman School of Public Health, April 17, 2006, doi.org/10.7916/D8VD76V8.

43 **to call them "refugees,":** Katy Reckdahl, "The Lost Children of Katrina," *The Atlantic*, April 2, 2005, theatlantic.com/education/archive/2015/04/the-lost-children-of-katrina /389345/.

43 **working nor in school:** Denielle Dreilinger, "Unemployed, Out of Work Youth Cost Louisiana 1.7 Billion," nola.com, March 13, 2013, nola.com/education/2015/03/unemployed _out of-school_youth html.

CHAPTER 3: GETTING INTO COLLEGE, GETTING OUT OF DEBT

44 **would have been $5,500:** "B.U. Hikes Tuition, Blames Inflation As a Major Cause," *The Harvard Crimson*, January 8, 1980, thecrimson.com/article/1980/1/8/bu-hikes-tuition -blames-inflation-as/.

44 **over $46,000 per year:** Boston University Fact Sheet 2007/2008, "Summary of Data by Schools and Colleges," bu.edu/oir/files/2010/10/Fact-Sheet-2007-2008.pdf.

46 **most fully defined by it:** Board of Governors of the Federal Reserve System, Consumer Credit, federalreserve.gov/releases/g19/HIST/cc_hist_memo_levels.html.

46 **it's nearly $15,000:** YiLi Chien and Paul Morris, "Accounting for Age: The Financial Health of Millennials," Federal Reserve Bank of St. Louis, May 16, 2018, stlouisfed.org/ publications/regional-economist/second-quarter-2018/accounting-age-financial -health-millennials.

46 **most prestigious school they could find:** W. Norton Grubb and Marvin Lazerson, *The Education Gospel* (Cambridge, MA.: Harvard University Press, 2007).

46 **(roughly $15,000 in 2018 dollars):** National Center for Education Statistics, "Table 320, Average undergraduate tuition and fees and room and board rates charged for full-time students in degree-granting institutions, by type and control of institution: 1964-65 through 2006-07," n.d., nces.ed.gov/programs/digest/d07/tables/dt07_320.asp.

46 **it was in 1988:** Jennifer Ma, Sandy Baum, Matea Pender, and C. J. Libassi, "Trends in College Pricing 2018," College Board, n.d.

47 **men earned undergraduate degrees:** Dr. Jean M. Twenge, *Generation Me* (New York: Free Press, 2006), 239.

47 **than none at all:** Gretchen Livingston and D'Vera Cohn, "Record Share of New Mothers are College Educated," Pew Research Center, May 10, 2013, pewsocialtrends.org/2013 /05/10/record-share-of-new-mothers-are-college-educated/.

47 **have only a high school degree:** "Millennial Life: How Adulthood Today Compares with Prior Generations," Pew Research Center, February 14, 2019, pewsocialtrends.org /essay/millennial-life-how-young-adulthood-today-compares-with-prior-genera tions/.

47 **numbered nearly a million:** Patrick Barta, Te-Ping Chen, Diana Jou, Colleen McEnaney and Andrea Fuller, "How International Students Are Changing U.S. Colleges," *The Wall Street Journal*, n.d., graphics.wsj.com/international-students/.

47 **college than in the 1960s:** Nancy Gibbs and Nathan Thornburgh, "Who Needs Harvard?", *TIME*, cover story, August 21, 2006, content.time.com/time/magazine/article /0,9171,1226150,00.html.

48 **the students who sent applications:** Michael S. Lottman, "Admissions Office Faces Dilemmas; Continuing Search for Excellence Clashes with Concern for Feelings," *The Harvard Crimson*, June 15, 1961, thecrimson.com/article/1961/6/15/admissions-office -faces-dilemmas-continuing-search/.

48 **it was 20 percent:** M. Brett Gladstone, "Officials Pleased with New Admissions," *The Harvard Crimson*, April 17, 1976, thecrimson.com/article/1976/4/17/officials-pleased -with-new-admissions-pmonday/.

48 **hovered around 5 percent:** Daphne C. Thompson, "Harvard Accepts Record-Low 5.3 Percent of Applicants to Class of 2019," *The Harvard Crimson*, April 1, 2015, thecrimson .com/article/2015/4/1/regular-admissions-class-2019/.

48 **had twice the earnings:** "Millennial Life," Pew Research Center.

48 **"from the earliest years of life":** William Deresiewicz, *Excellent Sheep* (New York: Free Press, 2014), 12, 16.

49 **more than a dozen schools:** National Association for College Admission Counseling, chart provided to the author.

49 **in the next five years:** National Center for Education Statistics, Fast Facts, "Enroll-ment," nces.ed.gov/fastfacts/display.asp?id=98.

50 **the American Council on Education:** Thomas G. Mortensen, "State Funding: A Race to the Bottom," American Council on Education, Winter 2012, acenet.edu/the-presidency /columns-and-features/Pages/state-funding-a-race-to-the-bottom.aspx.

50 **over the same period:** "25 Years of Declining State Support for Public Colleges," *The Chronicle of Higher Education*, March 3, 2014, chronicle.com/interactives/statesup port.

50 **acceptance letters said yes:** National Association for College Admission Counseling, charts provided to the author.

51 **average of eighty-seven every day:** New England Center for Investigative Reporting and American Institute for Research: hechingerreport.org/ranks-of-nonacademic-staffs -at-colleges-continues-to-outpace-enrollment-faculty/.

51 **made more than $3 million:** Dan Bauman, Tyler Davis, and Brian O'Leary, "Executive Compensation at Public and Private Colleges," *The Chronicle of Higher Education*, July 14, 2019, chronicle.com/interactives/executive-compensation#id=table_private_2016.

51 **$7.5 million that year:** Michael Mitchell, Michael Leachman, Kathleen Masterson, and Samantha Waxman, "Unkept Promises: State Cuts to Higher Education Threaten Ac-cess and Equity," Center on Budget and Policy Priorities, October 4, 2018, cbpp.org /research/state-budget-and-tax/unkept-promises-state-cuts-to-higher-education -threaten-access-and.

51 **eligible for food stamps:** Lee Hall, "I Am an Adjunct Professor Who Teaches Five Classes. I Earn Less Than a Pet-Sitter," *The Guardian*, June 22, 2015, theguardian.com /commentisfree/2015/jun/22/adjunct-professor-earn-less-than-pet-sitter.

51 **doubled as a share of GDP:** Noah Smith, "Student Debt Loan Is Crushing Millennials," *Bloomberg*, November 2, 2018, bloomberg.com/opinion/articles/2018-11-02/student-loan -debt-hobbles-next-generation-of-u-s-workers.

51 **most of that is student debt:** Northwestern Mutual, "Planning & Progress Study 2018."

51 **their parents ever did:** Michael Hobbes, "FML: Why Millennials Are Facing the Scar-iest Financial Future of Any Generation Since the Great Depression," *The Huffington Post*, n.d., highline.huffingtonpost.com/articles/en/poor-millennials/.

52 **graduated with little or no debt:** Anne Helen Petersen, "Here's Why So Many Ameri-cans Feel Cheated by Their Student Loans," *BuzzFeed*, February 9, 2019, buzzfeednews .com/article/annehelenpetersen/student-debt-college-public-service-loan-forgive ness.

52 **be behind on their payments:** Diane Harris, "The Truth About Student Debt: 7 Facts No One Is Talking About," *Newsweek*, September 30, 2019, newsweek.com/2019/08/23 /student-debt-loans-truth-facts-cover-story-1453057.html.

52 **and a worthless degree:** Petersen, "Here's Why So Many Americans Feel Cheated by Their Student Loans."

52 **borrowers has considered suicide:** Alex Tanzi, "1 in 15 Borrowers Has Considered Suicide Because of Student Debt, Survey Says," *The Washington Post*, May 5, 2019, washingtonpost.com/business/economy/student-debt-has-increased-almost-61-billion-since-end-of-2017-survey-shows/2019/05/05/cf923122-6f90-11e9-8be0-ca575670e91c_story.html.

THOUGHTS & PRAYERS

53 **"still in the hospital tonight.":** HLN Breaking News, April 17, 2005, youtube.com/watch?v=L7H56tcAFlw.

53 **the second round of shootings:** Christine Hauser and Anahad O'Connor, "Virginia Tech Shooting Leaves 33 Dead," *The New York Times*, April 16, 2005, nytimes.com/2007/04/16/us/16cnd-shooting.html.

53 **DESK I CHOSE TO DIE UNDER:** David Maraniss, "That Was the Desk I Chose to Die Under," *The Washington Post*, April 19, 2007, washingtonpost.com/wp-dyn/content/article/2007/04/18/AR2007041802824_3.html.

53 **"if it wasn't for him.":** Erinn Hutkin, "Holocaust survivor blocked shooter, letting students flee," *The Roanoke Times*, April 17, 2007, roanoke.com/archive/holocaust-survivor-blocked-shooter-letting-students-flee/article_0a51fa1f-3fc5-580e-9134-e9cfc610e524.html.

53 **Bush told Katie Couric:** "Eye to Eye with Katie Couric," CBS News, April 18, 2007, youtube.com/watch?v=Kxxsw2Hglak

53 **"praying for you," he said:** "President Bush Offers Condolences at Virginia Tech Memorial Convocation," White House, April 17, 2007, georgewbush-whitehouse.archives.gov/news/releases/2007/04/20070417-1.html.

53 **TOUGHEN SCREENING OF GUN BUYERS:** Richard Simon, "Bush Signs Bill Geared to Toughen Screening of Gun Buyers," *Los Angeles Times*, January 8, 2008, latimes.com/la-na-guns9dec09-story.html.

CHAPTER 4: THE LAST DINOSAURS

55 **included three big shifts:** Walter Isaacson, *The Innovators: How a Group of Hackers, Geniuses and Geeks Created the Digital Revolution* (New York: Simon & Schuster, 2014).

56 **more likely to have one:** Eric C. Newburger, "Home Computers and Internet Usage in the United States: August 2000," Current Population Reports, US Census Bureau, September 2001.

56 **America experienced a technological:** Reuben Fischer-Baum, "What 'Tech World' Did You Grow Up In," *The Washington Post*, November 26, 2017, washingtonpost.com/graphics/2017/entertainment/tech-generations/.

57 **30 percent had internet:** Newburger, "Home Computers and Internet Usage in the United States: August 2000."

57 **by early 2010, three-quarters did:** "Millennials: Confident, Connected, Open to Change," Pew Research Center, February 2010, pewresearch.org/wp-content/uploads/sites/3/2010/10/millennials-confident-connected-open-to-change.pdf.

57 **nearly a quarter of millennials:** Hannah Fingerhut, "Millennials' Views of News Media, Religious Organizations Grow More Negative," Pew Research Center, January 4, 2016, pewresearch.org/fact-tank/2016/01/04/millennials-views-of-news-media-religious-organizations-grow-more-negative/.

57 **defining characteristic of their generation:** "Millennials: Confident, Connected, Open to Change," Pew Research Center.

59 **understanding how to interpret it:** Amy Mitchell, Jeffrey Gottfried, and Katerina Eva Matsa, "Millenials and Political News," Pew Research Center, June 1, 2015, journalism.org/2015/06/01/millennials-political-news/.

59 **during the 2016 election:** Andrew Guess, Jonathan Nagler, and Joshie Tucker, "Less Than You Think: Prevalence and Predictors of Fake News Dissemination on Facebook," *Science*, American Association for the Advancement of Science, January 9, 2019, advances.sciencemag.org/content/5/1/eaau4586.

59 **distinguishing facts from opinions:** Jeffrey Gottfried and Elizabeth Grieco, "Younger

Americans Are Better Than Older Americans at Telling Factual News Statements from Opinions," Pew Research Center, October 23, 2018, pewresearch.org/fact-tank/2018/10/23/younger-americans-are-better-than-older-americans-at-telling-factual-news-statements-from-opinions/.

59 **Americans of organized religion:** "Religion Among the Millennials," Pew Research Center, February 17, 2010, pewforum.org/2010/02/17/religion-among-the-millennials/.

59 **political parties, corporations, and:** Zachary Crockett, "Millennials Have Very Little Confidence in Most Major Institutions," *Vox*, September 28, 2016, vox.com/2016/9/28/13062286/millennials-confidence-in-government.

61 **rooted in white male grievance:** Angela Nagle, "The Lost Boys: The Young Men of the Alt Right Could Define American Politics for a Generation," *The Atlantic*, December 2017, theatlantic.com/magazine/archive/2017/12/brotherhood-of-losers/544158/.

62 **tiny picture of campus:** Buttigieg, *Shortest Way Home*.

CHAPTER 5: THIS IS THE WAR THAT NEVER ENDS

64 **the nearby Helmand Province:** Dan Zak, "Dan Crenshaw Started the Week as a Punchline and Ended It as a Star. The Real Story Came Before That," *The Washington Post*, November 11, 2018, washingtonpost.com/lifestyle/style/dan-crenshaw-started-the-week-as-an-snl-joke-and-ended-it-as-a-gop-star-the-real-story-came-before-that/2018/11/11/d68d5c5c-e46e-11e8-ab2c-b31dcd53ca6b_story.html.

64 **cover over uncleared ground:** Zak, "Dan Crenshaw Started the Week as a Punchline and Ended It as a Star."

67 **including roughly 200,000 civilians:** "Iraq Body Count," iraqbodycount.org/.

67 **didn't even remember 9/11:** Tara Copp, "Recruiting a Generation with No Memory of Sept. 11," *Military Times*, September 11, 2017, militarytimes.com/news/2017/09/11/recruiting-a-generation-with-no-memory-of-september-11th/.

67 **time as their sons:** Barbara O'Brien, "59-year old Grandpa, Son, Ended Up Serving in Iraq at the Same Time," *The Buffalo News*, July 30, 2018, buffalonews.com/2018/07/30/59-year-old-grandpa-soldier-son-ended-up-serving-in-iraq-at-the-same-time/.

67 **mothers with their daughters:** "Mother and Daughter Form Soldier's Bond in Iraq," NPR, "Weekend Edition Saturday," December 7, 2012, npr.org/2012/12/08/166758989/mother-and-daughter-form-soldiers-bond-in-iraq.

67 **before they were born:** Vera Bergengruen, "The US Military Is Now Recurring Soldiers to Fight in a War That Started Before They Were Born," *BuzzFeed*, October 9, 2018, buzzfeednews.com/article/verabergengruen/afghanistan-recruit-war-endless-911-sept-11.

67 **called the "forever war.":** Dexter Filkins, *The Forever War* (New York: Vintage, 2009).

67 **quarter had a military parent:** Mark Thompson, "Here's Why The Military Is a Family Business," *TIME*, March 10, 2016, time.com/4254696/military-family-business/.

68 **them on multiple tours:** Sebastian Junger, "What's the Matter with the American Military?" *The Atlantic*, February 23, 2015, theatlantic.com/international/archive/2015/02/whats-the-matter-with-the-american-military/385735/.

68 **didn't have a college degree:** "War and Sacrifice in the Post-9/11 Era: Chapter 6," Pew Research Center, October 5, 2011, pewsocialtrends.org/2011/10/05/chapter-6-a-profile-of-the-modern-military/.

68 **found that 40 percent:** Population Representation in the Military Services, Fiscal Year 2016 Executive Summary, Office of the Under Secretary of Defense, Center for Naval Analyses, cna.org/pop-rep/2016/summary/summary.html.

68 **studying abroad than joining the military:** James Fallows, "The Tragedy of the American Military," *The Atlantic*, January/February 2015, theatlantic.com/magazine/archive/2015/01/the-tragedy-of-the-american-military/383516/.

70 **still transportable by air:** Stuart Koehl, "Kevlar Coffins?," *The Weekly Standard*, November 18, 2009, weeklystandard.com/stuart-koehl/kevlar-coffins.

70 **in a $13 billion program:** Robert H. Reid and Anne Flaherty, "Stryker Losses in Iraq Raise Questions, *The Washington Post*, May 13, 2007, washingtonpost.com/wp-dyn/content/article/2007/05/13/AR2007050s51300552.html.

70 **built to withstand buried IEDs:** Robert Haddick, "This Week at War: Why Don't Stryker Brigades Work in Afghanistan," *Foreign Policy*, November 6, 2009, foreignpolicy .com/2009/11/06/this-week-at-war-why-dont-stryker-brigades-work-in-afghanistan/.

71 **make combat vehicles safer:** Terrence K. Kelly, et al., "The U.S. Combat and Tactical Wheeled Vehicle Fleets," Rand Corporation, National Defense Research Institute, rand.org /content/dam/rand/pubs/monographs/2011/RAND_MG1093.pdf.

72 **half of boomers agreed:** Pew Research Group, "The Generation Gap and the 2012 Election: Section 8," November 3, 2011, people-press.org/2011/11/03/section-8-domestic-and -foreign-policy-views./

72 **misunderstood by the American public:** Pew Research Group, "War and Sacrifice in the Post-9/11 Era," Pew Social Trends, October 5, 2011, pewsocialtrends.org/2011/10 /05/war-and-sacrifice-in-the-post-911-era/.

73 **increase among young veterans:** Dave Philipps, "Suicide Rate Among Veterans Has Risen Sharply Since 2001," *The New York Times*, July 78, 2016, nytimes.com/2016/07 /08/us/suicide-rate-among-veterans-has-risen-sharply-since-2001.html.

73 **three-quarters of baby boomers:** Trevor Thrall, et al., "The Clash of Generations?: Intergenerational Change and American Foreign Policy Views," Chicago Council on Global Affairs, June 2018, thechicagocouncil.org/sites/default/files/report_clash-of -generations 180625.pdf.

73 **Only about a third of millennials:** Katie Reilly, "A Generational Gap in American Patriotism," Pew Research Center, July 3, 2013, pewresearch.org/fact-tank/2013/07/03 /a-generational-gap-in-american-patriotism/.

74 **"very good blind dates.":** Pete Buttigieg, *Shortest Way Home* (New York: Liveright, 2019), 73–74.

75 **in the US Navy Reserve:** Buttigieg, *Shortest Way Home*, 78.

CHAPTER 6: THE ROCKET SHIP

81 **"are better days ahead.":** "Barack Obama's Remarks to the 2004 Democratic Convention," *The New York Times*, July 27, 2004, nytimes.com/2004/07/27/politics/campaign /barack-obamas-remarks-to-the-democratic-national.html.

85 **thirty-five times that year:** Jennifer Jacobs and Michael McNarney, "Saga of Hillary Clinton in Iowa," *Des Moines Register*, April 12, 2015, desmoinesregister.com/story /news/elections/presidential/caucus/2015/04/12/hillary-clinton-timeline-iowa /25676433/.

85 **have a snow shovel:** David Farenthold, "In 2008, Clinton Couldn't Buy Iowan's Love, So She Bought Them Snow Shovels," *The Washington Post*, June 6, 2015 washingtonpost .com/politics/in-2008-clinton-couldnt-buy-iowans-love-so-she-bought-them-snow -shovels/2015/06/06/742be0e0-07a6-11e5-95fd-d580f1c5d44e_story.html

85 **campaign in Iowa alone:** "Obama Draws Record Number Young People," NPR, *Day to Day*, January 4, 2008, npr.org/templates/story/story.php?storyId=17847196.

85 **skipping an AARP event:** David Von Drehle, "Obama's Youth Vote Triumph," *TIME*, January 4, 2008, content.time.com/time/politics/article/0,8599,1700525,00.html.

86 **"may have begun in Iowa.":** Joe Klein, "Obama's Historic Victory," *TIME*, January 4, 2008, content.time.com/time/politics/article/0,8599,1700132,00.html.

86 **won by just twenty thousand:** David Von Drehle, "It's Their Turn Now," February 11, 2008.

87 **as a sign of support:** Von Drehle, "It's Their Turn Now."

87 **the crucial swing state:** Von Drehle, "It's Their Turn Now."

88 **opponent to the status quo:** Roger Cohen, "Obama's Youth-Driven Movement," *The New York Times*, January 28, 2008, nytimes.com/2008/01/28/opinion/28cohen.html

89 **enough to legally vote:** Laura Fitzpatrick, "The Dems' Really Young Guns," *TIME*, September 1, 2008, content.time.com/time/magazine/article/0,9171,1834668,00.html.

89 **investor, told *The New York Times*:** David Carr, "How Obama Tapped into Social Networks' Power," *The New York Times*, November 9, 2008, nytimes.com/2008/11/10 /business/media/10carr.html.

90 **of them small contributors:** Michael Luo, "Obama Hauls in Record $750 Million for

Campaign," *The New York Times*, December 4, 2008, nytimes.com/2008/12/05/us/politics/05donate.html.

90 **participate in the 2008 campaign:** Aaron Smith, "The Internet's Role in Campaign 2008," Pew Research Center, April 15, 2009, pewinternet.org/2009/04/15/the-internets-role-in-campaign-2008/

90 **that much airtime on TV news:** Claire Cain Miller, "How Obama's Internet Campaign Changed Politics," *The New York Times*, November 7, 2008 https://bits.blogs.nytimes.com/2008/11/07/how-obamas-internet-campaign-changed-politics/.

90 **such as registering to vote:** Jonathan Alter, *The Center Holds* (New York: Simon & Schuster, 2013).

90 **share of the youth vote:** "Obama's Election Redraws America's Electoral Divide," CNN, Election Center 2008, November 5, 2008, cnn.com/2008/POLITICS/11/05/election.president/.

90 **band played the national anthem:** Julie Rowe, "Elated Campus Erupts After Obama's Historic Win," *The Michigan Daily*, November 5, 2008, michigandaily.com/content/2008-11-05/campus-erupts-after-obama-landslide.

91 **president of their lifetime:** Pew Research Center, "Obama Tops Public's List of Best President in Their Lifetime, Followed by Clinton, Reagan," July 11, 2008, people-press.org/2018/07/11/obama-tops-publics-list-of-best-president-in-their-lifetime-followed-by-clinton-reagan/.

CHAPTER 7: THE CRASH

93 **market value vanishing overnight:** Vikas Bajaja and Michael M. Grynbaum, "For Stocks, Worst Single-Day Drop in Two Decades," *The New York Times*, September 29 2008, nytimes.com/2008/09/30/business/30markets.html.

93 **jobs and health insurance:** John Cawley, Asako S. Muriya, and Kosali I. Simon, "The Impact of the Macroeconomy on Health Insurance Coverage," National Bureau of Economic Statistics, Working Paper 17600, November 2011, nber.org/papers/w17600.pdf.

93 **two million families had lost their homes:** Les Christie, "Foreclosures Up a Record 81% in 2008," CNN Money, January 15 2009, money.cnn.com/2009/01/15/real_estate/millions_in_foreclosure/.

93 **"than anyone on this planet.":** *Knock Down the House*, directed by Rachel Lears (2019; Netflix).

95 **know up from down:** *Knock Down the House*, directed by Rachel Lears.

95 **had lost their breadwinner:** Ada Chávez and Ryan Grim, "A Primary Against the Machine," The Intercept, May 22, 2018, theintercept.com/2018/05/22/joseph-crowley-alexandra-ocasio-cortez-new-york-primary/.

95 **the class of 2009 did:** Michael Hobbes, "FML: Why Millennials Are Facing the Scariest Financial Future of Any Generation Since the Great Depression," *The Huffington Post*, December 2017, highline.huffingtonpost.com/articles/en/poor-millennials/.

96 **was more than 30 percent:** Bureau of Labor Statistics, "Youth Unemployment and Employment in July 2009," August 28, 2009, bls.gov/opub/ted/2009/ted_20090828.htm?view_full.

96 **debt than their parents:** Hobbes, "FML: Why Millennials Are Facing the Scariest Financial Future of Any Generation Since the Great Depression."

96 **jobs they would not have:** Malcolm Harris, *Kids These Days* (New York: Back Bay Books, 2017).

96 **have a postsecondary degree:** "15 Economic Facts About Millennials," White House Council of Economic Advisers, October 2014, obamawhitehouse.archives.gov/sites/default/files/docs/millennials_report.pdf.

97 **them lived in poverty:** Hobbes, "FML: Why Millennials Are Facing the Scariest Financial Future of Any Generation Since the Great Depression."

97 **comparable boomer male breadwinner's:** Christopher Kurz, Geng Li, and Daniel J. Vine, "Are Millennials Different?," Finance and Economics Discussion Series, 2018, Board of Governors of the Federal Reserve System, Washington, DC, doi.org/10.17016/FEDS.2018.080.

97 **had been at their age:** Kurz, Li, and Vine, "Are Millennials Different?".

97 **found that nearly a decade:** "The Demographics of Wealth," Federal Reserve Bank of St. Louis, May 2018, stlouisfed.org/~/media/files/pdfs/hfs/essays/hfs_essay_2_2018 .pdf?la=en.

97 **55 percent of their wealth:** Rakesh Kochhar and Anthony Cilluffo, "How Wealth Inequality Has Changed in the U.S. Since the Great Recession," Pew Research Center, November 1, 2017, pewresearch.org/fact-tank/2017/11/01/how-wealth-inequality-has -changed-in-the-u-s-since-the-great-recession-by-race-ethnicity-and-income/.

98 **other sources of income:** Hobbes, "FML: Why Millennials Are Facing the Scariest Financial Future of Any Generation Since the Great Depression."

98 **their student loan payments:** Amy Adkins, "Millennials, The Job Hopping Generation," Gallup, n.d., gallup.com/workplace/231587/millennials-job-hopping-generation.aspx.

98 **halved since 1983:** Bureau of Labor Statistics, "Union Membership in the United States," September 2016, bls.gov/spotlight/2016/union-membership-in-the-united-states /home.htm.

98 **schedules just a few days in advance:** Lonnie Golden, "Irregular Work Scheduling and Its Consequences," Economic Policy Institute, April 9, 2015, epi.org/publication/irregular -work-scheduling-and-its-consequences/.

99 **specialty cronuts and fancy coffees:** Kathleen Elkins, "Here's How Millennials Spend Their Money, Compared to Their Parents," CNBC, June 30, 2017, cnbc.com/2017/06/30 /heres-how-millennials-spend-their-money-compared-to-their-parents.html.

99 **worked as freelancers:** Edelman Intelligence, "Freelancing in America: 2018," Upwork and Freelancers Union, October 22, 2018, slideshare.net/upwork/freelancing-in-america -2018-120288770/1.

99 **from under them again:** Allison Schrager, "The Financial Crisis May Have Scarred a Generation for Life," Quartz, September 15, 2018, qz.com/1386293/the-casualty-of-the -financial-crisis-risk-taking/.

99 **there will be just two:** Social Security History, "Ratio of Social Security Covered Workers to Beneficiaries," ssa.gov/history/ratios.html.

99 **their forties and fifties:** Congressional Research Service: "What Would Happen If the Trust Funds Ran Out?" June 12, 2019, fas.org/sgp/crs/misc/RL33514.pdf.

CHAPTER 8: FIX THE SYSTEM

102 **American industry since World War II:** Steven Rattner, *Overhaul* (New York: Houghton Mifflin, 2010).

102 **far more cars in American driveways:** R&T Staff, "More Cars Than Drivers in US," *Road & Track*, November 6, 2012, roadandtrack.com/car-culture/a9672/more-cars-than -drivers-in-us/.

102 **flying everywhere on private jets:** Karey Wutkowski, "Auto Execs' Private Flights to Washington Draw Ire," Reuters, November 19, 2008, reuters.com/article/us-autos-bailout -planes/auto-execs-private-flights-to-washington-draw-ire-idUSTRE4AI8C52 0081119.

102 **until after the election:** David M. Herszenhorn and David E. Singer, "Bush Approves $17.4 Billion Auto Bailout," *The New York Times*, December 19, 2008, nytimes.com/2008 /12/19/business/worldbusiness/19iht-20autoB.18826530.html.

103 **by corporate sob stories:** Rattner, *Overhaul*.

104 **LET DETROIT GO BANKRUPT:** Mitt Romney, "Let Detroit Go Bankrupt," *The New York Times*, November 18, 2008, nytimes.com/2008/11/19/opinion/19romney.html.

104 **would get the blame:** Rattner, *Overhaul*.

105 **more than 500,000 new jobs:** US Department of the Treasury, TARP Programs, Auto Industry, updated January 8, 2015, treasury.gov/initiatives/financial-stability/TARP -Programs/automotive-programs/pages/default.aspx.

106 **for that exact reason:** Ashley Parker, "And Now, Starring in the West Wing: Ax & Lesser, *The New York Times*, June 12, 2009.

106 **that followed the recession:** Jonathan Alter, *The Promise* (New York: Simon & Schuster, 2010).

106 **told Geithner in 2009:** Alter, *The Promise*, 314.

107 **to dramatize his objection:** Alter, *The Promise*.

108 **single-payer health care:** "More Support for Single Payer Among Those Under 30 Than Older Adults," Pew Research Center, June 23, 2017, pewresearch.org/fact-tank/2018 /10/03/most-continue-to-say-ensuring-health-care-coverage-is-governments -responsibility/ft_17-06-23_healthcare_age_640px/.

CHAPTER 9: FUCK THE SYSTEM

113 **three-quarter-acre pocket park:** Mattathias Schwartz, "Map: How Occupy Wall Street Chose Zuccotti Park," *The New Yorker*, November 18, 2011, newyorker.com/news /news-desk/map-how-occupy-wall-street-chose-Zuccotti-park.

113 **40 percent of the active participants:** Ruth Milkman, Stephanie Luce, and Penny Lewis, "Changing the Subject," Murphy Institute, CUNY School of Labor and Urban Studies, 2013, docs.wixstatic.com/ugd/90d188_f7367c3e04de4e94a6f86f9e6b1023ed.pdf.

113 **website were under thirty-four:** Hector R. Cordero-Guzman, "Mainstream Support for a Mainstream Movement," 2011, Baruch College School of Public Affairs.

114 **under thirty supported the movement:** Public Policy Polling, "Americans See Occupy Movement Better Than Tea Party," October 13, 2011, publicpolicypolling.com/wp-content /uploads/2017/09/PPP_Release_US_1013925.pdf.

114 **called "We Are the 99 Percent.":** "We Are the 99 Percent," October 14, 2013, wearethe 99percent.tumblr.com/.

114 **"doctor without health insurance.":** "We Are the 99 Percent," 2, wearethe99percent .tumblr.com/page/2.

114 **"I'm taking my future back.":** "We Are the 99 Percent," 2, wearethe99percent.tumblr .com/page/5.

114 **"and asked to borrow rent.":** "We Are the 99 Percent," 5, wearethe99percent.tumblr .com/page/5.

114 **750 cities around the world:** Simon Rogers, "Occupy protests around the world: full lists visualised," November 14, 2011, *The Guardian*, theguardian.com/news/datablog /2011/oct/17/occupy-protests-world-list-map.

114 **bailouts to student debt:** "Declaration of the Occupation of New York City," Occupy Wall Street, September 29, 2011, occupywallstreet.net/learn.

115 *The Occupied Wall Street Journal*: Jessica Firger, "Protesters' Newspaper Occupies a Familiar Name," *The Wall Street Journal*, October 4, 2011, blogs.wsj.com/metropolis /2011/10/04/protesters-newspaper-occupies-a-familiar-name/.

115 **out free ice cream:** "Occupy Wall Street Tour with Cenk of the Young Turks," youtube .com/watch?v=y1WepAc6IuM.

115 **Susan Sarandon to Kanye West:** Gabriel H. Sanchez, "26 of the Most Powerful Pictures from the Occupy Wall Street Movement," *BuzzFeed*, September 17, 2018, buzzfeed news.com/article/gabrielsanchez/occupy-wall-street-pictures.

115 **neighborhood bathrooms were overrun:** Chris Glorioso, "Occupy Wall Street Protesters Acknowledge Neighbors' Quality of Life Concerns," NBC.com, October 20, 2011, nbc newyork.com/news/local/Angry-Neighbors-Occupy-Wall-Street-Zuccotti-Park -Lower-Manhattan-Community-Board-1-132289418.html.

115 **living in his parka:** Lila Shapiro, "Zuccotti Park's Micro-Neighborhoods May Indicate Deeper Divisions," *The Huffington Post*, November 9, 2011, huffingtonpost.com/2011 /11/09/Zuccotti-park-splinters-i_n_1084521.html.

115 **statue by the stairs:** "Occupy Wall Street Tour with Cenk of the Young Turks."

115 **and wiggle their fingers:** N. R. Kleinfeld and Cara Buckley, "Wall Street Occupiers, Protesting Till Whenever," *The New York Times*, November 1, 2011, nytimes.com/2011 /10/01/nyregion/wall-street-occupiers-protesting-till-whenever.html.

116 **"He pointed at Bank of America":** "Occupy Wall Street Mic Check at Zuccotti Park," YouTube video, October 7, 2011, youtube.com/watch?v=kZt-mA34xXM.

116 UNCLEAR, GET USED TO IT.: Michael Woods, "Zuccotti Park Day 54," *The Huffington Post*, November 11, 2011, huffingtonpost.com/michael-woods/zuccotti-park-day-54 -no_3_b_1086067.html

116 **the way the activists wanted it:** Meredith Hoffman, "Occupy Tries to Settle on De-mands, if Any," *The New York Times*, October 16, 2011, nytimes.com/2011/10/17/nyregion/occupy-wall-street-trying-to-settle-on-demands.html

118 **dozens of US cities:** Matt Williams, "Trayvon Martin Protests Being Held in 100 US Cities," *The Guardian*, July 20, 2013, theguardian.com/world/2013/jul/20/trayvon-martin-protests-us-cities.

118 **bags over their mouths:** "A Week After Verdict, Throngs Rally for Trayvon Martin," *The New York Times*, July 20, 2013, nytimes.com/slideshow/2013/07/20/us/MARTIN/s/MARTIN-slide-WHVK.html.

118 **to be Trayvon's age:** Jelani Cobb, "The Matter of Black Lives," *The New Yorker*, March 6, 2016, newyorker.com/magazine/2016/03/14/where-is-black-lives-matter-headed.

118 **"Black people. I love you.":** Cobb, "The Matter of Black Lives."

118 **met on a dance floor:** Cobb, "The Matter of Black Lives."

118 **Twitter and Tumblr accounts:** Wesley Lowery, "Birth of a Movement," *The Guardian*, January 17, 2017, theguardian.com/us-news/2017/jan/17/black-lives-matter-birth-of-a-movement.

119 **white men the same age:** Becky Pettit and Bryan Sykes, "Pathways: State of the Union," Special Issue 2017, Stanford Center on Poverty & Inequality, inequality.stanford.edu/sites/default/files/Pathways_SOTU_2017.pdf.

119 **in school were black:** School-to-Prison Pipeline (Infographic), ACLU, n.d., aclu.org/issues/juvenile-justice/school-prison-pipeline/school-prison-pipeline-infographic.

119 **he was booed:** Philip Swarts, "Ferguson protesters confront Jesse Jackson: 'When you going to stop selling us out?' *The Washington Times*, August, 23, 2014, washingtontimes.com/news/2014/aug/23/ferguson-protesters-confront-jesse-jackson-when-yo/.

120 **"I wanted to be a part of it.":** Charlotte Alter, "Black Lives Matter Protest in New York Attracts New People," *TIME*, July 10, 2016, time.com/4400211/black-lives-matter-new-york-protest/.

120 **58 percent of millennials approved:** Susan Page and Karina Shedrofsky, "Poll: How Millennials View BLM and the Alt-right," *USA Today*, October 31, 2016, usatoday.com/story/news/politics/onpolitics/2016/10/31/poll-millennials-black-lives-matter-alt-right/92999936/.

120 **than their black peers:** Cathy J. Cohen, et al., "The 'Woke' Generation?" Millennial Attitudes on Race in the US," GenForward, October 2017, genforwardsurvey.com/assets/uploads/2017/10/GenForward-Oct-2017-Final-Report.pdf.

124 **overwhelmingly white, mostly male:** Brian Montopoli, "Tea Party Supporters: Who They Are and What They Believe," CBS News, December 14, 2012, cbsnews.com/news/tea-party-supporters-who-they-are-and-what-they-believe/.

124 **fears of generational change:** Vanessa Williamson, Theda Skocpol, and John Coggin, "The Tea Party and the Remaking of Republican Conservatism," *Perspectives on Politics* 9, no. 1 (March 2011), scholar.harvard.edu/files/williamson/files/tea_party_pop_0.pdf.

125 **drawn with devil horns:** "Lloyd Doggett's Meeting on Obamacare," YouTube video, August 1, 2009, youtube.com/watch?time_continue=5&v=a8UjY3YDlwA.

125 **or presented with nooses:** Glenn Thrush, "Rep. Kratovil Hung in Effigy by Health Care Protester," *Politico*, July 28, 2009, politico.com/blogs/on-congress/2009/07/rep-kratovil-hung-in-effigy-by-health-care-protester-update-020260.

125 **turned on his Facebook Live:** Braxton Winston, Facebook Live, September 20, 2016.

127 **had been shot with:** Ann Doss Helms, "Charlotte Uprising Says Keith Scott's Death Brought Resistance, Not Riots," *The Charlotte Observer*, September 18, 2017, charlotteobserver.com/news/local/article174070431.html.

127 **on anticipated Occupy protests:** Michael Gordon, "This Charlotte Protester Whose Photo Went Viral Is No Longer Facing Criminal Charges," *The Charlotte Observer*, March 1, 2017, charlotteobserver.com/news/local/crime/article135714318.html.

THE BIG ONE

129 **between Brooklyn and Manhattan:** Inae Oh, "The Night Hurricane Sandy Hit New York City," *The Huffington Post*, October 29, 2013, huffingtonpost.com/2013/10/28/sandy-anniversary_n_4170982.html.

129 **safer place to stay:** Raymond Hernandez, "Near Tears, Gillibrand Tells of 2 Boys Deaths," *The New York Times*, City Room (blog), November 29, 2012, cityroom.blogs .nytimes.com/2012/11/29/gillibrand-chokes-up-describing-death-of-2-boys-in-storm/.

129 **stalled the car's engine:** James Barron, Joseph Goldstein, and Kirk Semple, "Staten Island Was Tragic Epicenter of Storm's Casualties," *The New York Times*, November 1, 2012, nytimes.com/2012/11/02/nyregion/staten-island-was-tragic-epicenter-of-new-york -citys-storm-casualties.html.

129 **"one of those things," he said:** Tim Hume, "Young Brothers, "Denied Refuge," Swept to Death by Sandy," CNN, November 4, 2012, cnn.com/2012/11/02/world/americas/sandy -staten-island-brothers/index.html.

129 **At least 147 people died:** City of New York, "A Stronger, More Resilient New York," June 11, 2013, s-media.nyc.gov/agencies/sirr/SIRR_singles_Lo_res.pdf.

129 **homes in flood zones:** Robert Lewis and Al Shaw, "After Sandy, Government Lends to Rebuild in Flood Zones," ProPublica, March 6, 2013, propublica.org/article/after-sandy -government-lends-to-rebuild-in-flood-zones.

CHAPTER 10: THE LOCALS

131 **historic 675 state legislative seats:** Aaron Blake, "Which Election Was Worse for Democrats: 2010 or 2014? It's a Surprisingly Close Call," *The Washington Post*, November 5, 2014, washingtonpost.com/news/the-fix/wp/2014/11/05/which-election-was-worse-for -democrats-2010-or-2014/.

131 **toward Republicans in several states:** "'Gerrymandering on Steroids': How Republicans Stacked the Nation's Statehouses," WBUR, July 19, 2016, wbur.org/hereandnow/2016 /07/19/gerrymandering-republicans-redmap.

131 **lowest rungs on the political ladder:** Chris Cillizza, "Republicans Have Gained More Than 900 State Legislative Seats Since 2010," *The Washington Post*, January 14, 2015, washingtonpost.com/news/the-fix/wp/2015/01/14/republicans-have-gained-more -than-900-state-legislative-seats-since-2010/.

131 **considering running for office:** Shauna L. Shames, *Out of the Running* (New York: NYU Press, 2017), 5.

131 **political office in the mid-1980s:** "The Cost of Winning an Election, 1986–2016," Brookings Institution, n.d., brookings.edu/wp-content/uploads/2017/01/vitalstats_ch3_tbl1.pdf.

131 **seat cost $88,000:** Shames, *Out of the Running*, 36.

133 **he was actually elected:** Charlotte Alter, "'We Can Do It Better.' Meet the Millennials Taking Over City Hall," *TIME*, October 12, 2017, time.com/4979264/meet-millennials -taking-over-city-hall/.

133 **and talk with him:** Matt Steecker, "Ithaca's Mayor Transforms Parking Space into Tiny Park," *Ithaca Journal*, July 5, 2017, ithacajournal.com/story/news/2017/07/05/park-your -body-mayor-myricks-parking-space-park/422099001/.

134 **to oppose building more:** Jeff Stein, "Long-simmering Fight over Affordable Housing Plan Ends amid Mayor's Emotional Plea," *Ithaca Voice*, August 27, 2014, ithacavoice.com /2014/08/long-simmering-fight-affordable-housing-plan-ends-amid-ithaca-mayors -emotional-plea/.

135 **could have spent elsewhere:** David Marchan, "Time for a New Vision," Ithaca.com, March 13, 2019, ithaca.com/opinion/guest_opinions/time-for-a-new-vision/article _8dff857c-45ae-11e9-ba3b-57834ca9d289.html.

135 **$40 million affordable housing plan:** Sarah Mervosh, "Minneapolis, Tackling Housing Crisis and Inequity, Votes to End Single-Family Zoning," *The New York Times*, December 13, 2018, nytimes.com/2018/12/13/us/minneapolis-single-family-zoning.html

136 **held by people under forty:** Andrew Dunn, "Millennials Are About to Control the City Council. How will They Change Charlotte?" CharlotteAgenda.com, November 30, 2017, charlotteagenda.com/110521/millennials-control-city-council-will-change-charlotte/.

136 **gentrification and income inequality:** Charlotte Regional Business Alliance, The Growth Report, 2019, charlottechamber.com/eco-dev/the-growth-report/.

136 **45 percent since 2010:** Pam Kelley, "From Brooklyn to Ballantyne," *The Charlotte Observer*, June 17, 2019, updated, August 14, 2019, charlotteobserver.com/news/local/article231622193.html.

136 **social inequality in Charlotte:** J. Brian Charles, "Affordable Housing Reaches Tipping Point Crisis in Charlotte," *Governing*, February 15, 2019, governing.com/topics/urban/gov-charlotte-affordable-housing-lc.html.

137 **to higher-opportunity neighborhoods:** Kriston Capps, "How a Section 8 Experiment Could Reveal a Better Way to Escape Poverty," CityLab, August 4, 2019, citylab.com/equity/2019/08/affordable-housing-assistance-voucher-seattle-neighborhoods/595423.

137 **still hadn't been built:** Lauren Lindstrom, "City Claims Victory on Affordable Housing Goal, Though Almost Half Aren't Built Yet," *The Charlotte Observer*, July 18, 2019, charlotteobserver.com/article231928623.html.

137 **refused to drop his gun:** "Full Body Camera Video Shows What Happened After the Shooting of Danquirs Franklin," video, *The Charlotte Observer*, April 24, 2019, charlotteobserver.com/news/local/crime/article229621954.html.

137 **to treat the wounds themselves:** Ames Alexander and Anna Douglas, "Under criticism, Charlotte police push to get faster medical help to shooting victims," *The Charlotte Observer*, April 25, 2019, charlotteobserver.com/news/local/article229572044.html.

138 **than Chicago or Afghanistan:** Crimesider Staff, "Report: Stockton, Calif, Has More Murders Per Capita thank Chicago," CBS News, June 29, 2012, cbsnews.com/news/report-stockton-calif-has-more-murders-per-capita-than-chicago/.

138 **and an incarcerated father:** Edward-Isaac Dovere, "Can This Millennial Mayor Make Universal Basic Income a Reality," *Politico*, April 24, 2018, politico.com/magazine/story/2018/04/24/michael-tubbs-stockton-california-mayor-218070.

138 **work hard in school:** Roger Phillips, "My Three Moms," Recordnet.com, May 11, 2014, recordnet.com/article/20140511/a_news/405110320.

139 **kids out of poverty:** Alana Semuels, "Can Philanthropy Save a City?," *The Atlantic*, August 2, 2018, theatlantic.com/technology/archive/2018/08/stockton-philanthropy-michael-tubbs/566624/.

140 **homicides had dropped 40 percent:** "Stockton Sees Steep Drop in Homicides So Far in 2018," CBS Sacramento, September 10, 2018, sacramento.cbslocal.com/2018/09/10/stockton-homicides-2018-september/.

140 **cash transfers could alleviate poverty:** Steve Lopez, "Column: Stockton's young mayor has bold turnaround plan: Basic income and stipends for potential shooters," *Los Angeles Times*, May 26, 2018, latimes.com/local/california/la-me-lopez-stockton-money-05272018-story.html.

140 **who go to college:** "Mayor Tubbs announces new scholarship program for Stockton youth," University of the Pacific, January 17, 2018, pacific.edu/about-pacific/newsroom/2018/january-2018/stockton-scholars-program.html.

141 **it languished in committee:** "Sen. Lesser Recommits to Passing Student Loan Bill of Rights, Unveils Expanding Coalition Backing Effort," Website of State Senator Eric Lesser, March 6, 2019, senatorlesser.com/news/2019/3/8/sen-lesser-recommits-to-passing-student-loan-bill-of-rights-unveils-expanding-coalition-backing-effort.

142 **dropped by 2.5 percent:** Mainstreet, "America's Dying Cities," *Newsweek*, January 21, 2011, newsweek.com/americas-dying-cities-66873.

142 **stop Obama's Chrysler bailout:** Daniel Suddeath, "State treasurer hopeful says Mourdock misjudged Chrysler case," *News and Tribune*, September 18, 2010, newsandtribune.com/archives/state-treasurer-hopeful-says-mourdock-misjudged-chrysler-case/article_ce9d4093-422e-5472-8428-f33e5a77bf20.html.

143 **and other offices in the Old Studebaker plant:** Kevin Allen, "South Bend's Studebaker Project in Cleanup Phase to Become Data Center," *Indiana Economic Digest*, September 11, 2012, indianaeconomicdigest.com/MobileContent/Most-Recent/Industrial

-Development/Article/South-Bend-s-Studebaker-project-in-cleanup-phase-to-become
-data-center/31/71/66573.

143 **cut unemployment in half:** Louis Jacobson, "Did Unemployment Fall By Half Under Buttigieg?" Politifact, April 10, 2019, politifact.com/truth-o-meter/statements/2019/apr/10/pete-buttigieg/did-south-bend-unemployment-fall-half-under-mayor-/.

144 **diversifying the South Bend police department:** Paul LeBlanc and Dan Merica, "Buttigieg: South Bend Police Department Isn't Diverse Because 'I Couldn't Get It Done.'" CNN, June 28, 2019, cnn.com/2019/06/27/politics/pete-buttigieg-south-bend-police-diversity/index.html.

145 **racial inequality in South Bend:** Adam Wren, "What Mayor Pete Couldn't Fix About the South Bend Cops," *Politico*, June 22, 2019, politico.com/magazine/story/2019/06/22/pete-buttigieg-police-shooting-227206.

145 **"I was well into adulthood":** Pete Buttigieg, "South Bend Mayor: Why Coming Out Matters," *South Bend Tribune*, June 16, 2015, southbendtribune.com/news/local/south-bend-mayor-why-coming-out-matters/article_4dce0d12-1415-11e5-83c0-739eebd623ee.html.

THOUGHTS & PRAYERS

147 **We are following some breaking news:** "Breaking News: Tragedy at Sandy Hook Elementary School (WVIT-TV)," PeabodyAwards.com, 2012, peabodyawards.com/award-profile/breaking-news-tragedy-at-sandy-hook-elementary-school.

147 **of them are children:** "Newtown, Connecticut Shooting: 27 Killed, Gunman Dead at Sandy Hook Elementary Tragedy," ABC News, December 14, 2012, YouTube video, youtube.com/watch?v=zTeuAojMa3c.

147 **"students would say things":** Interview with Kaitlin Roig, ABC News, YouTube video, youtube.com/watch?v=TX8V_ZWwgb4.

147 **LANZA'S RIFLE STILL LEGAL:** Matthew Kauffman, "In State with 'Assault Weapons' Ban, Lanza's Rifle Still Legal," *The Hartford Courant*, courant.com/hc-newtown-assault-weapons-20121217-8-story.html.

147 **@SpeakerBoehner:** John Boehner, tweet, December 14, 2012, twitter.com/SpeakerBoehner/status/279674132080250880.

147 **@TedCruz:** Ted Cruz, tweet, December 14, 2012, twitter.com/tedcruz/status/279675746971172864.

147 **@SenJohnMcCain:** John McCain, tweet, December 14, 2012, twitter.com/SenJohnMcCain/status/279727832710660096.

147 **@NRA:** NRA, tweet, January 30, 2013, twitter.com/NRA/status/296649775892287488.

147 **TO BLOCK GUN CONTROL:** Joseph Gerth, "McConnell Vows to Block Gun Control Measures," *The Courier-Journal* (Louisville, KY), January 19, 2013, usatoday.com/story/news/nation/2013/01/19/mcconnell-vows-block-gun-control-measures/1848103/.

147 **DRIVE FOR GUN CONTROL:** Jonathan Weisman, "Senate Blocks Drive for Gun Control," *The New York Times*, April 17, 2013, nytimes.com/2013/04/18/us/politics/senate-obama-gun-control.html.

CHAPTER II: THE YOUNG GRAND OLD PARTY

148 **prepare Rep. Paul Ryan:** Alana Abramson, "Congresswoman Elise Stefanik Has a Plan to Get More Republican Women Elected," *TIME*, May 9, 2019, time.com/5586408/republican-women-congress-elise-stefanik/.

148 **New Hampshire, and Virginia:** Noam Scheiber, "The Internal Polls that Made Romney Think He'd Win," *The New Republic*, November 30, 2012, newrepublic.com/article/110597/exclusive-the-polls-made-mitt-romney-think-hed-win.

149 **Obama beat Romney with:** Pew Research Center, "Young Voters Supported Obama Less, But May Have Mattered More," November 26, 2012, people-press.org/2012/11/26/young-voters-supported-obama-less-but-may-have-mattered-more/.

149 **"the next 50-plus years,":** "Growth and Opportunity Project," 2012, documentcloud.org/documents/624581-rnc-autopsy.html.

150 **themselves Independents than older generations:** Pew Research Center, March 20, 2018,"Wide Gender Gap, Growing Educational Divide in Voters' Party Identification," people-press.org/2018/03/20/1-trends-in-party-affiliation-among-demographic -groups/.

150 **Democrats by roughly two to one:** CIRCLE, "Young People Dramatically Increase their Turnout to 31%, Shape 2018 Midterm Elections," CivicYouth.org, November 7, 2018, civicyouth.org/young-people-dramatically-increase-their-turnout-31-percent-shape -2018-midterm-elections/.

150 **widely rejecting organized religion:** "U.S. Becoming Less Religious," Pew Research Center, November 3, 2015, pewforum.org/2015/11/03/u-s-public-becoming -less-religious/.

150 **resisted military intervention abroad:** Christopher A. Preble, "A Clash of Generations over American Leadership," Cato Institute, June 27, 2018, cato.org/publications /commentary/clash-generations-over-american-leadership.

151 **a growing generation gap:** Kristen Soltis Anderson, *The Selfie Vote* (New York: Harper Collins, 2015), 24.

151 **"experiences during early adulthood.":** Keith R. Billingsley and Clyde Tucker, "Generations, Status, and Party Identification: A Theory of Operant Conditioning," *Political Behavior* 9, no. 4 (December 1987).

151 **Columbia political scientist Andrew Gelman:** Ghitza and Gelman, "The Great Society, Reagan's Revolution, and Generations of Presidential Voting."

152 **vote for Mitt Romney:** "A Different Look at Generations and Partisanship," Pew Research Center, April 30, 2015, people-press.org/2015/04/30/a-different-look-at-generations -and-partisanship/.

152 **political climate in their late adolescence:** Amanda Cox, "How Birth Year Influences Political Views," *The New York Times*, July 7, 2014, nytimes.com/interactive/2014/07 /08/upshot/how-the-year-you-were-born-influences-your-politics.html.

154 **risk getting left behind:** Wendy Naugle, "Meet U.S. Representative Elise Stefanik, the Youngest Woman to Ever Break into the Old Boys' Club of Congress," *Glamour*, January 6, 2015, glamour.com/story/us-representative-elise-stefanik-youngest-woman-to-join -congress.

154 **free-spending libertarian Paul Singer:** Andy Kroll, "The GOP's 'Fundraising Terrorist: Has a New Cause; Electing More Women," *Mother Jones*, April 30, 2014, motherjones .com/politics/2014/04/paul-singer-winning-women-barbara-comstock-elise-stefanik -martha-mcsally/.

155 **"perennial loser" on TV:** Thomas Kaplan, "Former White House Aide Wins GOP Congressional Primary in NY," *The New York Times*, nytimes.com/2014/06/25/nyregion /former-white-house-aide-wins-gop-congressional-primary-in-new-york.html.

155 **"No matter their party":** Elise Stefanik acceptance speech, Glens Falls, New York, November 4, 2014, awpc.cattcenter.iastate.edu/2017/03/09/elise-stefanik-acceptance-speech -nov-4-2014/.

155 **intern or a spouse:** Sheryl Gay Stolberg, "As Power Shifts in Congress, Lives of Freshman Transition," *The New York Times*, January 6, 2015, nytimes.com/2015/01 /07/us/politics/as-power-in-congress-shifts-to-gop-lives-of-freshmen-in-transition .html.

155 **more turnover within their ranks:** Dhrumil Mehta, "The Age of Tea Party Members in Congress," FiveThirtyEight, May 5, 2014, fivethirtyeight.com/features/the-age-of-tea -party-members-in-congress/.

156 **year-round Pell Grants:** HR 1485 (115th Congress), Flexible Pell Grant for 21st Century Students Act, govtrack.us/congress/bills/115/hr1485/text.

156 **such as coding boot camps:** Patricia Mazzei, "Can Carlos Curbelo Survive in Donald Trump's GOP?," *Miami Herald*, May 13, 2006, miamiherald.com/news/politics -government/election/article77367802.html.

157 **a 2018 Pew study:** Cary Funk and Meg Hefferon, "Many Republican Millennials Differ with Older Party Members on Climate Change and Energy Issues," Pew Research Center,

May 14, 2018, pewresearch.org/fact-tank/2018/05/14/many-republican-millennials-differ -with-older-party-members-on-climate-change-and-energy-issues/.

157 **largely underwater in thirty years:** "Study: Miami Beach, Florida Keys Could Be Underwater Within 30 Years," June 4, 2019, miami.cbslocal.com/2019/06/04/study-miami -beach-florida-keys-could-be-underwater-within-30-years/.

158 **under the age of forty-five:** Emily Wirzba, "Who Is in the Bipartisan Climate Solutions Caucus in the 115th Congress?," Friends Committee on National Legislation, n.d., fcnl .org/updates/who-is-in-the-bipartisan-climate-solutions-caucus-in-the-115th -congress-772.

158 **"adversely impact all Americans.":** HR 195 (115th Congress), "Expressing the Commitment of the House of Representatives to Conservative Environmental Stewardship," congress.gov/bill/115th-congress/house-resolution/195/text.

158 **releases and not much else:** Mark Hand, "Congress's 'Climate Peacocks' Care More About Image Than Action," Think Progress, June 15, 2017, thinkprogress.org/climate -caucus-avoids-action-3fc64b84a706/.

159 **science behind climate change:** Kristen Ellingboe, Tiffany Germain, Kiley Kroh, "The Anti-Science Climate Denier Caucus: 114th Congress Edition," Think Progress, January 8, 2015, thinkprogress.org/the-anti-science-climate-denier-caucus-114th-congress -edition-c76c3f8bfedd/.

159 **humans hadn't caused it:** Ellingboe, et al., "The Anti-Science Climate Denier Caucus: 114th Congress Edition."

159 **taken almost $2 million:** "James M. Inhofe, Senator (OK)," OpenSecrets.org, opensecrets .org/members-of-congress/summary?cid=N00005582.

159 **Pew found that more:** Jocelyn Kiley, "61% of Young Republicans Favor Same-Sex Marriage," Pew Research Center, March 10, 2014, pewresearch.org/fact-tank/2014/03/10 /61-of-young-republicans-favor-same-sex-marriage/.

159 **supported same-sex marriage:** Ben Shapiro, "How Conservatives Can Win Back Young Americans," *The Weekly Standard*, May 9, 2018, weeklystandard.com/shapiro-win-back- young-americans.

160 **just 38 percent of boomer:** George Gao, "63% of Republican Millennials Favor Marijuana Legalization," Pew Research Center, February 27, 2015, pewresearch.org/fact-tank /2015/02/27/63-of-republican-millennials-favor-marijuana-legalization/.

160 **shares of older generations:** Bradley Jones, "Majority of Americans Continue to Say Immigrants Strengthen Country," Pew Research Center, January 31, 2019, pewresearch .org/fact-tank/2019/01/31/majority-of-americans-continue-to-say-immigrants -strengthen-the-u-s/.

160 **sponsored his own version:** H.R. 1468 (115th Congress), Recognizing America's Children Act, congress.gov/bill/115th-congress/house-bill/1468.

160 **A Pew study from 2014:** "Beyond Red vs. Blue: The Political Typology," Pew Research Center, June 26, 2014, people-press.org/2014/06/26/the-political-typology-beyond-red -vs-blue/.

160 **were in their late:** Mehta, "The Age of Tea Party Members in Congress."

161 **their white boomer base:** Jim Spencer and Curtis Ellis, "Most Tea Partiers Are Baby Boomers Reliving the 1960s," *Los Angeles Times*, February 24, 2010, latimes.com/ar chives/la-xpm-2010-feb-24-la-oe-ellis25-2010feb25-story.html.

161 **One of the first bills:** H.R. 3112 (114th Congress), Be Open Act, govtrack.us/congress /bills/114/hr3112.

161 **out of Georgetown University:** 114th Congress, Lugar Center Bipartisan Index, thelugarcenter.org/ourwork-Bipartisan-Index.html.

161 **in the top twenty:** 115th Congress, Lugar Center Bipartisan Index, thelugarcenter.org /ourwork-Bipartisan-Index.html.

CHAPTER 12: HOUSE OF GLASS, 2016

166 **never for an election:** Charlotte Alter, "Inside Alexandria Ocasio-Cortez's Unlikely Rise," *TIME*, March 21, 2019, time.com/longform/alexandria-ocasio-cortez-profile/.

166 **among young voters in Iowa:** Chris Cillizza, "Bernie Sanders Crushed Hillary Clinton by 70 Points Among Young Voters in Iowa," *The Washington Post*, February 2, 2016, washingtonpost.com/news/the-fix/wp/2016/02/02/bernie-sanders-crushed-hillary -clinton-by-70-points-among-young-people-in-iowa-but/.

166 **78 percent of first-time voters:** Eric Bradner and Dan Merica, "Young Voters Abandon Hillary Clinton for Bernie Sanders," CNN, February 10, 2016, cnn.com/2016/02/10 /politics/hillary-clinton-new-hampshire-primary/index.html.

166 **underwater by more than twenty points:** Frank Newport, "Sanders, the Oldest Candidate, Looks Best to Young Americans," Gallup, April 8, 2016, news.gallup.com/poll /190571/sanders-oldest-candidate-looks-best-young-americans.aspx.

166 **were feeling the Bern:** Charlotte Alter, "Bernie Winning Feminists Even at Hillary Clinton's Alma Mater," *TIME*, February 16, 2016, time.com/4220427/bernie-sanders -wellesley-hillary-clinton-femisim/.

167 **among the under-thirty set:** Harvard IOP Spring 2016 Poll, iop.harvard.edu/youth -poll/past/harvard-iop-spring-2016-poll.

168 **with their young daughters:** Charlotte Alter, "Hillary Clinton Collides Again with the Highest Glass Ceiling," *TIME*, November 9, 2016, time.com/4564142/hillary-clinton -gender/.

169 **did the bare minimum:** Zach Hirsch, "Stefanik's Reputation as National Security Expert Complicated by Support for Trump," North Country Public Radio, October 12, 2016, northcountrypublicradio.org/news/story/32726/20161012/stefanik-s-reputation-as -national-security-expert-complicated-by-support-for-trump.

169 **"attacking Gold Star families":** "Timeline: Stefanik Often Sharply Critical of Trump, but Backs His Agenda," NCPR News, August 10, 2018, northcountrypublicradio.org /news/story/36791/20180810/timeline-rep-stefanik-often-sharply-critical-of-trump -but-backs-his-agenda.

169 **"his statements regarding Putin.":** Brian Mann, "Trump Visit: Stefanik Loyal to President Despite Sharp Differences on Policy, Ethics," NCPR News, August 10, 2018, northcountrypublicradio.org/news/story/36799/20180810/trump-visit-stefanik-loyal -to-president-despite-sharp-differences-on-policy-ethics.

169 **her "Elsie the Cow.":** Brian Mann, "As 'Groping' Controversy Grows, Stefanik Maintains Support for Trump," North Country Public Radio, October 7, 2016, northcountry publicradio.org/news/story/32715/20161007/as-quot-groping-quot-controversy-grows -stefanik-maintains-support-for-trump.

169 **"That is a moral decision.":** Jim DeFede, "Republican Curbelo Open to Voting for Clinton," CBS4 Miami, March 24, 2016, miami.cbslocal.com/2016/03/24/republican-curbelo -open-to-voting-for-clinton/.

169 **or voted third party:** Sean McElwee, Brian F. Schaffner, Jesse H. Rhodes, and Bernard L. Fraga, "Trump Is Driving Out Precious Republican Voters," *The New York Times*, February 16, 2016, nytimes.com/2019/02/16/opinion/sunday/trump-youth-vote.html.

170 **When a *Washington Post*:** Ben Terris, "Youngest Female Lawmaker Says Social Media Is Just Part of the Job," *The Washington Post*, September 13, 2016, washingtonpost.com /news/powerpost/wp/2016/09/13/youngest-female-lawmaker-says-social-media-is -just-part-of-the-job/.

174 **"hateful" on Facebook:** John McCormack, "Is Dan Crenshaw the Future of the GOP?," *Politico*, March 2, 2016, politico.com/magazine/story/2019/03/02/is-dan-crenshaw-the -future-of-the-gop-225257.

176 **"bring them to the table.":** "Elise Stefanik Reelected as U.S. Representative for New York," MyNBC5-WPTZ, YouTube video, youtube.com/watch?v=r_EHJgomQUk.

176 **white women had broken slightly for Trump:** Molly Ball, "Donald Trump Didn't Really Win 52% of White Women in 2016": *TIME*, October 18, 2018, time.com/5422644 /trump-white-women-2016/.

176 **voters over forty-five:** William H. Frey, "The Demographic Blowback That Elected Donald Trump," Brookings, November 10, 2016, brookings.edu/blog/the-avenue/2016 /11/10/the-demographic-blowback-that-elected-donald-trump/.

177 **overwhelmingly voted to remain:** Simon Schuster, "The U.K. 's Old Decided for the Young in the Brexit Vote," *TIME*, June 24, 2016, time.com/4381878/brexit-generation -gap-older-younger-voters/.

177 **of eligible voters over sixty-five:** Thom File, "Voting in America: A Look at the 2016 Presidential Election," United States Census, Census Blogs, census.gov/newsroom /blogs/random-samplings/2017/05/voting_in_america.html.

177 **mostly white and male:** CIRCLE Staff, "Young Voters in the 2016 General Election," Tufts University, Jonathan M. Tisch, College of Civic Life, civicyouth.org/wp-content /uploads/2016/11/CIRCLE-Full-Exit-Poll-Analysis_Final.pdf.

178 **"emotions regarding the election.":** Neil Thomas, "Donald Trump Is President: Crisis at Harvard Kennedy School?," Kennedy School Review, November 28, 2016, ksr.hkspublications.org/2016/11/28/donald-trump-is-president-crisis-at-harvard -kennedy-school/.

CHAPTER 13: THE PILGRIMAGE OF ALEXANDRIA OCASIO-CORTEZ

182 **their new "prayer camp.":** Saul Elbein, "The Youth Group That Launched a Movement at Standing Rock," *The New York Times Magazine*, January 31, 2017, nytimes.com/2017 /01/31/magazine/the-youth-group-that-launched-a-movement-at-standing-rock .html.

182 **them off the land:** Evan Simon, "Meet the Youths at the Heart of the Standing Rock Protests Against the Dakota Access Pipeline," *The Seventh Generation*, ABC News Digital, abcnews.go.com/US/meet-youth-heart-standing-rock-protests-dakota-access /story?id=45719115.

183 **drawn to Standing Rock:** Alexandria Ocasio-Cortez, Facebook Live, December 21, 2016.

184 **wasn't the one driving:** Ocasio-Cortez, Facebook Live, Planning Our Route, December, 19, 2016.

186 **to make it to Flint:** Ocasio-Cortez, Facebook Live, Pre-Dawn Talks, December 21, 2016.

186 **and smelled like gasoline:** Josh Sanburn, "The Toxic Tap," *TIME*, February, 1, 2016, time.com/magazine/us/4188304/february-1st-2016-vol-187-no-3-u-s/.

186 **since the water switch:** Sanburn, "The Toxic Tap."

187 **"That is how protest works.":** Ocasio-Cortez, Facebook Live, December 20, 2016, Road to Standing Rock, Day 2, Flint, Michigan.

187 **and began to cry:** Ocasio-Cortez, Facebook Live, "We've arrived in North Dakota!", December 21, 2016.

188 **Alexandria had ever seen:** Ocasio-Cortez, Facebook Live, December 21, 2016.

189 **"Trump's victory has blown":** Dyanna Jaye and Varshini Prakash, "How We Got Here: Sunrise Movement," Medium, May 3, 2017, medium.com/sunrisemvmt/welcome-sunrise -c63943c00f37.

190 **in their announcement video:** Welcome to Sunrise, Sunrise Movement, YouTube video, youtube.com/watch?v=an5GbckznRQ.

190 **released a report that warned:** IPCC Special Report, "Global Warming of 1.5° C," ipcc .ch/sr15/.

190 **"And yet you are stealing":** Greta Thunberg, speech at UN climate change, COP24 Conference, December 15, 2018, YouTube video, youtube.com/watch?v=VFkQSGyeCWg.

190 **the end of February:** Tara John, "How Teenage Girls Defied Skeptics to Build a Global Climate Movement," CNN, February 13, 2019, edition.cnn.com/2019/02/13/uk/student -climate-strike-girls-gbr-scli-intl/index.html.

190 **the Belgian environment ministers:** J. Lester Feder, Pascale Müller, and Zahra Hirji,"A Huge Climate Change Movement Led by Teenage Girls Is Sweeping Europe. And It's Coming to the US Next," *BuzzFeed*, February 7, 2019, buzzfeednews.com/article /lesterfeder/europe-climate-change-protests-teens.

191 **catastrophic hurricanes threatening their homes:** Emily Witt, "The Optimistic Activists for a Green New Deal: Inside the Youth-Led Singing Sunrise Movement," *The New Yorker*, December 23, 2018, newyorker.com/news/news-desk/the-optimistic-activists-for-a-green-new-deal-inside-the-youth-led-singing-sunrise-movement.

THE BIG ONE

193 **her dead mother's body:** Simon Romero and Julie Bosman, "Clinging to Her Drowning 'Mama,' a Little Girl Survives the Raging Flood," *The New York Times*, August 30, 2017, nytimes.com/2017/08/30/us/victims-harvey-death-toll-houston.html.

193 **themselves in shelters again:** Yousur Al-Hlou, "How a Mattress Store Became a Home for Harvey Victims," *The New York Times* video, n.d., nytimes.com/video/us/100000005398367/houston-harvey-mattress-shelter.html.

CHAPTER 14: "SENATOR, WE RUN ADS"

194 **than Obama's and Bush's:** Henry C. Jacobson, "Trump's Cabinet by the Numbers," *Politico*, January 24, 2017, politico.com/blogs/donald-trump-administration/2017/01/trumps-cabinet-by-the-numbers-234117.

194 **"and not fall asleep.":** Daniel Lippmann, "'It's a Disaster Over There': Commerce Reaches New Heights of Dysfunction," *Politico*, July 22, 2019, politico.com/story/2019/07/22/wilbur-ross-commerce-department-dysfunction-1424427.

195 **a "sick, sad joke":** Emily Stewart, "Mick Mulvaney Once Called CFPB a 'Sick, Sad Joke.' Now He Might Be in Charge of It," *Vox*, November 16, 2017, vox.com/policy-and-politics/2017/11/16/16667266/mick-mulvaney-cfpb-cordray-omb-joke.

195 **"and their financial futures.":** Cory Turner, "Student Loan Watchdog Quits, Says Trump Administration 'Turned Its Back' on Borrowers," NPR, *All Things Considered*, August 27, 2018, npr.org/2018/08/27/642199524/student-loan-watchdog-quits-blames-trump-administration.

195 **school with a black student:** Alan Judd, "For Trump's AG Nominee Jeff Sessions, Race Is Great Battle Not Fought," *Atlanta Journal-Constitution*, February 8, 2017, ajc.com/news/national/for-trump-nominee-jeff-sessions-race-great-battle-not-fought/9cpM4nR3NUFQTbuSPSDzXL/.

195 **past three election cycles:** Tom McCarthy and Lauren Gambino, "The Republicans Who Urged Trump to Pull Out of Paris Deal Are Big Oil Darlings," *The Guardian*, June 1, 2017, theguardian.com/us-news/2017/jun/01/republican-senators-paris-climate-deal-energy-donations.

196 **his anti-environmental agenda:** Justin Worland, "The White House's Climate Change Believers Are Headed Out the Door," *TIME*, March 15, 2018, time.com/5201421/rex-tillerson-climate-change-donald-trump/.

196 **sea levels into account:** Nadja Popvich, Livia Albeck-Ripka, and Kendra Pierre-Louis, "85 Environmental Rules Being Rolled Back Under Trump," *The New York Times*, September 12, 2019, nytimes.com/interactive/2019/climate/trump-environment-rollbacks.html.

196 **of any climate change language:** Somini Sengupta, "U.S. Pressure Blocks Declaration on Climate Change at Arctic Talks," *The New York Times*, May 7, 2019, nytimes.com/2019/05/07/climate/us-arctic-climate-change.html.

196 **to weaken environmental regulations:** Website of Senator Edward Markey, Report of the Senate Climate Change Task Force, "The Most Anti-Climate Administration in History," n.d., markey.senate.gov/imo/media/doc/ANTI-CLIMATE%20REPORT%20.pdf.

196 **sixty-one in the Senate:** "The 115th Congress Is Among the Oldest in History," Quorum, n.d., quorum.us/data-driven-insights/the-115th-congress-is-among-the-oldest-in-history/175/.

196 **Republicans in the House:** Nate Silver and Dhrumil Mehta, "Both Republicans and Democrats Have an Age Problem," FiveThirtyEight, April 28, 2014, fivethirtyeight.com/features/both-republicans-and-democrats-have-an-age-problem/.

197 **hearing were an average:** Emily Stewart, "Lawmakers Seem Confused About What Facebook Does—And How to Fix It," *Vox*, April 10, 2018, vox.com/policy-and-politics/2018/4/10/17222062/mark-zuckerberg-testimony-graham-facebook-regulations.

198 **to drive to Standing Rock:** Alexandria Ocasio-Cortez, Facebook, January 21, 2017.

199 **and her late father's watch:** Alexandria Ocasio-Cortez, Facebook, January 21, 2017.

202 **"with pink pussy hats.":** Micah White, "Without a Path from Protest to Power, the

Women's March will End Up Like Occupy," *The Guardian*, January 19, 2017, theguard
ian.com/world/2017/jan/19/womens-march-washington-occupy-protest.

202 **"Cannot believe I'm willingly"**: Leah Greenberg, tweet, January 29, 2017, twitter.com
/Leahgreenb/status/825506938188398594.

202 **"This Land is Your Land."**: Leah Greenberg, tweet, January 29, 2017, twitter.com
/Leahgreenb/status/825535687944462337.

202 **to the Houston airport**: Pete Buttigieg, tweet, January 29, 2017, twitter.com/PeteBut
tigieg/status/825527908768821248.

202 **at Terminal E with signs**: Lindsay Ellis, Keri Blakinger, Mihir Zaveri, "Protests
Against Muslim Ban Ripple Across Houston, Packing IAH Terminal to Capacity,"
Houston Chronicle, January 30, 2017, chron.com/houston/article/Protests-planned
-against-Muslim-ban-across-10892379.php.

202 **had clearly done herself**: Pete Buttigieg, tweet, January 29, 2017, twitter.com/PeteBut
tigieg/status/825537950423343104.

203 **"out to the airport tonight!"**: Jess Morales Rocketto, tweet, January 29, 2017, twitter
.com/JessLivMo/status/825536526184505345.

203 **resisters were middle-aged**: Jill Filipovic, "Trump's Worst Enemy: Middle-Aged
Moms," CNN, July 3, 2018, cnn.com/2018/07/03/opinions/trump-worst-enemy-middle
-aged-moms-filipovic/index.html.

203 **who did the lion's share**: Michelle Goldberg, "Women Might Save America Yet," *The
New York Times*, July 2, 2018, nytimes.com/2018/07/02/opinion/women-democratic
-party-grassroots-trump.html.

204 **"all-of-the-above approach."**: Charlotte Alter, "The Wave Makers," *TIME*, October 18,
2018.

205 **"into a political buzzsaw."**: "Make Them Shake: Indivisible CO's Statewide Recipe for
Retaking May 2017 Recess Week," n.d., docs.google.com/document/d/1BL1dJ2vENT
GCoONbOLxy7rxhk3AY95dgvv6F84S13PQ/edit.

205 **"Do your job!"**: Amber Phillips, "Republican Town Halls Are Getting Very Very Nasty,"
The Washington Post, February 10, 2017, washingtonpost.com/news/the-fix/wp/2017
/02/10/republican-townhalls-are-becoming-the-leading-edge-of-the-democratic
-resistance/.

206 **sit-ins in Senate offices**: Stephen Koff, "Ohioans Protest Health Care Bill with Sit-in at
Sen. Portman's Washington Office," Cleveland.com, June 21, 2017, cleveland.com/metro
/2017/06/ohioans_protest_healthcare_bil.html.

206 **offices in twenty-one states**: Kaila White and Alejandro Baharona, "'Die-in' Rallies in
Arizona Protest Trumpcare," AZCentral, May 11, 2011, azcentral.com/story/news/politics
/arizona/2017/05/10/die-in-rally-protest-trumpcare-arizona/316794001/.

206 **in his hostile district**: "New Jersey Protesters See Victory in Frelinghuysen Retirement," MSNBC, *The Rachel Maddow Show*, January 29, 2018, msnbc.com/rachel-maddow
/watch/ew-jersey-protesters-see-victory-in-frelinghuysen-retirement-11489910
43980.

206 **Indivisible sent potatoes instead**: Indivisible Bucks County, tweet, July 23, 2017, twitter
.com/IndivisibleBUX/status/889257459633860608.

206 **Rep. Dave Brat complained**: Vanessa Remmers and Patrick Wilson, "Meet the Woman
Who Are Up in Dave Brat's Grill," *Richmond-Times Dispatch*, February 19, 2017, richmond
.com/news/virginia/meet-the-women-who-are-up-in-dave-brat-s/article_c41b47cb
-736a-58e4-9448-b99e8f7bac11.html.

206 **protect people with preexisting**: Brenda Schory, "Hultgren Fields Questions from
Raucous Crowd," *Kane County Chronicle*, April 19, 2017, kcchronicle.com/2017/04/18
/hultgren-fields-questions-from-raucous-crowd/a7ykro9/.

206 **protests at the offices**: Statewide Visits to Susan Collins' Offices, Maine Resists, June
21, 2017, maineresists.org/event/statewide-visits-susan-collins-offices/.

207 **and 141 in Arizona**: Charlotte Alter, "How Women Helped Save Obamacare," *TIME*,
July 29, 201, time.com/4878724/donald-trump-gop-health-care-women/.

208 **places that leaned Democratic**: "'Gerrymandering on Steroids': How Republicans
Stacked the Nation's Statehouses," WBUR, July 19, 2016.

208 **"game," Catherine told me:** Charlotte Alter, "Never Mind Congress. These Democrats Want to Win State Legislatures," *TIME*, August 16, 2018, time.com/5368460/flippable -democrats-state-legislature/.

211 **Model UN in high school:** Charlotte Alter, "The Avengers," *TIME*, January 18, 2018, time.com/magazine/us/5107476/january-29th-2018-vol-191-no-3-u-s/.

211 **Youth turnout doubled from:** CIRCLE, "Virginia Youth Voter Turnout Doubled Between 2009 and 2017," CivicYouth.org., November 8, 2017, civicyouth.org/virginia-youth -voter-turnout-doubled-between-2009-and-2017-estimates-suggest/.

211 **them won their seats:** Jen Kirby, "Meet the Group That Just Put More Than 30 Local Progressives into Office," *Vox*, November 9, 2017, vox.com/policy-and-politics/2017/11 /9/16625966/run-for-something-progressives-local-election-virginia.

CHAPTER 15: MILLENNIAL RED

214 **recovery and Black Lives Matter:** David Remnick, "Alexandria Ocasio-Cortez's Historic Win and the Future of the Democratic Party," July 16, 2018, *The New Yorker*, new yorker.com/magazine/2018/07/23/alexandria-ocasio-cortezs-historic-win-and-the -future-of-the-democratic-party.

215 **higher than their grandparents:** "'Socialism' Not So Negative, 'Capitalism' Not So Positive': A Political Rhetoric Test," Pew Rearch Center, May 4, 2010, people-press.org /2010/05/04/socialism-not-so-negative-capitalism-not-so-positive.

215 **that baseline American Dream:** Peter Bergman, et al., "Creating Moves to Opportunity," OpportunityInsights.org., August 2019, opportunityinsights.org/wp-content /uploads/2019/08/cmto_paper.pdf.

217 **"undisguised state socialism,":** Roosevelt Institute, "Franklin D. Roosevelt: Socialist or 'Champion of Freedom'?", April 20, 2012, rooseveltinstitute.org/rediscovering -governmentfranklin-d-roosevelt-socialist-or-champion-freedom/.

217 **"a socialist, not a Democrat":** Sean Wilentz, "Fighting Words," *Democracy*, Spring 2018, democracyjournal.org/magazine/48/fighting-words/.

218 **League Dinner in 1936:** The Facts in the Case, Al Smith speech to the American Liberty League Dinner, Washington, DC, January 25, 1936, exploreuk.uky.edu/catalog/xt7w wp9t2q46_94_1#page/1/mode/1up/search/socialism.

218 **"of more than $25,000":** Sam Pizzigati, "How About a Maximum Wage? Taxation: F.D.R. wanted to cap incomes of the wealthy—an idea whose time may have come again," *Los Angeles Times*, April 8, 1992, latimes.com/archives/la-xpm-1992-04-08-me-457 -story.html.

218 **"about whether it works.":** MSNBC, *Morning Joe*, February 14, 2019.

219 **when Ronald Reagan slashed:** Glenn Kessler, "Ocasio-Cortez's 70-Percent Tax Rate: Not So Radical?," *The Washington Post*, January 31, 2019, washingtonpost.com/politics /2019/01/31/ocasio-cortezs-percent-tax-rate-not-so-radical/.

219 **inequality of any Western democracy:** Jill Lepore, *These Truths* (New York: W. W. Norton, 2018).

221 **they supported democratic socialism:** Harvard Fall 2018 National Youth Poll, iop.har vard.edu/spring-2018-national-youth-poll.

221 **had dropped twenty-three points:** Frank Newport, "Democrats More Positive About Socialism Than Capitalism," Gallup, August 13, 2018, news.gallup.com/poll/240725 /democrats-positive-socialism-capitalism.aspx.

221 **In one 2019 poll:** Axios/SurveyMonkey Poll, 2019 World Economic Forum, January 16–18, 2019, surveymonkey.com/curiosity/axios-davos-2019/.

222 **issues, she replied curtly:** CNN, "Nancy Pelosi Town Hall," February 3, 2017, YouTube video, youtube.com/watch?v=BBrk2Vz2ASk.

222 **she told 60 Minutes:** Ashley Turner, "House Speaker Nancy Pelosi Says Socialism Is 'Not the View' of the Democratic Party," CNBC, April 15, 2019, cnbc.com/2019/04/15 /nancy-pelosi-says-socialism-is-not-the-view-of-the-democratic-party.html.

222 **Fox News, with Sean Hannity:** "The Radical Far Left and the Dangers of Socialism," Fox News, *The Sean Hannity Show*, February 26, 2017, YouTube video, youtube.com /watch?v=pym3Gt5jivI.

222 **whole segments to ridiculing:** "Tucker Takes on Cornel West over Democratic Socialism," *The Tucker Carlson Show,* July 6, 2018, YouTube video, youtube.com/watch
?v=kuc6C2_Txmw.

222 **2019 State of the Union:** President Donald J. Trump's State of the Union Address, February 5, 2019, whitehouse.gov/briefings-statements/president-donald-j-trumps-state
-union-address-2/.

222 **allies, told *The New Yorker*:** Remnick, "Alexandria Ocasio-Cortez's Historic Win and
the Future of the Democratic Party."

223 **to some public housing residents:** Greg Kaufman, "Why Fixing Potholes Is Key to This
Mayor's Radical Agenda, *The Nation,* December 13, 2018, thenation.com/article/jackson
-mississippi-mayor-chokwe-antar-lumumba/.

223 **Young socialists won city:** John Nichols, "The Next Generation of Democratic Socialists Has Started Winning Local Elections," *The Nation,* April 20, 2017, thenation.com
/article/the-next-generation-of-democratic-socialists-has-started-winning-local
-elections/.

THE BIG ONE

225 **FEMA resources were depleted:** Suzy Khimm, "FEMA Is Nearly Out of Cash, Just as
Hurricanes Harvey and Irma Strike," NBC News, September 7, 2017, nbcnews.com
/storyline/hurricane-irma/between-hurricanes-harvey-irma-fema-nearly-out-cash
-n799386.

225 **pieces like a jackhammer:** Brian Resnick, "Why Hurricane Maria Is Such a Nightmare for Puerto Rico," *Vox,* September 22, 2017, vox.com/science-and-health/2017/9/21
/16345176/hurricane-maria-2017-puerto-rico-san-juan-meteorology-wind-rain-power.

225 **energy grid was essentially destroyed:** CBS News, "Last of Puerto Rican Customers
Reconnected to Island's Main Grid," CBS News, March 20, 2019, cbsnews.com/news
/puerto-rico-hurricane-maria-recovery-last-customers-reconnected-main-power
-grid-today-2019-03-20/.

225 **get through to his family members:** Luis Ferré-Sadurní, Lizette Alvarez, and Frances
Robles, "Puerto Rico Faces Mountain of Obstacles on the Road to Recovery," *The New
York Times,* Sept 21, 2017, nytimes.com/2017/09/21/us/hurricane-maria-puerto-rico
-recovery.html.

225 **threw rolls of paper towels:** Aaron Blake, "Trump favorably compared Puerto Rico's
death toll to Hurricane Katrina. A study now says twice as many died in Puerto Rico,"
The Washington Post, May 29, 2018, washingtonpost.com/news/the-fix/wp/2018/05
/29/trump-once-favorably-compared-puerto-ricos-death-toll-to-katrinas-a-new
-study-shows-more-than-twice-as-many-died/.

225 **more than 4,600 American:** Nishant Kishore, et al., "Mortality in Puerto Rico after
Hurricane Maria," *The New England Journal of Medicine* 379 (July 12, 2018), nejm.org
/doi/full/10.1056/NEJMsa1803972.

CHAPTER 16: THE PINK WAVE

226 **"this year or next year.":** Alexandria Ocasio-Cortez, Facebook, April 1, 2017, facebook
.com/alexandria.ocasiocortez/videos/10208330592767335/.

227 **entertainers would become politicians:** Irina Aleksander, "How Alexandria Ocasio-
Cortez and Other Progressives Are Defining the Midterms," *Vogue,* October 2017, vogue
.com/article/alexandria-ocasio-cortez-interview-vogue-november-2018-issue.

227 **"It's time to hand over the keys.":** Alexandria Ocasio-Cortez, tweet, March 18, 2018,
twitter.com/AOC/status/975513455804538880.

227 **"It's a HUGE problem":** Alexandria Ocasio-Cortez, tweet, April 10, 2018, twitter.com
/AOC/status/983834237278224384.

228 **data on the campaign:** Author's interview with Michael Carter, February 2019.

228 **given Crowley his clout:** *Knock Down the House,* directed by Rachel Lears (2019; Netflix).

228 **she said in the debate:** Gloria Pazmino, "Crowley, Ocasio-Cortez argue future of the
Democratic party in first and only primary debate," *Politico,* June 15, 2018, politico

.com/states/new-york/albany/story/2018/06/15/crowley-ocasio-cortez-stay-civil
-despite-differences-in-primary-debate-470236.

228 **a bullhorn in Spanish:** *Knock Down the House*, directed by Rachel Lears.

229 **earmarked for the general election:** Goldmacher, Shane "An Upset in the Making:
Why Joe Crowley Never Saw Defeat Coming," *The New York Times*, June 27, 2018, nytimes
.com/2018/06/27/nyregion/ocasio-cortez-crowley-primary-upset.html.

229 **about thirty-five points behind:** *Knock Down the House*, directed by Rachel Lears.

229 **lock herself in a closet:** *Knock Down the House*, directed by Rachel Lears.

230 **that showed her name:** Andy Newman, Vivian Wang, and Luis Ferré-Sadurní, "Alexandria Ocasio Cortez Emerges as a Political Star," *The New York Times*, June 28, 2018,
nytimes.com/2018/06/27/nyregion/alexandria-ocasio-cortez-bio-profile.html.

230 **the whiteness of Naperville:** Naperville Demographics and Key Facts, August 2018,
naperville.il.us/about-naperville/demographics-and-key-facts/.

230 **by a black police officer:** Brian Crooks, "What It's Like to Be Black in Naperville, America," *Naperville Sun*, July 18, 2016, chicagotribune.com/suburbs/naperville-sun/ct-nvs
-being-black-naperville-america-st-0715-20160714-story.html.

232 **Democratic primary in the fourteenth district:** Sophia McBain, "Meet Lauren Underwood, the 31-year-old Democrat hoping to shake up Illinois politics," *New States-
man*, October 15, 2018, newstatesman.com/world/north-america/2018/10/meet-lauren
underwood-31-year-old-democrat-hoping-shake-illinois.

233 **she became the campaign treasurer:** Haley Stevens for Congress, Federal Election
Commission, n.d., docquery.fec.gov/cgi-bin/fecimg/?C00638650.

234 **pictures of their sick kids:** Kathleen Gray, "Trott Town Hall Gets Rowdy, Raucous,
While Hundreds Left Out in the Cold," *Detroit Free Press*, March 18, 2017, freep.com
/story/news/politics/2017/03/18/dave-trott-town-hall-novi/99346084/.

235 **came out of her house:** Charlotte Alter, "A Record Number of Women Are Running for
Governor and Congress," *TIME*, August 8, 2018, time.com/5361122/women-congress
-2018-elections-record/.

238 **"movement after generations in retreat,":** "NPC Statement on 2018 Elections," Democratic Socialists of America, November 7, 2018, dsausa.org/statements/npc-statement-on
-2018-elections/.

238 **"It's not a baseball game.":** Sydney Ember and Alexandra Burns, "Bernie Sanders Is
Winning Converts. But Primary Victories Remain Elusive," *The New York Times*,
June 24, 2018, nytimes.com/2018/06/24/us/politics/bernie-sanders-midterm-elections
.html.

243 **350 percent since 2016:** Charlotte Alter, "The Avengers," *TIME*, January 18, 2018, time
.com/magazine/us/5107476/january-29th-2018-vol-191-no-3-u-s/.

244 **gender gap in a midterm election:** Exit Polls, CNN, 2018 Election, cnn.com/election
/2018/exit-polls.

244 **their turnout nearly doubled:** Anthon Cilluffo and Richard Fry, "Gen Z, Millennials,
Gen X Outvoted Older Generations in 2018 Midterms," Pew Research Group, May 29,
2019, pewresearch.org/fact-tank/2019/05/29/gen-z-millennials-and-gen-x-outvoted
-older-generations-in-2018-midterms/.

244 **supported Democrats by two to one:** CIRCLE, "Young People Dramatically Increase
their Turnout to 31%, Shape 2018 Midterm Elections," CivicYouth.org., November 7,
2018, civicyouth.org/young-people-dramatically-increase-their-turnout-31-percent-shape
-2018-midterm-elections/.

244 **parties, according to Pew:** Alec Tyson, "The 2018 Midterm Vote: Divisions by Race,
Gender, Education," Pew Research Center, November 8, 2018, pewresearch.org/fact
-tank/2018/11/08/the-2018-midterm-vote-divisions-by-race-gender-education/.

244 **voters chose the Democrats:** CIRCLE, "Young People Favor Democratic House Candidates by Historic Margin, Data Continue to Suggest High Youth Participation for
a Midterm," CivicYouth.org., November 7, 2018, civicyouth.org/young-people-favor
-democratic-house-candidates-by-historic-margin-data-continue-to-suggest-high
-youth-participation-for-a-midterm/.

244 **Young voters were decisive:** CIRCLE, "Young People Dramatically Increase Their Turnout to 31%, Shape 2018 Midterm Elections."

245 **hit a twenty-five-year low:** Susan Chira, "Banner Year for Female Candidates Doesn't Extend to Republican Women," *The New York Times*, November 15, 2018, nytimes.com /2018/11/15/us/politics/women-politics-republican.html.

245 **"reflective of the American public.":** Paul Kane, "House GOP Women Confront a Political Crisis—Their Party Is Mostly Men," *The Washington Post*, November 17, 2018, washingtonpost.com/powerpost/house-gop-women-confront-a-political-crisis—their -party-is-mostly-men/2018/11/17/34448a4a-e9ed-11e8-b8dc-66cca409c180_story.html.

THOUGHTS & PRAYERS

247 **@TheCaptainAidan:** Tweet, February 14, 2018

247 **Good evening, it began:** NPR, *All Things Considered*, February 16, 2018, npr.org/2018 /02/16/586616035/why-there-have-been-few-new-federal-laws-after-each-school -shooting.

247 **@ohstephany_:** Tweet, February 14, 2018, twitter.com/ohstephany_/status/963929938 142400512.

247 **@Melody_Ball:** Tweet, February 14, 2018, twitter.com/Melody_Ball/status/96389978 9070028800.

247 **@Sarahchadwickk:** Tweet, February 14, 2018, twitter.com/Sarahchadwickk/status /963901678528409601.

247 **SEETHING PARKLAND LEGISLATOR:** Mary Ellen Klas, "Seething Parkland legislator: 'You know what is going to happen after this? Nothing,'" *Miami Herald*, February 15, 2018, miamiherald.com/news/local/community/broward/article200279494.html.

247 **MY GENERATION WON'T STAND:** Cameron Kasky, "Parkland student: My generation won't stand for this," CNN, February 20, 2018, cnn.com/2018/02/15/opinions/florida -shooting-no-more-opinion-kasky/index.html.

247 **GUN LAWS WOULDN'T HAVE:** Maegan Vazquez, "Rubio: Gun laws wouldn't have prevented Parkland," CNN, February 15, 2018, cnn.com/2018/02/15/politics/marco-rubio -senate-floor-florida-shooting/index.html.

247 **@Sarahchadwickk:** Tweet, February 23, 2018, twitter.com/Sarahchadwickk/status /966924331086266369.

247 **STUDENTS LEAD HUGE RALLIES:** Michael D. Shear, "Students Lead Huge Rallies for Gun Control Across the U.S.," *The New York Times*, March 24, 2018, nytimes.com/2018 /03/24/us/politics/students-lead-huge-rallies-for-gun-control-across-the-us.html.

247 **AFTER PARKLAND, STATES PASS:** Matt Vasilogambros, "After Parkland, States Pass 50 New Gun-Control Laws," Pew Research Center, August 2, 2018, pewtrusts.org/en /research-and-analysis/blogs/stateline/2018/08/02/after-parkland-states-pass-50 -new-gun-control-laws.

247 **PARKLAND SHOOTING SURVIVORS RELEASE:** Adeel Hassan, "Parkland Shooting Survivors Release Ambitious Gun Control Plan," *The New York Times*, August, 21, 2019, nytimes.com/2019/08/21/us/march-for-our-lives-gun-control.html,

247 **@davidhogg111:** Tweet, August 21, 2019, twitter.com/davidhogg111/status/1164114156 364161025.

CHAPTER 17: DEFEND, DISTANCE, DEFECT, OR DEFEAT

249 **the rest were in the middle:** Pew Research, "The Generation Gap in American Politics," March 1, 2018, people-press.org/2018/03/01/the-generation-gap-in-american-politics/.

249 **among Republicans under twenty-five:** Axios/SurveyMonkey Poll, "Younger Republicans Want an Alternative to Trump," January 2018, axios.com/younger-republicans -want-an-alternative-to-trump-4538b9bf-edf7-4144-b2de-f3644be381fc.html.

249 **millennial Republicans did:** Axios/SurveyMonkey Poll, 2019 World Economic Forum, January 16–18, 2019, surveymonkey.com/curiosity/axios-davos-2019/.

249 **conservative thinker Ben Shapiro wrote:** Ben Shapiro, "How Conservatives Can Win Back Young Americans," *The Weekly Standard*, May 9, 2018, weeklystandard.com/shapiro -win-back-young-americans.

250 **"Trump on his values.":** Shapiro, "How Conservatives Can Win Back Young Americans."

250 **told journalist Eliza Gray:** Eliza Gray, "The Next Generation of Republicans," *The Washington Post*, July 16, 2018, washingtonpost.com/news/style/wp/2018/07/16/feature /the-next-generation-of-republicans-do-they-stand-with-trump/.

250 **155 votes to spare:** Jeremy Wallace, "Is Houston's Dan Crenshaw the secret weapon for GOP with Millennials?", *Houston Chronicle*, May 25, 2018, houstonchronicle.com /news/politics/texas/article/Is-Houston-s-Dan-Crenshaw-the-secret-weapon-for -12943989.php.

251 **"the ones that have to pay":** Dan Crenshaw interview with *TIME*, conducted by Alana Abramson, January 2019.

251 **"can forgive one another.":** Dave Itzkoff, 'S.N.L.': Dan Crenshaw Accepts Pete David-son's Apology and Delivers Some Zingers," *The New York Times*, November 11, 2018, nytimes.com/2018/11/11/arts/television/snl-pete-davidson-dan-crenshaw.html.

252 **"and demands for apologies,":** Dan Crenshaw, "SNL Mocked My Appearance: Here's Why I Didn't Demand an Apology," *The Washington Post*, November 13, 2018, washingtonpost.com/opinions/i-made-amends-with-pete-davidson-on-snl-but -thats-only-the-beginning/2018/11/13/e7314fb0-e77e-11e8-b8dc-66cca409c180_story .html.

252 **"She's about to learn a lot,":** @MattGaetz, Tweet, February 26, 2019 (now deleted).

252 **a "shithole country":** Sarah Ferris, "Rep. Matt Gaetz hires ex-White House aide ousted for white nationalist ties," *Politico*, April 19, 2019, politico.com/story/2019/04/19/matt -gaetz-aide-white-nationalists-1283314.

252 **described as Trump's protégé:** Stephanie Mensimer, "How Matt Gaetz Used Daddy's Money to Become Trump's Favorite Congressman," *Mother Jones*, September/October 2019, motherjones.com/politics/2019/07/how-matt-gaetz-used-daddys-money-to-become -trumps-favorite-congressman/.

252 **and legalizing marijuana:** "Matt Gaetz's Public Statements on Issue: Marijuana Legaliza-tion," VoteSmart.org, n.d., votesmart.org/candidate/public-statements/117101/matt-gaetz /101/marijuana-legalization.

252 **getting too "politically correct,":** NPR/PBS NewsHour/Marist Poll, December 2018, maristpoll.marist.edu/wp-content/uploads/2018/12/NPR_PBS-NewsHour_Marist -Poll_USA-NOS-and-Tables_Civility_1812051719.pdf#page=3.

252 **and in one Harvard poll:** Harvard IOP Survey of Young Americans' Attitudes Toward Politics and Public Service, March 2018, iop.harvard.edu/sites/default/files/content /Release%202%20Toplines.pdf.

253 **"the first place they go.":** Nancy Jo Sales, "They Say We're White Supremacists": Inside the Strange World of Conservative College Women," *Vanity Fair*, November 29, 2018, vanityfair.com/news/2018/11/conservative-college-women-university-of-north-carolina -republicans.

253 **reporter Astead Herndon observed:** Astead W. Herndon, "Trumpism Finds a Safe Space at Conservative Women's Conference," *The New York Times*, June 17, 2018, nytimes .com/2018/06/17/us/politics/women-conservative-trump.html.

253 **him to check in:** Lindsey Bevin, "SNL's Pete Davidson Posted an Alarming Message on Instagram. Dan Crenshaw Reached Out to Help," *The Washington Post*, December 19, 2018, washingtonpost.com/arts-entertainment/2018/12/19/snls-pete-davidson-posted -an-alarming-message-instagram-dan-crenshaw-reached-out-help/.

254 **"ride-along" with Border Patrol:** Rep. Dan Crenshaw: The Truth at the Southern Bor-der, February 9, 2019, YouTube video, youtube.com/watch?v=m_Yt5MQ6L9U,

254 **"their moral high horse.":** Dan Crenshaw, Facebook Live, July 3, 2019, facebook.com /CrenshawforCongress/videos/879006952459536/.

254 **defended Trump's meetings with Kim Jong Un:** Dan Crenshaw, tweet, March 1, 2019, twitter.com/dancrenshawtx/status/1101453692350484481.

257 **"campaign and the Russian government.":** Elise Stefanik, tweet, March 24, 2019, twitter.com/EliseStefanik/status/1109912856563249152.

257 **90 percent of the time:** FiveThirtyEight, "Tracking Congress in the Age of Trump: Elise Stefanik," n.d., projects.fivethirtyeight.com/congress-trump-score/elise-stefanik/.

257 **wasn't "exactly right on that.":** "Stefanik Opposes Southern Border Wall," *The Post-Star*, May 10, 2017, poststar.com/news/opinion/columns/maury_thompson/stefanik -opposes-southern-border-wall/article_db82bbcf-ff05-59ed-982b-b3fd5feba321.html.

257 **"contrary to our American ideals.":** Grace Segers, "New York Republicans Divided on Trump's 'Shithole' Comments," *City and State New York*, January 12, 2018, cityan dstateny.com/articles/politics/new-york-state-articles/new-york-republicans-divided -on-trump%E2%80%99s-%E2%80%98shithole%E2%80%99-comments.html.

257 **"with the president's assertion.":** North County Public Radio, "Timeline: Rep. Ste-fanik Often Sharply Critical of Trump, but Backs His Agenda,"August 10, 2018, north countrypublicradio.org/news/story/36791/20180810/timeline-rep-stefanik-often-sharply -critical-of-trump-but-backs-his-agenda.

258 **"We suggest she visit soon.":** *Post-Star* editorial board, "Stefanik Fails to Call Out Right from Wrong," *The Post-Star*, July 21, 2019, poststar.com/opinion/editorial/editorial -stefanik-fails-to-call-out-right-from-wrong/article_1e6fba27-df16-553f-a6d1-34b19 661cfb3.html.

258 **after multiple corruption scandals:** Alexander C. Kaufman and Igor Bobic, "Growing Number of Republicans Join Calls for Pruitt to Resign," *The Huffington Post*, April 3, 2018, huffpost.com/entry/carlos-curbelo-scott-pruitt_n_5ac3b87be4b04646b6470a31.

258 **helped get Trump elected:** William Gray, "Reps. Elise Stefanik (R-NY) and Kathleen Rice (D-NY) Sponsor Honest Ads Act," Issue One, July 24, 2018, issueone.org/reps-elise -stefanik-r-ny-and-kathleen-rice-d-ny-sponsor-honest-ads-act/.

258 **only about half the time:** FiveThirtyEight, "Tracking Congress in the Age of Trump," projects.fivethirtyeight.com/congress-trump-score/elise-stefanik/.

259 **hall in April 2018:** Elise Stefanik Town Hall, April 2018, YouTube video, youtube.com /watch?v=WGiqhbHTxdk.

259 **A Pew study found:** "Partisan Identification Is 'Sticky,' but About 10% Switched Parties Over the Past Year," Pew Research Center, May 17, 2017, people-press.org/2017/05/17 /partisan-identification-is-sticky-but-about-10-switched-parties-over-the-past-year/.

259 **17 percent of millennials identified:** Pew Research Center, "The Generation Gap in America: 1. Generations' Party Identification, Midterm Voting Preferences, Views of Trump," March 1, 2018, people-press.org/2018/03/01/1-generations-party-identification -midterm-voting-preferences-views-of-trump/.

260 **strongly approved of Trump:** NBCNews Gen Forward, "November 2017 Toplines," genforwardsurvey.com/assets/uploads/2017/11/NBC-GenForward-November-2017 -Toplines-Final.pdf.

260 **"It's all these old racist dog whistles":** Joanne Rosa, "Meghan McCain Slams 'Coward-ice' GOP Response to Trump's Democrat Congresswomen Tweets," abcnews.go.com /Politics/meghan-mccain-slams-cowardice-gop-response-trumps-democrat/story? id=64341609.

260 **cried when he missed:** Rachael Bade and Jennifer Haberkorn, "Amash cries after miss-ing first vote in Congress," *Politico*, March 10, 2017, politico.com/story/2017/03/justin -amash-cries-after-missing-vote-235928.

260 **particular strain of American exceptionalism:** Matt Kibbe, Free the People podcast, "Why the Swamp Gets It Backwards," April 10, 2019, YouTube video, youtube.com /watch?v=jWkcPwt4GDQ&feature=youtu.be.

261 **they weren't deep enough:** Nate Reens, "U.S. Rep. Justin Amash votes against Paul Rand's budget plan," MLive.com, March 22, 2012, mlive.com/news/grand-rapids/2012 /03/us_rep_justin_amash_votes_agai.html.

261 **"eliminate the ACA completely":** Maureen Groppe, "Republicans modify Obamacare repeal bill to win more GOP votes," *USA Today*, March 20, 2017, usatoday.com/story/news /politics/2017/03/20/republicans-modify-obamacare-repeal-bill-appease-conservatives /99427432/.

261 **opposed pretty much all environmental regulations:** National Environmental Score-card: Representative Justin Amash (R), LCV.org, n.d., scorecard.lcv.org/moc/justin-amash.

261 **dismantle the Department of Education:** "Rep. Massie Introduces Bill to Abolish Fed-eral Department of Education," Website of Congressman Thomas Massie, press release,

February 7, 2017, massie.house.gov/newsroom/press-releases/rep-massie-introduces
-bill-to-abolish-federal-department-of-education.

261 **Trump's overreach on immigration:** Malachi Barrett, "Rep. Justin Amash Hammers
Trump's 'Unlawful' Immigration Ban," MLive.com, January 19, 2019, mlive.com/news
/grand-rapids/2017/01/rep_justin_amash_trumps_unlawf.html.

261 **singling out particular organizations:** Glenn Kessler, "Michigan Lawmaker Inflates His
Conservative Cred," *The Washington Post*, July 8, 2014, washingtonpost.com/news/fact
-checker/wp/2014/07/08/michigan-lawmaker-inflates-his-conservative-cred/.

261 **opposing expanded government surveillance:** Charlie Savage, Eileen Sullivan, and
Nicholas Fandos, "House Extends Surveillance Law, Rejecting New Privacy Safe-
guards," *The New York Times*, January 11, 2018, nytimes.com/2018/01/11/us/politics
/fisa-surveillance-congress-trump.html.

261 **expressing support for ICE:** David Weigel, "The New 'Dr. No:' Justin Amash Ma-
rooned in Congress," *The Washington Post*, July 31, 2018, washingtonpost.com/powerpost
/the-new-dr-no-rep-justin-amash-marooned-in-congress/2018/07/31/5e9f9ca2-90e8
-11e8-8322-b5482bf5e0f5_story.html.

261 **engaged in "impeachable conduct.":** Timothy Gardner, "Republican lawmaker says
Trump engaged in impeachable conduct," Reuters, May 18, 2019, reuters.com/article/us
-usa-trump-amash/first-republican-lawmaker-says-trump-engaged-in-impeachable
-conduct-idUSKCN1SP01I.

261 **findings of the report:** John Bowden, "GOP lawmaker: Trump has engaged in multiple
actions that 'meet the threshold for impeachment,'" The Hill, May 18, 2019, thehill.com
/homenews/house/444416-gop-lawmaker-trump-has-engaged-in-multiple-actions
-that-meet-threshold-for.

261 **"depending on whether they're":** Justin Amash, tweet, May 18, 2019, twitter.com
/justinamash/status/1129831627872493574.

262 **rejection of partisan politics altogether:** Paul Kane, "Pro-Impeachment Amash Insists
He Hasn't Changed But Republican Party Has," *The Washington Post*, June 15, 2019,
washingtonpost.com/powerpost/pro-impeachment-amash-insists-he-hasnt-changed
-but-republican-party-has/2019/06/15/c0edfd8a-8ecc-11e9-8f69-a2795fca3343_story
.html.

262 **"No matter your circumstance,":** Justin Amash, "Our Politics Is in a Partisan Death
Spiral. That's Why I'm Leaving the GOP," *The Washington Post*, July 4, 2009, washing
tonpost.com/opinions/justin-amash-our-politics-is-in-a-partisan-death-spiral-thats
-why-im-leaving-the-gop/2019/07/04/afbe0480-9e3d-11e9-b27f-ed2942f73d70_story
.html.

262 **told reporters he felt liberated:** Craig Howie, "Trump lashes out as Justin Amash says
he is leaving the GOP," *Politico*, July 4, 2019, politico.com/story/2019/07/04/partisan
-death-spiral-justin-amash-says-he-is-leaving-the-gop-1398935.

262 **him with a standing ovation:** Haley Byrd, "Amash Greeted with a Standing Ovation at
Michigan Town Hall," CNN, May 29, 2019, cnn.com/2019/05/28/politics/justin-amash
-town-hall-trump-impeachment/index.html.

262 **jockeying for his seat:** Lissandra Villa, "In Donald Trump's America, Rep. Justin
Amash Sets an Independent Course," *TIME*, October 10, 2019. time.com/5696967/justin
-amash/.

262 **proposed a carbon tax:** Oliver Milman, "Republican Lawmaker Pitches Carbon Tax in
Defiance of Party Stance," *The Guardian*, July 23, 2018, theguardian.com/environment
/2018/jul/23/republican-carlos-curbelo-pitches-carbon-tax-climate-change.

263 **few Republicans who visited:** Andrew Desiderio, "Carlos Curbelo's Election Dilemma:
Walking the Line Between Love and Hate for Trump," *The Daily Beast*, August, 27, 2018,
thedailybeast.com/carlos-curbelos-election-dilemma-walking-the-line-between
-love-and-hate-for-trump.

263 **Carlos said he wouldn't:** Tal Kopan, "Republican Won't Vote for Government Funding
Without DACA Deal," CNN, November 28, 2017, cnn.com/2017/11/28/politics/daca-deal
-government-funding-carlos-curbelo/index.html.

263 **compromise immigration bill that:** Mike DeBonis, "House GOP Weighs Possible

Immigration Compromise with Border Wall Funds," *The Washington Post*, June 8, 2018, washingtonpost.com/powerpost/house-gop-weighs-possible-immigration-compromise -with-border-wall-funds/2018/06/08/68b82f22-6b3d-11e8-bea7-c8eb28bc52b1_story .html.

263 **so it didn't pass:** Rebecca Shabad, "House overwhelmingly rejects compromise immigration bill despite Trump support," NBC News, June 27, 1028, nbcnews.com/politics /congress/reversing-course-last-minute-trump-calls-house-gop-pass-immigration -n886916.

263 **"Why do you have to":** Alex T. Daugherty, "Carlos Curbelo Tries to Distance Himself from Trump—But They Have Something in Common," *Miami Herald*, October 12, 2018, miamiherald.typepad.com/nakedpolitics/2018/10/carlos-curbelo-tries-to-distance -himself-from-trump-but-they-have-something-in-common.html.

CHAPTER 18: LADIES OF THE HOUSE

265 **had a private text chain:** Sheryl Gay Stolberg, "'The Squad' Rankles, but Pelosi and Ocasio-Cortez Make Peace for Now," *The New York Times*, July 26, 2019, nytimes.com /2019/07/26/us/politics/aoc-squad-pelosi.html.

266 **live in the fourteenth district:** Thatiana Diaz, "Alexandria Ocasio-Cortez's Red Lipstick Is Sold Out at Sephora," July 2, 2018, *Refinery 29*, July 2, 2018, refinery29.com /en-us/2018/06/203073/alexandria-ocasio-cortez-red-lipstick.

270 **there were the military:** Melanie Zanona, Sarah Ferris, and Heather Caygle, "'It Is Like High School': Meet the House's Freshman Cliques," *Politico*, March 4, 2019, politico .com/story/2019/03/04/house-democrats-freshman-cliques-1197530.

271 **"test of roommate compatibility!":** Katie Hill, Instagram, December 30, 2018.

272 **to afford something in DC:** Azi Paybarah, "Alexandria Ocasio-Cortez Will Push Washington. Will Washington Push Back?" *The New York Times*, November 7, 2018, nytimes .com/2018/11/07/nyregion/ocasio-cortez-congress-washington.html.

272 **LEAST $15,000 IN SAVINGS:** Lukas Mikelionis, "Ocasio-Cortez Claims She Can't Afford DC Apartment, But Records Show She Has at Least $15,000 in Savings," Fox News, November 13, 2018, foxnews.com/politics/ocasio-cortez-claims-of-not-being-to-afford -dc-apartment-crumbles-under-scrutiny.

273 **"they're the naive ones.":** Sunrise Movement, Facebook Live, facebook.com/sun risemvmt/.

274 **said she was so nervous:** Interview with Alexandria Ocasio-Cortez, *60 Minutes*, January 6, 2019.

275 **favored something like this:** David Leonhardt, "The Secret to Winning in 2020," *The New York Times*, December 16, 2018, nytimes.com/2018/12/16/opinion/democrats-2020 -election-economic-populism.html.

275 **were flipped by women:** Catie Edmondson and Jasmine C. Lee, "Meet the New Freshman in Congress," *The New York Times*, November 28, 2018, nytimes.com/interactive /2018/11/28/us/politics/congress-freshman-class.html.

276 **a congressman from Colorado:** John A. Lawrence, *The Class of '74* (Baltimore: John Hopkins University Press, 2018).

276 **ended up deepening partisan divisions:** Lawrence, *The Class of '74*.

277 **disparities in maternal health:** Website of Congresswoman Lauren Underwood, "Black Maternal Health Caucus Celebrates Passage of Priorities in Appropriations Bill," June 24, 2019, underwood.house.gov/media/press-releases/black-maternal-health-caucus -celebrates-passage-priorities-appropriations-bill.

277 **the next major hurricane:** Sydney Kashiwagi, "East Shore Seawall Project," SILive .com, expo.silive.com/news/g66l-2019/03/7df730b8d11896/east-shore-seawall-project-11 -things-you-need-to-know.html.

277 **global leadership in manufacturing:** Website of Congresswoman Haley Stevens, "Rep. Stevens' American Manufacturing Leadership Act Passes Science Committee," May 1, 2019, stevens.house.gov/media/press-releases/rep-stevens-american-manufacturing -leadership-act-passes-science-committee.

277 **early childhood STEM education:** H.R. 1665 (116th Congress), Building Blocks of STEM Act, congress.gov/bill/116th-congress/house-bill/1665/text.

277 **"So how can we use that to our advantage?":** Melanie Zanona, "'We're Not Going To Sit Idly By': Freshman Dems Look to Seize Shutdown Optics," *Politico*, January 17, 2019, politico.com/story/2019/01/17/freshman-house-democrats-government-shutdown -1110462.

278 **every building in America:** Tara Golshan and Ella Nilsen, "Alexandria Ocasio-Cortez's rocky rollout of the Green New Deal, explained," *Vox*, February 11, 2019, vox.com/policy -and-politics/2019/2/11/18220163/alexandria-ocasio-cortez-green-new-deal-faq -tucker-carlson

280 **Aides said Pelosi moved:** Rachael Bade and Mike DeBonis, "Outright Disrespectful': Four House Women Struggle As Pelosi Isolates Them," *The Washington Post*, July 10, 2019, washingtonpost.com/politics/outright-disrespectful-four-house-women-struggle -as-pelosi-isolates-them/2019/07/10/a33c63a8-a33f-11e9-b7b4-95e30869bd15_story .html.

280 **"They didn't have any following.":** Maureen Dowd, "It's Nancy Pelosi's Parade," *The New York Times*, July 6, 2019, nytimes.com/2019/07/06/opinion/sunday/nancy-pelosi -pride-parade.html.

280 **she told *The Washington Post*:** Bade and DeBonis, "Outright Disrespectful': Four House Women Struggle As Pelosi Isolates Them."

281 **She told *The New York Times*:** Catie Edmondson, "How Alexandria Ocasio-Cortez Learned to Play by Washington's Rules," *The New York Times*, September 18, 2019, nytimes .com/2019/09/18/us/politics/alexandria-ocasio-cortez-washington.html.

281 **campaign with an attack:** Website of Nicole Malliotakis for Congress, nicolemalliotakis .com/landing/.

CHAPTER 19: THE DOUBLE HELIX

283 **an up-and-coming Democrat:** David Remnick, "Obama Reckons with a Trump Presidency," *The New Yorker*, November 18, 2016, newyorker.com/magazine/2016/11/28/obama -reckons-with-a-trump-presidency.

283 **the "first gay president.":** Frank Bruni, "The First Gay President?," *The New York Times*, June 11, 2016, nytimes.com/2016/06/12/opinion/sunday/the-first-gay-president .html.

283 **"the porn star presidency.":** CNN Live Event/Special, Townhall with Mayor Pete Buttigieg, CNN, March 10, 2019, transcripts.cnn.com/TRANSCRIPTS/1903/10/se.03.html.

283 **more than twenty-two thousand donors:** Dan Merica, "Buttigieg Feels Momentum After CNN Town Hall, with $600K Raised in 24 Hours, CNN, March 12, 2019, cnn.com /2019/03/11/politics/buttigieg-fundraising-townhall/index.html.

288 **her opposition to Amazon's expansion:** Billy Perrigo, "Alexandria Ocasio-Cortez Celebrated Amazon Pulling Out of New York—But the Governor Says It Cost the City 25,000 Jobs," *TIME*, February 17, 2019, time.com/5530386/aoc-amazon-new-york-hq2/.

288 **even made a comic book:** Josh Blaylock, et al., *Alexandria Ocasio-Cortez and the Freshman Force: New Party Who Dis?*, Devils Due Comics, devils-due-1first-comics.myshopify .com/products/alexandria-ocasio-cortez-and-the-freshman-force-new-party-who -dis-1.

290 **Pete said he thought AOC:** Jason Lemon, "Alexandria Ocasio-Cortez's Arrival 'Was a Really Important Moment' for America, Democratic 2020 Candidate Says," *Newsweek*, newsweek.com/alexandria-ocasio-cortez-president-2020-election-1324770.

INDEX